STUDIES IN CHRISTIAN HISTORY AND THOUGHT

Our Sovereign Refuge

The Pastoral Theology of Theodore Beza

STUDIES IN CHRISTIAN HISTORY AND THOUGHT

A full listing of titles in this series
appears at the end of this book

STUDIES IN CHRISTIAN HISTORY AND THOUGHT

Our Sovereign Refuge

The Pastoral Theology of Theodore Beza

Shawn D. Wright

Foreword by John L. Farthing

Wipf & Stock
PUBLISHERS
Eugene, Oregon

Wipf and Stock Publishers
199 W 8th Ave, Suite 3
Eugene, OR 97401

Our Sovereign Refuge
The Pastoral Theology of Theodore Beza
By Wright, Shawn D.
Copyright©2004 Paternoster
ISBN: 1-59752-772-6
Publication date 6/10/2006
Previously published by Paternoster, 2004

This Edition Published by Wipf and Stock Publishers
by arrangement with Paternoster

Paternoster
9 Holdom Avenue
Bletchley
Milton Keyes, MK1 1QR
Great Britain

STUDIES IN CHRISTIAN HISTORY AND THOUGHT

Series Preface

This series complements the specialist series of *Studies in Evangelical History and Thought* and *Studies in Baptist History and Thought* for which Paternoster is becoming increasingly well known by offering works that cover the wider field of Christian history and thought. It encompasses accounts of Christian witness at various periods, studies of individual Christians and movements, and works which concern the relations of church and society through history, and the history of Christian thought.

The series includes monographs, revised dissertations and theses, and collections of papers by individuals and groups. As well as 'free standing' volumes, works on particular running themes are being commissioned; authors will be engaged for these from around the world and from a variety of Christian traditions.

A high academic standard combined with lively writing will commend the volumes in this series both to scholars and to a wider readership.

Series Editors

Alan P.F. Sell, Visiting Professor at Acadia University Divinity College, Nova Scotia, Canada

David Bebbington, Professor of History, University of Stirling, Stirling, Scotland, UK

Clyde Binfield, Professor Associate in History, University of Sheffield, UK

Gerald Bray, Anglican Professor of Divinity, Beeson Divinity School, Samford University, Birmingham, Alabama, USA

Grayson Carter, Associate Professor of Church History, Fuller Theological Seminary SW, Phoenix, Arizona, USA

Christo et ecclesiae

Contents

Foreword	xiii
Preface	xvii
Chapter 1 Theodore Beza in Context	1
Statement of this Study	2
Beza's Context	6
Beza's Self-Identity	11
Beza the Christian	11
Beza the Pastor	14
Beza the Trainer of Pastors	18
Beza's Eschatological Vision	21
The Vie de Calvin	21
The Fact of the Spiritual Battle	24
The Battle for the Truth	25
Satan's Schemes in Human History	27
The Eternal Stakes of the Battle	27
God's Sovereignty: Solace in the Battle	30
Conclusion	34
Chapter 2 Beza's Interpreters	36
Summary of Beza Research	37
Specific Doctrines	38
Biblical Exegesis and Preaching	39
Scholasticism and Humanism	39
John Calvin and Theodore Beza	41
Studies of Beza's Theological Method	46
Evaluation of Methodology Studies	55

Studies of Beza's Doctrine of Predestination	55
Studies Emphasizing Scholasticism	56
"Central Dogma" Studies	63
Contextual Studies	65
HISTORICALLY CONTEXTUAL	65
THEOLOGICALLY CONTEXTUAL	66
LITERARILY CONTEXTUAL	68
EVALUATION OF CONTEXTUAL STUDIES	69
Studies of Beza's Doctrine of Assurance of Salvation	71
Deviation from Calvin Scheme	71
Contextual Deviation	75
Evaluation	80
Conclusion	81
Looking Forward	82
Chapter 3 Beza's Pastoral Systematic Theology	**84**
Presuppositions	84
Beza's Theological Method: His Theory and his Practice	87
Sermon 9 in Sermons sur la Resurrection	88
The Role of the Holy Spirit in Theology	96
The Centrality of the Bible	98
THE SUFFICIENCY OF THE BIBLE	98
THE BIBLE'S ROLE IN THE SPIRITUAL BATTLE	102
The Need for Right Biblical Interpretation	105
BEZA'S HUMANISTIC INTERPRETATION	106
BEZA'S USE OF RHETORIC	110
BEZA'S QUALIFIED APPROPRIATION OF PHILOSOPHY	111
Conclusion	114
The Salvific Thrust of Beza's Systematic Theology	115
Confession de la foi Chrestienne *(1559)*	115
Altera brevis fidei confessio *(1559)*	122
Quaestionum et responsionum *(1570)*	126
Petit Catéchisme *(1575)*	130
Conclusion	132

Chapter 4 God's Sovereignty for His People: Comfort in the Spiritual Battle — **134**

Beza's Political and Theological Context — 136
The Providence of God Explained and Defended — 138
   Providence in the Systematic Treatises — 138
   Providence in the Polemical Treatises — 139
Application of Providence in the Spiritual Battle: *Treatise on the Plague* and *Lectures on Job* — 143
   De Peste Quaestiones duae Explicatae *(1579)* — 143
   Jobus, Theodore Bezae partim Commentariis partim Paraphrasi illustratus *(1589)* — 149
The Pastoral Application of God's Providence — 161
The Doctrine of Predestination Explained and Defended — 167
   The Sum of the Gospel According to Beza — 167
   Predestination and Genre — 172
      SYSTEMATIC WORKS — 172
      POLEMICAL WORKS — 173
      PASTORAL WORKS — 176
   Predestination: Anchor in the Battle — 177
Conclusion — 185

Chapter 5 Pastoral Implications of God's Sovereignty: Assurance in the Spiritual Battle — **187**

Assurance in Context — 187
Assurance in Light of the Previous Discussion — 192
Assurance and God's Sovereignty in the Spiritual Battle — 194
   The Confession — 194
   The Bezan Corpus — 199
The *Loci* of Assurance for Weary Christians — 203
   God's Character and Promises — 204
   Jesus Christ — 205
   Faith — 208
   The Holy Spirit — 209
   The Church — 212
   Prayer — 213
   Heaven — 214
   Conclusion — 216

The "Practical Syllogism" 217
Perseverance and Sanctification in the Battle 226
   Sanctification 226
   Perseverance 228
Conclusion 231

Conclusion **232**

Appendix 1: Tables of Beza's Works 235
Appendix 2: *Sermons* sur *l'Histoire de la Resurrection*: Sermon 9 243
Appendix 3: *The Treasure of Truth* 259

Bibliography **279**

Subject Index 303
Modern Author Index 307

Foreword

Since the theological task involves critical reflection on the Christian proclamation, theology finds its *raison d'être* in the mission and ministry of the Church. Pastoral work and theological creativity are symbiotic. On the one hand, theology finds its proper sphere in service to the pastoral activity of the pilgrim Church. On the other hand, the life of worship, prayer, proclamation, and apologetics provides the raw materials for theological reflection. To detach the theological from the pastoral, therefore, is to impoverish both of them.

At its best, Christian theology is far more than a dazzling display of systematic abstractions, an intellectual artifice to be admired simply for its own explanatory power and internal coherence. When it is done well, theology is not merely contemplative; it is an urgently practical response to imperatives arising from the experience of living in the confrontation between law and grace, promise and fulfillment, action and piety, society and person, the seen and the unseen, this world and the next. Theology is an eminently practical response to a wide variety of tensions arising at the intersection between the present journey of faith and the future life of the Kingdom in its fullness. To be a pastor is to stand with the faithful community on the boundary between the "two cities," negotiating a precarious passage between the here-and-now, on the one hand, and the coming Kingdom, on the other. Theology emerges in response to the questions that are unavoidable in the attempt to live, faithfully and authentically, on the boundary between the sacred and the secular. In an important sense, therefore, the phrase *practical theology* involves a redundancy, since theology is itself a practice that is integral to the pastoral dimension of the Church's life.

At its best, theology serves the community of faith in ways that can only be described as pastoral. A primary pastoral concern is to show how it is possible to remain persons of integrity in the act of faith, affirming the faith in ways that do not involve a sacrifice of intellectual honesty. Such integrity of faith requires a theology that integrates heart and head, faith and reason, learning and piety. Christian theology is a matter of *fides quaerens intellectum* ("faith seeking understanding"); a thoughtful pastor can hardly avoid the imperative to model for the faithful ways of integrating belief and behavior, on the one hand, and Christ and culture, on the other.

Leading the Church in the praise of God, a pastor is never far removed from the theological task. Thinking clearly about the divine is, after all, a way of loving God with the mind; when it is done well, theology is an act of worship. Theology has a liturgical dimension, and liturgy devoid of theological depth inevitably becomes bland and lifeless. Leading the faithful in loving mercy and doing justice, a pastor is both priest and prophet. Thus the pastoral role is always *integrative,* pressing toward an integration of thought and worship, feeling and action, faith and works, maintenance and mission, comfort and challenge. The pastoral meets the theological in this shared task of integration. That is why the theological dimension of the pastoral role is inescapable: the pastoral function of theology is fundamental.

It is not surprising, then, that some of the most profound articulations of theological vision have emerged in contexts that bear the unmistakable imprint of hands-on involvement in day-to-day pastoral ministry. "Pastor-theologian" is the phrase that best describes some of the most cogent voices in the history of Christian thought: Augustine comes immediately to mind, along with Martin Luther, John Calvin, Friedrich Schleiermacher, Jonathan Edwards, Walter Rauschenbusch, Dietrich Bonhoeffer, Reinhold Niebuhr, and Karl Barth, among many others.

Now Shawn Wright has made it overwhelmingly clear that Theodore Beza must be numbered among the great pastor-theologians of the Reformed tradition. Indeed, it is impossible to understand Beza's religious thought in a comprehensive way, or to provide a full description of his place in the history of Reformed theology, without taking into account the pastoral matrix in which Beza's theology took form and the pastoral motivations underlying his system. *Our Sovereign Refuge* makes it clear that Beza's work and thought involve a rich symbiosis of theological positions and pastoral concerns.

Wright argues persuasively that Beza's pastoral interests were pivotal in shaping his theological perspective. Through an empathetic reading of the Bezan corpus, in sensitive dialogue with recent scholarship, Wright shows how Beza's work as a pastor at Geneva became the principal source for his doctrine of divine sovereignty. In making that important contribution to our understanding of Reformed theology, Wright shows how historical scholarship ought to be done. *Our Sovereign Refuge* is the work of a competent, well-trained historian who reads the primary sources carefully, paying close attention to matters of context and genre. Above all, Wright has done what any historian is most fundamentally obliged to do: he has encountered Beza within the structures and dynamics of Beza's own world, rather than offering us the caricature that is bound to result when Beza is viewed through the prism of the values and assumptions of the post-Enlightenment secular culture of the West. When Wright challenges historians to practice a methodology of empathy, he does more than just talk the talk; he provides an exemplary case-study in the kind of historical scholarship that lets the evidence speak to us in its own terms rather than stretching it upon a rack of anachronistic assumptions.

Our Sovereign Refuge clarifies a number of patterns and connections in Beza's theology that until now were only dimly sensed or suspected. While the pastoral dimension of Beza's theological work has been noted by some scholars, only now can we say with assurance that Beza's pastoral concern is not just one of many factors underlying his thought but rather the leitmotif of his doctrine of divine sovereignty. That marks an important step forward in our understanding of the genius of Reformed theology.

Shawn Wright's work promises to enliven the dialogue among pastors and theologians who continue living and believing on the boundary that provided the setting for Theodore Beza's crucial contributions to the Reformed tradition in the late-sixteenth century. Beza's career as a pastor-theologian brought together effective pastoral care and discipline, on the one hand, and a rich theological creativity, on the other. Even though some of Beza's conclusions will seem problematic to many contemporary believers, his fruitful symbiosis of pastoral concern and theological insight offers a model still worth considering, even in a postmodern age.

John L. Farthing
Hendrix College
Pentecost, 2004

Preface

This book is a revised edition of my dissertation that was completed at The Southern Baptist Theological Seminary in 2001. It has been a community project from the start. My doctoral committee members were unflagging in their support of my initial efforts. Tom Nettles, my supervising professor, consistently encouraged me and enriched my study with his theological acumen. Bruce Ware helped me at an early stage to sharpen the focus of my study. His suggestions saved me much heartache. Gregory Wills encouraged me to pursue a study of Beza in the first place and challenged me to write on him lucidly. I have profited tremendously from observing not only the scholarship, but also the lives, of these three men. Additionally Tom Schreiner and Brian Vickers – dear friends and now my colleagues – encouraged me greatly during the dissertation-writing process.

Numerous persons helped me obtain necessary Bezan materials. Margaret Simmons of The Southern Baptist Theological Seminary's James P. Boyce Centennial Library procured numerous materials that were important for my study through inter-library loan. Bruce Keisling, the Associate Librarian, supported my research by having the library purchase some Bezan materials I needed. Scholars from other institutions also provided important materials, treatises I could not otherwise procure. My thanks go to Irena Backus of Institut d'histoire de la Réformation, Paul Fields of Calvin College's Meeter Center, and Scott Manetsch of Trinity International University, who all assisted me greatly in this regard. Additionally, Alan Savage of Wheaton College graciously helped me make sense of some of Beza's French.

Several scholars encouraged me and helped me to sharpen the focus of my study as I revised it into its present form. In this regard, my thanks go especially to Joel Beeke of Puritan Reformed Theological Seminary and Richard Muller of Calvin Theological Seminary. John Farthing of Hendrix College, who initially served as the external reader for my dissertation, has helped the final product greatly through his careful reading of my work. I am extremely thankful for his willingness to write the introduction to this book. Others also helped to make the book better. Two in particular took time out of their schedules to improve the final product of this book. First, Anne-Marie Karpinsky, lecturer in French at Bellarmine University and Indiana University

Southeast, gave me many hours of her expertise to help me better understand Beza's sermon found in appendix two. Second, Michael Pohlman, a doctoral student in church history at Southern Seminary, spent many hours helping to make the older English translations of Beza's work found throughout the book more readable. Jeremy Pierre also aided me with some of his editorial expertise. My friend, Michael Carter, helped me by laying out the book for publication. At Paternoster, David Wright served me greatly through his perceptive reading of my manuscript. My editor, Jeremy Mudditt, has been very helpful and encouraging throughout the process of getting the book to press.

My family supported me very tangibly as I wrote this book. My parents, Robert and Irma Wright, supported my family financially and with abundant encouragement as I wrote this dissertation. Paul and Heidi Parisi, my family by marriage, regularly encouraged me to persevere. Their financial support enabled me to speed up the writing of this dissertation. My sons, Benjamin, Jonathan, Aaron, Nathan, and Stephen have been tremendous joys to me throughout the entire process of writing this book. Each one of them is a precious treasure to me. I pray that they will adore and serve the same God whom Theodore Beza loved.

Words cannot express the debt I owe to my wife, Gretchen. She supported me in countless ways as I initially wrote the dissertation and then revised it for publication. It cannot be easy when one's husband is distracted or anxious about deadlines—or when he has to stay up to all hours of the night, again—but Gretchen has never complained. She has supported my academic interests and eagerly read every word of the dissertation. Her suggestions and comments made the final product much better than it would have been otherwise. Additionally, Gretchen and I have had occasion recently to reflect on the fact that God is our sovereign refuge, even in the midst of the trials of this life. It is the greatest blessing of my life to be married to one who is a devoted partner with me on the pilgrimage to the celestial city.

My hope is that this work will stimulate further discussion about the life and thought of Theodore Beza. I also hope that Christ's church will profit by learning from the example of a man who tried to be a faithful pastor in the midst of very tumultuous times. *Soli Deo gloria.*

Shawn D. Wright
Louisville, Kentucky
June 2004

CHAPTER 1

Theodore Beza in Context

At the age of sixty-eight, after having shouldered the burden of leading the Genevan Reformation for over twenty years, Theodore Beza needed rest. But as he scanned the horizon in April, 1588, no calm appeared. He had experienced tremendous stresses over the last few years. Just two years earlier, the aggressive and Catholic Charles-Emmanuel of Savoy besieged Geneva and blockaded its access to Lac Léman. Almost squeezing the life out of Geneva for a year, he only let up when his troops were ravaged by the plague. Under pressure from the blockade, the Genevans moved to close the doors of their famous Academy. Beza, who felt a special responsibility for the school, pleaded with the magistrates to keep the school open; they agreed, but he ended up being the sole professor for eight months until the blockade ended.[1] Also, Lutheran opponents continued to vex Beza. In 1586 he had traveled to Montbéliard to debate the Lutheran theologian Jacob Andreae over christology and the eucharist. Quickly Andreae turned the issue of debate to the thorny issue of predestination. Andreae, who would not agree to have minutes of the debate recorded, published his version of the debate in 1587, calling forth Beza's response. In the midst of the controversy, Beza complained to a friend that all he had done was take his doctrine "from the Word of God and from the writings of other great men."[2] Adding to his woes, Beza was in bad health, plagued by "colds and pains in his legs."[3] Superseding all these troubles, Beza's wife, Claudine, died in April of 1588 at the age of sixty-six. She had been Beza's wife and companion for some forty years, since before he had

---

1   Scott M. Manetsch, *Theodore Beza and the Quest for Peace in France, 1572-1598*, Studies in Medieval and Reformation Thought, vol. 79 (Leiden: Brill, 2000), 132-34.
2   Paul-F. Geisendorf, *Théodore de Bèze* (Geneva: Alexandre Jullien, 1967), 354. For details of the Colloquy of Montbéliard, see Geisendorf, *Théodore de Bèze*, 351-56; Jill Raitt, "The French Reformed Theological Response," in *Discord, Dialogue, and Concord: Studies in the Lutheran Reformation's Formula of Concord*, ed. Lewis W. Spitz and Wenzel Lohff (Philadelphia: Fortress, 1977), 178-90; idem, *The Colloquy of Montbéliard: Religion and Politics in the Sixteenth Century* (New York: Oxford University Press, 1993).
3   Geisendorf, *Théodore de Bèze*, 357.

proclaimed his allegiance to the Reformation cause.[4] He grieved deeply over his loss.

Yet Beza's services were needed. Soon after Claudine's death, Bern sent a messenger to Geneva to retrieve Beza to help settle a debate over predestination caused by the contentious Samuel Huber, who had accused Beza's treatise on the plague of propagating "a new doctrine, unknown until then."[5] The Genevan Company of Pastors judged the situation serious enough to warrant Beza's presence; besides, the journey would probably do him good in light of his recent mourning, they argued.[6] Beza went willingly. Upon his arrival in Bern, he and his companions later noted that "Satan had prepared a lot of pain, so much that [Beza] was nearly out of hope of reestablishing everyone, because Huber had spoiled and corrupted the doctrine of predestination" in Bern.[7] After he satisfactorily refuted Huber's errors, Beza confirmed the Reformed understanding of predestination in Bern. This incident from Theodore Beza's life raises an important question that I will try to answer in this study: Why was Beza so concerned about the doctrine of predestination that even during an incredibly troubling period in his life he felt compelled to defend it?

Statement of this Study

The point of this study is to prove that Theodore Beza was a pastoral theologian. Rather than attempt to delineate the contours of his entire theology, however, I will tackle what is often disparaged as the most abstract and theoretical aspect of his theology: namely, the doctrine of God's sovereignty. My thesis is that for Theodore Beza the doctrine of God's sovereignty was a pastoral doctrine. It was pastoral because Beza employed it to encourage his listeners in the midst of the troubles of life; it was meant to comfort, not to breed undue rationalizing. Depending on his context and on the genre in which he chose to communicate, Beza explained the doctrine in different degrees of exactness. His treatises to refute scholarly opponents who attempted to overturn belief in God's absolute sovereignty, for example, employed exact and technical language, whereas his sermons whose purpose was to comfort listeners during times of intense trouble were replete with affectionate language and were rarely technical. As a pastor, Beza expressed himself differently in various genres of writings which were called forth by changing pastoral concerns. But whatever his context or the genre of writing, Beza's fundamental intention in his handling of the doctrine of God's sovereignty was his hearers' and readers' edification, not abstract speculation. He intended even his most

---

4   Ibid., 324.
5   Ibid., 356.
6   Ibid., 357.
7   Ibid., 357.

technical treatments both to protect his audience from false doctrine and to build them up in the knowledge of biblical truth. While his purpose was not to change John Calvin's doctrine, he applied the same doctrines to a changing situation, all for the benefit of Christians. Beza's handling of the doctrines of providence, predestination, and assurance was motivated by his fundamental pastoral intention of strengthening Christians so that they might arrive safely in heaven.

Beza's pastoral doctrine of God's sovereignty was fueled by his belief in two eschatological realities: first, that all persons would spend eternity in either heaven or hell, and second, that a Christian's time on earth was a pilgrimage on the way to heaven marked by fierce spiritual conflict between God and Satan. Beza's main concern in life was to make certain that he and his parishioners and students stood firm in the midst of the spiritual battle raging around them and arrived safely in their eternal bliss. Rather than being a digression into metaphysical speculation, Beza's treatment of God's sovereignty was integral to his pastoral vision. Only God's powerful hand could uphold Christians in the midst of life's battles. Beza's vision of God's complete sovereignty was intensely pastoral.

Beza thus counseled that in times of trouble a Christian should rest in God's sovereign power. In 1568 the wife of the French Protestant leader Gaspard de Coligny died, and Beza wrote a letter of condolence, stressing that Christians could rest contentedly in God's perfect will and almighty strength:

> But the sovereign remedy is that which you have taken, namely the power, the wisdom, the good will of the Lord: power to assure you that he lacks no means; wisdom to enable you to understand well that he knows better than anyone, even you, what is best for you and yours; good will which is proper to God's elect, namely, that he who has chosen us by his eternal and unchangeable council (to which our vocation is an infallible witness resounding in our ears by the preaching of his word accompanied by his sacraments and in our hearts through the Holy Spirit), and since he can do all, he wishes nothing and consequently does nothing except for the salvation of his own.[8]

According to Beza, God's total sovereignty was purposive in believers' lives. God's omnipotent care for his people made their safe arrival in heaven certain, even though they might undergo severe trials in their lives. Beza yearned for God thus to uphold and care for him in life's battles and ultimately to transport him to heaven. These words from one of his prayers are

---

8   Theodore Beza, *Correspondance de Théodore de Bèze*, ed. H. Meylan, A. Dufour, C. Chimelli, and B. Nicollier (Geneva: Librarie Droz, 1978), 9:97-98, translated by Jill Raitt ("Theodore Beza, 1519-1605," in *Shapers of Religious Traditions in Germany, Switzerland, and Poland, 1560-1600*, ed. Jill Raitt [New Haven: Yale University Press, 1981], 99).

representative of his hope in God's protective power:

> O God of patience . . . as there is nothing in your word, but serves to our learning, and to the guiding of our temporal life, as a means to obtain the possession of heavenly joys, so does it principally insist in this, to lift up our hearts to an earnest meditation, and firm expectation of eternal life. . . .
>
> This virtue therefore is the firm pillar of our hope, which teaches us, not to love the things of the earth, as any felicity, but constantly to look up into heaven, where our peace and joy do remain. . . . [T]he present sorrow of your children, is unto them the watch of some future joy at hand, and that all adventures, the last of their most painful days, is the first of their eternal rest, in the second life.
>
> But whether I walk, or stand still, whether I do, or suffer, grant, O Lord, that I may always walk as in your presence, to the glory of your holy name, and that my soul may take counsel, and be satisfied in your righteousness, while in all patience I wait for my deliverance from all pain, and the perfection of my happiness, at my departure from this carnal habitation, when according to your promise I shall be received into your kingdom, in the company of the angels and saints, there to behold your glory eternally. So be it.[9]

These sentiments were the very lifeblood of all that Beza was and did. He saw his earthly existence as transitory. His longing, instead, was fixed on the "firm expectation of eternal life," for he believed that one's "peace and joy do remain" only in contemplating the certainty of heaven. In heaven he was sure he would receive "deliverance from all pain and the perfection of my happiness." There all would be right and joyful. Thus in his exposition of Psalm 4 he taught Christians to look forward with intense longing to heaven. Although God provided them with other comforts, the certainty of paradise was the chief bulwark for them in the midst of suffering:

> When the wicked do rage, we ought not only not to despair, or be discouraged, but rather boldly to reprove our adversaries, resting upon the power of God, whereof we have had so often experience, and trusting to the goodness of our cause, and chiefly to the most assured promises of the life to come, upon the which we must

---

9 Theodore Beza, *Maister Bezaes Houshold Prayers*, trans. John Barnes (London: n.p., 1603). The first paragraph quoted is from page K5v; there is no pagination for the remaining excerpts, all of which come from the prayer "For obtaining the Virtue of Patience." When citing primary sources, I will note all translators; if none is noted, the translation is mine. When I quote older English translations, I have modernized the spelling and punctuation. I have occasionally made stylistic changes to clarify the meaning. Some early books have inconsistent page numbering; when pages were not numbered, I have tried adequately to indicate the source of the reference.

always have our eyes bent, and never depend upon the transitory commodities of this world.[10]

As I will demonstrate later, Beza's sentiments expressed here were repeated throughout his numerous works. They were based on a supernatural worldview, a vision of reality that encompassed God and Satan as major actors on the stage of history. The literal realities of eternal punishment in hell for unbelievers and eternal bliss in heaven for those who trusted in Christ for salvation were also significant components of his pastoral vision.

My understanding of Beza's motivating force is not the common way of understanding his theology. In fact, as far as I can tell, this way of viewing Beza's life and work has only been hinted at before.[11] Interpreters have advanced various alternatives as keys to understanding him and his work. Scholars have characterized Beza as a scholastic and a humanist, as a political operative and as a leader of a burgeoning international movement, as an educational administrator, and as the one responsible for changing the direction of Calvinistic theology from its original moorings. Students of the history of doctrine have tended to approach Theodore Beza to answer the question of how theological method shifted from John Calvin (d. 1564) to Francis Turretin (d. 1687) who is often viewed as the pinnacle of Protestant scholasticism. In the process, however, his view of predestination particularly has frequently been studied in isolation and without adequate attention to Beza's pastoral context. The result of this question-answer approach to Beza has often been a misunderstanding of his thought. When they have examined his view of God's sovereignty, scholars have commonly failed to notice Beza's context, the genre of his writings, and his purpose in writing. The result is that rarely have they

---

10 Theodore Beza, *The Psalmes of David, truly opened and explaned by Paraphrasis, according to the right sense of everie Psalme. With large and ample Arguments before everie Psalme, declaring the true use thereof*, trans. Anthonie Gilbie (London: Henrie Denham, 1581), 5.
11 For example, Jill Raitt called for Beza's pastoral work to be examined carefully: "Beza as a pastor, as a shepherd of souls concerned for their growth in Christ, has not yet received attention. But it is through such a study that Beza's character becomes known to us. . . . [A]t the root of these [pastoral] activities was Beza's own life of faith nourished by Scripture and the Lord's Supper and shared with his flock and his students through a drama, commentaries and sermons, two manuals of prayer, and letters of spiritual advice and consolation" (Raitt, "Beza, Guide for the Faithful Life," *Scottish Journal of Theology* 39 [1986]: 83-84). In a sense, I am trying to follow (through a study of Beza, not Martyr) Marvin Anderson's lead "to penetrate beneath the level of description to the fundamental religious and nonspeculative roots of Martyr's thought" (Anderson, "Peter Martyr Vermigli: Protestant Humanist," in *Peter Martyr Vermigli and Italian Reform*, ed. J. C. McLelland [Waterloo, Ontario: Wilfred Laurier University Press, 1980], 67).

noted that above all Theodore Beza was a pastoral theologian.

As I explicate Beza's pastoral theology, I hope to rectify this failure. My goal is to let Theodore Beza speak for himself. To that end, I will deal not only with his better-known theological works but also with his specifically pastoral and occasional writings, many of which seem to have escaped scholarly attention until now. I intend to explicate Beza's pastoral use of the doctrine of God's sovereignty in five chapters. The first chapter will lay the foundation for the entire study. This will place Beza in his context and show the centrality of what I call his "eschatological vision" to all his work. Chapter two will consist of a survey of scholars' interpretations of Theodore Beza, especially his doctrines of predestination and assurance. Although these twin doctrines have received significant attention, I will note that many researchers have overlooked the pastoral dimension to Beza's thought. Then in chapter three I will demonstrate the importance that Beza placed on correct doctrine in view of the spiritual battle and the manner in which he understood all of theology, intrinsically, to be pastoral and useful for living. Chapter four will demonstrate that Beza viewed the doctrine of God's sovereignty, both its common sphere of providence and its particular salvific sphere of predestination, as essential for waging the spiritual battle. Finally, in the fifth chapter I will delineate the pastoral implications of God's sovereignty that Beza emphasized, especially the doctrine of assurance of salvation. My goal throughout this study is to listen to Theodore Beza.

Beza's Context

The pastoral application of Beza's theology was both derived from and directed to his context.[12] Specifically, Beza attempted to comfort Christians in his very troubled times by reminding and convincing them that their God was absolutely sovereign over all the affairs of their lives and their world.

In subsequent parts of this study I will try to place Beza in context when dealing with specific issues. For instance, I shall consider his conversion and

---

12 William Bouwsma helpfully made this point when speaking about Calvin. He argued that "theology is a *human activity* that is often remarkably sensitive to its historical context and can therefore tell us a good deal about the past; and conversely that theological discourse can often be understood only with some knowledge of the circumstances surrounding its expression" ("Calvinism as Renaissance Artifact," in *John Calvin and the Church: A Prism of Reform*, ed. Timothy George [Louisville: Westminster/John Knox, 1990], 28). Note Raitt's contention that Beza's work, even his "scholastic" productions, "grew out of critical pastoral situations in which souls and bodies were literally at stake" (Jill Raitt, "The Person of the Mediator: Calvin's Christology and Beza's Fidelity," in *Occasional Papers of the American Society for Reformation Research*, vol. 1, ed. R. C. Walton [n.p.: 1977], 70).

his early education, his responsibilities at the Geneva Academy, his preaching, the situations surrounding his polemical treatises on predestination, his experience of the plague, his involvement in and concern for France, and his experience when Savoy antagonized Geneva. In all of these situations Beza urged the great benefits of trusting in the omnipotent and good God. I merely intend here to introduce the theological and political world Beza lived in and to show the urgency of his pastoral application.

In the first place, the overall tenor of the time during which Theodore Beza ministered in Geneva was characterized by political insecurity. Beza served there for over forty-five years, from 1558 until his death in 1605, during most of which time he was at the helm of the Academy and the church. And these final decades of the sixteenth century brought with them a great deal of upheaval for the small city-state of Geneva. William Monter helpfully summarized the context in which Beza labored:

> The external history of the Republic of Geneva was extremely eventful during the forty years after Calvin's death. Isolated geographically from Bern, the city was forced to go farther afield and seek more secure guarantees for her independence. The course of her diplomatic activities became more intense; their goals, more serious. Finally, by the end of the sixteenth century, Geneva had to fight a four-year war with the Duke of Savoy. Even afterwards, no definitive peace was concluded. Only when Geneva repulsed a surprise attack from Savoy (the famous Escalade of December 1602, which is still celebrated annually in Geneva) did she attain some measure of political security.[13]

These circumstances account for the pastoral trajectory of Beza's theological expression.[14]

The course of Genevan politics during Beza's ministry was tumultuous. Geneva was a small, independent city-state and relied on alliances with other

---

13 E. William Monter, *Calvin's Geneva* (New York: John Wiley and Sons, 1967; reprint, Huntington, NY: Robert E. Kreiger, 1975), 194. Compare Jill Raitt's comment that "the political history of Europe in the last quarter of the sixteenth century is a complex weave out of which it is not easy to pluck the pertinent threads" (*Montbéliard*, 45).

14 They may also provide one clue as to why Beza's theology appears on the surface to be different from Calvin's: he wrote to address needs and times different from his master's. Hall helpfully pointed out that Beza "faced a world different from Calvin's and had to adjust to it politically, ecclesiologically and theologically" (Basil Hall, "Review Article: From Biblical Humanism to Calvinist Orthodoxy," *Journal of Ecclesiastical History* 31 [1980]: 341). Hall, however, proceeded to draw unwarranted theological conclusions from his sound observation, I think. See also Tadataka Maruyama, *The Ecclesiology of Theodore Beza: The Reform of the True Church*, Travaux d'Humanisme et Renaissance 166 (Geneva: Librairie Droz, 1978), 24-25.

states to maintain a détente with its Catholic neighbors.[15] Geneva was not a part of the Swiss Confederation and was separated by language from the stronger German-speaking Protestant states. She relied on Bern for protection during Calvin's tenure. But the year of Calvin's death brought trouble with Savoy, troubles which Beza would have to endure almost all his life.[16] Thus Monter commented that "the principal theme of the history of the republic [Geneva] from 1564 to 1603 was her search for political security."[17] Combined with the ravages of the plague in the city, this political and military uncertainty resulted in numerous dire situations in Geneva during Beza's ministry there. Beza contended that Savoy's continued opposition to Geneva was instigated by Satan's hatred for the Protestant state.[18] It was to this situation, a situation of almost perpetual war and fear on the part of the Genevans, that Beza applied his theology.

But Beza was also deeply concerned about affairs in France. Like Calvin, he was a native Frenchman who ended up in French-speaking Geneva because of the Catholic oppression of Protestants in France. Having remained in his homeland until his twenty-ninth year, he kept up a vigorous correspondence with the Protestants there.[19] It seems that Beza inherited, and perhaps even intensified, Calvin's intense desire for the advance of the Protestant cause in France.[20] Unlike Calvin, Beza traveled back to France several times. For example, he defended the Protestant cause at Poissy in 1561, stayed in France during the war of religion which soon followed, returned again to settle his

---

15 Scott Michael Manetsch, "Theodore Beza and the Quest for Peace in France, 1572-1598" (Ph.D. diss., University of Arizona, 1997), 52.
16 Geisendorf, *Théodore de Bèze*, 283-84.
17 Monter, *Calvin's Geneva*, 196.
18 Geisendorf, *Théodore de Bèze*, 288. For a summary of Geneva's relationship to Savoy during Beza's time in Geneva, see Monter, *Calvin's Geneva*, 196-207.
19 In addition to his correspondence with his French brethren, Beza kept Bullinger informed of developments in France from 1563 until the latter's death in 1575 (Geisendorf, *Théodore de Bèze*, 228). Reports on France occupy a large part of Beza's massive correspondence to Bullinger. Both Reformed leaders had great reason to be concerned about France, for as Greengrass pointed out, "France was by far the most populous country in sixteenth-century Europe with a population which may have approached 20 million" (Mark Greengrass, *The French Reformation*, Historical Association Studies [Oxford: Basil Blackwell, 1987], 42). It possessed the military power concomitant with its size.
20 Robert Kingdon conclusively demonstrated Calvin's, and Beza's, concern for the Protestant cause in France. See his *Geneva and the Coming of the Wars of Religion in France 1555-1563*, Travaux d'Humanisme et Renaissance 22 (Geneva: Librairie E. Droz, 1956) and idem, *Geneva and the Consolidation of the French Protestant Movement 1564-1572: A Contribution to the History of Congregationalism, Presbyterianism, and Calvinist Resistance Theory* (Madison: University of Wisconsin Press, 1967).

Theodore Beza in Context

dead brother's estate, and in both 1571 and 1572 participated in the Protestant synods there.[21] The latter part of the sixteenth century was a time of changing fortunes for Protestants in France, and Beza lived and suffered through these, attempting to minister to his countrymen during the trials they experienced. By the early 1560s, Protestantism was well entrenched in France, having among its adherents perhaps as many as two million persons, especially in the "Huguenot crescent" in the southern portion of the country. Not surprisingly, this was the area closest to Geneva.[22] Although the 1560s were difficult times, the Protestant cause flourished, so that the early years of the 1570s were in many ways the best years for the French Protestants.[23]

Hope of Protestant success in France gave way to despair after 1572. The St. Bartholomew's Day massacre of Protestants that year shattered the Protestants' dreams. Although the tragedy began as an organized action in Paris on 23 August, it evolved into mob outbursts against the Huguenots throughout much of France and lasted for several days. The mobs slaughtered thousands of Protestants, especially the leaders of the Reformation movement. The Protestant cause in France suffered a debilitating blow.[24] Understandably, Beza lamented the massacre of his brethren.[25] He despaired at the sufferings of his brethren, but he also saw behind the massacre an organized Catholic plot and suspected that the mobs might continue their frenzied search for Protestants all the way to Geneva. At that time he wrote to Henry Bullinger that "this is perhaps the last letter I will ever write to you. For it is abundantly clear that these massacres are the unfolding of a universal conspiracy. Assassins are seeking to kill me, and I contemplate death more than life."[26] The Catholic triumph over the Huguenots filled Beza with a bleak outlook for the viability of Protestantism in France. For the rest of the decade and into the 1580s, he did not think that the Huguenots had any future in his homeland.[27] Even though the Edict of Nantes (1598) provided some relief, Protestantism would never flourish in France again. For Beza, whose "concept of duty [to France] lay very

---

21 See, for example, Geisendorf, *Théodore de Bèze*, 120-80, 259, 299-305.
22 Greengrass, *French Reformation*, 43-44.
23 Kingdon, *Geneva and Consolidation*, 193; Geisendorf, *Théodore de Bèze*, 305.
24 Greengrass, *French Reformation*, 79.
25 Kingdon observed about Beza that "if his correspondence provides any index, he was never, in his entire tumultuous life, so near to real despair as in the first days after news of the massacres reached Geneva" (*Geneva and Consolidation*, 200). See also Geisendorf, *Théodore de Bèze*, 306-09.
26 Beza, *Correspondance*, 13:179, translated in Manetsch, *Theodore Beza*, 34.
27 Manetsch, *Theodore Beza*, 116. Greengrass claimed that after St. Bartholomew's Day massacre the *Histoire ecclésiastique* accounts "changed from being a confident record of the gradual revelation of God's truth in France to an account of the mysterious and incomprehensible workings of providence for an embattled minority" (*French Reformation*, 80).

close to the heart" of his self-understanding, events in France moved him to put his trust more and more in the mysterious sovereignty of God.[28]

Beza blamed the Catholics for the evil that transpired in France. From the time Beza defended his Protestant convictions to his father in his *Confession* of 1559 until the 1598 edition of his *Annotationes*, he regularly rebuffed Catholic opponents.[29] His fears were warranted, for Rome had increased its polemics against Protestants and was increasingly attempting to evangelize Protestants in the latter part of the century.[30] Of the many obstacles to Beza's aspirations for the gospel, the Catholic opposition especially signified to Beza that Satan was trying to stop him.[31] Against this Roman Catholic and demonic antagonism Beza sallied forth, wielding the doctrine of God's sovereignty.

More disconcerting to Beza in many ways than the attacks by the Catholics were the frequent assaults of Lutheran theologians against Calvinistic doctrines, especially the Reformed view of the eucharist.[32] Beza labored to answer his Lutheran opponents and wrote more on the Lord's Supper than on any other single subject, as Maruyama noted.[33] Beza directed much attention to Lutheran attacks throughout his ministry. For instance, as late as 1593, he published *De controversiis in Coena Domini* in order to set out the differences between the Reformed and Lutheran understandings of the eucharist and to argue that Lutheran problems with the Reformed view arose in large part from a misunderstanding of Reformed theology.[34] Beza's interactions with Lutheranism consumed much of his energy throughout his career.

What sustained Theodore Beza in these tumultuous years of struggle against

---

28 Manetsch, *Theodore Beza*, 39.
29 Ibid., 320.
30 Ibid., 310-11. For a record of Beza's interactions with a Jesuit in Geneva in 1580, see A. Lynn Martin, *The Jesuit Mind: The Mentality of an Elite in Early Modern France* (Ithaca, NY: Cornell University Press, 1988), 84-86. This work portrays Jesuit attempts to claim France for Rome, and thwart Protestant efforts there, in the late sixteenth century.
31 Manetsch, *Theodore Beza*, 119.
32 Thus Geisendorf characterized Brenz after Calvin's death as "the Lutheran theologian—the extremist—who, along with Andreae and Heshuss, did not stop polemicizing violently against the Calvinists" (Geisendorf, *Théodore de Bèze*, 266).
33 Maruyama, *Ecclesiology*, 1. Raitt similarly noted that from 1570 to 1594 both Beza's polemical works and his sermons were dominated by "the relation of the two natures to each other in the person of Christ, or the *communicatio idiomatum*" because of his on going debates with Lutherans ("Person of the Mediator," 59). For further discussion of these debates, see Jill Raitt, *The Eucharistic Theology of Theodore Beza: Development of the Reformed Doctrine*, American Academy of Religion Studies in Religion 4 (Chambersburg, PA: American Academy of Religion, 1972).
34 Raitt, *Montbéliard*, 126.

both Catholic adversaries and Lutheran challengers was his strong belief in the sovereignty of God. In fact, Beza's emphasis on the doctrine of God's sovereignty and his particular expression of this doctrine arose in this difficult pastoral context. And we have only touched the surface, passing over such monumental events as the death of his only child, his wife's passing, his many physical ailments, and his poverty in old age. Yet Beza's faith in his Sovereign was as affectionate as it was rational. He trusted and loved his God greatly. In the troubled political, military, and ecclesiastical times in which he lived, he perceived a spiritual battle raging between God and the powers of hell. Only this spiritual war, Beza argued, made sense of the turmoil surrounding him. And the Christian's affectionate trust in God's absolute sovereignty over all events in this life alone could afford peace for the soul and courage for action.

Beza's Self-Identity

Understanding who Beza thought himself to be is a necessary step in comprehending the utility he saw for the doctrine of God's sovereignty. Just as there were external factors during his lifetime that heightened the significance of God's power for Beza, so there were internal motivations that affected the ways in which he expressed his love for God's sovereignty. That is to say, the various genres of Beza's writings related to this doctrine flowed out of his three identities. Theodore Beza was a Christian, a pastor, and a teacher.

Beza the Christian

Important elements of Beza's identity appear in a biographical sketch he wrote in 1560, in letters from late in life, and in some of his devotional writings. The most pervasive element in each autobiographical reflection is Beza's conviction that above all else he was a follower of Jesus Christ, bound to him, and certain to spend eternity with him in heaven.

In 1559 Beza published his *Confession de la Foi Chrestienne* to clarify for his father why he had abandoned Catholicism. Later he translated the treatise into Latin for a wider audience and attached a biographical letter to Melchior Wolmar, his former instructor and dear friend.[35] The most important aspect of the biography was the theological analysis Beza offered of his life. He had been

---

35 "I wrote this *Confession of my Faith* at first in the French language, for the purpose of satisfying my own father, whom the calumnies of certain persons had alienated from me, as though I had been an impious man and a heretic, and with the further view of winning him, if possible, to Christ in his extreme old age. . . . I have put it in Latin" (Theodore Beza, "Autobiographical Letter of Beza to Wolmar," in Baird, *Theodore Beza*, 366). The Latin text is in Beza, *Correspondance*, 3:43-48. I will refer to this work as the *Confession* in subsequent discussion.

a rebel against God, he recounted. Then God had saved him, but later he had abandoned God because of the temptations of Satan. Finally, God had graciously brought Beza to himself once more. Beza viewed his life in the context of the spiritual battle raging in this world.

Beza wrote the letter to extol God for "so many examples of the divine providence for my preservation."[36] It is filled with examples of protection from the deadly schemes of the devil. When Beza was only two, God was "providing for my salvation," he recounted, by disposing Beza's uncle to provide him with a good education.[37] When Beza and a relative contemplated suicide as young boys in order to relieve themselves of tortuous medical treatments, he blamed it on Satan who was set "to effect our ruin." Yet the Lord had "compassion on us," and brought Beza's uncle to stop them, so that "the Lord rescued us as from the jaws of Satan himself."[38] After his conversion, Beza went first to Orleans where he got his law degree and then he returned to Paris where his uncle resided. Beza had committed himself to the Protestant faith, yet in Paris he was surrounded by affluence and promises of fame if he stayed within the folds of the Roman church. Beza recounted that "Satan suddenly threw all these things in my way."[39] Later he blamed the devil for throwing "about me a triple snare, namely, the allurements of pleasure that are so great in that city, the sweets of petty glory . . . and, lastly, the expectation set before me of the greatest honors, to which some of the leading members of the court called me, while my friends incited me, and my father and uncle did not cease from exhorting me."[40] Beza believed that the devil actively sought to destroy him, his faith, and his usefulness for the gospel.

Beza knew, though, that his faithful God had preserved him through all his trials. He told Wolmar, with whom he lived and studied for seven years, that it was "by far the greatest benefit I received at your hands, that you so imbued me with the knowledge of true piety sought in the knowledge of the Word of God, as in the most limpid fountain, that I should be the most ungrateful and churlish of men did I not cherish and honor you, I say not as an instructor but as a parent."[41] When tempted to renounce his commitment to the Reformation in Paris, the Lord remembered him. "It was God's will," he recounted, "that I who, wretched man that I was, had entered so perilous a path with my eyes open, should escape these dangers also."[42] "The Lord had compassion upon me" by inflicting "upon me a very severe illness, to such a point that I almost

---

36 Baird, *Theodore Beza*, 366.
37 Ibid., 356.
38 Ibid., 358.
39 Ibid., 362.
40 Ibid., 363.
41 Ibid., 360.
42 Ibid., 363.

despaired of life." The result was that "after infinite tortures of mind and body, the Lord, pitying His runaway slave, so consoled me that I entertained no doubts of the concession of His pardon to me. Therefore I renounced myself with tears, I asked for forgiveness, I renewed my vow openly to embrace His true worship—in short, I consecrated myself wholly to Him."[43] So, as soon as he could rise from his sickbed, Beza exclaimed that he "burst asunder every chain, collected my effects, forsook at once my native land, my kinsmen, my friends, that I might follow after Christ." He fled France first to Lausanne and then finally to Geneva.[44] Through it all, Beza had an eternal perspective. He celebrated the day of his conversion to Christ as "the beginning of all the good things which I have received from that time forward and which I trust to receive hereafter in my future life."[45] Theodore Beza saw his life as an example of God's sovereign protection of his people in the spiritual battle.

To be a Christian, Beza held, was to love God. It was a matter of the heart as well as the mind. His writings show him to be a Christian who had tremendous affection for God. For example, he exuded Christian zeal for the Lord in the preface to his *Houshold Prayers*:

> If we are endued with the true knowledge of our estate, and condition, as also, the efficacy of holy prayers, we should not need to be advertised often, to present ourselves before God, to offer unto him our vows, and to beseech his fatherly love, or direction, for guiding us, by his good spirit, unto the light of his truth, to increase in our hearts, faith, love, constancy, humility, and other of his heavenly gifts, to forgive us our debts, to mortify the corruptions of our nature, to clothe us with his spiritual armor, against the assaults of the devil, the world and the flesh, to provide for our necessities, to preserve us from infinite dangers, which compass us round about. To be short, to grant us his Holy Spirit, to guide the whole course of our life, to the glory of his name, and the peace and salvation of our own souls. For, he who has not a feeling of the great want of all these graces, or blessings, and consequently, the necessity of prayers unto God, for obtaining the same, knows not himself, but is senseless and void of all feelings. By prayer we bless God for his goodness, power, wisdom, justice, and mercy toward us. Because of our prayers, he blesses us, in doing us good, and distributing his benefits amongst us. It is unto us, as the soul of our souls. For that prayer quickens our affections, and lifts up our hearts unto heaven; which otherwise would be dead in sins and trespasses, by following the vanities of this wicked world. Prayer is as it were the key which opens unto us the treasury of our heavenly Father, as faith is the hand, laying hold upon those sure and permanent possessions of eternal life, the desire whereof, should cause us continually to pray unto, and fervently to love God.[46]

---

43 Ibid., 364-65.
44 Ibid., 365.
45 Ibid., 359.
46 Beza, *Houshold Prayers*, B1v-B3r.

Later Beza urged his readers to pray continually and so receive blessings from God. "Oh, how happy shall these men then be, whom the Lord shall find thus watching, and praying! for they shall depart unto him in peace, in the contemplation of his glory; which grace, God grant unto us all."[47] Beza was a Christian believer who communed with his Lord in prayer and was filled with affection for him.

Beza's sentiments here are striking when one considers that this collection of prayers was one of his last productions. He noted in them that he was "feeling myself toward the declining evening of my days." Yet he was spurred on by "a taste of so many solid, and permanent joys, as are daily to be found in prayer: and withal, being inflamed with a desire, to finish the rest of my course, in this sweet labor."[48] Beza was a passionate Christian. To him the idea of passionless faith was oxymoronic.

Beza the Pastor

Beza also understood himself to be a pastor. This aspect of his self-understanding influenced the manner in which he instructed and counseled others. He preached several times a week for most of his life as a Protestant.[49] His pastoral vision emerged in his labors as a shepherd of God's flock.

Beza's pastoral concern shines through in his writings in many ways. As an overseer concerned for the flock, he warned the readers of one of his biblical publications "how far they are deceived, that seek for contentment in any worldly thing."[50] Beza also offered pertinent pastoral advice about caring for the needs of others. Drawing on the example of Job's "counselors," Beza urged his students to be sensitive to the circumstances and needs of troubled persons they were going to need to help in pastoral ministry. He pointed out that "the saying of Terence is not always true, 'We that are well, can give good advise to those that are sick,'" for the poor counsel of Job's friends showed that

> it is not enough for us, when we will comfort others, to bring a good and loving mind, nor in some general terms to advertise them aright, unless moreover we observe these two things. First, that, as expert physicians use to do in diseases of the body, we labor to know the true and certain cause of the diseases of the mind,

---

47 Ibid., B9v.
48 Ibid., B8r-B8v.
49 Armand Dückert, *Théodore de Bèze: Prédicateur* (Geneva: n.p., 1891), 11; Michel Delval, "La Prédication d'un Réformateur au XVIe Siècle: l'Activité Homilétique de Théodore de Bèze," *Mélanges de Science Religieuse* 41 (1984): 65-66.
50 Theodore Beza, *Ecclesiastes, or the Preacher. Solomons Sermon Made to the people, teaching every man howe to order his life, so as they may come to true and everlasting happines. With a Paraphrase, or short exposition thereof, made by Theodore Beza* (Cambridge: n.p., n.d.), on Eccl 3:16.

not by any hasty and untimely judgment, not by every false and lying conjecture, not by common, but by proper and infallible signs. Secondly, that when once we have found out the truth and certainty of the disease, we have such a regard, as near as we may, both to the person diseased, and to the circumstances of time and place, that we temper sweet and sour together, and with discretion so mix our vinegar with sugar, and our sugar with vinegar, that if we chance to do him no good, the fault may lie wholly upon the patient himself, and not upon the physician.[51]

Beza's preface for his 1565 Latin New Testament concisely laid out his understanding of his calling as a pastor.[52] Remarkably, in a piece of astounding scholarship Beza first of all identified himself as a pastor. He pleaded, "Would to God that we (and I especially) who by God's grace minister in his church, might be free to be occupied with learning and teaching rather than in writing."[53] Beza considered himself a minister of the church.

What does that tell us about Beza's self-conception? First of all, Beza saw his "parish," in a sense, to encompass all those who would read his work. He was ministering to those who would use his translation. Beza could not justify studying and learning for its own sake when heterodoxy abounded. "We are compelled partly by the pestering of certain adversaries, whose efforts the lovers of truth must oppose in all ways, so that the simple and little ones should be deceived, and partly also by love which admonishes us to return for the benefit (*à l'utilité*) of our brothers all that we have received."[54] As a pastor charged with caring for the flock Beza had to strive for their good, in this case leading him to be a biblical scholar in order to be a faithful pastor.

In the second place, Beza labored as a Bible scholar because he knew that the Bible was one of a Christian's primary weapons in the spiritual battle. According to Beza, the purpose of the Bible was to show persons the way of salvation so that they might spend eternity with God. The Bible's authority was unequivocal; it alone taught the way of salvation. "It is therefore a certain thing that the doctrine of salvation contained in the word of God must be maintained orthodox (*saine*) and entire, not only in general, but also in each one of its parts

---

51 Theodore Beza, *Job Expounded by Theodore Beza, Partly in Manner of a Commentary, Partly in Manner of a Paraphrase* (Cambridge: n.p., 1589), L2v-L3r.
52 Beza, *Correspondance*, 6:254-70. According to the editors of Beza's correspondence, the letter Beza wrote to the Prince of Condé and other French Protestant nobility is an almost word-for-word French translation of Beza's Latin preface (ibid., 270). Quotations in the text are my translations of Beza's French letter. It was translated into English as "An Exhortation to the Reformation of the Church" in *A Confession of Faith Made By Common Consent of Divers Reformed Churches Beyond the* Seas (London: n.p., n.d.).
53 Beza, *Correspondance*, 6:267.
54 Ibid.

and particulars."⁵⁵ "We must decide all differences by the word of God," Beza exhorted, "and the false word by the true, as we also should discern by the word of God the legitimate Church from the bastard, and the councils governed by the Holy Spirit from those over which Satan presided. In short, the truth from a lie. Because we must not think that the truth would be disclosed to us elsewhere [than the word of God] in that which concerns our salvation."⁵⁶ The "pure word of God" (*la pure parolle de Dieu*) spoke only when the Bible was interpreted rightly, "by the comparison of passages, reconciling all interpretations by the analogy of faith, then finally nothing will present itself so difficult which will not easily be understood, nothing so obscure which will not be clear, nothing so doubtful which will not be rendered plain and evident."⁵⁷ Since previous Latin translations were erroneous at points, he had labored to provide a better translation, even though it "were to be desired" that everyone could read the original Hebrew and Greek.⁵⁸ Thus Beza's biblical scholarship flowed from his pastoral concern for persons to be saved. The "Church was nearly crushed" by doctrinal deviations over the centuries. But "the only path and means of redressing it was by disputing these differences by the pure word of God."⁵⁹ Only the pure Bible would lead people to salvation.⁶⁰ For these reasons, Beza

---

55 Ibid., 261.
56 Ibid., 265.
57 Ibid.
58 Ibid., 266.
59 Ibid., 265.
60 Beza's 1565 preface also gives us a glimpse into what he hoped to do in the remaining years of his life. Calvin had just died. Beza was forty-six years old, and he occupied a place of great power and influence. He was the president of Geneva's young Academy and the star faculty member there. He was the head of the Company of Pastors. He also had a very high reputation for his scholarship. What did Beza want to do with the remaining years of his life? As far as I know, the only other person who has noted the light this preface shines on the relationship between Calvin and Beza is Ian McPhee. See his "Conserver or Transformer of Calvin's Theology? A Study of the Origins and Development of Theodore Beza's Thought, 1550-1570" (Ph.D. diss., Cambridge University, 1979), 353.

Beza's answer to this question came when discussing the two kinds of biblical commentators. The first "does not properly consider what is said (that is to say, the words themselves) so they make the condition of declaring, changing so much only the language, in which words the thing is said." (Beza, *Correspondance*, 6:266). The second type, the better of the two, Beza judged, "explain things by more words, adjoining the reasons" (ibid.). Then he specifically evaluated Calvin's commentaries. He included Calvin in the second category, calling him "that noble John Calvin, man of glad memory and my father in Christ (*mon pere en Christ*)" who "surpassed by a great deal all the old and modern" commentators (*Correspondance*, 6:266). Then Beza explained how his own labors coincided with the high regard he had for Calvin's: "Though a few times I am not of the same opinion with him in certain points, not at all in those which concern doctrine (which I have always perceived to be writings of this man very pure and solid, so that never has there been another expositor like him), but in the explication of certain passages. Nevertheless, with regard to his commentaries, my advice is the same as the opinion of Cicero in a kind of writing very different concerning Julius Caesar's commentaries, be it known that he dissuaded through marvel the wisest men from writing after him" (*Correspondance*, 6:266-67).

Why, then, did Beza feel compelled to publish exegetical and expositional works? Here we must note Beza's context, for he said that the controversies of his day demanded his continued efforts to help Christians understand the Bible better. Many falsely interpret the Bible, he declared, by not paying attention to the order of words and sentences: "Leaving their [i.e., the Scriptures'] main purpose, one finds certain small observations confusedly and haphazardly gathered together, so that they have no regard or consideration for the sense of several passages which are of very great consequence." To correct this, Beza published his New Testament and *Annotationes*: "For this reason, so that I might remedy this sickness, I have tried in this work the most to annotate brief summaries of doctrine to the historical narratives, so that whoever shall navigate as it were in this sea, then may take refuge in the port situated before his eyes, which he can approach. And with regard to the epistles, I have done such that the point and the order of the arguments and finally the method and the native expositions (having distributed all things in order) can be known" (*Correspondance*, 6:267).

A key to understanding the relationship of Beza's works to Calvin's seems to be to try to understand the differences between their literary outputs. Calvin was able to write his *Institutes*, publish sermons, and write commentaries, as well as compose occasional theological treatises. In other words, he was able to write several works in various genres, all of which allows scholars to form a full-orbed picture of his theology. One reason Beza is often misunderstood, though, is that he was not able to write as much in the various genres as was Calvin. Beza's works, at least the ones scholars tend to focus on, are the occasional and polemical ones, because those are most of what he published. But that was not what Beza intended as he scanned the horizon and dreamt about his future labors as he took over the helm of the Genevan Reformation. In this preface, he wrote about what he hoped to do in the future: "And if God permits me that finally I can some day add two things that I am considering already, let it be known [that I want to write] a brief exposition of certain words which are found in the text, and also common places, each one in its place in a word, then truly I will think that I have done a masterpiece" (*Correspondance*, 6:267). Very importantly for the study of post-Reformation theological studies, then, one must note that Beza thought Calvin the best commentator of his day, that he felt driven to do his *Annotationes* because of the controversies raging still in his day, and that in the future he hoped to publish commentaries on the New Testament text itself as well as common place discussions of the difficult places in the commentaries. Thus, he hoped to mimic Calvin's theological productions. Beza never completed this task. There may be several reasons why he failed in this task, but I think the most obvious ones are that his times were quite different from Calvin's. Calvin lived in relative peace in

labored as a pastor in the face of much opposition and many difficulties for over forty-five years.

Beza the Trainer of Pastors

Much of Theodore Beza's energies were directed toward the Geneva Academy. For almost his entire stay in Geneva, he served as Rector and Professor of Theology, stepping down as professor in 1599 and ceasing from his pastoral duties in 1600.[61] The Reformer addressed the Academy at its first commencement in June of 1559. He declared, in part, "Since God has endowed us, as members of the human race, with intelligence, we are in duty bound to use this gift. We are intended to think things out, and to make orderly sense of what we see, and to understand that everything can be accommodated within a single comprehensive philosophy. But we cannot do this properly without training and hard work."[62] Then he explained why the upper school students must become acquainted with "good letters," or the classical authors, and why they had to be well-equipped in the "rational disciplines," or the use of rhetoric and dialectic.[63] The goal, according to Rector Beza, was not merely to create thoughtful and articulate young adults; rather, the point of this education was the glory of God. "Let us agree that the point of all philosophy is to pursue virtue," Beza said to the *scholastici*, the upper school students. Continuing, he argued:

> Virtue is that which is subordinated to the will of Almighty God. To this you must be obedient, and in that obedience, diligent in your studies. To be idle and negligent is a perfidious rejection of the gift of God. You are not here to take part in frivolous games, but in order that you may become imbued with true religion and equipped with all good arts, the better to amplify God's glory and to be a

---

    Geneva, rarely traveled, died hoping that events in France were going to result in Protestants' favor, and was capable of remarkable literary output. Beza, conversely, endured great military persecution against Geneva, had to deal with the onslaught of the plague several times, traveled extensively, was burdened with all aspects of the Academy, and lived through the darkest times for Protestants in his beloved France.

61 See Manetsch, *Theodore Beza*, 18.
62 Quoted in Gillian Lewis, "The Genevan Academy," in *Calvinism in Europe, 1540-1620*, ed. Andrew Pettegree, Alastair Duke, and Gillian Lewis (Cambridge: Cambridge University Press, 1994), 39. A complete English translation of the inaugural address is located in "Beza's Address at the Solemn Opening at the Academy of Geneva," trans. Lewis W. Spitz, in *Transition and Revolution: Problems and Issues of European Renaissance and Reformation History*, ed. Robert M. Kingdon (Minneapolis: Burgess, 1974), 175-79.
63 Lewis, "Genevan Academy," 39.

credit to your native land. Never forget that you have enrolled under the sacred military discipline of the great Commander himself.[64]

For Beza, then, the ultimate point of the Academy was religious instruction. Students were to learn there what true religion was and how to understand and defend it for the glory of God, in submission to his will.[65]

Only Beza's great concern for well-trained pastors in the midst of the spiritual battle can explain his almost Herculean efforts on behalf of the Academy. As Rector, Beza was very concerned with what was taught and who the teachers were at the Academy, showing a special interest in the teaching of theology. He alternated lecturing in theology every other week, giving one hour lectures on a book of the Bible on Monday, Tuesday, and Wednesday.[66] After Calvin's death he lectured three times a week in addition to his regular preaching responsibilities, until Lambert Daneau was brought in as adjunct instructor in 1572.[67] He kept at it for almost all his life, not least because the Genevan magistrates insisted. In 1590, suffering from very poor health at the age of seventy-one, Beza asked to be relieved of some of his duties. He was allowed to cease his weekday sermons, but was required to continue his alternate week theology lectures as well as his sermons on Sunday.[68] He did not cease lecturing until 1600.

Beza's role in the evolution of the theology curriculum at the Academy has been examined by a number of scholars. Beza argued that a second chair of theology could have negative effects, especially since a disagreement by the theology instructors over a point of doctrine in which one could not out-vote the other "could easily lead to division, disharmony, and even heresy," as

---

64 Ibid., 39-40.
65 "The tenor of Beza's inaugural address indicated that the Academy was not meant as a place where one would merely acquire a good education. Instead, the Academy was to provide goal-oriented training, with an especial, although not exclusive, focus on theology and on the mission which the students were called to fulfil, both as ministers and as laymen in the Calvinist world" (Karin Maag, *Seminary or University? The Genevan Academy and Reformed Higher Education, 1560-1620*, St. Andrews Studies in Reformation History [Aldershot: Scholar, 1995], 16).
66 Lewis, "Genevan Academy," 32. In February of 1564, Charles Perrot, a student at the Academy, wrote his brother of Beza's tireless labors there. Calvin, he said, "can scarcely manage to take his turn regularly because of illness, especially in the winter; in the summer he is a little better. This means that Theodore [Beza] carries almost all the weight of the School, which is testimony to his resilience: the more fields that are to be cultivated, the more the plough-ox shows his strength" (cited in Lewis, "Genevan Academy," 51).
67 Manetsch, "Theodore Beza," 189.
68 Manetsch, *Theodore Beza*, 213.

Manetsch argued.[69] Finally, though, a second professor was added in 1587 to teach *loci communes*, or "common places," to Academy students. Based on the desires Beza expressed in his 1565 preface to the New Testament and on the way in which theology continued to be taught under his watchful eye, one should not assume that this introduction of dogmatics to the curriculum materially changed the way in which theology was done at Geneva. Whatever the cause for the pedagogical innovation, Beza viewed it as a means to train pastors to wage war in the spiritual battle.[70] Thus, when the magistrates decreed that the Academy should close due the Savoyard blockade and the subsequent economic hardship in Geneva during 1586, Beza argued that the school must remain open for the sake of truth. Its closure would harm the churches, he said. Besides, it "would please their enemies and give a strong advantage to Catholic colleges." The Academy remained open, and Beza began lecturing on Job in order to encourage the students of God's sovereign wisdom and power during the upheaval.[71]

In all his efforts at the Academy, Beza's goal was not just to create well-equipped minds. He aimed to train pastors who would not only preach the truth, but also urge its utility for living. In fact, Beza was critical of those who had

---

69 Manetsch, "Theodore Beza," 189. One should also realize that due to plague infestation of Geneva in 1564 and again from 1568 to 1570, Savoy's blockade of Geneva in 1586, the rise of other Protestant academies, and also Beza's aging and Geneva's problem finding someone of his stature to replace him, the Academy's prestige, and importantly, its enrollment, had declined greatly. See Lewis, "Genevan Academy," 62; Maag, *Seminary or University?*, 31-32, 40, 61-65; Kingdon, *Geneva and Consolidation*, 30-32; and Manetsch, *Theodore Beza*, 215-16.

70 Lewis thinks it was so that the students would be prepared to defend the Protestant, specifically Reformed, faith in view of the many controversies of the late sixteenth-century ("Genevan Academy," 61). Those who are quick to chalk up the change in curriculum to Beza's scholasticizing tendencies would do well to remember the desires Beza expressed in 1565 about *loci communes*, specifically that he did not think dogmatics negated biblical exegesis, and they should note recent investigation into the nature of scholasticism. Marvin Anderson aptly noted that Vermigli's *loci* were exegetical, while Turretin's were not, but that the change was not Beza's fault: "The shift to elenchi such as that of Francois Turretin would be a more subtle process as fresh loci that focused on the nature and attributes of God replaced the exegetical ones of Vermigli. Zanchi himself denies that this theological interest in the nature of God came from Vermigli." Rather, "though the temptation was present already in Daneau and Zanchi to shift the focus from scripture to metaphysical speculation about God, that 'fall' did not occur in the first six decades of the Genevan Academy" (Anderson, "John Calvin: Biblical Preacher [1539-1564]," *Scottish Journal of Theology* 42 [1989]: 179, 181).

71 Manetsch, "Theodore Beza," 190-91. For a fuller discussion of Beza's lectures on Job, see chapter four.

only intellectual components in their teaching. Commenting on Psalm 39, Beza said, "the prophet throughout this psalm mixes prayers full of affections, that he might teach us that these things are not to be disputed coldly of us, as though we were in philosophers' schools. But we must use most vehement and earnest prayers, whereby we should ask of God, both to have our affections eased, and our faith continued."[72] Theodore Beza aimed at his students' affections in his teaching.

Beza's Eschatological Vision

Beza's eschatological, or pastoral, vision is evident throughout his writings. It permeated all that he did, including his historical, devotional, pastoral, and doctrinal treatises. This pastoral view of reality drove what Beza did as a Christian, a pastor, and a professor. In this section I will delineate the contours of that vision which undergirded and fueled everything that Beza accomplished. Understanding Beza's eschatological vision is essential to comprehending the utility of God's sovereignty in his thought. The realities of Satan, of a raging spiritual battle, of hell, and of heaven necessitated an omnipotent hand to preserve and guide Christians through their earthly pilgrimage.

The Vie de Calvin

Beza's *Vie de Calvin* offers a fitting introduction to his pastoral vision because in it God and Satan were the key actors along with Calvin. He initially wrote this in the year of Calvin's death, to commemorate the life of his "father in Christ" (*mon pere en Christ*).[73] Although it contains the requisite references to dates, places, and events, there is much more. The most surprising fact about the eulogy is the heightened spiritual activity that Beza noted around the life and labors of his beloved Calvin. Beza punctuated his prose with numerous evaluative judgments and assertions of divine or demonic causation of events in Geneva, showing that for him the fact of spiritual activity was a given. In fact, besides Calvin, God (the one providentially guiding all that went on, including

---

72 Beza, *Psalmes*, 77.
73 Beza, *Correspondance*, 6:266. Frédéric Gardy noted the three editions of this work during Beza's life and its translation from French into Latin, German, English, Dutch, and Hungarian, which suggest its popularity (*Bibliographie des Oeuvres Théologiques, Littéraires, Historiques et Juridiques de Théodore de Bèze* [Geneva: Librairie Droz, 1960], 104-26). William J. Bouwsma charged that "the canonization of Calvin began as early as Beza's *Life*, a work that, from an author who had known Calvin so long and so closely, is curiously lifeless and lacking in human insight" (*John Calvin: A Sixteenth Century Portrait* [New York: Oxford University Press, 1988], 238 n. 8). I am offering no judgment about Beza's merits as a biographer, but I am suggesting that this work clearly displayed his pastoral vision.

the schemes of Satan) and Satan (opposing Calvin and the truth at every turn) are the two key actors in this spiritual drama.[74]

Beza held that the conflict between God and Satan affected civic and ecclesiastical affairs in Geneva. He wrote that Satan was "exasperated (but in vain)" when Geneva adopted the Reformation in 1537, for "the Lord had anticipated Satan."[75] God's hand even stood behind Calvin's forced departure from Geneva to Strasbourg, for "the event showed that the purpose of Divine Providence was partly, by employing the labors of his faithful servant elsewhere, to train him, by various trials, for greater achievements" when he returned to Geneva.[76] With Satan opposing the Lord at every turn, God guided Calvin back to Geneva in 1541 and used his return to bring about Geneva's adoption of Calvin's ecclesiastical discipline. Beza commented that "these laws Satan afterwards made many extraordinary attempts to abolish, but without success."[77] Satan afterward promoted dissension and controversy to derail Calvin's efforts at reform. The devil would stop at nothing; thus Beza charged that Satan did an "almost incredible" thing, "making use especially of the very persons who were most desirous of suppressing [the devil's work]; I mean Farel and Viret."[78] The spiritual conflict raged throughout Calvin's career.

According to Beza, God and Satan were primarily battling over the truth because truth was the tool that bent the soul. Although he recounted the rise of factions and the ousting of persons, Beza's central theme in the *Vie* was the antagonism between truth and error. God empowered Calvin to adhere to the scriptures and teach the truth; Satan vigorously opposed this teaching, raising up heretics who tried to expunge the truth of God. Thus Beza lauded the almost superhuman efforts of Calvin, empowered as he was by divine aid: "The thing to be wondered at rather is, that a single man [Calvin], as if he had been a kind of Christian Hercules, should have been able to subdue so many monsters, and this by that mightiest of all clubs, the Word of God. Wherefore, as many adverseries as Satan stirred up against him, (for his enemies were always those

---

74 The only scholar of whom I am aware who has noticed elements of this spiritual battle motif in the *Vie* is Philip Holtrop. But his explanation—that Beza wanted to make Calvin a hero and all his opponents heretics in the context of the wars of religion in France—is not satisfactory given the centrality of spiritual combat and God's providential care throughout the *Vie*. See Philip C. Holtrop, *The Bolsec Controversy on Predestination, from 1551 to 1555: The Statements of Jerome Bolsec, and the Responses of John Calvin, Theodore Beza, and Other Reformed Theologians* (Lewiston, NY: Edwin Mellen, 1993), 1:786-88, 793.
75 Thedore Beza, *The Life of John Calvin*, in *Selected Works of John Calvin: Tracts and Letters*, vol. 1, ed. and trans. Henry Beveridge (1844; reprint, Grand Rapids: Baker, 1983), xxx.
76 Ibid., xxxiii.
77 Ibid., xxxviii.
78 Ibid., lii.

who had declared war against piety and honesty,) so many trophies did the Lord bestow upon his servant."[79] In Beza's estimation, then, Geneva was central to the Lord's purpose since it was the place where, "by the singular providence of God," the Lord had over and over again caused "the purest light to arise out of the thickest darkness."[80] Through Calvin's exposition of the truth, "the arch-enemy," Satan, "was most powerfully opposed."[81] Calvin's experience in Geneva proved that the spiritual battle for souls would be decided in the struggle for the truth.

This spiritual battle for the truth produced numerous deadly skirmishes in Geneva, according to Beza. For instance, Jérôme Bolsec's heretical opinions about predestination indicated spiritual attack. The Lord won this encounter, for "all that Satan gained by these dissensions was, that this article of the Christian religion, which was formerly most obscure, became clear and transparent to all not disposed to be contentious." Yet, "as if Satan himself had blown the trumpet," the opponents of the truth were roused from their slumber to oppose God through Bolsec's boldness.[82] Likewise, Beza blamed the devil for the controversy surrounding Michael Servetus who was "a monstrous compound of mere impiety and horrid blasphemy."[83] To Beza, then, God and the devil were engaged in martial combat, wielding the weapons of truth and heresy. Calvin manifested God's power because "in defending his doctrine," he "trusted solely to the power of truth."[84]

Beza's *Vie* delineates the contours of his pastoral vision. A spiritual battle was raging whose main combatants were God and Satan. The battle concerned the truth and therefore was waged with the weapons of correct doctrine and heresy. The outcome of each engagement meant the salvation or damnation of souls. For that reason the main locus of activity in the battle was the church, for God appointed it to preserve the truth. The stakes in this combat were eternal. For those who persevered, under God's providence, the reward was heaven; hence the time of Calvin's death, though "to us of the greatest and best founded grief," "was to him the commencement of perpetual felicity."[85]

This vision of reality was the basis of Beza's insistence that God had to be

---

79 Ibid., xcix.
80 Ibid., lxxvii.
81 Ibid., xlvi.
82 Ibid., lvii, lix.
83 Ibid., lxv.
84 Ibid., lx.
85 Ibid., lxxxii. Daniel Ménager noted that one of Beza's reasons for composing the *Vie* was to comfort (*consoler*) Protestants after Calvin's death ("Théodore de Bèze, Biographe de Calvin," *Bibliothèque d'Humanisme et Renaissance: Travaux et Documents* 45 [1983]: 232). He also rightly highlighted Beza's portrayal of God's providential activity in the eulogy (ibid., 240, 242, 254), so that it should perhaps be called a "praise of God" (*éloge de Dieu*) (ibid., 255).

completely sovereign in order to protect his children. The components of his pastoral vision previously noted in his *Vie* permeated Beza's writings, of all genres, as the following overview will demonstrate.

The Fact of the Spiritual Battle

Beza depicted Satan as active in the world, indefatigably trying to harm Christians.[86] So he indicted Satan as the foremost of "my enemies" in his meditation on Psalm 102. The devil was "that great devouring lion, who has spoiled, torn, and swallowed so many" Christians "from the beginning of the world."[87] Satan was the deadly aggressor in the spiritual battle.

Satan's schemes took many forms. In the first place, he was incessant in troubling Christians, and in tempting them to sin. "Satan, the prince of darkness, lays always in wait to hurt us, seeking principally to make a breach into our hearts when we stand least upon our guard," Beza warned. "Give us grace," he therefore prayed, "to be delivered from the temptations of the devil, from uncleaness . . . into which our infirmity leads us."[88] The devil also troubled Christians when they attempted to pray, "for besides that the devil at all times lies in wait, to seduce us, so does he, especially, at such times, seek to creep into our minds, to divert our thoughts elsewhere, that they may be polluted with many blemishes."[89] One of the prerequisites of fervent prayer was thus to abandon "Satan with all his baits."[90]

Only God could make Christians strong for the combat. They could not rely on their autonomous efforts in the spiritual battle. Indeed, one of the devil's favorite schemes involved making believers think they could stand against him in their own strength: "we have to learn how Satan," Beza urged his listeners, "is never more ready for us to surrender, than when we think we have won the upper hand."[91] Rather, the omnipotent God would protect his children. "Does Satan amaze you?" Beza asked his listeners when the Genevans feared a

---

86 Compare Manetsch's opinion that when Beza referred to Protestants' opponents as "Satan" his "use of biblical images like these often served as a barometer of his angst and anger. When the reformer wished to express his deepest pain, frustration, or indignation, he frequently appealed to scriptural characters and concepts, interpreting the data of his experience in light of the biblical drama of God's chosen people struggling against Satan and his minions" (*Theodore Beza*, 53-54).
87 Theodore Beza, *Christian Meditations upon Eight Psalmes of the Prophet David* (London: Christopher Barker, 1582).
88 Beza, *Houshold Prayers*, P3r-P3v.
89 Ibid., B6r.
90 Ibid., B5v.
91 Theodore Beza, *Sermons sur l'Histoire de la Passion et Sepulture de nostre Seigneur Jesus Christ, descrite par les quatre Evangelistes* (Geneva: Jean le Preux, 1592), 197.

Catholic attack in 1587.[92] If so, believers need not worry, for their Lord

> has vanquished him for you. Does the corruption of your nature astonish you? The Son of God making himself man has fully sanctified it for you. Do your sins make you afraid, which be fruits of this corruption? He has borne them all upon the tree, and has paid for your discharge. Which more is, his righteousness is yours, if he himself is yours. Are you afraid of men, if God is for you? Does death make you afraid? It is vanquished and turned into an entry of life. Behold then all your enemies scattered, behold quite under foot, all such as afflicted you within and without, because the Lord allows you for one of his servants and household.[93]

The battle was real, but God would protect his children and bring them safely to himself. Although Satan's schemes were evil and troubling, "it is not in the power of any to trouble us, except when and how far it pleases God they shall do it."[94] Thus, Beza urged his listeners to forgo trusting in their "imaginary powers" by partaking of the "real remedy" Christ modeled for them, namely, "to know prayer, provided that it is lifted up" to almighty God.[95]

The Battle for the Truth

Satan especially sought to destroy the church because God cared for it and appointed it the guardian of the truth. The devil attacked the church by trying to foster heretical beliefs in her midst. So Beza warned his listeners to "guard here of a great ruse of Satan, pushing us if he can, from one extreme to the other, which are as much as precipices. Therefore let us know that those are grandly self-deceived who want to subjugate the word of God to their own natural sense." Instead believers must lean "on the word of God understood, and not at all on our imaginations, whether they are old or new."[96] Satan moved in those "deceived who seek for the true religion in the crowd, in custom . . . as if there had not already been more fools than wise men." But, he went on to warn his listeners, "let us defend ourselves here from Satan's ambushes, and let us remember this, which the true Jesus Christ admonished us (Matt. 24:23) to

---

92 Raitt, "Beza, Guide," 97-98.
93 Beza, *Christian Meditations*, on Ps 143:12.
94 Theodore Beza, *Master Bezaes Sermons Upon the Three First Chapters of the Canticle of Canticles*, trans. John Harmar (Oxford: Joseph Barnes, 1587), 236.
95 Beza, *Sermons sur la Passion*, 129. Based on the devil's heightened activity against believers, Beza chided Christians: "let us be ashamed hereof, that Satan is more diligent in doing mischief, daily laboring to bring us to destruction, than we are careful in the whole course of our life, to perform the duties of our vocation, and to keep ourselves out of the danger of so deadly an enemy" (*Job*, on Job 1:13).
96 Beza, *Sermons sur la Passion*, 437.

know, that false christs and false prophets" would come.[97]

The conflict between orthodoxy and heresy heightened the importance of schools, for these were charged with instructing students in the truth. Again, Beza highlighted Satan's malicious schemes in the schools, especially "the school of divinity" because here "Satan has served his turn with sugar to turn it into most bitter and deadly poison." The devil "banished out of the school of divinity that which was the only subject thereof, I mean the reading and expounding of the text of holy Scripture, to thrust thereunto an abominable confusion of dreaming sophistications, some as vain as curious, others absurd, other full of impiety."[98] In another place, Beza identified a principal "craft" of Satan as "these human traditions and this glorious theology called 'scholastic'" which consisted of "so many buckets and stamps to oppose what is this truth of God."[99] Schools must teach the truth.

Satan not only drew people away from the Bible to human traditions; he also introduced outright heresy. Remarkably, when writing to the French Protestant leaders in 1565 exhorting them not to turn away from the Protestant cause in the face of persecution, Beza's chief concern was Satan who had been responsible for fomenting heresy throughout the history of the church. Satan, Beza averred, "still forges other secret mysteries, against which it is necessary that you resist and stand steadfast, by the sincerity and pure simplicity of Christian doctrine."[100] Advisors who promoted compromise were in league with the devil for "their words have a great show and a beautiful [one], but it proceeds from the spirit of Satan."[101]

Biblical truth was essential. If one did not believe certain truths, one would be damned eternally. That is why Beza prayed that the church would "be my whole desire, and the sole subject of my delights, that I may never depart from there, notwithstanding whatsoever assaults and temptations I am to endure." He yearned to remain in the church in the midst of the spiritual battle because "there is not any such mishap, or so much to be feared, as to be out of this holy temple, wherein only abides all light, truth, salvation, and life."[102] The church, Beza prayed to God, was "where your truth is lodged."[103] As such, it was the locus of salvation and life. Although the truth was being assailed by the schemes of the devil, it would prevail: from true doctrine "proceeds the stability of the Church, which the endeavors of Satan cannot shake, because the

---

97 Ibid., 325-26.
98 Beza, *Canticles*, 135.
99 Theodore Beza, *Sermons sur l'Histoire de la Resurrection de nostre Seigneur Jesus Christ* (Geneva: Jean le Preux, 1593), 188-89.
100 Beza, "Exhortation to Reformation."
101 Ibid.
102 Beza, *Houshold Prayers*, G2v-G3r.
103 Ibid., G1r.

foundation of her faith and doctrine is grounded upon the true, and immoveable rock, even the pure confession of the name of Christ."[104] Though Satan endeavored to destroy the church, the confession of the truth protected her in the midst of the spiritual battle.

Satan's Schemes in Human History

The spiritual battle also raged outside the confines of the church. Satan connived in secular affairs, trying through these mechanisms to oppose God and his truth. In the preface to his *Histoire ecclésiastique des églises réformées au royaume de France*, Beza noted two ways of reading history, one seeing God's providential hand and the other seeing only material causes.[105] "A very great mistake," he averred, was committed when one merely looked at "the boundary marks of this frail and transitory life." This was merely the secondary arena of history. The principal arena of history was God's "spiritual government, in which shines sovereignly and in a particular way the providence, wisdom, power, and infinite mercy of God. Persons were principally created and formed for the contemplation" of this providence.[106] Beza had two overriding purposes in composing this martyrology. In the first place, he wanted persons "to return the honor to [God] that belongs to him" when they had seen "the great works that he has done in our time." But, secondly, Beza thought his history would be a means of helping persons to persevere in the midst of the spiritual battle. He wrote it "to put before the eyes of those God opened, that which can and must infinitely encourage them not to grow weary, on account of any difficulty, of following the good path which they entered" when they were reminded of God's providential care in the midst of intense hardship.[107]

The Eternal Stakes of the Battle

Theodore Beza's pastoral vision was eternal in its scope. He had his eyes fixed on eternity as he lived and ministered in this life. He wanted himself and those under his care to go to heaven and not to have to suffer the perpetual torments of hell.

---

104 Ibid.
105 Although the compiler of *Histoire ecclésiastique* is not named, Beza probably oversaw its composition. See Manetsch, *Theodore Beza*, 139 n. 80, and Beza, *Correspondance*, 21:vii-xi.
106 Theodore Beza, *Histoire ecclésiastique des églises réformées au royaume de France,* ed. G. Baum and E. Cunitz (Paris: 1883; reprint, Nieuwkoop: B. de Graaf, 1974), 1:i.
107 Ibid., 1:x.

Beza acknowledged that eternity was an awesome experience to contemplate in this life. In the prayer "upon temporal death," he exhorted persons to dwell upon the inevitability of eternity so that they might escape God's judgment and resort to Christ for salvation:

> The longest time of our course – whereof sleep nibbles away a good part – is but three-score and ten years, or four-score for the strongest bodies, while in every moment of life, the nearest and smallest danger that threatens us, seems to be death, which as our shadow, follows us at the heels, and laughs at our good devices, until she has scattered them in the wind, and brought us into ashes. But which is worse, where is the man, so holy and perfect, that does not tremble and quake, if there be represented unto him, O Lord, the tribunal seat of your sovereign justice, where we all, after death, must appear? Your indignation against sinners is manifest, and there is none righteous, your vengeance is ready against rebellion, whereof we be all guilty, which does also cause, that death is unto us, not only as a temporal ending as concerning the flesh, whereat nature is moved and abashed, but also an interior feeling of the curse fallen upon sin, yea even an entry into eternal death, unless there be for us with you our Father, redemption in our Lord Jesus Christ.[108]

So those who did not receive redemption must certainly go to "the tribunal seat of [God's] sovereign justice" and experience God's "indignation against sinners" and his "vengeance [which] is ready against rebellion."[109]

Hell's torments would be excruciating for unbelievers. "These miserable men," he said, "depart this their earthly habitation, with great grief and trembling." Their eternal fate is foreshadowed in the misery and fear they experience on the brink of death which is "the proof that they are going to make, of the eternal torments with the devils in the burning lake of fire and brimstone, which is never quenched, given to the soul presently upon the temporal death." Their "eternal death" is "a death which continues without dying." And it will not only consist in torments of body but also of conscience, for "this pain is not the least to the damned . . . that they never have any motion of the spirit to repent or convert unto you the only and true God."[110] Yes, hell will be for them an eternity of intense emotional, physical, and spiritual pain, because "when they think upon death, they see nothing but fearful, horrible, damnable, all-intolerable pain, without diminution or end, an infernal, devilish, and endless torment, a gnashing of teeth, with blasphemy and despair, a perpetual disquiet both in body and soul, an eternity to their woe and damnation." But much more than that "a most merciful God, whom they shall know to be in heaven, and yet not to be their God, but their adversary, and

---

108 Beza, *Houshold Prayers*, in the prayer "Upon temporal death."
109 Ibid.
110 Ibid., N2v-N3v.

sovereign judge, to be as severe and rigorous to them, as he shall be gentle and favorable to his children."[111] Lest one argue with the deity that hell seemed an exorbitantly horrendous punishment for finite sins, Beza justified an eternal hell in Anselmian terms, "for your majesty being infinitely offended, ought also in justice to require a punishment without end."[112]

As hell should be abhorred and avoided at all costs, heaven should be desired and sought after with all of one's being. Heaven was a wonderful and joyful place, where a Christian would be freed from the trials of his or her earthly pilgrimage. In heaven Christians "may once for all, wholly be set free from so miserable bondage of sin" and "they may behold [God] as it were face to face, yea and more rightly serve and honor him, whom all their lifetime they have most earnestly sought."[113] Thus Beza prayed that the Lord would make a believer who was near death "with the eyes of his faith, to behold the eternal blessings you reserve for him in your paradise, to live happy for ever." Such a person could endure death since he knew he would soon "enjoy your presence in heaven."[114]

Having an eternal perspective fortified believers in the present spiritual battle, according to Beza. It empowered Christians to withstand the temptations of the world. "To the children of darkness," he commented, "the uncleanness of the flesh is a pleasant habitation. But to the children of light, to the immortal spirits, to the regenerate hearts, heaven is much more desirable." He thus prayed "Grant therefore, my God, that as I daily grow towards my end, so I may live the more cheerfully, learning in your school, to prefer your eternal life, before the light of the Sun, the glory of heaven, before the vanity of the earth, the glorious habitation in paradise, before the painful tumults of the world, the society of angels, before the fellowship of mortal men, the only blessed and permanent life, before the passing shadow of this life." He continued asking that he would "know how to prepare myself by continual meditation in these excellent Christian consolations, that happy are they that die in the Lord."[115] Similarly, in his prayer "For heavenly life," Beza asked the Lord "to give me grace, that withdrawing my affection more and more from the dark cloisters of the earth, sprinkled with tears, I may lift up my desires to the lightsome habitation of thy deity, where the treasures and incomparable joys of your paradise do remain in an eternal life." He prayed that he might comfort "myself incessantly night and day, in that the promise is made unto me through my savior Jesus Christ, to the end, that in my last hour – come out of my misery and entered into my felicity – I may with a happy flight go take my rest above

---

111 Ibid., N1v-N2r.
112 Ibid., Q5v.
113 Beza, *Job*, on Job 3.
114 Beza, *Houshold Prayers*, in the prayer, "At the visitation of the sick."
115 Ibid., in the prayer "Upon temporal death."

in your peace, O my God, which surmounts all understanding, and for to sing psalms of thanksgiving unto you without end."[116]

God's Sovereignty: Solace in the Battle

Beza's eschatological vision formed his pastoral view of reality. The times were precarious. The plague threatened and Catholic armies besieged the city; Lutheran antagonists repeatedly attacked the Reformed doctrine of the eucharist and predestination; fellow believers in his beloved France suffered death under Catholic rule; the future of the Geneva Academy appeared bleak. But above and behind all these concerns, Beza perceived a battle between God and Satan, a war which inevitably involved Christians. How could believers have confidence in such dangerous times? Their assurance of salvation and the certainty that they would persevere all the way to heaven, their survival in times of political turmoil, their strength in the midst of Satan's attacks, their very salvation—all these things depended on God's absolute sovereignty, according to Beza. God's sovereignty at its heart was a pastoral doctrine.

Beza's writings are replete with applications of the truth of God's sovereignty to his listeners and readers. He did not, to be sure, shy away from very technical discussions about predestination and providence in his teaching or his polemics. But his overriding concern remained the comfort and assurance of believers. Later chapters of this study will delineate the contours of Beza's doctrine of God's sovereignty, but the following survey of the pastoral uses Beza made of this doctrine will demonstrate that he taught that God's sovereignty was the ultimate source of joy, assurance, and salvation for Christians in the midst of the battle raging all around them.

Beza produced a litany of pastoral applications of God's sovereignty. All of them were based upon his firm belief that the present life of Christians would be hard but that the eternal glory which awaited them in heaven was stunning and filled with eternal joy. The vehicle God employed to uphold his servants in the midst of their sufferings consisted of his promises to them in the Bible, all of which stood firmly on the solid foundation of God's goodness, wisdom, and omnipotence. God's sovereign ability to keep these promises was thus the anchor for his hurting people.

So Beza urged Gaspard de Coligny to trust in the Lord as he led the Protestants during precarious times in France. Beza exhorted his friend to be "assured of the faithful guidance of such a Guide, who will lead you through the right path, whatever difficulty there is of unknown and inaccessible places." He counseled him to rely "upon that faithful Leader, who can lead you through a sure path in the midst of impassable and inaccessible places."[117] And in the

---

116 Ibid., in the prayer "For heavenly life."
117 Beza, *Correspondance*, 6:19.

midst of evil, indeed sometimes inexplicable evil, Beza insisted that even when they did not understand God's ways, Christians must seek to trust in him and his providential control over all things. "If you see in a country oppression of the poor, and defrauding of right and equity, think not too much upon this manner of doing whatsoever men list. For he that is higher than the highest works these things, and there are that are higher then they," he wrote. Rather, he cautioned his listeners not "to begin to doubt of that providence of God. For however these things seem to be tossed up and down, as if the world had no governor, yet be sure there is one above all these, that abuse the honor whereunto they are advanced, who has also standing by him innumerable and most mighty ministers, whom in due time he may set a work to execute his decrees upon these proud men."[118] In another place, Beza wrote that "it pleases God to temper the life of man by giving sometimes prosperity, sometimes adversity," but that persons "are not able to attain to his wisdom" in these matters. The only proper course, and the only avenue open to prospering in adversity, was to rest wholly in God's wisdom: "the only means to escape out of all these straights" is "neither profanely inquiring into God himself" nor "wickedly scorning at that, which he can not conceive, but falling down before the majesty of God, which we cannot comprehend." Such persons "rest wholly in his will."[119] God would take care of his people, even when they did not understand his ways.

The schemes of Satan were especially vexing to God's people. The devil tried to keep Christians apart from Christ and incited heinous evil against believers through those who opposed the Protestants. But God in his sovereignty would prevail over Satan and judge the wicked. In 1586 Beza described the two sorts of "mountains" that might tend to separate believers from the Lord, whom Beza identified with the "bridegroom" in his exposition of Canticles:

> For first of all Satan and his accomplices do what lies in them to hinder that this bridegroom and this spouse should never see each the other, leaving no kind of cruelty unpracticed, nor any kind of subtle and crafty sly means unattempted to work this division and divorce, which is verified throughout the whole sacred history. But to go no farther for proof hereof, what has been done in this behalf in our time by kings and emperors enchanted and bewitched by that whore of Rome, and by her slaves? And what does the world still every day? Read we over all the histories of the ancient persecutions, no one excepted, shall we find the like unto that which has been practiced in our time? For there is neither fire, nor water, nor air, nor earth, which have not all of them been employed to suck the life of our poor brethren: there is no kind of cruel death through which they have not passed, neither have the hands of the hangmen only been wearied with their slaughter, but

---

118 Beza, *Ecclesiastes*, on Eccl 5:8.
119 Beza, *Ecclesiastes*, C4-C5.

the people also have been employed to imbrue themselves with the blood of the poor, meek and innocent, without distinction of age or difference of sex, or any privilege of nature whatsoever. And this licentiousness has been permitted, to any that would dye his hands red with innocent blood, not in time of war and hostility, but in the greatest appearance and confidence that might be of peace and friendship.[120]

So Beza encouraged his listeners to trust their Lord: "Let us therefore know and hold this for an irrefragable point and undeniable, and altogether resolved upon . . . that the Lord is never late or slack in coming, that is to say, fails not to come at the point, yea and that leaping over all that which might seem to slack and stay his coming."[121]

God's control, Beza asserted, reached right down to ordering the deeds the devil should do. Rather than causing consternation among believers, though, Beza argued this truth should comfort them: "This doctrine is full of excellent comfort. For thereby we understand, that by the power of our God, the rage of that hungry lion is abated and bridled, and that God will never suffer him to do anything against his children, which shall not be to their good and profit, as the apostle tells us (Rom. 8:28) and also teaches us by his own example (2 Cor. 12:17)."[122]

Beza argued that God's sovereignty assured Christians of their salvation. Their Sovereign was the author of salvation from its very beginning until the time he brought his children to be with him in heaven. As believers held on to this promise, Beza argued, it would produce comfort and joy, even during times of earthly conflict. Thus Beza offered a prayer "To obtain the gift of faith":

> So great is the vanity, ignorance, and infirmity of our nature, that if you, O most merciful God, work not that in us, which you command us to do, if you do not teach us that we may know, if you do not convert us, that we may cleave to your word, if you do not give us to your Son, that he may keep us yours, if he bring us not clothed in his righteousness to the throne of your grace, and if your spirit leads us not in the paths of your kingdom, holding us fast in the effects of his gifts, upon the way of your truth, we cannot hearken to this voice of the shepherd of our souls, neither in our hearts conceive such and so lively a faith, that all uncertainty might be banished, and the same sealed with his own efficacy: much less can we feel the peace and joy that true faith brings with it.[123]

It was absolutely essential, Theodore Beza argued, that God be sovereign in salvation. Beza took great pains to controvert those who "utterly take away the supernatural grace of God, which is the first ground and foundation of our

---

120 Beza, *Canticles*, 246-47.
121 Ibid., 247.
122 Beza, *Job*, on Job 1:6.
123 Beza, *Houshold Prayers*, in the prayer "To obtain the gift of faith."

salvation." These false teachers who had been "rightly condemned and detested," charged that the Genevan ministers "transform men into blocks and stones, depriving them utterly of understanding and will."[124] They failed to notice why God must be absolutely sovereign in salvation, Beza argued.

> For, on the contrary, there is in our nature nothing but most desperate and most obstinate rebellion, until the spirit of God do drive away, first, the darkness of our understanding, which cannot, nor will not of itself, so much as think upon the things of God (2 Cor. 3:5) and that secondly it correct the forwardness of our will, which is an enemy of God, and of whatsoever is truly good (Rom. 5:10 and 8:7). And this is the cause why the apostle (Eph. 2:1) says not simply, that we are wounded, but that we are naturally dead in our sins and offences.[125]

Christians' hopes, then, rested in the Lord who had sovereignly saved them in love.

And as he had saved them, so God would grant his children the grace to persevere, Beza argued. Believers could take great comfort in their Lord's continuing sovereign grace in their lives. "He who has obtained the gift of true faith and has trusted in that same goodness of God," Beza urged, "must also be concerned about his perseverance. Yet he should not doubt, but should rather call on God in every kind of temptation and affliction, with the sure hope of attaining what he asks, at least as far as it is expedient, since he knows himself a child of God, who cannot fail him."[126] They would persevere because God who required holiness in his people would sanctify them sovereignly as well. So Beza urged his listeners when they were troubled about their standing to call upon the Lord: "Have recourse unto him which has made us, and who alone can make us anew, by the same power, which is his holy spirit, enlightening the eyes of our understanding (Eph. 1:18, Acts 26:18), framing a clean heart within us (Ps. 51:12), creating in us both to will and to do (Phil. 2:13), in a word, making us from the head to the feet new creatures (2 Cor. 5:17), that is to say, such as this spouse is set before us here to be, which is at large described unto us by Ezekiel."[127] The grand result of God's sovereignty for a believer in this life was assurance of salvation, Beza argued. In the troubles of life, believers could trust that God, in his power, would uphold them, and they could hope that God would grant them a sense of his love:

---

124 Beza, *Canticles*, 57.
125 Ibid., 56.
126 Theodore Beza, *Tabula Praedestinationis*, in *The Potter and the Clay: The Main Predestination Writings of Theodore Beza*, trans. Philip C. Holtrop (Grand Rapids: Calvin College, 1982), 58.
127 Beza, *Canticles*, 36-37.

> It may please the Lord who has drawn us out of darkness into this light of his truth, and has placed and preserved us most miraculously here in this holy rest and peace of conscience, waiting for the full accomplishment of his promises, to settle and engrave in our minds this holy assurance of his mighty power in good will towards us, that we be never astounded by the assaults of Satan, and of such his adherents as he employs and uses against us: but that contrariwise we persevere and continue in this holy profession of his truth, as well by mouth, as also by an holy and Christian life, until we come unto the real enjoying of all that, which he has made us to believe and hope for, according to his most holy and most assured promises. Conformably unto which doctrine acknowledging our over great negligence here and laziness in our duty, with other infinite faults and offences of ours, we will crave mercy at his hands.[128]

Ultimately, though, Beza looked forward to heaven as the answer to the vicissitudes of the earthly pilgrimage. The prospect of eternal felicity might seem remote during one's earthly life, but it was certain because of God's sovereign action on behalf of his people. So while he was praying "That we may well use afflictions," Beza exuded confidence in God's eternal goal for his people:

> Especially grant, O Lord, that I may attain to this reason of true wisdom, always to be content with your will, the sovereign and just cause of all things; namely, in that it pleases you, that the livery of your household should consist in carrying their cross after your Son, to the end, that I should never but be seasoned to drink the wholesome myrrh which purges the soul from the lusts of the flesh, and replenishes the same with the desires of eternal life. Also that I learn in whatsoever my estate, cheerfully to submit myself to the conduct of your providence, as being well assured, that whatsoever I suffer, all the crosses of my life shall be unto me so many blessings and helps from you my Father, to make me go the right way into your kingdom, and increase unto me the price of glory in the same.[129]

The sovereign Father would certainly bring his children to himself for eternity.

Conclusion

Theodore Beza has emerged in this chapter as first and foremost an affectionate and committed follower of Christ. His goal was not a cold, intellectual knowledge of God. Rather, he was engaged in an active piety, in drawing utility from the Bible to demonstrate God's absolute sovereignty through all the affairs of life. And his context, as we have seen, was a troubled one personally, politically, and theologically. More than these complications, though, Beza

---

128 Ibid., 358.
129 Beza, *Houshold Prayers*, K3v-K4v.

believed that Satan was vigorously opposing Christians through their entire earthly pilgrimage. In the midst of the spiritual battle between God and the devil—which formed Beza's eschatological and pastoral vision—Beza relied on God's control over all the vicissitudes of life, and he encouraged others to do the same. God would faithfully usher his people to eternal felicity. The goal of this life to Beza, therefore, was a Christian's safe arrival in heaven, supported by the goodness and omnipotence of God. The truth of God's sovereignty comforted Beza and his listeners in their troubled context.

CHAPTER 2

Beza's Interpreters

> Three evils principally reigned [in biblical interpretation before the Reformation]. First, they that had been brought up in philosophy did not remember that most grave and apostolic sentence: "Take heed, lest anyone spoils you through philosophy." For besides the fact that they had many vain speculations, as in the applying to the angels the imaginations of Plato, concerning the intelligences and spirits . . . they did manifestly waste the word of God unto those lessons that they had learned of the philosophers. Here sprang the opinions of the power and free will of man, which are altogether Aristotelian, by which at this day the church of God is shaken, and had been trodden down long ago had not Augustine – provoked by Pelagius – set himself against it. . . . [A]nother evil (the worst of all that as with a deadly disease all men's minds were infected) was a marvelous desire to turn and transform all the Scriptures into allegories, in the invention of which every man thought everything in this point to be lawful to himself. Origen surely seems to have given occasion to both those evils – of following the philosophers and also of allegories – who was the most impure writer (as I do take him) that ever did write upon the Scriptures, whom though many, as he well deserved, did abhor, yet some of the other side, had him in great admiration because he was very excellent in the knowledge of the languages, arts, and sciences. And some pursued him rather of envy than of upright judgment.[1]

Theodore Beza frequently evaluated his predecessors. Throughout his corpus, he looked at those who came before him, citing some as authorities who agreed with him but excoriating others for their heretical opinions.

As historical evaluation and criticism was important to Beza, it is to us. In this chapter I will summarize and evaluate Beza's recent interpreters. This chapter is important, for it places my evaluation of Beza's intention in his theological works in a wider context. Many historians and theologians have researched Theodore Beza. And I have profited from much of their work. I will first give an overview of Bezan scholarship. Then I will note studies on the three topics of Bezan theology that are pertinent for my study. My conclusion is twofold. First, profitable research has been performed on numerous aspects of Beza's thought. Second, no one has attempted to explicate, from the whole Bezan corpus, the eternal focus that informed and motivated all that Beza was

---

1   Beza, "An Exhortation to the Reformation of the Church," n.p.

and did, as I tried to outline in the first chapter. Unlike many scholars' opinions who have researched Beza, my conclusion is that Theodore Beza was above all a pastoral theologian.

Summary of Beza Research

Beza has undergone extensive scrutiny at the hands of several scholars, especially recently, as the question of the relationship between the Reformation and post-Reformation Reformed Orthodoxy has come to prominence. Yet, given his significance both historically and theologically, relatively little comprehensive attention has been paid to Beza's life or thought. When Paul-F. Geisendorf surveyed the biographies of Beza that preceded his own, he found that almost all of them were short and dated treatments.[2] Four works deserve comment. Henry Baird's biography of Beza is the only extended work in English. The primary focus was Beza's role in the wars of religion in France.[3] Although it is rich in detail about developments in France and Beza's role in promoting Protestantism there, Baird's work neglects Beza's thought. The short compass of Clavier's recent biography – only fifty-six pages – and its reliance on secondary sources also renders it relatively unhelpful in understanding Beza's context and thought.[4] Geisendorf's monograph outshines all others as a sourcebook of Beza's life and derived from a careful examination of Beza's corpus. However, Geisendorf himself acknowledged two significant weaknesses in his work: it did not explicate Beza's theology and it did not adequately place Beza in his historical context.[5] Finally, Scott Manetsch's recently published dissertation contains a wealth of information on the latter years of Beza's life, a period curiously neglected by many other students. Drawing on numerous unpublished manuscript sources, Manetsch attempted to

---

2   Geisendorf, *Théodore de Bèze*, v-ix. Among the older histories Geisendorf noted are Jérôme Bolsec, *Histoire de la vie, moeurs, doctrine et débordements de T. de Bèze* (Paris: n.p., 1582); Johan Wilhelm Baum, *Theodor Beza nach handschriftlichen Quellen dargestellt*, 2 vols. (Leipzig: Weidmann'sche Buchhandlung, 1843-1851); Heinrich Heppe, *Theodor Beza: Leben und ausgewählte Schriften* (Elberfeld: R.L. Friedrichs, 1861); and Auguste Bernus, *Théodore de Bèze à Lausanne* (Lausanne: Georges Bridel, 1900).

3   Baird, *Theodore Beza*. Other helpful biographical sketches of Beza in English include the following: Robert M. Kingdon, "Beza, Theodore," in *New Catholic Encyclopedia* (New York: McGraw-Hill, 1967), 2:379; Jill Raitt, "Bèze, Théodore de," in *Oxford Encyclopedia of the Reformation*, ed. Hans J. Hillerbrand (New York: Oxford University Press, 1996), 1:149-51; idem, "Theodore Beza: 1519-1605," 89-104.

4   H. Clavier, *Théodore de Bèze: Un aperçu de sa vie aventureuse, de ses travaux, de sa personnalité* (Cahors: A. Coueslant, 1960).

5   Geisendorf, *Théodore de Bèze*, viii-ix.

demonstrate Beza's continued involvement in affairs in France until the end of his life and gave little attention to Beza's thought.[6] These scholars have done admirable work, even though more study of the driving force behind Theodore Beza's pastoral theology is still warranted.

Although no one has adequately studied Beza's pastoral theology, scholars have examined several aspects of his thought. Beza's treatment of select doctrines, his biblical hermeneutics, his homiletics, and his fidelity to Calvin's teaching have received extended treatment, as the following survey will demonstrate.

Specific Doctrines

Beza's views concerning certain Christian doctrines have received very adequate attention. With her studies of Beza's beliefs about the eucharist, christology, and baptism, Jill Raitt spearheaded these investigations.[7] In addition, Tadataka Maruyama and Glenn Sunshine have examined Beza's ecclesiology.[8] Still other scholars have tried to explicate Beza's views of the relationship between the church and civil government.[9]

---

6 Manetsch, *Theodore Beza*. Another, though somewhat dated, study of Beza's involvement with French Protestantism is Robert M. Kingdon, *Geneva and the Consolidation of the French Protestant Movement 1564-1572*). Two helpful works concerning the French Reformation, which include discussions of Geneva's involvement, are Mark Greengrass, *The French Reformation*, and Mack P. Holt, *The French Wars of Religion, 1562-1629*, New Approaches to European History (Cambridge: Cambridge University Press, 1995).

7 Raitt, *Eucharistic Theology of Theodore Beza*; idem, "The Person of the Mediator"; idem, "*Probably* They are God's Children: Theodore Beza's Doctrine of Baptism," in *Humanism and Reform: The Church in Europe, England, and Scotland, 1400-1643*, Studies in Church History, subsidia 8, ed. James Kirk (Oxford: Blackwell, 1991), 151-70.

8 Maruyama, *Ecclesiology*; Glenn S. Sunshine, "Reformed Theology and the Origins of Synodical Polity: Calvin, Beza and the Gallican Confession," in *Later Calvinism: International Perspectives*, Sixteenth Century Essays and Studies, vol. 22, ed. W. Fred Graham (Kirksville, MO: Sixteenth Century Journal, 1994), 141-58; idem, "Discipline as the Third Mark of the Church: Three Views," *Calvin Theological Journal* 33 (1998): 469-80.

9 Robert M. Kingdon, "Calvinism and Democracy: Some Political Implications of Debates on French Reformed Church Government, 1562-1572," *American Historical Review* 69 (1964): 393-401; idem, "The First Expression of Theodore Beza's Political Ideas," *Archiv für Reformationsgeschichte* 46 (1955): 88-100; Richard C. Gamble, "The Christian and the Tyrant: Beza and Knox on Political Resistance Theory," *Westminster Theological Journal* 46 (1984): 125-39; and Jean-Blaise Fellay, "Un Presbyterianisme de Droit Divin: l'Eglise, le Pouvoir et l'Etat dans l'Ecclesiologie de Theodore de Beze," in *Visage de l'Église: Cours*

Biblical Exegesis and Preaching

Irena Backus has prolifically drawn attention to Beza's method of biblical interpretation.[10] Other researchers have followed her, attempting to clarify Beza's hermeneutic.[11] Their efforts notwithstanding, Beza's exegetical method has not received due attention. This is unfortunate since Beza was known as one of the premier biblical scholars of his day.[12] Similarly, his preaching has been neglected. Jill Raitt has contributed a few recent studies of Beza's homiletics, but the only other treatments are quite short considerations.[13]

Scholasticism and Humanism

Closely related to the re-evaluation of Protestant scholasticism going on in Reformation studies, and in some ways the precursor to such reconsideration, has been a movement to re-examine the relationship of Renaissance humanism

---

d'ecclésiologie, ed. Patrick de Laubier (Fribourg: Éditions Universitaires Fribourg, 1989), 125-40.

10 Irena Doruta Backus, "'Aristotelianism' in Some of Calvin's and Beza's Expository and Exegetical Writings on the Doctrine of the Trinity, with Particular Reference to the Terms ουσια and υποστασις," in *Histoire de l'Exégèse au XVIe Siècle: Textes de Colloque International Tenu a Genève en 1976*, ed. Olivier Fatio and Pierre Fraenkel (Geneva: Libraire Droz, 1978), 351-360; idem, *The Reformed Roots of the English New Testament: The Influence of Theodore Beza on the English New Testament*, Pittsburgh Theological Monograph Series 28 (Pittsburgh: Pickwick, 1980); idem, "Piscator Misconstrued? Some Remarks on Robert Rollock's 'logical analysis' of Hebrews 9," *Journal of Medieval and Renaissance Studies* 14 (1984): 113-19; idem, *Les Septs Visions et la Fin des Temps: les Commentaires Genevois de l'Apocalypse entre 1539 et 1584*, Cahiers de la Revue de Théologie et de Philosophie 19 (Lausanne: Revue de Théologie et de Philosophie, 1997); idem, "The Church Fathers and the Canonicity of the Apocalypse in the Sixteenth Century: Erasmus, Frans Titelmans, and Theodore Beza," *Sixteenth Century Journal* 29 (1998): 651-65.

11 Pierre Fraenkel, "Matthias Flacius Illyricus and His *Gloss* on Hebrews 9," *Journal of Medieval and Renaissance Studies* 14 (1984): 97-111; Luc Perrottet, "Chapter 9 of the Epistle to the Hebrews as presented in an unpublished course of lectures by Theodore Beza," trans. Irena Backus, *The Journal of Medieval and Renaissance Studies* 14 (1984): 89-96; and John L. Farthing, "Beza, Theodore," in *Historical Handbook of Major Biblical Interpreters*, ed. Donald K. McKim (Downers Grove, IL: InterVarsity, 1998), 153-57.

12 Maruyama, *Ecclesiology*, 1-2.

13 Raitt, "Beza, Guide," 83-107; idem, "Lessons in Troubled Times: Beza's Lessons on Job," in *Calvin and the State: Papers and Responses Presented at the Seventh and Eighth Colloquia on Calvin and Calvin Studies*, ed. Peter De Klerk (Grand Rapids: Calvin Studies Society, 1993), 21-45; Dückert, *Théodore de Bèze*; Delval, "La Prédication"; idem, "Orthodoxie et Prédication."

to scholasticism in general. Paul Oskar Kristeller led this movement by demonstrating that the Renaissance was not homogenous. It contained diverse streams, all equally part of the Renaissance, however different they were from one another.[14] Additionally Charles Schmitt showed that Renaissance Aristotelianism was not a uniform movement, but was employed by persons who held quite different views from one another.[15] At the same time, scholasticism has been shown not to encompass a set of rigid beliefs but rather to refer to a method of instruction.[16] The bearing of these studies on Beza scholarship cannot be overlooked, especially as it relates to Beza's role in establishing the Geneva Academy's curriculum. Since many scholars now believe that scholasticism affected the method of teaching more than its content, one can no longer label Beza a "scholastic" merely because he used Aristotle to instruct theology students.[17] Further complicating the picture, Beza was a premier humanist of his day.[18] Yet, in light of recent studies, it is no longer absurd to argue that Beza was a "scholastic humanist."

---

14 Paul Oskar Kristeller, *Renaissance Thought: The Classic, Scholastic, and Humanist Strains* (New York: Harper Torchbooks, 1961). Kristeller summarized his thesis in "Humanism," in *The Cambridge History of Renaissance Philosophy*, eds. Charles B. Schmitt, Quentin Skinner, Eckhard Kessler, and Jill Kraye (Cambridge: Cambridge University Press, 1988), 113-37. Kristeller's conclusions have been qualified, though. See, e.g., Erika Rummel, *The Humanist-Scholastic Debate in the Renaissance and Reformation* (Cambridge, MA: Harvard University Press, 1995), 16-17.
15 Charles B. Schmitt, "Towards a Reassessment of Renaissance Aristotelianism," *History of Science* 11 (1973): 159-93.
16 I. C. Brady, J. E. Gurr, and J. A. Weisheipl, "Scholasticism," in *New Catholic Encyclopedia* (New York: McGraw-Hill, 1967), 12:1153-70; and Richard A. Muller, *Scholasticism and Orthodoxy in the Reformed Tradition: An Attempt at Definition* (Grand Rapids: Calvin Theological Seminary, 1995).
17 Richard Stauffer, "Calvinism and the Universities," in *University and Reformation: Lectures from the University of Copenhagen Symposium*, ed. Leif Grane (Leiden: E. J. Brill, 1981), 76-98; Marvin W. Anderson, "Theodore Beza: Savant or Scholastic?" *Theologische Zeitschrift* 43 (1987): 320-32; and Robert D. Linder, "Calvinism and Humanism: The First Generation," *Church History* 44 (1975): 167-81. For recent studies concerning aspects of the Geneva Academy, see Ganoczy, *La Bibliothèque de l'Académie de Calvin*; Maag, "Education and Training"; idem, *Seminary or University?*; Lewis, "The Genevan Academy."
18 Natalie Zemon Davis, "Peletier and Beza Part Company," *Studies in the Renaissance* 11 (1964): 188-222; Kirk M. Summers, "Theodore Beza's Classical Library and Christian Humanism," *Archiv für Reformationsgeschicte* 82 (1991): 193-207; idem, "Theodore Beza's Reading of Catullus," *Classical and Modern Literature* 15 (1995): 233-45.

John Calvin and Theodore Beza

The bulk of recent Beza research has sought to answer a question of historical theology: Did Theodore Beza change the contours of John Calvin's theology? After examining Beza's writings on predestination and assurance of salvation, many scholars have argued that Beza introduced the doctrines of limited atonement and supralapsarianism into Reformed thought and gave it a highly rationalistic theological method. These innovations, they have argued, were foreign to Calvin's theology.

Two broad positions have been taken. First, some researchers argue that Beza changed Calvin's thought materially. Even in his lifetime Beza had to answer the charge that he differed theologically from his Genevan predecessor and mentor, so this criticism has a long pedigree.[19] This mutation theory, which reigned during the nineteenth and twentieth centuries, pitted the biblical Calvin against the Bezan, rationalistic Calvinists.[20] The works of Ernst Bizer, Jürgen Moltmann, Johannes Dantine, and especially Walter Kickel have been especially influential recently.[21] Anglophones have also adopted this interpretative scheme. Thus the nineteenth-century Scottish Presbyterian, William Cunningham, suggested that Beza deviated from Calvin's theology, albeit mildly.[22] More recently, Basil Hall, Brian Armstrong, and R. T. Kendall have set up a sharp divide between Calvin and Beza. Hall and Kendall argued that the deviations were primarily theological, while Armstrong argued that they derived from differing methods: Calvin was a humanist, but Beza a

---

19 Theodore Beza, *Response aux cinq premieres et principales demandes de F. Jean Hay* (Geneva: Jean le Preux, 1586).
20 See Richard A. Muller, "Calvin and the 'Calvinists': Assessing Continuities and Discontinuities between the Reformation and Orthodoxy," *Calvin Theological Journal* 30 (1995): 345-59, for a helpful overview of the history of research.
21 Jürgen Moltmann, "Zur bedeutung des Petrus Ramus für philosophie und theologie im Calvinismus," *Zeitschrift für Kirchengeschichte* 68 (1957): 295-318; Ernst Bizer, *Frühorthodoxie und Rationalismus*, Theologische Studien, 71 (Zurich: EVZ-Verlag, 1963); Johannes Dantine, "Das christologische Problem im Rahmen der Prädestinationslehre von Theodor Beza," *Zeitschrift für Kirchengeschichte* 77 (1966): 81-96; idem, "Les Tabelles sur la Doctrine de la Prédestination par Théodore de Bèze," *Revue de théologie et de philosophie* 16 (1966): 365-77; and Walter Kickel, *Vernuft und Offenbarung bei Theodor Beza: Zum Problem des Verhältnisses von Theologie, Philosophie und Staat*, Beiträge zur geschichte und lehre der Reformierten Kirche, no. 25 (Neukirchen-Vluyn: Neukirchener Verlag des Erziehungsvereins, 1967).
22 William Cunningham, "Calvin and Beza," in *The Reformers and the Theology of the Reformation*, ed. James Buchanan and James Bannerman (1862; reprint, Edinburgh: Banner of Truth, 1967), 349-50, 359-66, 396-400.

scholastic.²³

In the second place, several scholars have advocated a more nuanced judgment of the relationship between Calvin's and Beza's thought. Many have noted the ways in which the change in Beza's context from Calvin's necessitated that Beza change his doctrinal expression, though without changing the doctrine materially.²⁴ A change in the method of teaching theology to meet the demands of the day did not necessarily mean a change in doctrine itself. Several scholars have challenged the "Calvin versus Beza" thesis head-on, though it is still the reigning historiography of the era.²⁵ Paul

---

23 Kendall stated his thesis clearly: "The one man more than any other who was the architectural mind for English Calvinism was Calvin's successor at Geneva, Theodore Beza (1519-1605). Beza perhaps would not have wanted his theology to be known as Calvinism, but his systematizing and logicalizing theology had the effect of perpetuating a phenomenon that bore Calvin's name but was hardly Calvin's purest thought" ("The Puritan Modification of Calvin's Theology," in *John Calvin: His Influence in the Western World*, ed. W. Stanford Reid [Grand Rapids: Zondervan, 1982], 201). See also Basil Hall, "Calvin Against the Calvinists," in *John Calvin*, Courtenay Studies in Reformation Theology 1, ed. G. E. Duffield (Appleford: Sutton Courtenay, 1966), 19-37, and Brian G. Armstrong, *Calvinism and the Amyraut Heresy: Protestant Scholasticism and Humanism in Seventeenth-Century France* (Madison: University of Wisconsin Press), 32-33, 38-39, 41-42. Armstrong explained further: "This new outlook [Beza's method] represents a profound divergence from the humanistically oriented religion of John Calvin and most of the early reformers. The strongly biblically and experientially based theology of Calvin and Luther had, it is fair to say, been overcome by the metaphysics and deductive logic of a restored Aristotelianism" (*Calvinism*, 32). Armstrong acknowledged his dependence upon Kickel: "Suspicion of Beza's scholastic orientation and his role in leading Reformed Protestantism in that direction receives almost decisive corroboration in Walter Kickel's *Vernuft und Offenbarung bei Theodor Beza*" (*Calvinism*, 39). Although he qualified some of Kickel's conclusions, Armstrong followed Kickel in locating Beza's evolution of Calvin's thought in the doctrine of God (*Calvinism*, 39-41).

24 Robert Letham well expresses this cautious approach to the change between Calvin's and Beza's theology: "Certainly, Beza gave a warmer welcome to scholastic methodology than Calvin. His prominent supralapsarianism may be symptomatic of that. He firmly defends limited atonement which Calvin, whatever his views on the question, did not do. However, his overall thought on predestination and on its relationship to Christology, his formulations on faith and assurance in connections with election, Christ, sanctification and the Spirit all undermine the idea of a deep-seated departure from his predecessor ("Theodore Beza: A Reassessment," *Scottish Journal of Theology* 40 [1987]: 39-40).

25 An unqualified adoption of the "Calvin versus Beza" thesis in two recent surveys of historical theology proves its continuing popularity. Thus Alister McGrath followed Armstrong's schema of scholasticism and made this judgment about the post-Calvin Reformed theologians: "It seems to be a general rule of history that periods

Helm and others have attempted to draw attention to the theological biases and flawed methodology of Kendall's research in particular.[26] In addition, various researchers have tried to prove that Calvin believed in definite atonement, thus maintaining that Beza and later Calvinists were in line with their predecessor in this belief.[27] Still other historians have argued, contra Kendall, that although Calvin and Beza may have emphasized different aspects of the doctrine of assurance of salvation, they were not fundamentally at odds with each other.[28]

---

of enormous creativity are followed by eras of stagnation. The Reformation is no exception." And Beza's works "present a rationally coherent account of the main elements of Reformed theology, using Aristotelian logic" (Alister McGrath, *Historical Theology: An Introduction to the History of Christian Thought* [Oxford: Blackwell, 1998], 169, 172). Roger Olson's negative judgment of Beza's contribution is even starker: "Many of the Reformed scholastics like Beza were fascinated with questions about the decrees of God. . . . Beza and other post-Calvin Reformed theologians began to wonder and speculate about the 'order of the divine decrees.' . . . Beza and certain other Calvinists were obsessed with the doctrine of predestination more than Calvin himself ever had been" (Roger E. Olson, *The Story of Christian Theology: Twenty Centuries of Tradition and Reform* [Downers Grove, IL: InterVarsity, 1999], 456-57).

26 Paul Helm, "Calvin, English Calvinism and the Logic of Doctrinal Development," *Scottish Journal of Theology* 34 (1981): 179-85; idem, *Calvin and the Calvinists* (Carlisle, PA: Banner of Truth, 1982; William Young, "Calvin and Westminster," *The Bulwark* (May/June 1980): 15-18; George Harper, "Calvin and English Calvinism to 1649: A Review Article," *Calvin Theological Journal* 20 (1985): 255-62.

27 Roger Nicole, "John Calvin's View of the Extent of the Atonement," *Westminster Theological Journal* 47 (1985): 197-225; Jonathan H. Rainbow, *The Will of God and the Cross: An Historical and Theological Study of John Calvin's Doctrine of Limited Redemption* (Allison Park, PA: Pickwick, 1990); Paul Noel Archbald, "A Comparative Study of John Calvin and Theodore Beza on the Doctrine of the Extent of the Atonement" (Ph.D. diss., Westminster Theological Seminary, 1998). W. Robert Godfrey showed that there was no consensus about this doctrine early in the seventeenth century among Calvinists ("Tensions within International Calvinism: The Debate on the Atonement at the Synod of Dort, 1618-1619" [Ph.D. diss., Stanford University, 1974]). Kendall's thesis has received recent approval, though, in at least two studies: G. Michael Thomas, *The Extent of the Atonement: A Dilemma for Reformed Theology from Calvin to the Consensus (1536-1675)*, Paternoster Biblical and Theological Monographs (Carlisle: Paternoster, 1997); and Kevin Dixon Kennedy, "Union with Christ as Key to John Calvin's Understanding of the Extent of the Atonement" (Ph.D. diss., The Southern Baptist Theological Seminary, 1999).

28 Joel R. Beeke, *Assurance of Faith: Calvin, English Puritanism, and the Dutch Second Reformation*, American University Studies, series 7, Theology and Religion, vol. 89 (New York: Peter Lang, 1991), 78-81; R. W. A. Letham, "Saving Faith and Assurance in Reformed Theology: Zwingli to the Synod of Dort" (Ph.D.

By paying particular attention to the post-Reformation Reformed theologians' historical and theological context, a growing coterie of researchers has attempted to correct the Bizer-Kickel-Armstrong-Kendall thesis. Richard Muller, especially, has averred that historians must pay more careful attention to literary genre and must eschew the tendency to create a facile divide between humanism and scholasticism.[29] Following Muller's lead, several scholars are reinvestigating the post-Reformation orthodox theologians in light of new discussion about the meaning and impact of scholasticism.[30] Marvin Anderson's conclusion in this respect is apropos, since he specifically chided those who pitted Beza against his mentor and dear friend, Calvin, without reading from a variety of the Bezan corpus: "The burden of proof still lies with those who see Theodore Beza as Calvin's bête noir. They have yet to demonstrate their contention from the full range of Beza's writings that the methods he used to defend Calvin were the Achilles heel of the Reformed Tradition."[31]

Certainly it is an important avenue of research to seek to answer the

---

diss., University of Aberdeen, 1979), 153-54; idem, "Faith and Assurance in Early Calvinism: A Model of Continuity and Diversity," in *Later Calvinism: International Perspectives*, Sixteenth Century Essays and Studies, vol. 22, ed. W. Fred Graham (Kirksville, MO: Sixteenth Century Journal, 1994), 355-88.

29 Among Muller's prodigious output, the following works pay special attention to Beza: "Perkins' *A Golden Chaine*: Predestinarian System or Schematized *Ordo Salutis?*," *Sixteenth Century Journal* 9 (1978): 69-81; *Christ and the Decree: Christology and Predestination in Reformed Theology from Calvin to Perkins*, Studies in Historical Theology 2 (1986; reprint, Grand Rapids: Baker, 1988), 79-96; "Review of *The Bolsec Controversy on Predestination, From 1551 to 1555*, by Philip C. Holtrop," *Calvin Theological Journal* 29 (1994): 581-89; "Calvin, Beza, and the Exegetical History of Romans 13:1-7," in *The Identity of Geneva: The Christian Commonwealth, 1564-1864*, Contributions to the Study of World History 59, ed. John B. Roney and Martin I. Klauber (Westport, CT: Greenwood, 1998), 39-56; and "The Use and Abuse of a Document: Beza's *Tabula Praedestinationis*, The Bolsec Controversy, and the Origins of Reformed Orthodoxy," in *Protestant Scholasticism: Essays in Reassessment*, ed. Carl R. Trueman and R. S. Clark (Carlisle: Paternoster, 1999), 33-61. Muller has been accused of over-emphasizing the continuities between the medieval period, the Reformation, and the post-Reformation periods, though. See, e.g., Ronald N. Frost, "'Scholasticism, Reformation, Orthodoxy, and the Persistence of Christian Aristotelianism': A Brief Rejoinder," *Trinity Journal*, n.s., 19 (1998): 97-101.

30 See, e.g., Lyle D. Bierma, *German Calvinism in the Confessional Age: The Covenant Theology of Caspar Olevianus* (Grand Rapids: Baker, 1996); Carl R. Trueman and R. S. Clark, eds., *Protestant Scholasticism: Essays in Reassessment* (Carlisle: Paternoster, 1999); and Carl R. Trueman, *The Claims of Truth: John Owen's Trinitarian Theology* (Carlisle: Paternoster, 1999).

31 Anderson, "Theodore Beza," 332.

question, Was Theodore Beza faithful to John Calvin's theology or did he deviate from his friend and colleague's doctrine? To answer it, scholars have especially investigated three aspects of Beza's thought. Scholars have researched his theological method, his doctrine of predestination, and his teaching on the means by which Christians could find assurance of their salvation. These three, of course, are closely related. Beza's method for arriving at theological conclusions inevitably influenced his understanding of God's role in salvation, which in turn impacted his view of assurance of salvation. Although the answers to the posed question vary, the consensus scholarly opinion has been that in these three areas Beza showed an evolution in thought from his mentor, John Calvin. However, the answers that have been tendered have generally not been satisfactory.

Three fundamental errors of many researchers call their conclusions about the relationship of Beza to Calvin into question, resulting in facile characterizations of Beza's thought at worst or incomplete accounts of his beliefs at best. First of all, some scholars have failed to read Beza empathetically. They have imposed their own ideas and thought-forms on Beza before trying to understand him on his own terms. They judge Beza guilty for not thinking as they do. In other words, they study and critique Beza as theologians or philosophers, not as historians.

In the second place, other researchers have failed to pay careful attention to context when studying Beza. Some have not paid enough attention to the history of doctrine and its development when examining one of Beza's doctrinal commitments. Some have not located Beza and his work firmly enough in their historical context, in the circumstances that called forth his work. Others have failed to read his words in context, lifting phrases or points out of a treatise as if they were self-contained units and not pieces of a larger exposition.

In the third place, other scholars have failed to take account of the genre of Beza's treatise they were examining. They have read Beza's works as if his mode of expression were uniform, when in fact Beza wrote several different types of treatises. The emphases he made in a polemical work, for example, might not be matters of emphasis at all in a systematic work, and they might not even be points he mentioned in a pastoral work.

My purpose in this chapter is to show how much recent Beza research, even that which is very good, is deficient because it is limited in one of these areas. Of course, even though errors have been committed, many positive contributions have been made in the scholarship on Beza. So as I examine and critique the research under the three heads mentioned above – theological method, predestination, and assurance – I will also note the valuable contributions others have made. I will not, of course, be able to be exhaustive. Nor will I be able to handle each scholar's contributions equally. I will spend more time on some than others, in the hope that I might offer a balanced view of the major positions that have been set forth on Beza. This chapter is important in the flow of my study, for after critiquing other scholars here, my final three chapters will offer a new evaluation of Beza's thought in the three areas under investigation.

Studies of Beza's Theological Method

In order to explain what is often perceived to be a radical change in doctrine from Calvin's, scholars have scrutinized Beza's theological method. Three commentators in particular – Ernst Bizer, Walter Kickel, and Brian Armstrong – have exercised tremendous influence. But they have fundamentally misunderstood Beza's theological method. Each of them took little notice of Beza's context or the genre of his works. And none of them attempted to read Beza sympathetically. More recently, Jill Raitt, Ian McPhee and Donald Sinnema offered a more prudent evaluation of Beza's method. An accurate explanation of Beza's theological method must place him squarely in his place in the sixteenth century and evaluate his theological method in light of his whole thought.

According to Bizer, Beza was the cause for the almost imperceptible (*unvermerkten*) movement from the Reformation's biblical orientation to Enlightenment rationalism.[32] Beza's logical emphases unknowingly fostered a move toward a rationalistic spirit in subsequent generations of Reformed thinkers. Kickel followed his mentor Bizer and argued that Beza's work over the course of fifty years was responsible for the change from Reformation thought to Protestant orthodoxy. Following Bizer's lead, he maintained this shift occurred because Beza was guided by Aristotelian dialectic in his theological exposition.[33] Kickel employed the criteria of reason and revelation as the keys to measuring the mutation from the Reformation to the rationalistic spirit of orthodoxy.[34]

Armstrong argued that Beza was the "most influential" orthodox theologian who led the Reformed away from Calvin's method "and for this reason one may lay much of the blame for scholasticism at his feet."[35] The polemical requirements of Beza's day necessitated the "movement of Beza away from Calvin's basic theological position and towards scholasticism."[36] Armstrong offered four characteristics of scholasticism, which we will note, given their continuing influence. According to Armstrong, Protestant scholasticism was characterized by:

---

32 Bizer, *Frühorthodoxie und Rationalismus*, 6.
33 Kickel, *Vernuft und Offenbarung*, 10.
34 Ibid., 11.
35 Armstrong, *Calvinism and the Amyraut Heresy*, 38.
36 Ibid., 129.

(1) that ideological approach which asserts religious truth on the basis of deductive ratiocination from given assumptions or principles, thus producing a logically coherent and defensible system of belief. Generally this takes the form of syllogistic reasoning. It is . . . invariably based upon an Aristotelian philosophical commitment and so relates to medieval scholasticism. (2) the employment of reason in religious matters, so that reason assumes at least equal standing with faith in theology, thus jettisoning some of the authority of revelation.
(3) the sentiment that the scriptural record contains a unified, rationally comprehensible account and thus may be formed into a definitive statement which may be used as a measuring stick to determine one's orthodoxy.
(4) a pronounced interest in metaphysical matters, in abstract, speculative thought, particularly with reference to the doctrine of God. The distinctive scholastic Protestant position is made to rest on a speculative formulation of the will of God.[37]

Armstrong averred that this methodological shift, which Beza began, had deleterious effects on the focus of Calvinistic theology. The deviation from Calvinism to scholasticism

> manifested itself primarily in the approach to theological issues. No longer was the primary approach the analytic and inductive, but rather the synthetic and deductive. Theology was explained not as experienced by man and from his viewpoint but as determined by God and from the perspective of God. This approach was, then, primarily interested in the logical explication of the source of theology—that is, the counsel of God. It would, paying lip service to Calvin's principle, caution against excessive speculation concerning the incomprehensible counsel of God. Nevertheless, they would then proceed to discuss theology by taking as their starting point the decrees of God, indeed in terms of a specific order in these decrees, giving the impression that there was nothing incomprehensible about them.[38]

Beza was thus responsible for shifting theology's starting point from the Bible to God's eternal decree.

Bizer's, Kickel's, and Armstrong's attempts to clarify Theodore Beza's theological method, however, fail. First of all, and perhaps most significantly,

---

37 Ibid., 32.
38 Ibid., 136. Armstrong devoted three pages to outlining Kickel's conclusions regarding Beza's culpability for the shift in methodology, especially focusing on Kickel's critique of Beza's understanding of the relationship between the doctrine of God and predestination (ibid., 39-41). Besides altering the placement of predestination, Armstrong charged that "Beza introduced other rigid teachings into Reformed theology, among them supralapsarianism, a limited atonement, and the immediate imputation of Adam's sin. These all, to some degree, represent a distortion of Calvin's teaching" (ibid., 41-42).

none of these three succeeded in reading Beza's words empathetically. Bizer's work offers a couple of illustrations of this fault. After a very brief discussion of Beza's *Tabula praedestinationis*, Bizer postulated that the connections Beza made between the acts of God's grace and damnation were logical, although not distinctly Christian.[39] Ignoring Beza's expressed intention to be biblical, Bizer argued that Beza's logic proceeded merely from the idea of God (*Gottesgedankens*) that he had formulated rationally.[40] Bizer noted, for example, that Beza held that the origin of evil in light of God's sovereign goodness exceeded human capacity; rather than struggling to figure it out, Beza insisted that persons should marvel at the mercy of God towards sinners. Yet, instead of reporting this anti-speculative reasoning of Beza, Bizer attacked it. He censured Beza, arguing that "so much has been said about [evil by Beza], that the question [of its origin] has become inevitable."[41] It seems that Ernst Bizer, not Theodore Beza, was the rationalist. Bizer maintained his antagonism in his summary of the *Tabula*. He chastised Beza for not being specifically Christian in his argumentation.[42] Beza's explanations were, rather, a rationalistic attempt to explain the Reformer's preconceived concept of God. Thus Bizer maintained that Beza's method was inherently unbiblical, since his *Tabula*, with its parallel lines showing the fate of both the elect and the reprobate, agreed completely with reason.[43] Beza's theology was derived from human ratiocination, not the Bible, in Bizer's opinion. Had Bizer examined more than the chart in Beza's *Tabula*, he would have noted that each of Beza's aphorisms (which stated his theological theses) was followed by multiple Scripture quotations (*Probationes ex Dei verbo*), sometimes consisting of several pages.[44]

In the second place, these three scholars failed to notice the genre of the treatises they employed. Bizer, for instance, discussed a few of Beza's systematic treatises as if they comprised the sum of his thought. The preponderance of his discussion concerned one occasional and polemical treatise, Beza's *Tabula*. His twelve references to Beza were all to the

---

39 The *Tabula praedestinationis*, which Beza wrote in 1555 to refute Bolsec's views about predestination, is also known as the *Summa totius christianismi*. In subsequent references, I will refer to it as the *Tabula*.
40 Bizer, *Frühorthodoxie und Rationalismus*, 10.
41 Ibid., 9.
42 What Beza tried to ground in Scripture, Bizer judged "not specifically Christian" (*nichts spezifisch Christliches*) (ibid., 10).
43 Ibid., 12.
44 See Theodore Beza, *Tractationum Theologicarum, in quibus plerasque Christianae Religionis dogmata adversus haereses nostris temporibus renovatas solide ex Verbo Dei defenduntur*, (Geneva: Vignon, 1582), 1:170-205.

Reformer's early works.[45] Likewise when he explicated Beza's method, Kickel referenced Beza's works forty-eight times.[46] But two works dominated. He referenced *Ad Sebastiani Castellionis calumnies* and *De haereticis* eleven times each. So these two occasional treatises – the first Beza's refutation of Sebastian Castellio's treatise on predestination, the second a defense of orthodox christology – comprised almost half of Kickel's proof in the formative part of his monograph.[47] The purpose of these polemical treatises explains the form they took. In the first, for example, Beza refuted Castellio's contention that Calvin's doctrine of predestination was erroneous. Beza's reply was determined by Castellio's work. He listed each of Castellio's points (*Castellionis argumentum, calumnia*) in turn, and then countered with the orthodox doctrine of the matter (*refutatio, responsio*). Although his responses were filled with biblical quotations, they were dominated by dialectical argumentation attempting to display the faulty logic that Castellio had employed. The purposes of these polemical treatises explain their logical structures. They do not prove what Kickel assumed, namely, that in Beza's theological method reason triumphed over revelation. Finally, Armstrong's use of Bezan primary sources was nonexistent. In fact, Armstrong made only two passing references to Beza's "'chart' of salvation" in his footnotes to prove his assertions about Beza's scholastic tendencies.[48] Beyond this, he never referenced Beza directly. Instead, he uncritically accepted Amyraut's contention that Beza used a *methode particuliere*, as opposed to Calvin's biblicism.[49]

In the third place, these scholars did not read Beza contextually. Bizer excoriated Beza for his rationalistic view of the necessity for Christ's incarnation, that is, that Jesus had to become human in order to save persons from sin. Beza, he charged, explained the unity of the human and divine in Christ as a logical necessity (*mit logischer Notwendigkeit*), and he cited Beza's

---

45 Of the twelve references to Beza, Bizer cited the *Summa totius Christianismi* (1555) two times, the *Quaestionum et Responsionum* (1570) on five occasions, the *Confession* (1559) four times, and Beza's *Catechismus* (1575) once.
46 Kickel, *Vernuft und Offenbarung*, 15-68.
47 This is surprising given the fact that Kickel had noted that one of the reasons such little work has been done on Beza is the occasional nature of Beza's writings (ibid., 8). Yet Kickel did not pay enough attention to those works of Beza which are more systematic, where he developed a fuller-orbed picture of his theology and his methodology.
48 Ibid., 39 n. 114; 136 n. 53.
49 Armstrong, *Calvinism and the Amyraut Heresy*, 159 (citing Moïse Amyraut, *Defense de la doctrine de Calvin. Sur le sujet de l'election et de la reprobation* [Saumur: Isaac Desbordes, 1644], 206). Armstrong also noted his agreement with Bizer and Kickel (Armstrong, *Calvinism and the Amyraut Heresy*, 39).

Petit Catéchisme to prove this point.[50] But Bizer failed to note that previously in the *Petit Catéchisme* Beza had specifically claimed that all doctrine necessary for salvation must come from the Bible.[51] Beza believed his doctrines were dependent on Scripture, not reason.[52] Similarly, Bizer complained of Beza's logical necessitarianism surrounding the incarnation. But he failed to note that Beza attempted to ground what he said on the words of Scripture, not his own logic.[53] Bizer incorrectly accused Beza of rationalization, ignoring Beza's stated intention to be biblical.

Kickel's work is also marred by a lack of concern for Beza's context. One example will suffice. He argued that Beza's letters to Polish heretics were instances of his putting reason on equal footing with biblical revelation, thus paving the way for Protestant Scholasticism.[54] He complained that these letters, which contained little Scriptural exposition, demonstrated that soon after Calvin's death Beza deviated from the former's biblicism. Kickel, though, disregarded Beza's reason in writing them. Nancy Conradt's later study

---

50 The two questions and answers Bizer noted are these: "Q. If he had not been God, could he have been our Saviour. A. No, for it belongs to God only to pardon and forgive sins, and to give eternal life," and "Q. Why do you say for Jesus Christ's sake? A. Because we being altogether corrupted and wholly perverse in ourselves, God could not love us, but in respect of him only" (Theodore Beza, *A Little Catechisme, That is to Say, A Short Instruction Touching Christian Religion* [London: Hugh Singleton, 1579], A3r-A3v).

51 Ibid., A1r-A1v.

52 Thus, explaining the point of Christ's incarnation in the longer *Quaestionum et Responsionum*, Beza referred to several biblical verses as proof that Jesus had to be both human and divine in order to save persons. He cited Matt 1:21 and Mark 2:7 as proof of the necessity of Jesus' divinity and Gal 4:45 (?) and Heb 2:9, 14, 15 as showing the requirement that Jesus be God; then John 1:14, Heb 2:16, and 1 John 1:7 were given as proof of the God-man character of Jesus (Beza, *Tractationum Theologicarum*, 1:655).

53 Bizer cited Beza's words in the *Confession* III, 20, but he referenced only Beza's notation of Rom 5. He overlooked Beza's references to Isa 43, Hos 13, Jer 17, John 14, and 2 Cor 5 (Bizer, *Frühorthodoxie und Rationalismus*, 64-65 n. 10). See Beza, *Tractationum Theologicarum*, 1:4; Theodore Beza, *The Christian Faith*, trans. James Clark (Lewes: Focus Christian Ministries, 1992), 11. This manner of expressing the Christian doctrine concerning Christ goes back at least to Anselm and was also used by Calvin (Reinhold Seeberg, *Text-book of the History of Doctrines*, trans. Charles E. Hay [Grand Rapids: Baker, 1952], 2:66-69.) On the similarity of Beza's doctrinal expression to Anselm's, see Richard A. Muller, "Predestination and Christology in Sixteenth Century Reformed Theology" (Ph.D. diss., Duke University, 1976), 197.

54 Kickel, *Vernuft und Offenbarung*, 26-30.

corrected this oversight.⁵⁵ She summarized Beza's approach: "While this change [not to argue at length from Scripture but to refute error logically] may have been due partially to a scholasticization of Calvin's doctrines which several scholars insist that Beza introduced, in this case it was a tactical judgment."⁵⁶ Beza decided that because of his opponents' obstinacy and their misuse of Scripture, the safest tack was merely to repeat the doctrine of the Trinity as it had been held through the centuries by the orthodox church. Kickel's inattention to the historical context contributed to his erroneous conclusions.⁵⁷

Three scholars in particular have recently evaluated Theodore Beza's theological method more sensitively. Raitt's, McPhee's, and Sinnema's investigations are much more careful than those of the scholars discussed above. As a consequence their conclusions are better.⁵⁸ Jill Raitt's examination of Beza's theological method is much more credible than the studies surveyed previously. Raitt showed awareness of context and genre. Early in his career, Beza had downplayed the ability of human ratiocination, she maintained. Thus, speaking of Beza's opinion of reason as expressed in his 1559 *Confession*, Raitt claimed that

> Beza affirms that this mystery of religion is the heart of true religion. It is only in the light of the knowledge of Christ as he has been revealed to us by God that we can know God as merciful and just, and by faith in this redeemer put on Christ's innocence and justice; and so know and practice true religion. This point should be kept well in mind. It is essential to an understanding of Beza's development. That God is just and merciful is revealed to us in Christ. Once we know it, we can use reason to argue it, but reason cannot discover these attributes of God by its own powers, especially after the fall of Adam.⁵⁹

---

55 For example, on at least one occasion Beza made a tactical decision not to argue at length with the Polish heretics; arguing would simply give them more fuel with which to burn their heretical fires and would serve only to confuse the common people. So in 1565 Beza decided merely to repeat the orthodox doctrine of the Trinity against the antitrinitarian heretics without much use of Scripture or any attempts to show the falsity of their biblical interpretations (Nancy Conradt, "John Calvin, Theodore Beza and the Reformation in Poland" [Ph.D. diss., University of Wisconsin-Madison, 1974], 103).
56 Ibid., 228.
57 Note, however, McPhee's criticisms of Conradt ("Conserver or Transformer of Calvin's Theology?, 88, 125).
58 One might also note Olivier Fatio's short discussion of Beza's dialectic in his monograph on Lambert Daneau's theological method. See Olivier Fatio, *Méthode et Théologie: Lambert Daneau et les débuts de la scolastique réformée*, Travaux d'Humanisme et Renaissance 147 (Geneva: Librairie Droz, 1976), 38-42.
59 Raitt, "The Person of the Mediator," 60-61.

Noting that Beza's career from 1570 to 1594 was dominated by his controversies with Lutherans over the *communicatio idiomatum*, Raitt saw a progressive evolution in Beza's appropriation of dialectic.[60] Beza was faithful to Calvin's biblical orientation up to 1570, she argued. In that year, she noted an increase in Beza's use of technical, logical language in his *Questionum et responsium*.[61] By the end of that decade, she argued, it was clear from Beza's increased proficiency in dialectics that he had been reading Aristotle and Aquinas.[62]

Did Beza become a "scholastic," then? Raitt proffered a generally negative response. She described the nature of scholasticism. This movement in theology was not so much a way of thinking as it was a pedagogical necessity in the polemical times of the late sixteenth century. In this regard, she approvingly quoted Brian Gerrish, who said, "What we need to attempt, I think, is a non-pejorative way of stating the nature of the shift [from Calvin to Beza]. Why must we say, with some of Beza's critics, *e.g.*, Kickel, that Beza *rationalized* Calvin's theology? Why not say: he *professionalized* it, detaching it from the task of edification and striving after the highest standards of precision?"[63] Raitt was unwilling to stop there, though. To her, Beza was as much a pastor as a professor. She added, "Lest one then charge Beza with lack of pastoral concern, let it be remembered that every effort to be more precise grew out of critical pastoral situations in which souls and bodies were literally at stake."[64]

Continuing her pastoral focus, Raitt commented that in Beza's later sermons he appeared more like his predecessor than in his academic tomes. "The spirit here," she maintained, "is quite different, and the disciple of Calvin speaks with his mentor's tones."[65] This admission, of course, makes one wonder how to reconcile the "scholastic" Beza of polemical debate with the "biblical" Beza of the sermons? Raitt offered a tentative answer. "Can it be that the opposition established by some Calvin scholars between Ciceronian rhetoric and Aristotelian logic," she asked, "is misleading and that in the sixteenth as well as in the earlier centuries, both were used for different purposes? E.g., rhetoric for sermons and logic for disputations?"[66]

Ian McPhee explained that recent scholarship had made great strides in understanding the relationship of humanism to scholasticism, along with the

---

60 Ibid., 59.
61 Ibid., 64.
62 Ibid., 68.
63 Ibid., 70, quoting B. A. Gerrish's response to Raitt's paper when it was read at the joint meeting of the AAR/ASRR on 1 November 1975 in Chicago.
64 Ibid.
65 Ibid., 71.
66 Ibid., 74 n. 47.

role that Aristotelianism played in both.[67] He concluded that it would have been consistent in the sixteenth century for Beza to be a humanist who employed Aristotelian logic, especially as very polemical times called forth a reasonable defense of the Reformed faith. Indeed, as McPhee argued, Beza "was even more deeply rooted in French humanism than Calvin had been."[68] McPhee's summary of the relationship of reason to revelation in Beza's theological method is insightful:

> Beza expressed little interest in the metaphysics of God's being and attributes. His primary concern was *Deus ad nos*, an orientation which influenced every aspect of his thought and no less so than in his treatment of the relationship between reason and revelation. On this topic Beza provided no ambitious scheme to reconcile the two, or to offer proofs for God's existence, or to elaborate on God's attributes. . . . Without doubt he did admit a degree of harmony between faith and reason, but 'harmony' is never a goal in the sense that a natural knowledge of God might become prolegomenon to faith. Rather, Scripture, the Holy Spirit and faith represent the exclusive basis of Beza's theological noetic. Genuine knowledge of God finds no assistance from reason or natural theology; instead, like Calvin, Beza stands firmly within Gilson's spiritual family of Augustinians who stress the primacy of faith in the attainment of true wisdom.
> This did not mean, of course, that reason was wholly abandoned, for it served as an auxiliary of theology. Beza, even more than Calvin, employed reason and philosophy in his elaboration and explanation of theology. Since Beza held that there was one objective body of truth, he was not afraid to use dialectic and philosophy in the defence of the Calvinist faith. In his polemics, biblical exegesis and confessional writings, Scripture formed the sole content of theological formulation. Nevertheless, the gifts of dialectic and reason were placed in the service of theology to define and clarify doctrinal points, to refute faulty reasoning, to provide coherence in the understanding of doctrinal relationships and, most importantly, to ensure a defensible body of teaching.[69]

Donald Sinnema argued that Beza's discussions of theological method and

---

67 McPhee, "Conserver or Transformer of Calvin's Theology?," xvii-xxvi.
68 Ibid., v. Compare Letham's helpful statement in this regard: "There is considerable uncertainty and confusion over what exactly Protestant scholasticism was. . . . The lines between scholasticism and humanism were, in any case, often blurred. 'All kinds of adjustments and combinations between humanism and scholasticism were possible and were successfully accomplished.' To say that a particular writer was influenced by scholasticism is not so significant a statement as has often been thought, since the vast bulk of the academic curriculum in the sixteenth century was governed by Aristotelian philosophical categories. Moreover, even if Beza was influenced by scholastic methodology his humanist interests were lifelong and more pronounced by far" (Letham, "Saving Faith and Assurance," 2:77 n. 199, quoting Kristeller, *Renaissance Thought*, 116).
69 McPhee, "Conserver or Transformer of Calvin's Theology?," 220-21.

his use of Aristotelianism must be understood in light of the pedagogical debate that was going on in the latter years of the sixteenth century. In this regard, Sinnema argued that Beza's use of Aristotle was a didactic, not a philosophical or theological, decision. Sinnema noted the "growing scholastic orientation" of "Reformed orthodoxy" in the latter sixteenth century, including its "attempt to present the Christian faith as a logically coherent and rationally defensible system," the "increased role given to reason and logic in presenting and defending religious truth," and its "dependence upon the methodology and philosophy of Aristotle."[70]

Sinnema delineated the contours of Beza's theological method from his preface to *Christianae Isagoges*, a theological text written by Lambert Daneau in 1583.[71] "After bewailing the miserable state of medieval theology, its neglect of the Scriptures, and its debates over thorny questions drawn from Lombard's Sentences," Sinnema remarked, "Beza states that the Lord brought renewal—surprisingly, he does not point to the preaching of the Word—by the restoration of languages and the good arts in the schools, especially 'that true and genuine logic explained by the Peripatetics alone.' . . . According to Beza, this renewal of languages and good arts prepared the way for the driving out of the 'idolomania' of popular medieval religion."[72]

Beza was adamant that a minister must be able to reason properly. But he "did not mean to mix the sacred with the profane or to bind divine wisdom to the rules of dialectic," because he "denied that the content of theology may be derived from pagan philosophy."[73] What use did Beza have for Aristotle, then? Sinnema argued that "for the purposes of orderly reasoning and teaching, Beza gave Aristotelian logic a firm place in theology." Sinnema referenced Beza's words to prove this point:

---

70 Donald Sinnema, "Aristotle and Early Reformed Orthodoxy: Moments of Accomodation [sic] and Antithesis," in *Christianity and the Classics: The Acceptance of a Heritage*, ed. Wendy E. Helleman (Lanham, MD: University Press of America, 1990), 119. Aristotelian logic was accepted uncritically by many theologians, he averred: "Logic as the art of reasoning was commonly assumed to be a necessary tool for theologians and, though Ramist logic made strong inroads in Reformed circles, many leading orthodox theologians were committed to Aristotelian logic. Since it was thought that logic, as a gift of God, does not influence theological content, it was easy to assume that Aristotelian logic was neutral with respect to the Christian faith" (ibid., 143).

71 See Olivier Fatio, "Lambert Daneau: 1530-1595," trans. Jill Raitt, in *Shapers of Religious Traditions in Germany, Switzerland, and Poland, 1560-1600*, ed. Jill Raitt (New Haven: Yale University Press, 1981), 115-17.

72 Sinnema, "Aristotle," 129.

73 Ibid., 130.

> This I impress again and again (said Beza) upon all students, if indeed they wish to be considered teachers of the truth and refuters of falsehood in the Church, that especially in this time they should continue diligently to learn, practice, and use logic, not that new-fangled logic of the very clever sophists . . . which turns men into pseudo-dialecticians in three days, while overturning the foundations of both the art itself and of nature, but that true and genuine logic such as has been taught most perfectly by Aristotle.

Sinnema continued, "When students have learned this art, Beza pointed out, they need go no further than the apostle Paul for the perfect example of the practice of logic," for he said that logic could "'be learned either from the most perfect teacher of it himself, Aristotle, or (if anyone does not think that he needs to know the individual details which Aristotle teaches so precisely and accurately) from any learned compedium, but that the practice of the art be observed in our Paul.'"[74]

Evaluation of Methodology Studies

Scholars thus have very different judgments about Beza's theological method. Bizer and Kickel, basing their evaluations on a very limited survey of the Bezan corpus charged Beza with introducing rationalism and an unhealthy use of logic into Reformed thought. Armstrong followed them. Sinnema showed, conversely, that Beza intended to be explicitly biblical in his theology; logic was important but, after all, it was also essential to the Bible's writers. McPhee, through a study of much of the Bezan corpus, argued that Beza intended to base his doctrine on Scripture. Sinnema and McPhee also attempted to place Beza in his historical and intellectual context. Sinnema showed the developing pedagogy of Beza's era. Raitt likewise noted the pedagogical and polemical forces that led Beza to express his theology in an increasingly logical manner. McPhee traced Beza's humanistic training. Although Sinnema's, McPhee's and Raitt's research was superior, their studies also have limitations. Sinnema's evaluation consisted of only one of Beza's very short works. McPhee limited himself to Beza's pre-1571 works. Raitt's research examined just one aspect of Beza's theology. In addition, she did not pursue her very insightful question about the cause for Beza's use of rhetoric and dialectic.

Studies of Beza's Doctrine of Predestination

Scholars have probably investigated Theodore Beza's teaching on predestination more than any other *locus* of his theology. Many scholars charge that here Beza exhibited the starkest deviance from Calvin's balanced theological position. However there are two weaknesses with many of these

---

74 Ibid.; quoting Beza's preface to Lambert Daneau, *Christianae Isagoges ad Christianorum theologorum locos communes* (Geneva: Vignon, 1583), fols. iii-iiii.

studies. First, several scholars have judged Beza by preconceived criteria, without giving his assertions a fair hearing. These researchers have especially averred that Beza's whole theological tenor was scholastic. Second, other scholars' works have lacked sufficient attention to the genre of Beza's productions. These researchers, especially, have charged Beza with making predestination the central dogma of his system. Noting the shortcomings of both of these approaches, other researchers have tried to understand Beza's use of scholastic language in his historical context while also demonstrating the subservient place predestination had in his system as a whole. They have been more successful. Yet, their focus on a small number of Beza's works warrants still more research on Beza's doctrine of God's sovereignty in salvation.

Studies Emphasizing Scholasticism

Philip Holtrop, Walter Kickel, and John Bray opined that Beza increasingly appropriated scholastic ideas and language in his theology, in contrast to Calvin's essential biblical humanism. This resulted in Beza's over-emphasis on predestination, they maintained. Their analyses were flawed from the start, however, because of their presuppositions about the nature of scholasticism.

Holtrop's study is massive. Yet it is misguided at key points. Holtrop's analysis exhibits several of the recent inaccuracies in the study of Beza's theology. According to Holtrop, Calvin wrestled with both scholastic and humanistic tendencies, struggled to remain biblical, and during his controversy with Bolsec succumbed to a philosophical and dogmatic (and anti biblical) position. Beza made Calvin's eccentricity habitual. Beza is thus the full-blown scholastic, the one who gave up all pretenses of being biblical in favor of a dogmatic Aristotelianism, and who ushered in the era of Protestant Scholasticism. Beza, Holtrop charged, exaggerated the "scholastic side" of his predecessor, so that his treatises on predestination were dominated by Aristotelian language and concepts.[75] But Holtrop's deductions from Beza's Aristotelian language are unwarranted. His claims manifest three deficiencies, all of which reinforced his faulty view that Beza emphasized Aristotelianism.

First, Holtrop disregarded genre. Beza certainly did use logic in his treatises on predestination. But that does not prove that Beza's whole pastoral and theological enterprise was dominated by Aristotelian categories. Nor does it explain why Beza filled these works with biblical citations and allusions.

---

75 Holtrop developed this thesis in a lengthy appendix titled "Calvin, Beza, and the Early Development of Reformed Scholasticism" (Holtrop, *Bolsec Controversy*, 1:822-92). Undeniably, there is grist for the scholastic mill in Beza's predestinarian writings. As Holtrop demonstrated vigorously, Beza used several elements of Aristotelian logic—especially his scheme of causality—in his predestinarian treatises (ibid., 1:842-59).

Holtrop had no warrant to claim categorically that "from the beginning to the end of his career, [Beza] used the causality framework of Aristotle and saw all reality in that light—starting with the 'highest cause,' through 'secondary causes,' and ultimately the 'final cause' or 'goal.' For Beza, causality was more than a 'formal' concern; it was the key for understanding the history of redemption."[76] A comparison Holtrop made between Calvin and Beza showed the results of Holtrop's inattention to genre:

> Throughout the *Institutes* Calvin put a stronger accent than Beza on God's salvation *pro nobis*. In his non-polemical writings in general he defined God's glory relationally, while Beza saw it as God's realizing in history his essential nature as merciful and just. The following is a typical pronouncement in Beza: "Hence that statement that he loves some and hates others; he has created some for his glory and others for shame; he has elected some and rejected others. That is to say: He elects some freely, and loves them, and endows them with eternal salvation—but he rejects others rightly, and hates them, and has determined to destroy them by his eternal judgment." If all that sounds rather clinical—and antiseptic—we should remember that God is a God of order, who acts in accord with who he *is*. "And indeed, in either case, he acts for the revelation of his glory."[77]

Holtrop allowed for Calvin's "non-polemical writings," but failed to examine such non-polemical treatises composed by Beza. The quotation from Beza's *De praedestinationis* is not "a typical pronouncement" of his entire thought.[78] Holtrop ignored Beza's pastoral writings.

Second, Holtrop's scheme of the "relational" Calvin mutating into the "scholastic" Beza led him to postulate historical inaccuracies. According to his thesis, Beza's use of scholasticism increased over time. So, Holtrop argued that in one of Beza's "early" treatises, "An Exhortation to the Reformation of the Church," Beza "warned against the 'imaginations of Plato concerning intelligences and spirits' and the 'opinions of the power and free will of man—which are completely Aristotelian, and with which the church today is convulsed.'"[79] Yet "by the time [Beza] gave his inaugural *Discours* at the Genevan Academy—in 1559," Holtrop asserted that Beza "appreciated Plato

---

76 Ibid., 1:842.
77 Ibid., 1:851.
78 In a similar vein Holtrop unfavorably compared Beza's use of Thomistic language in his 1588 *Ad acta* to Calvin's thought. In the *Ad acta*, "The argument is heavy and thoroughly Aristotelian," but, he charged, "it is different from the generally rhetorical, relational, personal, and more 'biblical' tone in Calvin's *Institutes*" (ibid., 1:841). Yet Holtrop had previously labeled the *Ad acta* "polemical" (ibid., 1:840). It was inappropriate for him to compare two works of such varied genres.
79 Ibid., 1:834.

and Aristotle profoundly."⁸⁰ Actually, though, Beza penned the "Exhortation" six years after he gave the *Discours*.⁸¹ Holtrop's chronological scheme is mistaken.

Third, Holtrop's notion of the Platonic Calvin versus the Aristotelian Beza is a false dichotomy. In the first place, it is incorrect descriptively. Holtrop argued that "Beza was primarily a theologian of the 'head,' while Calvin focused primarily on the 'heart.' In the polemics during the [Bolsec] controversy, Calvin was argumentative. But when he wrote for the believing community he was more celebrative than cerebral, and more doxological than dialectical. In line with that, he was more Platonic than Aristotelian."⁸² Holtrop made this assertion the basis for his evolutionary argument: "The pattern was now set. Beza became increasingly Aristotelian as he moved along."⁸³ The issue, rather, seems to be that Beza's (and Calvin's) use of Aristotle was nuanced. Seeing some good in Aristotle, Beza nevertheless critiqued him at points.⁸⁴ Additionally, Beza was often very affectionate in his pastoral works. However, Holtrop failed to notice any of this genre of Beza's treatises.⁸⁵ This is akin to judging all of Calvin's theology by looking only at his *De aeterna Dei praedestinatione*. Contrary to Holtrop's assertion, Beza's many pastoral and devotional works were "more celebrative than cerebral, and more doxological than dialectical." Holtrop's work fails to give us a full picture of Beza's

---

80 Ibid.
81 See Beza, *Correspondance*, 6:254, 270.
82 Holtrop, *Bolsec Controversy*, 1:835. Paradoxically, Holtrop was here sensitive to the genre of Calvin's works, even though he disregarded genre in his discussion of Beza.
83 Ibid. The issue seems to be, rather, what use did Beza make of Aristotle? Holtrop argued that Beza's use of logic showed he was no longer concerned with deriving truth *a posteriori* from the Bible (ibid., 837). Following Sinnema, though, I believe the issue for Beza was that correct logic was useful and, indeed, essential because it helped one to understand the Bible correctly.
84 See chapter three below.
85 Beza's works cited by Holtrop were (followed by the number of references): *De praedestinationis doctrina* (49); *Questionum et responsianum* (30); *Ad acta (pars altera)* (29); *Summa totius christianismi* (24); *Confession* (19); *Ad sebastiani castellionis calumnias* (15); *Prefatio* to Danaeus's *Isagoges* (11); *Jobus* (11); *Theses theologicae* (10); *Epistolarum theologicarum* (2); "Discours du Recteur Th. de Bèze" (2); *Altera brevis fidei confessio* (2); *Questionum et responsionum pars altera* (1); *Joannis Calvini vita* (1); *Berne Colloquy* (1); and, *Summa doctrinae de re sacramentaria* (1). The fact that 24 percent of Holtrop's references were to one of Beza's works devoted to predestination, and that three of the top four (49 percent of the total references) were polemics defending predestination, calls his conclusions into question. Of course Beza would speak much about predestination here, perhaps often in great "scholastic" detail.

doctrine of God's sovereignty.[86] In the second place, Holtrop's bifurcation between the "relational" Calvin and the "scholastic" Beza is inaccurate. Calvin used the very kind of scholastic terms that Holtrop despised; and Calvin used them throughout his various works, not just during the heat of the Bolsec controversy.[87] Calvin also promoted Beza's method of defending the doctrine of predestination in the *Tabula*.[88] Additionally, Calvin and Beza both received a similar French humanistic education, some of it from the same mentor, Melchior Wolmar. Calvin was more scholastic, and Beza more humanistic, than Holtrop allowed.

Walter Kickel's thesis was that Beza placed human reason on equal footing with biblical revelation. Eventually reason gained ground over revelation in Beza's thought, appropriating Aristotelian concepts. By giving room to reason when handling predestination, Kickel argued that Beza unwittingly allowed

---

86 The source of many weaknesses in Holtrop's analysis is that his historical investigation was partisan. His theological agenda unhelpfully skewed his analysis. He wanted to move Reformed theology away from a "decretal theology" to one that was more "relational," focused not on God-in-himself but on "God the Father in relation to us" (Holtrop, *Bolsec Controversy*, 1:858). This agenda is seen clearly in his appendix, "Toward a Biblical Conception of Truth, and a New Mood for Doing Reformed Theology" (ibid., 1:893-920). Cf. P. C. Holtrop, "Decree(s) of God," in *Encyclopedia of the Reformed Faith*, ed. D. McKim (Edinburgh: St. Andrews, 1992), 97-99.

87 See, for example, David C. Steinmetz, "The Scholastic Calvin," in *Protestant Scholasticism: Essays in Reassessment*, ed. Carl R. Trueman and R. S. Clark (Carlisle: Paternoster, 1999), 16-30, and Stephen R. Spencer, "Reformed Scholasticism in Medieval Perspective: Thomas Aquinas and Francis Turrettini on the Incarnation" (Ph.D. diss., Michigan State University, 1988), 89-90. Holtrop did not deny that Calvin used scholastic terminology, but he did argue that this was out of character with "Calvin's 'voluntarism' and accent on God the Father in relation to us (as in the *Institutes*)" (Holtrop, *Bolsec Controversy*, 1:858). In his review of Holtrop's book, Muller noted, though, that Calvin's works were filled with scholastic language, and he argued that Beza probably borrowed it from Calvin at points (Muller, "review of *The Bolsec Controversy*," 588).

88 For example, in 1562 Calvin's sermons on predestination from his ongoing exposition of Genesis were published. Calvin included an appendix titled "An Answer to certain slanders and blasphemies, wherewith certain evil disposed persons have gone about to bring the doctrine of God's everlasting Predestination into hatred" (John Calvin, *Sermons on Election and Reprobation*, trans. John Fielde [London: 1579; reprint, Audubon, NJ: Old Paths, 1996], 305). After pointing out numerous reasons the opponents of predestination were wrong, Calvin said he could not deal adequately in this place with all the Bible had to say about this doctrine. So he recommended that his readers "consider those places which are gathered in a little book that our brother master Beza has made thereof, and you shall be fully satisfied therein" (ibid., 310-11).

human ratiocination to trump biblical truth.

Kickel's thesis has two closely-connected weaknesses. First, Kickel created his reason-revelation paradigm and then conformed Beza's writings to this pattern. This is seen clearly in Kickel's final statements in his survey of Beza's doctrine of predestination. Kickel concluded that

> philosophical reason along with Aristotelian philosophy, whose foundational structure, especially its concept of science, its concept of causation, and its idea of God, determined the development of Beza's doctrine of predestination. The consequence of these Aristsotelian influences is the removal of Christ and of the Word from their central place in theology as well as the substitution of a rational system of final causation in the place of Christocentrism. . . . We must therefore conclude that Beza's doctrine of predestination is not in accord with revelation. It. . . removes Christ from his position as the foundation and criterion of knowledge for theology. Beza's claim that his doctrine of predestination is identical with the teaching of Christ, so that opposition against his doctrine amounts to opposition to Christ, cannot therefore be upheld. The introduction of reason in theology . . . has therefore practiced a long-range and ominous influence in theology. The seemingly formal principles of Aristotelian philosophy, which in actual fact are based on metaphysical presuppositions, push through their own character within theology. They are not smashed by the truth of revelation; instead they split and deform the truth of revelation. The official introduction of reason has therefore turned into a surreptitious position of sovereignty.[89]

Kickel was driven by his reason-revelation dichotomy. He also fundamentally misunderstood Beza's intention in his writings on predestination, erecting them as the pinnacle and controlling principle of all of the Reformer's theological expression. For example, Kickel wrongly interpreted the *Tabula*, asserting that the "doctrine of predestination" promoted there "represents the entire theology of Beza."[90]

Second, Kickel neglected a large part of Beza's corpus. Although Kickel included one hundred and forty-two references to Beza's works (some of them extended quotations) these were from just seven different treatises. And three of Beza's works – the *Tabula*, *De praedestinationis*, and *Ad Sebastiani Castellionis calumnies* – dominated his discussion.[91] Two of these were polemical defenses of predestination and the other a very detailed technical

---

89 Kickel, *Vernuft und Offenbarung*, 167-68.
90 Ibid., 99. See also McPhee, "Conserver or Transformer of Calvin's Theology?," 301, and John S. Bray, *Theodore Beza's Doctrine of Predestination*, Bibliotheca Humanistica and Reformatorica 12 (Nieuwkoop: B. De Graaf, 1975), 95-97, for additional critiques of Kickel.
91 Kickel referenced the *Tabula* thirty-eight times (27 percent of his references), *De praedestinationis* fifty-eight times (41 percent), and *Ad Sebastiani Castellionis calumnies* thirty times (21 percent).

exposition of Romans 9. Disregarding these genre issues, though, Kickel used them as 89 percent of his prooftexts in his discussion.[92] Certainly it is appropriate to use treatises Beza wrote specifically on predestination while attempting to explicate this component of his thought. But to fail to use any of Beza's pastoral works, where he dealt with predestination and applied it to his listeners, is too selective. Combined with Kickel's *a priori* characterization of Beza as a rationalist, his lack of attention to a wide range of Beza's works weakens his conclusions.

John Bray's conclusions were better nuanced but retraced much of the same ground.[93] Through an investigation of Beza's appropriation of scholasticism, Bray attempted to decide if Beza changed Calvin's theology. He argued that

> Beza was, in no sense of the word, a full-blown scholastic. Many of the emphases found in scholasticism are absent from his work, and Beza denounced the very methodology into which he was partially drawn. Bizer, Kickel, and Dantine have overemphasized the scholastic element in Beza's theology and have underplayed the biblical component. This may have been the result of their neglect of Beza's non-systematic works in favor of his systematic studies. . . . Beza, with his penchant for systematization, was unusually well equipped for the theological demands of his era. He did move beyond Calvin and, in a very real sense, established a precedent for the rigid systems of the Reformed scholastics. His use of scholastic terminology and, at times, methodology, in his role as Calvin's successor resulted in granting to scholasticsm a respectability in the Reformed tradition that would later be eagerly seized by others.[94]

The outlines of Bray's study were formed by Armstrong's characterizations of scholasticism. In fact, Bray began with the list of "basic tendencies" of scholasticism formulated by Armstrong.[95] And he ended by summarizing his opinions of Beza's adherence to scholastic methodology.[96] Although he

---

92   He also referenced the *Confession* nine times and the *Questionum et responsium* three times. Three additional references were to Beza's *Correspondance*. But Kickel noticed none of Beza's pastoral works.

93   Bray's positive contributions should be noted too. For instance, he argued helpfully that much damage has been done in Bezan studies by falsely understanding the Reformer's intention in his *Tabula*. Rather than teaching that "for Beza the doctrine of predestination summarized all of Christian theology," as Kickel taught, the *Tabula* "should be interpreted to mean the sum total of the Christian life or of the redemption promised to the faithful," according to Bray (*Beza's Doctrine*, 72). He also tried to understand Beza in his historical context (ibid., 22-68), although his later characterizations of Beza's theology disregarded the implications of his own historical introduction.

94   Ibid., 141-42.

95   Bray expanded Armstrong's four tendencies into six (ibid., 12-16).

96   Ibid., 137-43.

qualified Beza's adherence to these scholastic "tendencies," Bray's discussion was framed by Armstrong's criteria.[97]

Bray helpfully summarized his conclusions as follows: Calvin was biblical in his doctrinal presentation (including his teaching about the doctrine of predestination). Beza presented "predestination as the foundation of all doctrine and spoke of it as being more important than justification by faith" in several works, although he "warned specifically that one should not employ predestination as a metaphysical principle which would be used to explain all phenomena of belief and unbelief." "Predestination played a greater role in Beza's theology than had been the case with Calvin," probably because of his perceived need to defend Calvin's doctrine. "Beza was more of a systematizer than was Calvin," and he appropriated Aristotle and Aquinas more than Calvin had. Beza emphasized "the role of reason and logic" resulting in "a much greater confidence on the part of Beza concerning man's ability to reason and to employ logic in the solution of theological problems. Beza's references to the mysterious elements involved in the execution of predestination became minimal. He also became much bolder in his theological assertions and was willing to take a position on issues that Calvin felt had not been clearly resolved in Scripture" with the result that "Beza's theology became so philosophical that even the actions of God were viewed in terms of logical, rational necessity." Finally, however, Beza limited his philosophical and speculative language to his polemical and systematic treatises, whereas his devotional and pastoral treatises used biblical categories.[98]

The cornerstone of Bray's argument was that there was an evolution in Beza's thought. Early, Beza was biblical in his argumentation; as time progressed, he became more scholastic in his reasoning.[99] This interpretation has several problems. First, Bray assumed, but did not attempt to prove, Armstrong's list of scholastic "tendencies." Should these be faulty summaries of scholasticism, Bray's conclusions are problematic. Second, although Bray noted the importance of genre in Beza research, the bulk of his attention was to works Beza devoted to the doctrine of predestination. Third, Bray was dependent on other scholars, more than Beza himself, and was unsympathetic to the Reformer. In this regard, note his characterization of the relationship of the *Tabula* to the later *De praedestinationis*, along with his judgmental attitude towards Beza:

---

97 Ibid., 119-31.
98 Ibid., 140-41. The seeming incongruity of some of Bray's conclusions makes his thesis hard to pin down.
99 "Beza's growing confidence in this selective use of reason was one of the basic distinctions between his theological method and that of Calvin" (ibid., 92-93).

Although there are strong similarities between the *Tabula* of 1555 and Beza's *De Praedestinationis doctrina* of 1582, the differences are consistent and significant. By 1582 it appears that the scholastic, rationalistic tendencies within Beza have come more to the fore. The basic terms used in both works—decree, predestination, foreknowledge—are given a more precise, rationalistic definition. By 1582 Beza has dropped such anthropencentric terms as "love" and "hate". There has been an infusion of Thomistic terminology. And, perhaps most significantly, Beza's earlier strictures which reminded one of the mystery involved in predestination are almost entirely absent from this later work. It would appear that now the only mystery consists of determining who is to be included in the ranks of the reprobate.

In spite of the fact that the lectures upon which *De Praedestinationis doctrina* was based were, ostensibly, an exegesis of Romans 9, in fact, the text of Romans 9 has been exploited by Beza as an opportunity to expound his theory of predestination. Thus one discovers that Beza has read into the text of Romans 9 controversies in which he himself was involved; he has sought justification in Romans 9 for his own theories concerning predestination; and he has drawn conclusions from the text far beyond what many exegetes would view as justified. At the same time, one must remember that Romans had provided an opportunity earlier for Luther and Calvin to expound their theories of predestination. The difference is that Beza's comments were far more systematic and scholastic.[100]

Significantly, Bray cited Johannes Dantine after the first paragraph and Kickel after the second. His subsequent exposition of the *De praedestinationis* contained little actual reference of the Bezan text but a lot of dependence upon Kickel. In the final analysis Bray's study is not convincing because he assumed, but did not prove, many of his points, especially the nature of scholasticism and Beza's use of it.

"Central Dogma" Studies

The notion that Beza placed predestination at the center of his theological system has an impressive pedigree.[101] Two scholars, especially, have advocated this "central dogma" theory in recent decades. According to Johannes Dantine and R. T. Kendall, supralapsarian predestination (with its concomitant, limited atonement) was Beza's doctrinal passion. These scholars, however, did not pay sufficient attention to genre when they made this claim.

Dantine argued that Beza's attempts to clarify the doctrine of predestination, in his *Tabula* and his later *De praedestinationis*, led him into increased speculation. Originally dependent on Calvin, Beza increasingly borrowed from

---

100 Ibid., 72-73.
101 See Richard A. Muller, "Calvin and the 'Calvinists': Assessing Continuities and Discontinuities between the Reformation and Orthodoxy," *Calvin Theological Journal* 30 (1995): 345-58, and 31 (1996): 151-57.

Aquinas and employed scholastic language. The result was Protestant Orthodoxy, a far cry from the theology of Calvin.[102] Whereas Calvin intentionally treated predestination as a mystery and placed it under the doctrine of salvation, Beza emphasized it "in a sense exactly opposite to that of Calvin."[103] Similarly, Kendall argued that Beza mutated Calvin's biblical predestinarianism into an unhealthy supralapsarianism. He claimed that Beza was the first of the Reformed theologians "to make the doctrine of predestination central to his system."[104] Not only did Beza heighten the importance of predestination, but he also changed it into a supralapsarian scheme which was foreign to Calvin's doctrine.[105]

The theological problem that Beza faced, according to Dantine, was how to reconcile the following two statements: first, "God is the author of faith, which he decided from eternity"; second, "one cannot say that God is also the author of sin, of unbelief, of eternal condemnation."[106] Dantine argued that in the *Tabula* especially "the methodological principle of the distinction between the eternal decree and its execution permitted Beza to see all the problems of predestination as resolved."[107] Beza developed his works on predestination, then, "with this principle," showing how God's use of secondary causes allowed him to execute his decree without being culpable for sin.[108]

Yet both Dantine and Kendall created a canon within the canon of Beza's works in order to substantiate their claims. To Dantine, Beza's scheme in the *Tabula* became the criterion by which to judge all his other works.[109] Dantine noted that other treatises by Beza were arranged differently, but he argued that

---

102 Dantine, "Les Tabelles," 365, 371-72.
103 Ibid., 372.
104 R. T. Kendall, *Calvin and English Calvinism to 1649* (New York: Oxford University Press, 1979; reprint, Carlisle: Paternoster, 1997), 30.
105 As we shall see below, Kendall argued that the logical extension of Beza's supralapsarianism was the doctrine of a limited atonement, that is, the view that Christ died only for those who had been chosen by God from eternity. This new doctrine, Kendall averred, was foreign to Calvin's view (Ibid., 30-31).
106 Dantine, "Les Tabelles," 367.
107 Ibid., 374.
108 Ibid., 367, 369. See Raitt, *Montbéliard*, 148-50. But whereas Beza may have stressed this formula more than other theologians, Muller has shown that he was drawing on an historical expression of the doctrine that included Calvin (see Muller, "Use and Abuse," 47-48), while McPhee noted that the distinction between the decree and its execution was not an instance of Beza's rationalism, but was rather called forth by the controversy with Bolsec (McPhee, "Conserver or Transformer of Calvin's Theology?," 84).
109 Dantine also engaged in unwarranted psychoanalysis when he postulated that Beza needed a rigorous system because of the dissolute life he lived before his conversion ("Les Tabelles," 366).

they deviated from Beza's norm. For example, the *Confession*, originally written to convince Beza's father of Protestantism, obviously downplayed the potentially controversial doctrine of predestination, he argued. Likewise, although the *Quaestionum et responsium* was arranged differently from the *Tabula* (Beza used an analytic method here, which was "different from Beza's normal and preferred method"), Dantine concluded that even here we see "predestination as the base of all theological reflections."[110] In sum, Dantine erected predestination as the focus of Beza's entire theological enterprise after examining just two treatises, works that Beza intentionally devoted to predestination. He then judged all of Beza's theology according to this predestinarian canon. Kendall's claims were likewise derived from a quick survey of just six of Beza's works.[111] It seems that neither Dantine nor Kendall examined enough of Beza's treatises to corroborate their theses about Beza's view of predestination. Beza's main doctrinal concern in his *Tabula* and his *De praedestinationis* was certainly predestination. Dantine and Kendall were guilty of elevating his presentation of predestination in these two works (the first a polemical work against Bolsec's denial of the doctrine, and the second a very technical lecture in the Academy on Romans 9) above all his other productions. Beza's stress on predestination here is understandable given his purpose in composing these two works. He did not, however, emphasize predestination equally in other genres.

Contextual Studies

Other scholars have investigated Beza's doctrine of predestination more sympathetically, avoiding the mistakes of earlier research. Their studies were marked by careful attention to context. Raitt, Muller, and McPhee tried to put Beza's predestinarian works in their historical context. Muller, Sinnema, and McPhee placed them in their theological context. Beeke showed their literary context and noted the importance of genre. These various contextual studies resulted in much better results than the studies surveyed above.

HISTORICALLY CONTEXTUAL

Jill Raitt successfully placed one of Beza's predestinarian treatises in its historical context. Before recounting the specifics of Beza's interchange with the Lutheran Jacob Andreae at the Colloquy of Montbéliard in 1586, Raitt elucidated the complex theological and political background which informed

---

110 Ibid., 375. In chapter three, I will argue for an alternative understanding of the *Quaestionum et responsium*.
111 See my critique below of Kendall's use of the Bezan corpus regarding assurance.

the debate.[112] Raitt's work showed that Beza did not theologize *ex nihilo*.[113]

Richard Muller's evaluation of Beza's *Tabula* is a model of contextually sensitive research. He averred that "the primary basis for a right understanding of the *Tabula* must be consideration of its genre and purpose in its historical context, not the purpose to which it might be directed by nineteenth-century theologians in search of their own central dogmas."[114] An understanding of Beza's purpose for writing this treatise (that the doctrine of predestination would be "methodically treated" in an effort to refute the errors of Bolsec)[115] and of its structure (Beza began by showing the pastoral use of the doctrine of election, presupposed a distinction between the decree and its execution, focused all of the doctrine around Christ, inserted biblical proofs for his doctrine after each statement, and culminated the treatise by showing the manner in which it should be preached)[116] is prerequisite to "understanding" Beza's doctrine of predestination.

THEOLOGICALLY CONTEXUAL

Muller noted a consistent Christocentrism in Beza's predestinarian scheme. He also elaborated on the contextual reasons for Beza's oft-maligned *Tabula*. In his extended survey of Reformation thought, for example, Muller was at pains to demonstrate that Beza's use of the doctrine of predestination did not detract from Calvin's consistent Christocentrism. The conclusion of Muller's section dealing with Beza is noteworthy:

> In neither of his major systematic efforts [i.e., the *Confession* and *Questionum et responsium*] did Beza attempt to set forth a predestinarian system. . . . Beza's predestinarianism really serves only to clarify and to ground his conception of the *ordo salutis*. . . .
>
> In conclusion, Bizer, Kickel, and Dantine have overstated their case greatly. Fully developed Reformed orthodoxy does not appear in Beza's theology nor does a thoroughly rationalistic and necessitarian perspective on theology. . . . Beza was

---

112 Raitt, *Montbéliard*, 11-72. See also her "French Reformed Theological Response," 178-90. Similarly, Robert Letham contended that context was the key to understanding Beza's doctrine of predestination: "Those works in which Beza uses predestination as a governing principle were written in a polemical context, amidst the controversies raging around the views of Bolsec, Castellio and Andraeus." So, he continued, "they should be measured against the overall tenor of his entire output. . . . Many other theological works give no foundational function to predestination" (Letham, "Theodore Beza," 27).

113 Raitt commented that the debate between Beza and Andreae "was sometimes scholastic, sometimes scriptural," but the heart of the matter consistently gravitated around the issue of assurance of salvation (*Montbéliard*, 150).

114 Muller, "Use and Abuse," 61.

115 Ibid., 39.

116 Ibid., 45-59.

a transition figure. He moved beyond Calvin in his use of scholastic terminology and in the precision of his doctrinal statements. But his 'scholasticism' was moderate even by sixteenth-century standards as set by Vermigli, Zanchi, Ursinus, and Polanus, to name only a few.... Beza's role in the development of Reformed system may better be described as a generally successful attempt to clarify and to render more precise the doctrinal definitions he had inherited from Calvin and the other Reformers of the first era of theological codification.[117]

Sinnema very thoroughly explicated the place of reprobation in Beza's doctrine of predestination, showing in the process the manner in which Beza differed from his predecessor in Geneva. Calvin clearly taught double predestination.[118] Reprobation, according to Calvin, is "a positive rejecting or predestining to eternal damnation or destruction."[119] He taught that the ultimate cause of reprobation was God's will.[120] In the process, Calvin emphasized the difference between proximate and remote causes (*causae propinquae et remotae*) in the damnation of sinners: "Though the remote cause of damnation and destruction is God's will, the proximate cause is man's original corruption and sin. Thus the blame for their destruction remains in the reprobate themselves, not in God. How God could be the remote cause and yet not be the author of sin was for Calvin a mystery known to God alone."[121]

According to Sinnema, Beza softened Calvin's doctrine of reprobation by making a distinction between God's decree and its execution. Sinnema outlined Beza's doctrine in this manner:

> As there is a difference between the *decree* of reprobation and its *execution* (damnation), so their respective causes differ. The cause of the decree to reprobate, hidden to us, is found in God's will alone, not in sin or in a foreknowledge of unbelief. It is God's will alone that determines why some rather than others are destined to destruction. On the other hand, the causes of damnation and eternal destruction are well-known: the original corruption of Adam, in which the reprobate are born, and its sinful fruits. God is not the cause of damnation; neither is his decree of reprobation its cause, although the reprobate are not condemned apart from his decree.[122]

Sinnema averred that Beza's desire to show the reasons for damnation explains the chain of causes found in his table of predestination and reprobation: "While

---

117 Muller, *Christ and the Decree*, 95-96.
118 Donald W. Sinnema, "The Issue of Reprobation at the Synod of Dort (1618-19) in Light of the History of this Doctrine" (Ph.D. diss., University of St. Michael's College, 1985), 59.
119 Ibid., 60, citing Calvin, *Institutes* 3.21.5.
120 Ibid., 61.
121 Ibid., 62.
122 Ibid., 69; my emphasis.

Beza considered the decree of election to be the efficient cause of faith, he denied that the decree of reprobation is the efficient cause of unbelief, which, however, does not occur apart from the decree. Man's will is the efficient cause; God can only be called its deficient cause (*causa deficiens*). For unbelievers do not believe as (*sicut*) it pleases God to desert them in their unbelief."[123]

McPhee's is the most cogent study of Beza's doctrine of predestination in its historical and theological context. McPhee concluded his evaluation of Beza by noting that

> the historiography on Beza, by concentrating too exclusively on the *form* of his doctrine of predestination, has overlooked the christological and ethical dimension of his thought. To focus solely on the rational, or so-called scholastic side of Beza's presentation of divine omnipotence has led to serious distortion. When Beza's *intention*, as well as the polemical demands confronting him, are taken into account, one discovers that the form was placed in the service of Beza's pastoral and practical concern. In short, there was a vast underworld of soteriological and ethical thinking behind the rational form of his doctrine. Moreover, it is also evident that Beza was not entirely the prisoner of Aristotelian ontology and logic, for in his less systematic works, and particularly his annotations he was heavily informed by biblical categories of thought.
>
> Conversely, the rational and logical side of Beza's doctrine of predestination cannot be minimized. Both in terms of his developments of Calvin's teaching, and his influence on the course of Reformed theology, Beza's clear-cut supralapsarianism, his emphatic doctrine of limited atonement and his shift in emphasis in the doctrine of assurance: all of these reflect Beza's systematic genius.[124]

McPhee rightly noted that Theodore Beza was more than an Aristotelian rationalist. He was a pastor who was concerned with biblical living in the world. His writings on predestination, though they were sometimes scholastic, also included pastoral treatments. All of them were informed by Beza's biblicism.

LITERARILY CONTEXTUAL

Joel Beeke briefly evaluated Beza's doctrine of predestination through an examination of Beza's *Tabula, Confession*, and *De praedestinationis*. Beeke emphasized the context of Beza's works, as well as his pastoral intent in their composition. First, both Beza's supralapsarianism and his differences from Calvin "can easily be overestimated." Second, "Beza's attempt to move from a Christological to a trinitarian framework was not mere speculation, but a

---

123 Ibid., 70-71.
124 McPhee, "Conserver or Transformer of Calvin's Theology?," 350.

serious attempt to make an improvement upon, and enlargement of, Calvinian theology *in toto*." And finally, "Some of the confusion of scholarship's widely varied interpretations of Beza's thought must be charged to Beza himself," because he expressed himself differently in various works.[125] Beeke also stressed the importance of genre. Beza wrote in varied styles, and scholars cannot assume that a single work represents the Reformer's complete thought.

EVALUATION OF CONTEXTUAL STUDIES

All of the above-mentioned scholars have furthered our understanding of Beza's doctrine of predestination. However, although many of these studies are excellent in their own right, each of them also has limitations. McPhee's research was limited in time and in purpose. Raitt's and Muller's studies were limited in the number of Beza's works used in their investigations. Sinnema's research was limited to merely one aspect of the doctrine of God's sovereignty in salvation. As valuable as their studies are, then, more work still needs to be done on Beza's doctrine of predestination.

In the first place, then, McPhee's research was limited to a relatively short time period. He stopped his investigation at 1570 for "in a real sense 1570 represented the end of Beza's theologically creative period," he averred.[126] He argued that a number of historical situations after 1570 (the heightened activity of the Catholic Counter Reformation, growing Lutheran intransigence, Catholic victories in France, Beza's debate with Morely over ecclesiology, among them) "forced Beza more on the defensive. Thus, it would appear legitimate to treat Beza's post-1570 theology separately as these political and eccelesiastical [*sic*] changes may have shaped his thinking considerably."[127] But McPhee limited his study too drastically. By neglecting Beza's works composed after 1570 he bypassed most of Beza's pastoral works, almost all of which were published

---

125 Joel R. Beeke, "Did Beza's Supralapsarianism Spoil Calvin's Theology?" *Reformed Theological Journal* 13 (1997): 64-66.

126 McPhee noted at the outset of his examination of Beza's doctrine of predestination that "Where greater progress needs to be made is in the recovery of the ethical and religious side of Beza's doctrine of predestination. In an ironic way the critics who claim that Beza developed the rational side of Calvin's teaching at the expense of the religious are guilty of the same fault. Not even Bray's more sensitive study has explored the religious roots of Beza's doctrine of predestination. So much stress has been laid on the rational form of his doctrine that little or no effort has been made to understand the underlying motives of his teaching on divine omnipotence" ("Conserver or Transformer of Calvin's Theology?," 290-91). To this end, however, he mainly examined Beza's *Tabula*, *Confession*, *Questionum et responsium*, *Annotationes*, and his lectures on Romans. This is a very small sample of Beza's works.

127 McPhee, "Conserver or Transformer of Calvin's Theology?," xxviii.

later in his life.[128] It is in these works, however, treatises written during the heat of controversy and often when Beza was forced to question God's sovereignty on behalf of Geneva and France, that Beza's pastoral application of the doctrine of God's sovereignty is apparent to a degree not present in his previous compositions.

McPhee also had a very limited purpose: to discover if Beza was faithful to Calvin doctrinally.[129] He argued convincingly that Calvin and Beza were very similar in their theological content. Beza's expression of that doctrine, however, was different because of the different needs of his day, especially the urgency to buttress the Reformed faith in the midst of increasing attacks.[130] But the narrow focus of his investigation meant that McPhee could not examine the breadth of issues surrounding Beza's doctrine of God's sovereignty. His narrow focus was important and enlightening. But he was not able to be as broad in his treatment of Beza as might be desired.

Raitt's and Muller's studies were based on a small sampling of Beza's works. Raitt's examination highlighted the importance of historical context for Beza's pastoral concern. It was limited to one of Beza's doctrinal debates. Although Muller has been prolific in his attempts at explicating Beza's thought,

---

128 See appendix one. McPhee also denied himself the opportunity to examine Beza's *De praedestinationis*, which was included in the third volume of Beza's collected theological works in 1582. McPhee's inattention to Beza's pastoral works is surprising given the fact that he noted the "biblical, soteriological and ethical centre of Beza's teaching" on predestination and the fact that Calvin and Beza had very similar form and content in their respective presentations of this doctrine ("Conserver or Transformer of Calvin's Theology?," 351). I do not think his study of all editions of Beza's *Annotationes*, up to the last one in 1598, rectifies this shortcoming, since Beza was deliberately concise in these explanatory notes on the New Testament.

129 Note the title of his dissertation: "Conserver or Transformer of Calvin's Theology? A Study of the Origins and Development of Theodore Beza's Thought, 1550-1570."

130 McPhee summarized his reasoning in this way: "Beza's thought bore the imprint of his defensive strategy and method. The emphasis on dialectical thoroughness and skill, the greater openness to Neoplatonic and Aristotelian metaphysics, the greater dependence on patristic authority: these served to re-shape Calvin's theology into a more tightly argued, logically unassailable body of doctrine. However, to compare Calvin and Beza in terms of scriptural exposition versus rationalist synthesis is too simplistic. Calvin's theology was not merely the product of faithful biblical exposition; it too was influenced by philosophy, rational selection and organization. Nevertheless, it is true that Calvin could permit a series of dialectical tensions to exist within his theology, contradictions and antinomies that made life very frustrating for supporters like Beza who had to deal with mounting attack on critical points of doctrine. Thus, in Beza's thought rational explanation of such tensions became a matter of some urgency" (ibid., 355).

he has not considered the full range of the Bezan corpus. On two occasions, he interacted at length with the *Tabula*.[131] His primary study of Beza's theology (which is a survey of two doctrinal *loci* from Calvin to Perkins) was also limited to just a handful of Beza's more systematic works.[132] Finally, Sinnema limited himself to one theological point, the doctrine of reprobation. And, like Muller's studies, Sinnema's dealing with Beza's doctrine came in the midst of a survey of the developments within this doctrine during the Reformation and post-Reformation periods.

Studies of Beza's Doctrine of Assurance of Salvation

The point at issue in discussion about the doctrine of assurance is how the "practical syllogism" arose in Reformed thought and what specifically Beza's role was in promoting it. This question-answer scheme narrowed the focus of most of the evaluations offered. Most of these studies have two *foci*, Calvin and Beza. Even more than studies of Beza's doctrine of predestination, research on Beza's view of assurance has been severely hampered by lack of attention to the full scope of Beza's corpus. Barth and Kendall (who chastised Beza for his views) as well as Bray, Muller, and Beeke (who were much more sympathetic in their evaluations) based their opinions on a small sampling of Beza's works. Letham's contextual study was helpful, yet it was hindered by its preoccupation with a prior historical-theological question. Although helpful as far as it went, McPhee's evaluation was once again limited by the chronological parameters of his study. In this most pastoral focus of the doctrine of God's sovereignty, Beza the pastor has often remained concealed.

Deviation from Calvin Scheme

Three scholars in particular – Karl Barth, R. T. Kendall, and John Bray – argued that Beza deviated from Calvin's doctrine of Christian assurance. Barth averred that most commentators had misread Calvin's doctrine. Instead, "what was later called the *syllogismus practicus* did constitute one element in the

---

131 See Muller, "Use and Abuse," and idem, "Perkins' *A Golden Chaine*."
132 Muller examined primarily Beza's *Questionum et responsionum, Petit Catéchisme, Altera brevis fidei Confessio, De praedestinationis doctrina, Propositions and Principles of Divinitie, Summa totius christianismi*, and the *Confession* ("Predestination and Christology," 195-216, 219-28; cf. *Christ and the Decree*, 79-96). But he did this with the caveat that Beza "wrote no system. Apart from his confessions and his catechism he gave no indication of the structure he would have given to a system of doctrine" ("Predestination and Christology," 189). Additionally, Muller studied Beza's *Annotationes* of Romans 13 (Muller, "Calvin, Beza, and the Exegetical History of Romans 13:1-7").

theology of Calvin himself."[133] But Calvin set up three safeguards for its use: first, "the testimony of 'works' must not take the first place and assume the role of a crown witness"; second, "the testimony of 'works' must not be separated from faith, as if *this* 'fruit' could detach itself from *that* tree and be considered by itself. It is not to be treated as a self-supporting (in some sense 'existential') decision of empirical self-examination and self-evaluation, distinguishable from the testimony of the Holy Spirit"; third, "the testimony of 'works' must not be detached from the self-testimony of Christ, from the promise of the forgiveness of sins, or in general from the objective Word of God, as if it had power in itself to penetrate its mystery, or as if there were a kind of pipeline between God's decree on the one hand, and human piety and morals on the other."[134] According to Barth, Beza defied these warnings. In support of this contention, Barth cited just one point in Beza's *Quaestionum et responsionum*.[135] Barth referenced the question, "In the perilous temptation of particular election, where should I flee for succor?," which Beza answered, "To the effects whereby the spiritual life is rightly discerned, and likewise our election, just as the life of the body is perceived from its feeling and moving. . . Therefore, that I am elect, is first perceived from sanctification begun in me, that is, by my hating of sin and my loving of righteousness. To this I will add the testimony of the Spirit, comforting my conscience."[136] From this one citation, Barth argued that Beza radically departed from Calvin's balanced view of Christian assurance.

Kendall similarly argued that there was a radical shift between the doctrines of Calvin and Beza. He explained his view in this way:

> Fundamental to the doctrine of faith in Theodore Beza (1519-1605), Calvin's successor in Geneva, is his belief that Christ died for the elect only. Beza's doctrine of a limited atonement makes Christ's death that to which the decree of election has particular reference and that which makes the elect's salvation efficacious. It must therefore be argued that, as a result of this soteriological position, Beza's doctrine (1) inhibits the believer from looking directly to Christ's death for assurance; (2) precipitates an implicit distinction between faith and assurance; (3) tends to put repentance before faith in the *ordo salutis*; and (4) plants the seed of voluntarism in the doctrine of faith. In a word: Beza's doctrine

---

133 Karl Barth, *Church Dogmatics*, ed. G. W. Bromiley and T. F. Torrance, vol. 2, *The Doctrine of God*, pt. 2, trans. G. W. Bromiley et al. (Edinburgh: T. & T. Clark, 1957), 335.
134 Ibid., 335-36.
135 Ibid. See Beeke's criticism of Barth's comments (Beeke, *Assurance of Faith*, 83).
136 Theodore Beza, *A Little Book of Christian Questions and Responses, In which the Principal Headings of the Christian Religion are Briefly Set Forth*, trans. Kirk M. Summers (Allison Park, PA: Pickwick, 1986), 96-97.

requires the use of the practical syllogism in order for one to be persuaded he is one of those for whom Christ died.[137]

According to Kendall, Calvin discouraged persons from seeking assurance based on their sanctification because he believed that Christ died for everyone indiscriminately. Doubting persons must look to Christ. Beza advocated the opposite, though, since his doctrine of limited atonement "makes trusting Christ's death presumptuous."[138] The only ground for assurance was to look at oneself, that is, to look for proof of one's salvation by means of the "practical syllogism." Thus Kendall argued, "it is as though Beza says: all who have the effects [of salvation] have faith; but I have the effects, therefore (the infallible conclusion) I have faith."[139] So Kendall concluded: "Beza's doctrine of faith substantially diverges from that of Calvin; the difference is not quantitative but qualitative. The origin of this departure is linked to Beza's doctrine of limited atonement; when Christ is not held forth to all men as the immediate ground of assurance, the result is not only introspection on our part but a need to assure ourselves upon the very grounds Calvin warns against."[140] Calvin urged persons to find assurance in Christ. Beza urged them to find it in themselves.

Agreeing with Kendall's assertion, Bray asserted "it is possible to trace within Beza's doctrine of assurance subtle, yet significant, movement from Calvin's doctrine. For Calvin, assurance was based upon faith and the person of Christ; for Beza the primary factors were works and perseverance."[141] Calvin and his protégé were very different, according to Bray: "What might appear at this point to be a minor difference of emphasis between Calvin and Beza is in fact symptomatic of a crucial difference in their theological orientation. The lessened Christocentrism in Beza's treatment of the question is a correlate of his more rationalistic theological methodology."[142] Beza's increased rationalism led him to seek assurance through a syllogism, not in Christ: "For Beza, the rock of assurance was not to be found in the person and work of Christ, as it had been for Calvin. . . . In his search for a means whereby the believer could gain assurance Beza eventually seized upon an application of the *syllogismus practicus*." Bray concluded by asserting that "one discovers in

---

137 Kendall, *Calvin and English Calvinism*, 29.
138 Ibid., 32.
139 Ibid., 33.
140 Ibid., 38.
141 Bray, *Beza's Doctrine*, 107.
142 Ibid., 108. In a later article, Bray made the divide between Calvin and Beza even starker. His thesis was that "Beza did, in fact, place a value upon works that one does not find in Calvin's theology. In so doing Beza did alter the theology of his master" (John S. Bray, "The Value of Works in the Theology of Calvin and Beza," *Sixteenth Century Journal* 4 [1973]: 79).

Beza's works a bald, almost brutal, demand for good works."[143]

Tracing development in the history of any doctrine is very complex. It requires that one pay careful attention to the thought of various thinkers in different historical, ecclesiastical, and theological contexts. This task becomes even more difficult when one does not examine enough of the primary sources to conclude accurately what a person's view was on a particular subject.[144] Yet that is what these three scholars did. Barth drew only one citation from one of Beza's works. This is far from conclusive proof that this was the sum of Beza's view on assurance. Similarly, at the crucial points in both their arguments, Bray and Kendall only referenced one question in Beza's *Petit Catéchisme* as proof of his devolution into the "practical syllogism" scheme. Kendall noted that Beza asked, "But how may a man know whether he has faith or not?" and answered "By good works."[145] According to Kendall, "It seems that it is not faith which assures but the conclusion that proves faith is there."[146] By failing to pay attention to the broader context of Beza's comments within the *Petit Catéchisme*, let alone his numerous other treatises that touch on assurance, Kendall drew an inaccurate conclusion about Beza's doctrine.[147] Although he noted that to arrive at valid historical interpretations one must range widely in the primary sources, Kendall disregarded his own prescription. Thus while he stated that his "study [would] draw from several writings of Beza," he only used six works.[148] Although he claimed that "Beza's other works are largely

---

143 Bray, *Beza's Doctrine*, 108. Paradoxically, though, Bray concluded with a relatively positive evaluation of Beza's doctrine vis-à-vis Calvin's. He claimed that "Beza moved beyond Calvin on the question of assurance by virtue of his tendency to systematize, his emphasis upon the *syllogismus practicus*, and his lessened Christocentrism. And yet the difference between the two treatments was quantitative, not qualitative" (ibid., 111, citing Barth, *Church Dogmatics* II/2, 335-36). Bray's ambiguous evaluation has been noted by other scholars as well. See, e.g., McPhee, "Conserver or Transformer of Calvin's Theology?," xxvi.

144 In my opinion, this highlights the danger of coming to Theodore Beza in order to discover if he deviated from Calvin's thought. Whereas Calvin's works are readily available and have been studied by numerous scholars, most of the Bezan corpus is not easy to obtain and much of it has not been studied.

145 Kendall, *Calvin and English Calvinism*, 33 n. 3.

146 Ibid.

147 Other scholars have similarly argued that this question in Beza's *Catéchisme* showed his penchant for the "practical syllogism" (see, e.g., Bray, *Beza's Doctrine*, 108, and Muller, *Christ and the Decree*, 85). In chapter five, I will offer an alternate interpretation of the *Petit Catéchisme*'s teaching on assurance.

148 These works were *A briefe and pithie summe of the christian faith, A Little Catechisme, A Booke of Christian Questions and answeares, A Briefe Declaration of the chiefe points of Christian religion set forth in a Table, A Discourse of the true and visible Markes of the Catholique Church,* and *Sermons upon . . . Canticle of Canticles* (Kendall, *Calvin and English Calvinism*, 29 n. 1).

irrelevant for this study," Kendall offered no proof for this assertion.[149] This selective use of Beza's works weakens Kendall's thesis.[150] Related to Kendall's weakness was Bray's disregard of genre. Even though he hinted at the importance of accounting for differences in genre, he disregarded his own warnings.[151] So while showing Beza's penchant for the *syllogismus practicus*, he stated categorically that "the clearest statement of Beza's doctrine of assurance is to be found in" his *Tabula*.[152] But he pointed out that Beza's later sermons were also instructive for arriving at a clear picture of the contours of Beza's doctrine.[153]

Contextual Deviation

Other scholars, while again assessing the doctrinal changes from Calvin to Beza, have noted that the differences in their doctrinal expressions were the result of changing pastoral needs. Beza ministered in quite different times than Calvin, so he taught Christians to find assurance differently. To one degree or another, the scholars in this group also noticed the pastoral intent of Beza's explication of Christian assurance.

Neither Robert Letham nor Joel Beeke found a substantial difference between Calvin's and Beza's doctrines. Summarizing the findings of his research, which ranged from Zwingli to the Synod of Dort nearly a century later, Letham argued that "Reformed theology before Dort saw the development of two qualitatively distinct understandings of saving faith." Calvin represented the first opinion which "held that faith was equivalent to assurance of God's favour and of ultimate salvation" since neither faith nor assurance was "dependent on the vacillating nature of introspection." In the second view assurance was "subsequent to faith, and owed its increasing popularity to the rise of the conditional covenant theology of Bullinger" and

---

149 Ibid.
150 G. Michael Thomas recently stated that "Kendall has been criticized for basing his conclusions on a narrow band of Beza's writings (those that are more systematic, and are available in English translation), and it has been suggested that a survey of Beza's homiletic literature would create a more balanced picture." But, inexplicably, Thomas went on to aver, "Whether or not this is the case, it is difficult to argue with the main outline of Kendall's account of Beza" ("Calvin and English Calvinism: A Review Article," *Scottish Bulletin of Evangelical Theology* 16 [1998]: 113-14). How Thomas can assert this, while only citing one more of Beza's works and referring to some of his letters, mystifies me.
151 Bray, *Beza's Doctrine*, 141-42.
152 Ibid., 108 n. 13.
153 Ibid., 111.

others.[154]

Letham turned Kendall's conclusions about Beza on their head:

> Beza's supralapsarian construction of election eclipses the covenant and encourages him to adopt a strong defence of limited atonement. He gives a prominent place to sanctification as a means of assurance of election. However, his attempt at making election Christocentric enables him to focus assurance on Christ. He does not give sanctification an independent function in relation to assurance. All this fits in with his doctrine of faith which he sees as certain knowledge or assurance of God's favour. While he gives a greater stress than Calvin to faith as act, his is not a voluntaristic view of faith and he makes faith prior to repentance. The differences between Calvin and Beza have been exaggerated.[155]

According to Letham, then, although Beza and Calvin had different emphases, they were united in stressing the preeminent place of Christ in Christian assurance. Even Beza's supralapsarianism, with its doctrine of definite atonement, was Christocentric and encouraged struggling pilgrims to look to Christ for assurance of salvation. Letham did argue, however, that rationalistic views Beza held concerning assurance later in his life influenced the move in later Reformed Orthodoxy away from Calvin's biblical opinions:

> There appears to be evidence that in later years Beza's scholasticism and rationalism may have hardened. Certainly, there seems to be an element of change in some of his writings published towards the end of his life. Thus, in the 1589 edition of his annotated *Novum Testamentum* he tends to emphasise faith as an act more than in earlier editions. In the *Theses theologicae*, first published under his direction in 1588, he makes considerable use of sanctification as the basis of assurance. The *Eximia tractatio de consolandis qui circa praedestinationem tentatur* (1599), published along with William Perkins' *Armilla aurea* to help those perplexed by the doctrine of predestination and the question of whether they were elect, makes pervasive use of the practical syllogism and introspection as the solution. There is a marked absence of Christocentricity. At no time in the work is Christ seen as the basis of assurance. The same applies to his work *De remediis adversus praecipuos insultus Satanae*. The very titles of these works and the problems with which they are concerned indicated the root of this change. Beza's supralapsarianism created a pervasive dehistoricising tendency through which the promise in Christ was inhibited from fulfilling a central role in relation to

---

154 Letham, "Saving Faith and Assurance," 1:x. See Letham, "Faith and Assurance,", 355-88.

155 Letham, "Saving Faith and Assurance," 1:153-54. Like most researchers, Letham was concerned to show the way that Beza's thought related to Calvin's. In his nuanced view, although there was not much variation between the two Genevans, they were not replicas of each other. Beza's thought showed a more-Scholastic bent and paved the way for Reformed Orthodoxy. See Letham, "Theodore Beza," 35-36.

assurance. As Beza's rationalistic method gained ground so this tendency became increasingly acute.[156]

Thus Letham argued that Bezan assurance was Christocentric early but moved toward introspection in his later years.

Whereas Kendall concluded that Beza's and later Calvinism's works manifested a *qualitative* departure from Calvin's views, Beeke argued throughout his study that "Calvinism's wrestlings with assurance were *quantitatively* beyond, but not *qualitatively* contradictory to, that of Calvin." He averred that

> notwithstanding differences in *matters of degree* on the doctrine of assurance between Calvin and the Calvinists, there is little difference *in substance*. By setting assurance more clearly within a Trinitarian (as well as a Christological) framework, Reformed orthodoxy did not negate Calvin's Christology. Rather, Calvin's Christology was theologically advanced in the process, thereby augmenting rather than detracting from his theology as a whole.[157]

Beeke's monograph exhibits three strengths in particular. First, Beeke demonstrated Calvin's nuanced view of Christian assurance. On the one hand, Calvin asserted that assurance is of the essence of faith. On the other hand, he qualified this, by acknowledging "that assuring faith is neither retained without severe struggle against unbelief, nor left untinged by doubt and anxiety."[158] Importantly for the comparison with Beza's doctrine, Beeke charged that even though "Calvin did not use the *syllogismus practicus* in a formal sense," he "did utilize the principles of the syllogism in a practical sense." Beeke concluded: "The real issue at stake in the *syllogismus practicus* is not its presence in the thought of Calvin and the Calvinists, but the form it takes within their systems and the message it implies for both doctrine and life. In Calvin's theology even the occasional syllogism used never detracts from Christ."[159]

Second, Beeke demonstrated that Beza's emphases, although different from Calvin's, did not substantially deviate from his predecessor's. Beza never intended to separate the evidence of works from the need to trust in Christ alone for salvation. Beeke argued that Beza "is not saying that sanctification-works is the primary witness, nor does he intend to separate his full-blown

---

156 Letham, "Saving Faith and Assurance," 1:154.
157 Beeke, *Assurance of Faith*, 2.
158 Ibid., 51.
159 Ibid., 72, 76. Beeke cited several excerpts from Calvin's writings showing his point (ibid., 72-76). For the view that Calvin had no place for the practical syllogism, see Wilhelm Niesel, *The Theology of Calvin,* trans. Harold Knight (Philadelphia: Westminster, 1956), 169-81.

syllogismus practicus from saving faith, much less from Jesus Christ and a Trinitarian framework rooted in the promise and Word of God. In fact, he is not so far removed from Calvin as is usually assumed, for Calvin also stresses that proof of election may be fortified in the presence of works that flow out of faith."[160]

Third, Beeke argued that Beza did place greater emphasis than his predecessor on the "practical syllogism." But his motives in using it were pastoral: "Whereas Calvin always maintained a secondary status at best for assurance by works, Beza comes closer to equalizing all three grounds of assurance [the promise of the gospel in Jesus Christ, the internal witness of the Holy Spirit, and sanctification][161] by utilizing the *syllogismus practicus* more freely than Calvin, particularly in the case of tried believers."[162] Beeke thus noticed differences between Calvin and Beza regarding assurance of salvation, but more importantly he saw overwhelming similarities.

Richard Muller and Ian McPhee also emphasized Beza's pastoral sensitivity with regard to his doctrine of Christian assurance. Muller maintained that rather than hindering assurance, predestination was meant to comfort Christians in Beza's scheme. He pointed out that Beza's goal was pastoral, not metaphysical, even in his *Tabula*: "Beza emphasizes not the development of a predestinarian system of theology but the application of election to the life of piety. His purpose in preaching and teaching election, even in preaching the doctrine of the double decree, is the assurance of the elect."[163] He drew his conclusion from the first chapter of the *Tabula*. According to Muller, at this point (1555), for Beza "assurance results from the inner testimony of the Spirit of adoption, who cries 'Abba, Father' in our hearts and whose power and efficacy perform their work in us." At this early date, he argued, Beza "had no concern to press toward the *syllogismus practicus*."[164]

Yet Muller claimed that Beza's doctrine of assurance developed over time. By the time of his 1570 *Quaestionum et responsionum* Beza showed "a tendency toward the adoption of an analytic method in discussing predestination, a more speculative, *a posteriori*, argument than witnessed by his earlier thought leading within five years to the *syllogismus practicus* of the *Catechismus compendarius*."[165] Yet the "practical syllogism" was only one

---

160 Beeke, *Assurance of Faith*, 83.
161 Ibid., 81.
162 Ibid., 84. Beeke's conclusion demonstrated sensitivity to both Calvin's and Beza's contexts: "For Beza and Calvin, the critical point is *faith in Christ*. There are no *essential* differences between their views on assurance, though their *emphases* and *methods* vary considerably—no doubt in some measure due to their being in different milieus" (ibid., 86).
163 Muller, *Christ and the Decree*, 80.
164 Ibid.
165 Ibid., 85.

aspect of Beza's multi-faceted approach to assurance, according to Muller. Since Beza believed in present forensic justification and perfect sanctification only in heaven, "the empirical *syllogismus*" could not "enter the picture as sole ground of assurance." Yet, when Beza thought about the type of life "that results from faith, justification, and sanctification, proceeding, that is, from the divine cause to its human effects, he more pointedly even than Calvin, demands that good works follow." Muller argued that this proved a tension in Beza's thought "between the spiritual and the empirical grounds of assurance." For example, in his late work on Ecclesiastes, Beza denied the syllogism, whereas in the *Petit Catéchisme* "the syllogism rears its head in unabated form."[166]

McPhee, more than any other scholar, attempted to demonstrate the pastoral intent of Beza's teaching on Christian assurance. Although he noted that "the view that Beza departed from the christological basis of Calvin's doctrine of assurance has won almost universal acceptance,"[167] McPhee concluded that "there is a peculiar tidiness about this separation of Beza and Calvin which arouses suspicion."[168] Calvin's emphasis that "election cannot be understood apart from Christ," made him recoil "from any suggestion that assurance may be derived from speculation into the decree of God."[169] Christ is merely one side of the coin. "The other ground of assurance is the nature of faith itself."[170] For Calvin, since faith was created only by the powerful work of the Spirit in one's life, faith itself was bound up with assurance.[171] The regenerating power of the Spirit in one's life, creating faith, was what assured one of salvation.[172]

---

166 Ibid. See, though, Muller's more guarded statement in his dissertation. Beza, he argued there, made the *syllogismus practicus* "a primary ground of assurance. This is his most obvious departure from Calvin's line of argument; but the *syllogismus practicus*, however much it detracts from the piety and the devotional quality of Calvin's doctrine of assurance, does not at all represent a tendency toward metaphysical speculation or to rationalization based upon a doctrine of the decrees. It is anti-speculative and empirical with a vengeance. It looks only to tangible effects. . . . [and one must see that it] is not a structure which appears consistently even in the thought of Beza: it is absent from the *Tabula*" (Muller, "Predestination and Christology," 197-98).
167 McPhee, "Conserver or Transformer of Calvin's Theology?," 330.
168 Ibid., 332.
169 Ibid., 333.
170 Ibid., 334.
171 "Faith was for Calvin a full persuasion that God is benevolent toward men in Christ. It was characterized by certainty, so much so that he called it 'a firm and certain knowledge'" (ibid., 334, citing Calvin, *Institutes* 3.2.7).
172 McPhee, "Conserver or Transformer of Calvin's Theology?," 336. Following Barth, though, McPhee chided Calvin: "His appeal to Christ, as the source of assurance, was menaced by the *decretum absolutum*, not, I think, on account of a separation of Christ from the foundation of the decree, but simply because it was a *double decree*" (ibid., 337).

It was this tradition, "this tension between christology and anthropology," that Beza inherited, according to McPhee.[173] Several aspects of Beza's thought showed his affinity with Calvin. First, Beza also had a dynamic view of the Spirit's work: "Following Calvin's example Beza placed great stock in the doctrine of efficacious calling as a pledge of faith, and thus, of election."[174] Second, Beza emphasized "Christ as the object of faith." Even though "one does not find in Beza the constant appeal to Christ the mirror of election that one does in Calvin," McPhee urged, "Beza by no means set aside the christological basis of assurance."[175] Beza in fact "related the two poles of assurance more effectively than Calvin." By "locating Christ the mirror of election within the orbit of the believer's experience of faith, Beza strengthened Calvin's doctrine of assurance."[176]

McPhee contended that Beza's intent was always pastoral. In the *Tabula*, Beza "predicates assurance on effectual calling."[177] The Holy Spirit's witness to one's conscience "is one proof of our adoption and thus our election. The corollary to the first basis of assurance is the reality of the Spirit's presence demonstrated by his work of sanctification in the believer."[178] This same pastoral intent was present in the *Confession* where Beza reiterated the twofold basis of assurance: the internal witness of the Holy Spirit and the proof of union with Christ as seen in an increasingly sanctified life.[179] God's eternal decree is never where believers should look for assurance. Therefore the fact that one questions his election should not lead to utter despair:

> If the effects of faith are temporally quenched Beza encourages his readers [in the *Confession*] to remember when they *were* evident. If they are still tempted to doubt their faith, it must be remembered that God's purpose is never frustrated. If they were once sure of their union with Christ, it is certain that it will triumph to the end, for true faith cannot be separated from perseverance.[180]

Beza was a trained pastor, a wise casuist, argued McPhee.

Evaluation

The positive advances these scholars made in our understanding of Theodore Beza based on their contextual studies notwithstanding, their research was still

---

173 Ibid.
174 Ibid., 341.
175 Ibid.
176 Ibid., 342.
177 Ibid., 343.
178 Ibid.
179 Ibid., 344.
180 Ibid., 346.

too limited to offer a complete picture of Beza's doctrine of assurance of salvation. It was limited primarily in the number of sources consulted. For instance, Beeke acknowledged that his Beza research would have to be "painted in broad strokes," and would be derived from Beza's "major doctrinal confessions."[181] Beeke's notes reveal that he relied on just a few of Beza's systematic works.[182] Muller likewise only used a sampling of the Bezan corpus. McPhee's conclusions about Beza's doctrine of assurance were limited by his terminus. Many Bezan materials, especially his later-published pastoral works, were not considered. In addition, McPhee limited himself to a few of Beza's doctrinal works written before 1570.[183] Letham's investigation was dominated by an attempt to fit Beza within a survey of the history of the doctrine of assurance. This fact limited his ability to interact sufficiently with the Bezan corpus. Letham alone discussed the later Bezan works. But though he referenced these treatises, he did not here interact with any of Beza's pastoral or devotional treatises.

Conclusion

Beza's doctrines of predestination and Christian assurance have undergone much scrutiny by scholars. The debated point is the degree to which Beza adopted Aristotelian (i.e., "scholastic") methodology and hence deviated from Calvin's consistent biblical humanism. Bizer, Kickel, and Armstrong advanced the deviation view forcefully, while Sinnema and McPhee tried to check it by appealing to Beza's context. Many scholars incorrectly judged that Beza raised predestination to a central place in his theology and deviated from Calvin's attempts to derive his theology from Scripture rather than human ratiocination. Dantine, Holtrop, and Kickel were especially guilty in this regard. Muller, McPhee, and Sinnema, among others, answered these charges effectively. Certainly Beza had different emphases from Calvin, they maintained, but he did not make predestination the doctrine from which all others flowed. Nor did he rationalize the mysterious elements in this difficult doctrine. Several other researchers, Kendall and Barth among them, argued that Beza substantially changed the locus of assurance from Calvin's Christ to the good works of the

---

181 Ibid., 2.
182 He referenced the *Summa totius christianismi* seven times, the *Questionum et responsionum* and the *Confession* five times each, the *Annotationes* twice, with one reference to both the *Petit Catéchisme* and *De Praedestinationis* (ibid., 100-04).
183 According to my calculations, while he was dealing with Beza's doctrine of assurance, McPhee only cited the following works: *Confession* (12 times), the *Summa totius christianismi* (9), *Quaestionum et responsionum* (4), *Ad Sebastiani Castellionis* (1), as well as a couple of references to Beza's *Annotationes* and lectures on Romans.

person, leading the way to an anthropocentric theology at odds with the Reformation principle of *sola fide*. But Letham and Beeke answered these criticisms, arguing that Beza may have emphasized aspects of assurance that Calvin did not. The change was quantitative, however, not qualitative.

In addition to helping resolve the question of theological development between Calvin and Beza, a few scholars have been especially useful in placing Beza in his historical context. Sinnema showed the relationship of Aristotelian thought to Ramism and its impact on the Academy and Beza's method. Raitt demonstrated the way that Beza's ongoing arguments with Andreae influenced his doctrinal expression at Montbéliard. Muller attempted to place Beza in the line of development of Reformed theology from Calvin to early Puritanism. McPhee, especially, succeeded in showing how Beza's location in history influenced his doctrinal expression.

Looking Forward

In the first chapter I argued that Theodore Beza was an affectionate follower of Christ. As a Christian, a pastor, and a teacher, Beza exuded great love for God and confidence in his sovereign care in the turbulence of life. Beza turned to God in the midst of the spiritual battle he perceived raging all around him. His eschatological vision led him to trust in God's absolute sovereignty in this life, leading to the eternal bliss of heaven. Beza was a passionate pastor.

The scholars surveyed in this chapter almost completely neglected this central, defining component of Beza's identity. Why? There are several reasons, I think. Some scholars have deductively, I would argue, attempted to fit Beza into an Aristotelian mold (e.g., Kickel and Holtrop). Some have relied too much upon questionable historical reconstructions (e.g., Bray). Many have failed to pay much attention to Beza's location in history. Others have shown little regard for the genre of Beza's works. The result of these errors is that in large part the real Beza has eluded scholarship.

In the next chapter, I will try to correct some of these deficiencies by arguing that historians must empathize with their subject if they hope to understand it. I will also note the need for historians to be cognizant of their distance in time and thought from the subject of their research. Empathy and awareness of distance will go a long way toward rectifying the oversights I noted in much of the Bezan historiography.

Now, though, it will be helpful to note the errors emanating from genre insensitivity. With the exceptions of McPhee and Bray, no scholar I surveyed in this chapter showed adequate awareness of the wide variety of Beza's writings. Several researchers thus proffered that Beza was a dispassionate, rational theologian. This false view arose from focusing too narrowly on a small number of Beza's writings, usually his polemical treatises. In appendix one, I have included three tables, all drawn from the standard bibliography of Beza's works.[184] The first table of the appendix lists Beza's writings in chronological order, along with one of six categories to which I assigned it. In my opinion, Beza wrote six types of treatises: humanistic, polemical, doctrinal, biblical, historical, and pastoral.[185] The second table shows the different categories of Beza's works published each year. Although the polemical works dominated, Beza's other interests were significant. Here we see, for example, that his penchant for humanistic productions was consistent throughout his life. This should give pause to those who argue for a "humanistic to scholastic" change in Beza over time. We also see that Beza's pastoral works almost all came late in his life. A study limited to Beza's early career will necessarily neglect this part of his corpus. The third table may suggest how Beza was perceived in his own lifetime by showing the rate of re-publication and translation of his works. We see there, for instance, that Beza's humanistic works were well-received throughout his life. Also, his doctrinal treatises seemed to have been better received than his polemical works, on average.

These facts suggest that an adequate analysis of Beza's thought must be derived from a wide reading in his works, specifically targeting various genres of his treatises. This will allow the complete Theodore Beza to speak. I hope to listen widely to him in the remaining chapters.

---

184 Gardy, *Bibliographie*.
185 Of course, these categories are my creation. Beza (unfortunately) did not neatly categorize his various works. I think, however, that my categories are a fair representation of the contents of Beza's numerous works.

CHAPTER 3

Beza's Pastoral Systematic Theology

O God, O God? And do you dare name this most sacred name, you mischievous mouth of so mischievous a man? . . . You traitorous tongue against your faithful servant Uriah, can you not pronounce this word, "God," who is most true? Your hands imbrued with many murders, presume you so fare as to follow that bold tongue, heaving up yourselves toward him, whom you have so shamefully profaned. Your heart, guilty of the whole law broken at one blow, are you so hardy as to address yourself to him, who has already judged you? O king, so many ways perjured against him, that of a poor shepherd boy, promoted you above the throne of all this world's monarchs: You hypocrite towards him, who has performed for you infinitely more than ever he promised you: wretched man, which has trampled under feet the covenant of eternal life, to make an adulteress of a chaste wife: unhappy man, who has laid that most precious name open to the blasphemies of infidel nations. O you ingrate, which has rendered to your loyal servant death for his wages. O you unworthy one, that, where you owed to your people all justice, has showed them the way to all mischief. Do you live yet? Do you speak yet? Dare you call upon your God yet? Yes, my God, so great is your patience.[1]

This chapter makes one point: for Beza, all theology, even the most technical and scholastic, was pastoral. Theology assisted persons to withstand the spiritual assaults against them. Satan attacked them by promoting falsehood. They therefore needed truth from God. Since God's truth resided in the Bible, Christians were to read the Bible, while pastors were to interpret and apply the Bible properly. The Bible, God's living word, was central to all that Theodore Beza did because it was the means of arriving at comfort in the midst of the spiritual battle.

Presuppositions

I am guided in what follows by two hermeneutical principles: empathy and recognition of distance. Concerning the first point, I draw on Marvin Anderson's methodology. Anderson was involved in a hermeneutical debate with John Patrick Donnelly and J. C. McLelland regarding the proper

---

1   Beza, *Christian Meditations*, Eiir-Eiiir.

interpretation of Peter Martyr Vermigli.² Donnelly attempted to characterize Vermigli as a proto-scholastic, but Anderson argued that the Italian Reformer was a humanist. Anderson chided Donnelly for taking note only of those places in Vermigli's writings where he specifically made use of scholastic terminology. In addition, he complained that Donnelly conveniently ignored Vermigli's very pointed critique of much of the received scholastic tradition. Donnelly restricted himself to a small corpus of Vermigli's writings. Anderson examined a larger sampling and different genres of Vermigli's writings.³ He argued that "where Martyr disassociates himself from the late medieval scholastic tradition one should take him at his word unless the texts suggest otherwise."⁴ Anderson here argued persuasively for the importance of "empathy" in interpretation.⁵ Anderson also noted the fundamentally religious character of Vermigli's work. Failing to take that defining aspect of his motivation into account necessarily led to skewed interpretations of his purpose. Anderson lamented the "failure of some recent Vermigli studies to penetrate beneath the level of description to the fundamental religious and non-speculative roots of Martyr's thought."⁶ He pointed to flawed methodology as the culprit, arguing that scholars would notice Martyr's religious intentions if they read his *loci* as they appeared in his commentaries rather than as they were posthumously abstracted and arranged in his *Loci communes*.⁷ The key for Anderson was "empathy," letting Martyr's words in their context express his true intention. This applies also to the interpretation of Beza.

An important element of empathy is letting the subject under consideration determine the historian's conclusions. This involves letting the historical author say what he or she intends. It includes taking the words of the texts seriously and letting them determine the historian's conclusions. In this regard Quentin Skinner well expresses my approach here:

> The essential question which we therefore confront, in studying any given text, is what its author, in writing at the time he did write for the audience he intended to address, could in practice have been intending to communicate by the utterance of

---

2   See Frank A. James, *Peter Martyr Vermigli and Predestination: The Augustinian Inheritance of an Italian Reformer*, Oxford Theological Monographs (Oxford: Clarendon, 1998), 7-17, for an overview of the debate. My purpose here is not to enter into the debate about whether or not Vermigli was a humanist or a scholastic. I am concerned rather to show what, in my opinion, were sound hermeneutical principles elaborated by Anderson.
3   See Anderson, "Peter Martyr Vermigli," 65-84.
4   Ibid., 67.
5   Anderson also cogently argued for the importance of noting context in proper interpretation (ibid., 67-68).
6   Ibid., 67.
7   Ibid.

this given utterance. It follows that the essential aim, in any attempt to understand the utterances themselves, must be to recover this complex intention on the part of the author. And it follows from this that the appropriate methodology for the history of ideas must be concerned, first of all, to delineate the whole range of communications which could have been conventionally performed on the given occasion by the utterance of the given utterance, and, next, to trace the relations between the given utterance and the wider *linguistic* context as a means of decoding the actual intention of the given writer.[8]

Regarding the second point, Carl Trueman and Scott Clark recently argued that one factor influencing wrong interpretations of the post-Reformation period is the inability of modern and postmodern historians and theologians to relate to the thought patterns of pre-Enlightenment figures. Since the influx of Enlightenment rationalism was cosmic in its effects, it creates a tremendous divide between the contemporary interpreter and pre-Enlightenment figures. The most important matter was

> the Enlightenment's dethronement of Aristotle and the subsequent collapse of the Enlightenment project under the searching light of Immanuel Kant's critical philosophy. To the historian, the continuities in philosophical worldview between the thirteenth and the seventeenth centuries, combined with the watershed nature of the Kantian development would suggest that the theology of Calvin, his Protestant contemporaries and those who succeeded him in the later sixteenth and seventeenth centuries should be assessed in terms of the ongoing Western pre-Kantian tradition, rather than by the criteria formed by post-Kantian theology.[9]

---

8 Quentin Skinner, "Meaning and Understanding in the History of Ideas," *History and Theory* 8 (1969): 48-49, quoted in Carl T. Trueman, "Puritan Theology as Historical Event," in *Reformation and Scholasticism: An Ecumenical Enterprise*, ed. Willem J. van Asselt and Eef Dekker (Grand Rapids: Baker, 2001), 257-58. I also draw on E. D. Hirsch's admonition that valid interpretation of a document should be based "on the sensible belief that a text means what its author meant" (E. D. Hirsch, Jr., *Validity in Interpretation* [New Haven: Yale University Press, 1967], 1). Beyond mere hermeneutical theory, though, I also agree with Harry Stout's contention that historians' judgments about the rightness or wrongness of their subject matter influences their evaluations: "philosophical commitment does make a difference in the characters and themes of history stories. In the final analysis, point of view directs the script and selects the themes in ways that invariably point back to the ultimate values of the story-tellers" (Harry S. Stout, "Theological Commitment and American Religious History," *Theological Education* 25, no. 2 [1989]: 52). I hope my empathy with Beza's Christian perspective will allow me to treat him fairly in the following exposition.

9 Carl R. Trueman and R. Scott Clark, "Introduction," in *Protestant Scholasticism: Essays in Reassessment*, ed. Carl R. Trueman and R. Scott Clark (Carlisle: Paternoster, 1999), xiii. Similarly, Alister McGrath pointed out the difficulty that

These two methodological presuppositions form the basis for what I hope to do. First, I will try to read Beza sympathetically, taking his words and conclusions at face value. Second, recognizing that Beza is far removed from me in time and thought, I will try not to impose post-Enlightenment presuppositions about truth on him. As a historian, my goal is to report, not to judge. I will try to let Theodore Beza speak for himself.[10]

Beza's Theological Method: His Theory and his Practice

Theodore Beza was a humanist. That is, he derived theological truth from a careful study of the Bible, studying the words of Scripture in their original languages, in their immediate contexts, and in the context of the whole Bible. His humanistic bent manifested itself in his emphasis on utility, that is, his insistence that the Bible was useful for the Christian life. Indeed, to Beza it was essential. Only the word of God could strengthen and protect God's people in the midst of the ongoing spiritual battle. It was this humanistic—we might better say "pastoral"—emphasis of Beza that led to his denunciations of scholasticism and philosophy. The scholastic method too often came between the biblical interpreter and the actual text of the Bible, he argued. Its conclusions were useless in the raging spiritual battle. So Beza's methodology, influenced by his impeccable education, was humanism in service of pastoral ends. He was a pastor who used the tools of humanism in order to hear God and be equipped for the spiritual battle. In other words, he was a pastoral humanist.

In this chapter we are going to traverse two major steps. First of all, we will examine Beza's theological methodology in some detail from his own writings. We will begin with an important sermon Beza preached on theological method. From that we will deduce that for Beza there were three central components of theological methodology: first, theology was a spiritual enterprise; second, the Bible was central in theology; and, third, right biblical interpretation was of paramount importance. We will then see instances of these emphases in Beza's other writings, including his nuanced and theologically-driven critique and utilization of philosophy.[11] Having shown that Beza's methodology was

---

Enlightenment rationalists have understanding Christianity, whose belief-structure is based on more than just individualistic reflection. See Alister E. McGrath, *The Genesis of Doctrine: A Study in the Foundations of Doctrinal Criticism* (Oxford: Basil Blackwell, 1990), 177, 199.

10 In chapter two I noted the burgeoning secondary literature on Beza and collateral issues related to him. In the text of this chapter, I will not be able to interact extensively with the secondary literature. My methodological decision to let Beza speak for himself is warranted, I believe, by the fact that Beza's actual words have so often been ignored in the historiography.

11 In a sense, I am making a claim parallel to that of James who argued, concerning Peter Martyr Vermigli, that Martyr used both humanistic and scholastic methods,

humanistic at its core and driven by his eschatological vision, in the second place, I will then discuss four of Beza's most systematic theological treatises. After a careful analysis of these, we will see that for Beza all theology was pastoral. Even very technical doctrinal treatises were meant to lead persons to salvation.

Sermon 9 in Sermons sur la Resurrection

The ninth sermon Beza preached on the resurrection of Christ to his listeners in Geneva in 1593 offers a fitting introduction to his theological methodology. As far as I know, no one has examined this sermon previously.[12] Scholars' lack of interaction with Beza's sermons has fostered their view of him as a scholastic. The sermons generally portray Beza as a pastoral humanist instead. Its genre also makes this sermon especially suited to study Beza's theological methodology, for it is not an abstract and technical *disputatio*, but a passionate and logical sermon.[13] Here we see Beza doing the very thing about which he was preaching. This is a sermon to future preachers. It was a combination of biblical exegesis, logic, and rhetoric applying the truth to his listeners' lives. Here we discover the complex Beza. He is a "scholastic" (in his use of dialectic or reason) and also a "humanist" (in his exegesis and rhetoric).[14] But most

---

but both served his Augustinian theology (Frank A. James, "Peter Martyr Vermigli: At the Crossroads of Late Medieval Scholasticism, Christian Humanism and Resurgent Augustinianism," in *Protestant Scholasticism: Essays in Reassessment*, ed. Carl R. Trueman and R. S. Clark [Carlisle: Paternoster, 1999], 73). On the relationship between pastoral and scholastic theology, see also Donald Sinnema, "The Distinction Between Scholastic and Popular: Andreas Hyperius and Reformed Scholasticism," in *Protestant Scholasticism: Essays in Reassessment*, ed. Carl R. Trueman and R. S. Clark [Carlisle: Paternoster, 1999], 127-43.

12 In 1977 Jill Raitt noted that in this sermon "Beza stresses what reason may not do and how it is abused." She said that she hoped to examine it in the future (Raitt, "The Person of the Mediator," 77 n. 38). I do not think Raitt subsequently examined this homily by Beza.

13 On *disputatio*, and other scholastic devices, see Spencer, "Reformed Scholasticism in Medieval Perspective," 18-64.

14 I am dependent, in making this claim, on a number of scholars who have recently studied scholasticism and humanism in the Renaissance and Reformation periods. In the first place, I have profited from the recent historiography which has shown that "scholasticism" referred not to a particular set of beliefs but to a particular method of teaching in the schools. Note Muller's definition of "scholasticism" as "a highly technical and logical approach to theological system, according to which each theological topic or locus was divided into its component parts, the parts analyzed and then defined in careful propositional form. In addition, this highly technical approach sought to achieve precise definition by debate with adversaries and by use of the Christian tradition as a whole in arguing its doctrines. The form of

theological system was adapted to a didactical and polemical model that could move from biblical definition to traditional development of doctrine, to debate with doctrinal adversaries past and present, to theological resolution of the problem. This method is rightly called scholastic both in view of its roots in medieval scholasticism and in view of its intention to provide an adequate technical theology for schools, seminaries and universities. The goal of this method, the dogmatic or doctrinal intention of this theology was to provide the church with 'right teaching,' literally, 'orthodoxy.' . . . [It was] a discipline characteristic of theological system from the late twelfth through the seventeenth century. Since scholasticism is primarily a method or approach to academic disciplines it is not necessarily allied to any particular philosophical perspective nor does it represent a systematic attachment to or concentration upon any particular doctrine or concept as a key to theological system" (Richard A. Muller, *Dictionary of Latin and Greek Theological Terms, Drawn Principally from Protestant Scholastic Theology* [Grand Rapids: Baker, 1985], 8, 18). Others promoting this general view include J. A. Weisheipl, "Scholastic Method," in *New Catholic Encyclopedia* (New York: McGraw-Hill, 1967),12:1145-46; Schmitt, "Towards a Reassessment," 161; and Spencer, "Reformed Scholasticism in Medieval Perspective," 8.

Beginning with Kristeller, other scholars have noted the complex nature of "humanism" in the Reformation era. In one place Kristeller explained that by the middle of the fifteenth century "humanism" stood for "a well-defined cycle of studies, called *studia humanitatis*, which included *grammatica, rhetorica, poetica, historia* and *philosophia moralis*" but unlike "the liberal arts of the earlier Middle Ages, the humanities did not include logic or the *quadrivium* (*arithmetica, geometria, astronomia* and *musica*)." Thus, "humanism does not represent, as often believed, the sum total of Renaissance thought and learning, but only a well-defined sector of it. Humanism has its proper domain or home territory in the humanities, whereas all other areas of learning, including philosophy (apart from ethics), followed their own course, largely determined by their medieval tradition and by their steady transformation through new observations, problems or theories" (Kristeller, "Humanism," 113-14). See also W. J. Ong, "Humanism," in *New Catholic Encyclopedia* (New York: McGraw-Hill, 1967), 7:216-21; Lewis W. Spitz, "Humanism and the Reformation," in *Transition and Revolution: Problems and Issues of European Renaissance and Reformation History*, ed. Robert M. Kingdon (Minneapolis: Burgess, 1974), 153-67; and Marvin W. Anderson, *The Battle for the Gospel: The Bible and the Reformation, 1444-1600* (Lexington, MA: Ginn, 1987), 15-16.

Additionally, several scholars have noted the complex relationship of "scholasticism" to "humanism." The two often overlapped in the same person, as Spitz remarked: "The battle of the *viae* in the universities in late medieval times and the struggle between scholasticism and humanism during the Renaissance period have been wildly exaggerated. It is easier to define scholasticism and humanism in the abstract than it is to specify which person followed the one or the other discipline. There were half-scholastic humanists and half-humanist scholastics, and the conflicts at the universities were as often as not about who should be given which chairs than about the intellectual differences involved" (Lewis W. Spitz, significantly we here encounter Beza the passionate Christian pastor who was concerned that his listeners heed the instruction of the Scriptures.

Beza's preaching schedule included several sermons a week, and sometimes more than one in a day. In Paris, after defending the Protestant cause at Poissy, he preached to crowds of nearly 25,000.[15] As we saw in chapter one, he did not finally relinquish his preaching duties until 1600, although repeated illnesses in the late 1590s affected the regularity of his preaching and teaching in the final years of his life.[16] Beza preached *Sermons sur la Resurrection* during a lull in Geneva's conflict with Savoy. Delivered toward the end of Beza's life, they consist of straightforward expositions of several texts in the Gospels.[17] Beza did not shy away from imitating *disputatio* at points, but for the most part these sermons were homiletic devices that stressed application much more than abstract reasoning.[18]

Beza's main point throughout the sermon was that the Bible must assume the place of honor in all theological discussions.[19] Reason had value within certain carefully defined fields but the Bible was always the final judge of the truth. And this biblical truth should run its course in the lives of Christians. Thus when he set the account of the biblical passage under consideration, Beza time and time again applied the Bible's truths to his listeners. Although the two disciples were ignorant, Jesus did not excuse their unbelief, but he reproved them for their tardiness to believe the women who had seen the empty tomb. In the present situation, therefore, Christians must simply believe the words of the Holy Spirit in the Bible rather than trusting in vain philosophy or depraved thinking, Beza argued. Unlike those engaged in such haughty intellectual pursuits, Christ employed simple language. So, Beza pointed out, preachers must seek to imitate their Lord by learning their rhetoric from the Scriptures. Their rhetoric must be Bible-like oratory that is weighty and supports the reality of God and his authority; rhetoric for the sake of eloquence alone must be eschewed.

"Humanism and the Protestant Reformation," in *Renaissance Humanism: Foundations, Forms, and Legacy*, ed. Albert Rabil Jr. [Philadelphia: University of Pennsylvania Press, 1988], 2:393). In this regard, see also Charles Trinkaus, "Italian Humanism and Scholastic Theology," in *Renaissance Humanism: Foundations, Forms, and Legacy*, ed. Albert Rabil Jr. (Philadelphia: University of Pennsylvania Press, 1988), 2:333; Ong, "Humanism," 216; and James, "Peter Martyr Vermigli," 70-71.

15 Dückert, *Théodore de Bèze*, 9, 11.
16 Manetsch, "Theodore Beza," 400-01.
17 From the text before him, Beza made several points—not always connected—in a point-by-point manner. "The plan consisted merely in the exposition of a certain number of points that he developed successively" (Dückert, *Théodore de Bèze*, 62).
18 Dückert, *Théodore de Bèze*, 27, 43, 63, 65; Delval, "La Prédication," 83.
19 See my English translation of this sermon in appendix two.

After this initial exhortation, Beza made ten points from this short passage. All these points, he said, were what "the Holy Spirit wants to engrave well on the heart of each" listener from the Scriptures.[20] In the first place, Beza argued that to preach like Christ is more than just to explain the text and answer questions of doctrine. As a physician, the preacher must also apply the medicine of consolations and reproofs to his patients. To do this, he had to posses substantial learning to understand the Bible, discretion to know what actions require reproof, and "for the true use of the language of God, not just to speak, but to speak frankly as one must speak" in order to rebuke evil biblically.[21]

Second, the Scriptures were the source of correct doctrine. Jesus went to the Old Testament prophets to prove his identity to his two disciples, even though he had inspired the prophets. By referring to them, he left Christians an example of proper hermeneutics. Third, Beza argued that the canonical Scriptures alone were divine revelation. Christ specifically referred to the books of the Old Testament canon, so those who add to the revelation found in the Bible are actually demonic instruments.[22] In this regard, Beza laid down two keys for the proper interpretation of the Bible. In the first place, the Apostles' Creed was a barometer of allowable doctrine. Second, one must interpret the "true texts," that is, the Bible, by the Scriptures themselves.[23] The Bible was so important that all Christians must be allowed to read and hear God speaking in the Bible since it is "the word of the Lord" and "the incorruptible seed of the church in general and of each member of the church in particular."[24] Believers must listen to God's voice in the Bible.

Fourth, Beza cautioned that one must come to the biblical text with a humble attitude, with a willingness to submit to God's word there regardless of one's preconceived notions. Since the Bible was God's living voice, it could be understood and obeyed only with his assistance. So Beza encouraged his listeners to begin their Bible study by asking for God's help to understand the text so that they would hear God speaking there and not end up trusting in their reason.

In the fifth place, Beza noted the spiritual dimension of biblical interpretation. Unbelievers hate the truth and will not submit to it. Seeing Jesus in person and hearing him speak would not even make persons trust him unless the Lord chose to give them life, filling them with love for the truth. Following close on this, in the sixth place, Beza differentiated between intellectual credence and heartfelt belief. The Lord abhors mere intellectual assent but

---

20 Beza, *Sermons sur la Resurrection*, 246.
21 Ibid., 247.
22 Ibid., 250.
23 Ibid., 251.
24 Ibid., 252.

rejoices when persons love and cling to the truth revealed in Scripture. He "wants to have all or nothing" of a person. Those who love him and his truth from the heart will be with him for eternity, while those who "do not want to believe him" will "feel to their own cost" the sentence of the Judge before whose tribunal "there is no appeal."[25] The Bible's ultimate point was to lead persons to eternal salvation.

The seventh point consisted of a polemic against Roman practice. The Catholics' contention that one need merely to have "indefinite" belief in the Church's teaching was wrong, Beza contended, because of the example of Jesus with the bewildered disciples. God wanted all the words of the prophets and apostles to be taught in the churches and believed by the people. The Bible, not the church, determined truth.[26]

Beza's eighth and ninth points elaborated his understanding of the relation of reason to revelation. In the eighth place, he argued that those who sought for religious truth through their own reason had been duped by Satan. Since all people are sinful, their judgment of what is true or untrue cannot be trusted. Beza castigated people for following "false philosophy," which he also called "artificial folly." Such falsehood originated from their "natural sense." Jesus' example here proved that God desired for Christians not to pull "out just a little of the Scriptures." Rather, Beza urged, "let us search there [in Scripture] for our principles and our conclusions far away from all profane curiosity."[27] Since humans were fallen, persons could not sound God's depths on their own. Humility required that they seek the truth only in the Bible.[28]

The ninth point was an extended discourse about the relationship between the Bible and reason, and the role of rationality in confirming what God said in the Scriptures. Beza here argued that the Bible was the highest authority in religious matters since its authority had been established by God. It is, Beza urged, "the only true and immutable support of the true faith." More than that, though, Scripture sat as the final judge of all human reasoning: "it is the only rule of all true reason."[29] Rationality still had a place in religious matters, though, for it confounded mockers and confirmed biblical truth. Thus Jesus sometimes demonstrated "some reason on which the contents of the Scriptures were founded" as did Paul when he confuted the philosophers in Athens.[30] Therefore the church fathers and the apologists of Beza's day stood in good company when they, "in order to confound mockers, confirm themselves in our

---

25   Ibid., 256-57.
26   Ibid., 257.
27   Ibid., 257-58. Here Beza twice cited the apostle Paul's polemic against vain philosophy in Col. 2.
28   Ibid., 258.
29   Ibid., 259.
30   Ibid., 259-60.

religion by many good and very visible reasons."[31]

However, even "good" pagan knowledge made persons more guilty, because rather than leading them to salvation it did not change them. Unaided reason could not arrive at "knowledge of the true God" and the way to be reconciled to him. Human reason is intricately connected with the entire person, which, apart from God's grace, is opposed to the Lord. So Beza lamented that "our mind not only does not see anything. But which is more, it is so doggedly resistant" that it will never arrive at the truth by itself.[32] God must intervene first of all to give a person "the grace of knowing his folly" and, secondly, to draw the person to himself and by the Holy Spirit allow the individual to understand God's truth.[33]

These things are proved, Beza argued, by what Jesus explained about himself in the text under consideration. Then Beza inserted a detailed argument for the logic of Christ's atonement. The logical connections in his summary statement of the reason for Christ's salvific work are striking. Beza reasoned that

> in order to save those whom God had destined to salvation, the Savior had to be God, different in person than he who struck him, which is the Son. And he had to be still a true son of Adam in unity of person, and by consequence conceived by the virtue of the Holy Spirit, who carried in his body and in his soul all the punishment owed to our sins, dying as the just one who was pledged for the unjust, and who after he abolished death by his resurrection took possession of eternal glory for himself and for his own.[34]

Preachers, though, did not concoct these notions; rather, they concluded them from the authoritative revelation of God in Scripture. Indeed, Beza urged that such truths were beyond our capacity to discern. Instead they were founded on God's wisdom "which must be the true and only foundation of our faith."[35] Beza's logical interlude proved that there are "apparent reasons left in man" to confirm the truth and to confute opponents of the truth.[36]

The Lord's practice was the antidote. Jesus' example pointed to the correct balance between trusting in biblical revelation and relying on human reason. Christ did not act as the false teachers, Beza stressed, who go to "their unwritten words, their traditions, antiquity, and the mask of councils put forward" as dispensers of the truth. Rather, there is only one "touchstone" (*pierre de touche*) of religious truth, the Bible. Indeed Jesus, who himself inspired the biblical writers, went through all the Old Testament to prove his

---

31 Ibid., 258.
32 Ibid., 260-61.
33 Ibid., 261.
34 Ibid., 264.
35 Ibid., 265.
36 Ibid., 265.

identity to the two disciples. The Bible is absolutely sufficient in relating the truth to persons, Beza argued, for "the Holy Spirit omitted nothing which might be necessary" in it.[37] Human reason was doomed in finding the truth because it was joined to fallen persons who opposed the God of all truth. Even when used correctly when searching for religious certainty, reason merely confirmed the truth found in the Bible.

Finally, in the tenth point of the sermon, Beza engaged in an extended ethical discourse about lying. Beza derived this discourse from the final phrase of the passage: Jesus "made as though he would have gone farther," a part of the passage that is clearly not the main point of the text. Yet, from it Beza raised the question of whether or not it is ever right "to speak or to do something contrary to what one has at heart, always presupposing that the thought is good and right."[38] He answered, first, that one may never lie. Second, though, he reasoned "that not to say or not to represent all that one thinks, or not to say or represent a thing of the way that one thinks, is another thing than to lie, either by words or by actions." This was more than situational ethics, though, for Beza grounded his belief on biblical examples of just such partial concealment of the totality of truth, such as God's commands to Isaiah and Jonah to threaten their listeners in God's name with destruction, a calamity that God knew would not befall them.[39] In forecasting this destruction, however, God did not lie "because," as Beza argued, God "is the truth itself." Rather than showing God's mendacity, these instances demonstrated that the Lord "did not want to say all that he had decreed. Therefore he kept silent the condition that he had opposed to his decree."[40] So God did not lie, but he did conceal the fullness of what he intended to do. In the same way, Beza argued, believers must not tell falsehoods. In certain circumstances, however, such as spying in times of war, they might rightly not tell all of the truth.

In the conclusion to the sermon, Beza reiterated four points. First of all, he said, all persons need to be taught by the Lord, just like the two disciples under consideration. Second, one must see the Lord's description of the problem and take the medicine he prescribes for our souls. "This malady," Beza charged, "is our natural sense wanting to make itself the critic and judge of the wisdom of God, made known in his holy Word." To counteract this wrong-headed hubris on the part of all persons, God spoke authoritatively in the Scriptures by his Spirit and he continued in Beza's day to speak through the faithful preaching of those Scriptures: "The Holy Spirit is the only doctor, having here spoken by the lips of the Master, as he speaks in his church by the lips of his faithful

---

37 Ibid., 265-66.
38 Ibid., 267.
39 Ibid., 268.
40 Ibid..

servants."[41] Related to this, and in the third place, Beza encouraged his listeners to evaluate human teachers based on their faithfulness to the words of Scripture. The Bible determined "which drugs are used by the true doctors." They should hold on only to those which "grow and originate in the field of the Scriptures of the prophets and apostles." The supreme example of correct biblical interpretation is Jesus Christ. In this place, "by the comparison of passages that should provide the text and the gloss, everything being brought back to the articles of faith," the Lord had modeled the Reformation interpretive principle, the "analogy of faith."[42] Last, Beza reminded his listeners that understanding and obeying the Bible was ultimately more than an intellectual exercise. For this reason Beza urged them to "learn to ask God for a spirit of discretion, in order to keep ourselves from contravening in anything this simplicity and truth so recommended to Christians."[43]

This sermon, preached in Theodore Beza's seventy-fourth year, portrays his developed theological methodology. He particularly developed three themes related to proper biblical methodology. These themes were interrelated, of course, but they constitute the foundation of what Beza taught about theological method during his long and productive career. First of all, Beza noted the spiritual dimensions of theology: the living God spoke, Satan opposed the truth, sinful persons could not understand and would not submit to the truth without the aid of God's Spirit. In the second place, the Bible was the locus of God's revelation. Beza consistently promoted the Reformation principle of *sola scriptura*, not because it was sacrosanct, but because it was essential if Christians were to hear from God and be strengthened in the spiritual battle.[44] Third, Beza held a nuanced position concerning the value of human reason and philosophy. On the one hand, reason and philosophy were of no value because they were adversely affected by the fall. On the other hand, though, if used by regenerated Christians, they aided the proper interpretation of the Bible and the pastoral charge to refute error. Combined, these three themes show that Beza was a pastoral theologian. His primary concern was not to dispute or to polemicize, although both of these tasks had their proper place. His major goal was to hear God speak in the Bible and, concomitantly, to refute error and understand the Scriptures properly. His humanism was pronounced because of

---

41 Ibid., 271.
42 Ibid., 272. On different types of *gloss*, see Spencer, "Reformed Scholasticism in Medieval Perspective," 22-23.
43 Beza, *Sermons sur la Resurrection*, 272.
44 For a clear exposition of the Reformation principle of *sola scriptura*, especially showing its relation to reason and tradition, see Anthony N. S. Lane, "*Sola Scriptura*? Making Sense of a Post-Reformation Slogan," in *A Pathway into the Holy Scripture*, ed. P. E. Satterthwaite and D. F. Wright (Grand Rapids: Eerdmans, 1994), 297-327.

his desire properly to understand God's word. But it was subservient to his greatest desire, the urge to hear from the living God.

In subsequent sections of this chapter I will look at these three key elements to Beza's theological methodology: the spiritual nature of theology, the centrality of the Bible, and the necessity of proper interpretation. Drawing on many of Beza's pastoral sources while surveying these key areas, I will show that Beza was consistent in emphasizing these elements throughout his pastoral career. Subsequent interaction with his systematic treatises will confirm this pneumatological, biblical, and humanistic character of Beza's theology.

The Role of the Holy Spirit in Theology

Beza's emphasis on the spiritual nature of theology is no where more apparent than in the role he assigned to the third Person of the Trinity in the theological task. The Holy Spirit was vital in theology. Without the Spirit's work in regeneration, no Christians would exist to do theology. Without his enlivening of their hearts to seek for truth in God's word, none would want to do theology. And without his illumining their minds to understand God's word, no believers would ever arrive at correct theology.

Beza stressed the priority of God's grace throughout his theology.[45] One example must suffice here. The Holy Spirit only illuminated the elect, according to Beza. "Christ calls all men unto him by his gospel, spreading forth to that effect, his light throughout the whole world," he said. "But his sheep only do hear his voice, and follow him; as also he knows them and gives unto them life everlasting, even by the mere efficacy of his Spirit which quickens and lightens all your elect, O God, to make them in your word to behold the only lamp of your kingdom, [and] the knowledge of salvation."[46]

The Reformer also noted that the Spirit must give God's people a desire for the truth of his word. God alone was powerful enough to give persons a desire for the truth: "it is God alone who can put into men's minds, a true earnest desire of seeking the truth, he only is able to persuade them that it is the best and most glorious kind of victory to give place to the truth."[47] He also besought God "above all things" to "give us grace to desire, and especially to seek the spiritual bread of your word, wherewith our souls may be fed eternally in the name, and to the glory of the Father, Son, and Holy Ghost, one only and true

---

45 See chapter four.
46 Beza, *Houshold Prayers*, in the prayer "For obtaining the gift of the Holy Ghost."
47 Beza, *Job*, preface to Job 15. According to Beza this truth explained much of the contentiousness of doctrinal debate since "So hard a thing it is especially in disputing and reasoning to avoid self-love, as even in these times experience daily teaches us" (ibid.).

God."[48]

Beza's recognition of the necessity of the Spirit's work in theology also included an emphasis on his role in illuminating the biblical text to Christians so that they might properly understand it. Several of the Reformer's prayers demonstrate this. "I beseech you therefore, my God, vouchsafe to direct and guide me in the understanding of this eternal truth, through the operation of your Spirit," Beza prayed, "that being by him instructed, I may accomplish and make myself perfect in these four chief principles of the doctrine of salvation, which are fully taught at large. . . . Whereby I may obtain the end of my being . . . which is to know you, to glorify you for my God, to believe you, and in you, Jesus Christ, and in Jesus Christ, to love, fear, and serve you, according as you do command us, and in all things to observe equity towards all men."[49] In a different place, he spoke to God, saying that although "all people may read your sacred writings, only they can gather the sense to the peace of their souls, whom it pleases you, as a Father to illuminate from above."[50] The role of the Holy Spirit was to teach Christians divine truth, and he did this through opening the Scriptures to them: "I beseech you," he prayed, "let your eternal wisdom reach to me even through the light of your spirit. . . . to lift them up by the effects of his gifts, unto the sanctuary of your super-celestial palace, there to make them see, hear, and worship, in spirit and truth, the divine marvels of your kingdom, and the mysteries of the adoption of your elect. So that being thus taught by the most sacred oracles, I believe in heart, and with understanding meditate upon the true and eternal existence of you."[51] The Spirit, then, revealed divine truth through "the most sacred oracles."[52]

The Holy Spirit used the means of the Scriptures, but those means would be of no avail without his work of illuminating Christians' understandings. Thus Beza closed a sermon by urging his listeners to beseech

---

48 Beza, *Houshold Prayers*, in the prayer "Before meat, among the Family."
49 Ibid., in the prayer "To crave of God the light of his word."
50 Ibid., F1r.
51 Ibid., in the prayer "To one only God in Trinity of Persons."
52 In another place, Beza argued, "That we may consent unto the points of Christian religion, as unto true grounds, and much more that we may apply them unto ourselves, it behooves surely that we should have our ears elsewhere opened, a fleshly heart given us, to be short, that we should elsewhere be taught than of flesh and blood, because the church is the congregation of them that must be taught of God, and to whom the arm of the Lord is revealed. And that men may understand, what the prophets and apostles, have briefly thought and taught, concerning every article of our religion, they have need, not only of a wit of some measure sharpened, but also of the knowledge of tongues, and of careful and diligent reading" (Theodore Beza, *A Discourse, of the true and visible Markes of the Catholique Churche* [London: Robert Waldegrave, 1582], n.p.).

him which had shown us so great favor, as to have brought us into his Church, out of the filthy pollutions of this world and so many idolatries and superstitions, that he will give us his spirit the better to consider of, and to understand his holy doctrine taught in his Church, that we may profit thereby more and more in the knowledge and true fear of him, considering the bottomless depths of his great mercies. . . . Wherefore let us not grieve or make sad the spirit of sanctification, but on the contrary suffer him to work mightily and powerfully in us, waiting for his second coming, which shall be the accomplishment of that which we must presently hope for.[53]

"What are the great secrets which are comprised in these words?" Beza spoke of a text in the Song of Songs. "Let us pray unto God he will vouchsafe to teach them [to] us thoroughly."[54] In his prayers and practice as a preacher Beza emphasized that only those who were illuminated by the sovereign Spirit of God would have the desire to understand divine truth and they alone would comprehend it. This pneumatological emphasis was balanced by Beza's word-centeredness, as we shall now see.

The Centrality of the Bible

To Beza the spiritual battle necessitated *sola scriptura*. The living God had revealed himself and his ways, and continued to speak, through his word, the Bible. But, as Beza repeated continually, the devil vigorously opposed God's living voice in Scripture. If Christians were to withstand the wiles of the devil, they must be girded by truth from God. Roman Catholic, heretical, and any other human ideas that came between the individual and the Bible must be abandoned. The Bible had to be believed and proclaimed.

THE SUFFICIENCY OF THE BIBLE

For Beza, the Bible's sufficiency derived from its authorship. The Scriptures were God's own voice to his people. As such they were authoritative and sufficient for God's people. "Does this word contain all that which we must believe and do?" Beza asked at the head of his catechism. The necessary response was "Yes, without having any need to adjoin anything thereto, or to take anything therefrom."[55] It was sufficient because God himself had written it. So, Beza argued that the eighth psalm's true meaning was found in three New Testament verses "as the Holy Ghost interprets it."[56] "The Son of God," he said elsewhere, "has left us his lively portrait in his doctrine written by the Apostles, comprising whatever is necessary for us to know, either touching his

---

53 Beza, *Canticles*, 12.
54 Ibid., 276-77.
55 Beza, *Little Catechisme*, A1.
56 Beza, *Psalmes*, 11.

person, or touching all the counsel of God his Father concerning our salvation."[57] Similarly, in his prayer, "To crave of God the light of his word," Beza said, "you have so far graced us, that this your word of life has been, and still remains among us, faithfully collected in the sacred registers of the holy scripture, so to be unto us, the image of your glory, the law of your kingdom, the ladder of heaven, the gate of paradise, the trumpet of salvation, to be brief, the treasury of piety, virtue, wisdom, consolation, and perfection."[58]

Since the Bible was God's word, fidelity to the Bible was the mark of fidelity to Christ, Beza maintained. He taught that "Christ is the true, perpetual, necessary, and to be short, the only mark of the Church; yes, I say, the true Christ, that is, such a one, as he from the beginning has most perfectly, touching the matter and manner of salvation revealed himself, both in the writings, of the prophets and of the apostles." Jesus was known only through the Scripture. The Bible was much more than just accurate historical reporting, though. Christ spoke now, indeed, he ruled his church now, by means of his written word: "Therefore, wherever that word is heard, as it ought to be, there indeed Christ reigns, and where Christ reigns, there indeed we judge the Catholic, visible Church to be."[59]

This Bezan emphasis on God's active speaking through the Bible explains the usefulness he saw for the Scriptures in the church. Satan was active in the world, especially attacking the church. His major ploy was to entice persons to trust the power and accuracy of their unaided reason. This was a dangerous evil, Beza warned in a sermon to his students. The God-given protection against this demonic scheme, significantly, was found in biblical doctrine:

> But let us guard here of a great ruse of Satan, pushing us if he can, from one extreme to the other, which are as much as precipices. Therefore let us know that those are grandly self-deceived who want to subjugate the word of God to their natural sense; in this manner they do not transgress less dangerously who under the pretext that our faith should charm our natural sense, forge the articles of supernatural faith to their appetite. Instead faith should . . . lean on the word of God understood, and not at all on our imaginations, whether they are old or new.[60]

Pastors, therefore, must allow God's people to hear his words to them in Scripture. "By what means," Beza asked rhetorically, should pastors guard their flocks from heretics? The prescribed antidote was "pitching the hays of the word of God, to catch and entrap [heretics] therein, shutting them up in their dens and caves by this word also, compared unto fire consuming the chaff of falsehood and lies. . . . For it is properly by the spirit of the Lord's mouth, that

---

57 Beza, *Canticles*, 31.
58 Beza, *Houshold Prayers*, in the prayer "To crave of God the light of his word."
59 Beza, *True and visible Markes*, D2r-D2v.
60 Beza, *Sermons sur la Passion*, 437-38.

the vineyard of the Lord is planted, husbanded and preserved."[61]

The living voice of God in the Bible required a response from its hearers. Because God addressed sinful persons in the Scriptures, salvation stood in the balance when they heard God's word expounded, according to Beza. How they responded determined their eternal destiny:

> To be short, every man fattens himself so gross, that it will be impossible hereafter to pass through the strait gate – a thing lamentable, and of which I warn you in the name of God, while he yet says, "Come unto me," and while the door is yet open, or at the least only half shut. If we will not, God will show us to our cost – and we are very blind if we do not perceive that he already prepares himself thereunto – that if we think not on it, he will think on it, and when we shall cry, it shall be answered us, as it was them which were invited to the banquet.[62]

The Bible's divine origin and its usefulness meant, for Beza, that it must be heard by all God's people. It must, therefore, be translated. Although Rome charged that Scripture should not be translated into vulgar languages, "since, they say, in doing this each one would want to make himself a teacher and expositor of the Scriptures," Beza rebutted that this was "An argument very false in every way!" He argued that "the means of preventing that heresies would not happen . . . is not to prevent the reading of the Scriptures by which alone the truth is discerned from falsehood." Rather, "it is the duty of faithful Pastors to teach, to reprove, to exhort, to comfort their sheep by this living Word."[63]

The Bible was useful for Christians in all of life. For example, it challenged them to be diligent in their obedience to God. Comparing Christians' zeal to that of Satan, Beza maintained that the devil's zeal should make followers of Christ embarrassed. "Let us," he exhorted his listeners, "be ashamed of our own slothfulness and security, in that we are not by many degrees so diligent and

---

61 Beza, *Canticles*, 292. Beza delineated the value of the Bible in combat with Satan in one of his final sermons on the Song of Songs. The "threescore men of gard" in the text, he said, referred to those men "whose ministery God has used for the building of that arsenal and artillery house from which we are to take all our spiritual weapons with which the apostle arms his spiritual ritter (Eph. 6:13). I mean the holy scriptures uttered to the pen of the prophets by the Holy Ghost (2 Pet. 1:21), and yet in more greater abundance and with greater efficacy delivered unto the apostles, in whose writinges are to found all these weapons set in order and prepared for every one that will use them, taking them and learning the use of them, from the hands of the true pastors and dispensers of them. You see what these *gard* are, you see what these weapons are, with which whoever arms and aids himself cannot choose but see Satan, the world, the flesh, and sin cast down and trampled under his feet" (ibid., 357).
62 Ibid., 63.
63 Beza, *Sermons sur la Passion*, 781-82.

watchful in doing well and performing our duties, as Satan is in working all manner of wickedness and mischief. To this effect tend all those exhortations unto continual watchfulness, so often beaten upon and repeated in the holy Scriptures."[64]

The Scriptures also addressed matters of civic decorum, Beza believed. His sermons are replete with instances of his rebuking his parishioners for their disobedience to God's will for proper social order. For example, Pastor Beza castigated and warned his listeners:

> You dissolute, you idle and do-nothings, coming to sermon for a show and countenance only, or to sleep when you are there, when will you learn why you came into the world before you go out of it? You gamesters and wasters both of your own and others, will you forget the sermon which some of your companions made on the scaffold not long ago? . . . What shall I say more? God give you grace and mercy, God give you grace to cast far from you these filthy rags, to be adorned with his jewels and chains received of him and before his face.[65]

The Scriptures, God's living word, must therefore be the constant diet of his people. Summarizing the "principal end" of Psalm 119, Beza reiterated the divine origin and the sufficiency of the Bible, as well as the vital need for God's Spirit to apply the Scriptures to Christians. The purpose of this psalm was

> that men ought to be enticed to the careful study of the heavenly doctrine. . . . And the whole doctrine may be brought to these four principal heads. (1) That those things are signified by the name of the heavenly doctrine, which are revealed of God himself, and comprehended in the holy scriptures – whether we understand that part which commands that which we ought to do, and forbids the contrary, the name of the Law being taken in a more straight signification, or whether we understand that other part, wherein it is taught what we must believe to salvation, which we call the gospel. (2) That this doctrine is declared from heaven, not that we should comprehend it in our understanding only, but that every one should follow it with an earnest care, without fainting, as the rule of his whole life. (3) That we may be both willing and able to embrace and follow it, we must of necessity pray for the Spirit of God, which may both drive away darkness from our understanding, and amend our affections that are wholly corrupted. (4) Though the world being terrified, partly with the fear of dangers, partly with the greatness of calamities, and partly also deceived with a feigned show of profit, does rather go some other way, yet they only do wisely, which stick unto that way which is set down in the word of God, what difficulties so ever do offer

---

64 Beza, *Job*, 11r.
65 Beza, *Canticles*, 176. For further instances of Beza's applicatory sermons, see *Canticles*, 173, 372.

themselves in this life, so that at the last they shall have the fruition of true and everlasting life.[66]

To Beza the Bible was of supreme usefulness for God's people because of its divine origin. It alone contained "heavenly doctrine" from God himself.

THE BIBLE'S ROLE IN THE SPIRITUAL BATTLE

We have seen instances above of Beza's belief that Satan actively opposed God's revelation in Scripture. As he surveyed the contemporary landscape, Beza noticed Satan's machinations behind Rome's heretical doctrines. The battle between Protestants and Catholics, therefore, mirrored the battle between God and the devil over the truth. Beza also noted the spiritual dimension of other heresies in his day. The central fact to notice is the way that all of these demonic falsehoods were countered, in Beza's reasoning, by the holy Scriptures. Much more than just a formal doctrinal statement, then, for Beza *sola scriptura* meant that the living God spoke truth in the midst of heretical confusion to strengthen and protect his people.[67]

In his sermons on the Song of Songs, for instance, Beza noted the demonic origin of Roman doctrine. He rebuked the Catholics for "their false and cursed doctrine" which they attempted to cover with "their lies and falsehoods." This practice, he argued, originated with "Satan their father" and was carried on "in the school of these foxes, or rather these wolves, which are the talents and the

---

66 Ibid., 284-85.
67 Beza, like the Reformers in general, was quick to point out that Protestants had not invented their doctrines *ex nihilo*. Protestant beliefs came from the Bible, but they were also in line with the early creeds of the Church. Unlike Roman belief, though, Protestant doctrine had to be judged by the touchstone of Scripture. Beza said at one point, then, that Protestants adhered to the ecumenical creeds of the church: "Now lest these men should again complain, that whatever has been established by council after council, in the ancient church, should by this means be called into doubt. We confess, that we do acknowledge the creeds, which were always approved by the common consent of the whole church, namely, the Creed of the Apostles, Nicea, Athanasius his creed, the creed of Constantinople, Chalcedon, together with the curses pronounced in the second Council of Ephesus against Nestorius" (*True and visible Markes*, D1r-D2r). The power of the creeds, though, derived from their faithfulness to Christ's voice in his word. His voice was powerful enough to refute heresies, Beza pointed out, saying, "we both with mouth and heart detest, all heresies, which either by open or secret consent of the whole church, were out of that word of God condemned in those four councils, and also overthrown in the fifth and sixth councils of Constantinople. And also all other heresies whatever, which afterward, either newly sprung up, or are newly polished, not that the truth hangs upon any synods or creeds, but because we acknowledge that the things which are prescribed and established in them may be rightly judged by the writings of the prophets and apostles" (ibid., D2r).

teeth of that great monster of Rome."[68] In another place, he warned his flock to "take diligent heed of Satan's and his ministers' subtlety, who would bear us in hand that all old wine is good, and must be received: which is most false. For there is as well old wine mingled and poisoned, as new wine, which we must warily take heed of."[69] The sure antidote against such demonic poison, Pastor Beza noted, was to judge everything by the sure canon of the Bible, "to consider well whether it be drawn out of the true vessels of . . . the writings of the prophets and Apostles, otherwise called, the Old and the New Testament, and so consequently reject and refuse without all exception whatever wine is drawn elsewhere."[70]

Satan's opposition to the truth flourished in Catholic theology schools, Beza maintained. His contempt for Roman theological method was palpable. Regarding the divinity schools where these falsehoods were inculcated, Beza charged that

> this is there where Satan has served his turn with sugar to turn it into most bitter and deadly poison – having banished out of the school of divinity that which was the only subject thereof, I mean the reading and expounding of the text of holy Scripture, to thrust therein an abominable confusion of dreaming sophistications, some as vain as curious, others absurd, other full of impiety. In such sort, that to be a doctor in such a thing is no more but to be farther off from pure and sound doctrine, as the apostle so diligently warns us (1 Tim. 1:4 and 4:7) while Satan goes forward in the utter overthrow of all their clergy having transformed them into shops and brothels of sodomy and instruments unto all sacrilege and simony.[71]

Likewise in a sermon to students at the Academy, he charged Satan with introducing false theological method into Catholic schools of theology. Beza labeled this wrong method "scholasticism ."[72] The devil's schemes paralleled

---

68 Beza, *Canticles.*, 290.
69 Ibid., 230.
70 Ibid.
71 Ibid., 135.
72 At this point, it is pertinent to mention the curriculum of the Geneva Academy. The Geneva Academy was organized to offer students a humanist education, squarely based on the mastery of the classical languages and French, and on the study of rhetoric. "At the school's opening Calvin's fairly brief remarks and Theodore de Beze's Address at the Solemn Opening of the Academy in Geneva suggested the way in which the reformers would combine religion with humanistic classical culture. The distribution of the twenty-seven weekly lectures indicates the emphasis given: three on theology, eight on Hebrew, three on Greek ethics, five on Greek orators and poets, three on physics or mathematics, and five on dialectic or rhetoric" (Spitz, "Humanism and the Protestant Reformation," 392). As Richard Stauffer remarked, referring to Borgeaud's study of the Geneva Academy, it

the heinous machinations of those in Beza's sermon text who spread the heretical rumor that Jesus' body had been stolen from the tomb.

> And what other craft does Satan do in all times, and indeed without going more remote, what has come to pass in the world since about eighty years, and that we see still every day, is it not like a living representation of this narrative? Because all these human traditions and this "glorious" theology called "scholastic," which have they not been another thing than so many buckets and stamps to oppose what is this truth of God, shrouded in the cavern of ignorance and of barbarity of so many centuries, not able to extricate. And this giant stone set at the grave by Joseph, yet not with a bad intention, is it not represented to us by this false primate attributed to this glorious bishop of Rome, as the principal priest . . . . This "glorious" Council of Trent, is it not a living representation of this council mentioned in this narrative . . . to make to be good their faults and evil machinations until this day? But take courage, my brothers. He who was raised to life in spite of all his enemies, and who has raised to life his truth in our times in our hearts, and among all those to whom he pierced their ears, is still and will be ever also drawing up against all his adversaries, and also careful of the salvation

---

consisted of a "'theological seminary [the *schola publica*], to which was joined a 'College in three languages' [the *schola privata*] which more or less imitated that of Erasmus" (Richard Stauffer, "Calvinism and the Universities," in *University and Reformation: Lectures from the University of Copenhagen Symposium*, ed. Leif Grane [Leiden: E. J. Brill, 1981], 82). For the founding documents of the Academy which lay out its curriculum in both schools, see W. Stanford Reid's translation of the *Ordre de l'Ecole* in "Calvin and the Founding of the Academy of Geneva" *Westminster Theological Journal* 18 (1955): 22-33. Why was there such an emphasis on humanism? Here one must recollect the humanist training of the two most important individuals at the fledgling Academy, Calvin and Beza, as well as the humanistically trained persons whom Calvin sought to fill the posts and provide the foundation of the Academy. Reid mentions, for example, Budé, Wolmar and Lefebvre as some of Calvin's early teachers and de Govreau and Sturm with whom he was friends in college. Calvin saw Sturm's educational principles in action during his exile to Strasbourg from 1538 to 1541 (Reid, "The Academy of Geneva," 4-5). The boon which both Calvin and Beza saw in humanistic education was its emphasis on languages and the developing in students of the ability to think clearly and express their ideas persuasively. Lewis's evaluation is certainly right: "Dialectic will enable the student to question definitions and to break down problems into their constituent parts. This skill will equip him to spot unacceptable implications in propositions put forward by those who offer to the faithful erroneous and perverted readings of the Word." So the students' studies were designed to prepare them to handle Scripture facilely: "He will then embark upon the figures of rhetoric, not for idle pleasure but so that he will be better able to persuade others of the Gospel message and to convince them that what he has to offer is the true reading of God's Word" (Lewis, "Genevan Academy," 43).

of his church by the reign of his truth, that he will be then when this history comes to pass.[73]

Rome was not the only trouble spot, though. Heresy also came from other quarters. "The Lord had no sooner begun in our time, to take his vineyard into his own hands," Beza maintained,

> but Satan thrust into it those foxes, the Anabaptists and Libertines of many sorts, from whom sprang those vile and filthy heretics of the family of love. . . . On the other side, are crept into the world the Arians. . . . In a word, I know not whether there be at all any one old heresy which Satan endeavors not to set a broach among us, or new yet to be invented which he hammers not in the forge, so to break in upon this vineyard being yet young and tender, to hinder her fruit to come to maturity and ripeness.[74]

The only weapon strong enough to defeat this demonic, heretical foe was God's word, according to the Reformer. He urged his listeners to "take diligent heed of Satan's and his minister's subtlety, who would bear us in hand that all old wine is good, and must be received: which is most false." Such heresy could only be confounded as Christians went to the Old and New Testament Scripture "and so consequently reject and refuse without all exception whatsoever wine is drawn elsewhere."[75] According to Theodore Beza the Bible was the weapon Christians needed to wield in the spiritual battle.

The Need for Right Biblical Interpretation

Nowhere did Beza's humanism show itself more clearly than in his repeated insistence that the Bible must be interpreted correctly. Thus he emphasized the importance of interpreting the Bible in its original languages using proper hermeneutical technique. It is in this regard that he also used Aristotle. The Peripatetic, Beza believed, had left students helpful tools for proper interpretation. We will notice these briefly in the following exposition. Also, Beza believed in the appropriate use of rhetoric by preachers. However, Beza's humanism and his appropriation of philosophy were very qualified. First, Beza

---

73 Beza, *Sermons sur la Resurrection*, 188-89, 191. We see here some of Beza's motivation behind nearly single-handedly keeping the Geneva Academy going in times of extreme hardship. Beza's desire did not stem from political hubris. Nor was it from a desire for job security. Rather, it was motivated by and founded on his eschatological vision. The living God spoke in the Bible, but Satan—in the schools and in the Catholic church—opposed the truth at every turn. The church must hear God speaking through his living word, so pastors must be trained to understand it and preach it faithfully.

74 Beza, *Canticles*, 291.

75 Ibid., 230.

argued that Christians' knowledge would not be complete during their early pilgrimage. Second, philosophy, for all its benefits, was unhelpful in curbing and shaping one's affections. Ultimately, philosophy, especially logic, was licit as long as it did not come in between the interpreter and the text of the Scripture. In this way, Theodore Beza showed himself to be fundamentally a biblical humanist. In other words, as I will show below, he was a pastoral theologian.

BEZA'S HUMANISTIC INTERPRETATION

Beza's training in humanism has been well documented.[76] He did not lose his interest in humanistic endeavors when he converted to Protestantism, nor even when he took the helm of the church and Academy in Geneva.[77] The Reformer's background in humanism shines through in his instructions on proper biblical interpretation. In his exposition of Job, for instance, Beza lauded the rediscovery of the knowledge of the biblical languages in his day. In fact, God, he said, was to be praised for this: "God be thanked that in these days he has restored the knowledge of the Hebrew tongue, through ignorance whereof those that are unskillful will hardly believe how often and how greatly the most learned Greek interpreters have erred in the true exposition of all the sacred books of the Old Testament. . . . it has pleased God in this age to make the Hebrew tongue so familiar unto us, lest with the Fathers in many places they err from the true and natural sense of the Scriptures."[78] Thus Beza urged the study of the biblical languages at the Academy, for Christian schools, he argued, were to be "a preparation of students in theology with the knowledge of the languages and humane letters (*bonnes lettres*)."[79]

Having read the Bible in its original tongue, the interpreter should then seek to understand the relationship of the words to one another and of the context of the passage to the broader context of the book. In so doing, Beza argued, the Bible reader would correctly ascertain the meaning of the Bible.[80] This, in fact,

---

76 See Clavier, *Théodore de Bèze*, 40; Linder, "Calvinism and Humanism" 167-81; McPhee, "Conserver or Transformer of Calvin's Theology?," v; Letham, "Theodore Beza," 26-27; Summers, "Theodore Beza's Classical Library," 193-207; and Muller, "Calvin, Beza, and the Exegetical History of Romans 13:1-7," 52.
77 See appendix one.
78 Beza, *Job*, on Job 1:5.
79 Beza, *Sermons sur la Resurrection*, 414.
80 Backus's comments about Beza's interpretation are pertinent at this point. She said, "It is by now an established fact that Biblical commentators in the second half of the sixteenth century paid greater attention than their predecessors to the internal coherence of the Scriptural text. The exact nature of this preoccupation is very clearly stated by Theodore Beza in his unpublished and undated *Ratio studii theologici*. There, after emphasising the importance of the study of the Scriptures, Beza says that the commentator should first of all understand the meaning of the

explained Beza's biblical expositions. In his prefatory letter to his exposition of Job, Beza explained his method of interpretation, showing the importance he placed on context when interpreting Scripture. Beza recorded that

> I have written a full commentary upon the two first chapters thereof, wherein I have soundly and plainly so far as I could, unfolded and laid open many questions of no small importance, and specially that controversy of the providence of God. I have moreover set down before the beginnings of all the other chapters following, both the sum of those things which are handled in them, as also the manner how every argument therein contained, is disposed. The ignorance or rather contempt of such method, I dare be bold to say, has brought many both false and also foolish expositions, not only into this book of Job, but also into the writings of the prophets and apostles.[81]

But Beza's judgment of right hermeneutical techniques was clearly determined by his humanistic training. He was concerned, for instance, with understanding words in their context and in their relationship to one another. In order to understand a biblical book correctly, Beza argued that one must "favorably weigh the intent and meaning of the speaker."[82] In the introduction to his *Annotationes* on the New Testament, he therefore argued that many persons wrongly interpret the Bible for want of paying close attention to the arrangement of the words themselves: "they leaving the scope and purpose, wander to certain notes and observations, confusedly and without order heaped together so that in many places of most importance no regard is had to the sentence itself."[83] In the case of the interpretation of Paul's epistles, for example, this tactic will not do, for the apostle "had as great a skill and judgment in writing as any writer that ever did write," Beza argued.[84] This led to his negative judgment concerning the schoolmen who were unable to understand Paul, since they failed to comprehend the logical ordering of his words: "certainly this most excellent declarer of God's secrets [Paul], was no more known in the schools than if he had left no monuments nor writings. Yes, many did flee from him as from a rock, for fear of shipwreck."[85]

Beza's was a *biblical* humanism. There is perhaps no more concise

---

section of text he is studying and the relationship between it and the sections that precede and follow. Having done that, he can then offer an interpretation of the section in accordance with the *analogia fidei*. It is only after this examination of the internal structure that he should turn his attention to the study of the individual words and other commentators" (Backus, "Piscator Misconstrued?," 113). See Theodore Beza, *Ratio studii theologici*, in Fatio, *Méthode et Théologie*, 119-21.

81 Beza, *Job*, A5r.
82 Ibid., preface to Job 35.
83 Beza, "Exhortation to the Reformation of the Church," Eiiv.
84 Ibid.
85 Ibid.

statement of Beza's expressed concern for proper biblical interpretation than his 1592 exhortation to the Academy's students, many of whom were preparing to spend their lives in the preaching ministry. Beza reminded them that the Church had been plagued in the past by those who set themselves up as the authoritative judges of truth. A wise determiner of truth was needed.

> And who will be this except the Lord? And how will the Lord do this, but by the Scripture itself? Or do we want him to descend again from heaven? But, they say, how will the Scriptures be the judge since [the interpretations of Bible people have are different]. . . . I respond first that in the matter of religion it is to make a very great fault to have recourse elsewhere than to the holy Scriptures which we know to be dictated by the Holy Spirit (*dictées du S. Esprit*). Because it is as much as to oust him from his throne. It is not a lesser fault also to think that the Holy Spirit wanted to speak more clearly by the mouth of a living man, than by those who were his very faithful and certain secretaries who recorded all the truth required for salvation. Thirdly, several other beautiful passages of the ancient Greek and Latin fathers teach us to compare the passages of Scripture which prove some difficulty (St. Paul, Rom. 12:6). They give us a very certain rule to discern false interpretations from true ones. We must give an account of the consistency of all the articles of our faith, confessed and defended, since it is very assured and infallible that the Holy Spirit is not contrary to himself because he is the teacher of truth. . . . In sum therefore the holy Scriptures should furnish the text and the gloss, and it is necessary to continue in these limits. Thus Isaiah called the false teachers of his time back to the Law and the testimony (Isa. 8:20). It is there also and no other that David sends us again (Ps. 19:8 and all of Ps. 119), though the old covenant could not compare to the full light of the Gospel. Thus what the apostles taught are confirmed by the writings of the prophets (Acts 17:11), seeing in these the traces of their master and ours (Jn. 5:39). It is there that Abraham recalled those who want to be teachers (Lk. 16:29, 31). It is thus in this manner that the ancient Fathers at the true councils combated and demolished the heresies of their times.[86]

We see here that, according to Beza, the necessary judge in the church is holy Scripture. But the Bible is more than a book, for in it the Lord himself speaks. It, he exclaimed, was "dictated by the Holy Spirit." To look elsewhere than Scripture therefore is more than a wrong hermeneutical tactic. It is blasphemy, a wrong-headed attempt to remove God "from his throne." In order to let God speak, Beza charged that the Bible alone must be the foundation of the truth in the church. The key to proper interpretation, he maintained, was to let Scripture interpret itself, since the Holy Spirit who spoke it would not contradict himself. In other words, the Bible must be supreme in the church. The word of God, not human fancies or constructs, must "furnish both the text and the gloss." In other words, it was to be the document being interpreted as well as the commentary

---

86 Beza, *Sermons sur la Passion*, 546-48.

read to help in the interpretative process.

It is in this context that we must note Beza's use of allegory. Like his contemporaries, Beza employed allegorical interpretation. He used it temperately, though, arguing in one place that "it is apparent by the whole course of this his speech" that a section of Job was not allegorical.[87] The context of a passage, then, determined how it should be analyzed by the exegete. When Beza understood a passage figuratively, he did it because of other biblical warrant. Thus his understanding of Psalm 68 as primarily teaching about Christ was informed by his reading of two New Testament passages. "This Psalm," Beza exposited,

> than the which nothing could be written more divinely, more full of majesty, or more eloquently by any man. . . . [T]he prophet stood not fixed only in that matter, which was then in hand, but by divine inspiration did insinuate mystically . . . therefore by that ark is mystically understood, that the Son of God, in whom the fullness of the Godhead remains, has put upon him our flesh. By Zion is meant the tabernacle, not made with man's hand. By bringing in of the ark, the ascension of Christ into heaven. By leading away of the captives, that Satan, sin, and death, are overcome. Lastly, by the temporal blessings continually poured upon Israel, the spiritual and everlasting gifts of Christ daily bestowed upon the Church, by the holy ministry and work of the gospel, is here figuratively described, as Paul witnesses (Eph. 4:8) and almost throughout the epistle to the Hebrews.[88]

The entire Bible must be interpreted properly, Beza argued, so that Christians might be edified. This included even the difficult, doctrinally-sophisticated parts of Scripture, such as those dealing with predestination. So in the conclusion to the *Tabula*, Beza's defense of the Calvinistic understanding of predestination, he included a chapter titled "In What Way This Doctrine Can Be Set Forth Publicly, in a Fitting Manner." Here Beza excoriated his opponents who created unbiblical distinctions and were thus "entangled, until they can never emerge from those labyrinths." That did not mean, though, that the doctrine of predestination should be eschewed by preachers, "since no subject is more fittingly taught, in a pure and sincere way, in God's church." Rather, Beza argued that proper interpretation was the key to understanding this thorny doctrine biblically. "No manner of speaking should be used that are foreign to Scripture," he argued, "as far as that is possible (for in the interest of teaching we must sometimes hazard something in a holy and reverent way). The teachings that are found in the Word of God should be explained by proper interpretation (*quae in verbo Dei occurrunt, commoda interpretatione explicentur*), so that one who is less sophisticated will not have reason to

---

87 Beza, *Job*, on Job 1:21.
88 Beza, *Psalmes*, 145-46.

stumble."[89]

Even Theodore Beza's concern for proper biblical interpretation cannot be rightly appreciated apart from knowledge of Beza's eschatological view of reality. He was much more than a Renaissance humanist. Earlier in the sermon referenced above, he had asserted that Satan tried to ensnare persons in merely the natural knowledge of God, the conception of him they would get merely from looking at God's creation.[90] Through the biblical writers, however, Christ revealed the true, supernatural knowledge of God. This is the eschatological context in which we should understand Beza's call for his students to take up arms, that is, the Bible correctly interpreted, in order to combat and demolish the heresies of their day, just as the early church had done. For Beza, correct interpretation of the Bible was essential since the church was at war with Satan.

BEZA'S USE OF RHETORIC

What, then, of rhetoric?[91] Calvin's rhetoric has received much attention; rightly so, for in his search for *brevitas et facilitas*, Calvin had not abandoned his humanistic (or homiletic, we might better say) bent towards taking the Scripture and applying it in an understandable and moving way to the heads and hearts of his listeners.[92] Beza faithfully followed Calvin's model in this regard, even though he was not as successful in it as his mentor had been.[93] For example, in a telling pastoral application to his students, Beza hammered the point of the Bible's utility home:

> Jesus Christ did not simply assure his Apostles that he would really be raised, but taught them when and what the fruit which they should receive from this resurrection would be, showing in this what the duty of the faithful teachers of the Church is, and of true hearers also. It is not therefore enough to teach, nor to believe the sacred histories contained in the old and new testament: but it is necessary that the teachers show the use contained in them, and by the manner of speaking smash the shell in order to show in it the stone of the fruit: and that they the listeners from the speakers receive it and eat and digest by this true faith.[94]

---

89 Beza, *Tabula*, in *The Potter and the Clay*, 74-45; *Tractationum Theologicarum*, 1:197.
90 Beza, *Sermons sur la Passion*, 531-32.
91 On rhetoric see G. F. Drury, "Rhetoric," in *New Catholic Encyclopedia* (New York: McGraw-Hill, 1967), 12:458.
92 See Richard C. Gamble, "*Brevitas et facilitas*: Toward an Understanding of Calvin's Hermeneutic," *Westminster Theological Journal* 47 (1985): 1-17.
93 On Beza's use of rhetoric, see Summers, "Beza's Classical Library," 198-99.
94 Beza, *Sermons sur la Resurrection*, 404-05. Spitz rightly noted that the Reformers emphasized rhetoric because they had a complete view of persons being those who need to be moved in their affections as well as taught intellectually ("Humanism

We have already noted several examples of Beza's attention to rhetorical devices. In the section to follow, we shall see several more. At this point, however, we should notice that Beza did not adopt the use of rhetoric uncritically. In one of his sermons to future pastors, for instance, he argued that since Christ and the evangelists were simple and vulgar in their speech, no "virtue should be attributed to any human eloquence nor to artificial rhetoric." His ultimate proof for this assertion derived from the apostle Paul's words to "those beautiful orators of Corinth" in which he said that he did not "come to you with the excellence of speaking well, and my preaching was not in the attractive words of human wisdom, but in the effectiveness of the Spirit and of power (1 Cor. 2:1, 4)." From this, Beza concluded that "The simplicity of preaching does not at all detract from the majesty of the Scripture, but on the contrary shows that the building of the Church is an edifice, founded entirely on only one virtue of the inner God. Such was also the Apostles' language, which neither the wisdom of the philosophers nor the eloquence of the orators could resist." Following the apostolic example, Beza sought for the final solution in the Scripture. Thus, in conclusion, he said, "Therefore the Holy Spirit has his rhetoric in the past [in the Bible]," and he is "displeased" and "disgusted" with those "who are not able to take any taste of the language of the holy Scriptures: and yet love more to use their lives in the reading of orators and poets, and other profane writings."[95]

In a sense, Beza's view of rhetoric prepares the way for us to examine his nuanced view of philosophy. Rhetoric as practiced in the secular schools, based on the reading and emulating the classical orators and poets, was vapid. Worse than that, it was dangerous, for it could easily obscure the simple but pointed rhetoric of the Spirit, the living word of God. As long as the preacher's words did not cloud the meaning of that divine word but sought to explicate and apply its truth to the pastor's audience, rhetoric was licit.

BEZA'S QUALIFIED APPROPRIATION OF PHILOSOPHY

Beza saw a positive use of logic and received philosophical traditions when they helped one to arrive at the true meaning of a biblical passage.[96] Thus while

---

and the Protestant Reformation," 394). Cf. Bouwsma, "Calvinism as Renaissance Artifact," 32-35.
95 Beza, *Sermons sur la Resurrection*, 292-93.
96 Several scholars, I contend, have misconstrued Beza's intention in using logic in his polemical treatises as evidence of his philosophical bent. In addition to the internal proofs I offer in the above exposition to counter this idea, there are historical data that call this idea into question. First of all, Beza (like his mentor, Calvin) was self-taught theologically, with little or no training in the scholastic discipline (Robert M. Kingdon, *Adultery and Divorce in Calvin's Geneva*, Harvard Historical Studies 118 [Cambridge, MA: Harvard University Press, 1995], 166-67). Second, some of Beza's debates with Lutheran opponents demonstrate that he was out of his element

writing against the Catholic view of the church, Beza argued that "men should demand what the church should be before they determine of the bounds of her authority. Which order they that do not follow, commit truly that gross error, and worthy of stripes, which they call *Petitio principii*. But who is so far void of all reason," Beza continued, "that he sees not here again, *Petitio principii*, and the thing in controversy to be taken as granted?"[97] After disproving papal succession from the Bible, Beza lamented the typical Catholic way of arguing for their position: "What can be more corrupt than this subtle kind of reasoning? For this is that which is well known, even to children, which they are want to call *elench* or a fallacy of composition and division."[98]

Yet Beza was not a rationalist. He placed strict limits on reason's power. He realized that his knowledge of spiritual reality would be incomplete in this life. Only in eternity, he prayed, would he "obtain full knowledge of those things that you have given me to believe, and in the perfect contemplation of the same."[99] In another place, commenting on Jesus' call to discipleship, Beza maintained it was "necessary for us to renounce our own nature and reason, and to abandon our own affections, to suffer you and your love, O our God, to live and reign in us."[100]

As Beza's own practice of biblical interpretation and polemics showed, his point in saying this was not that Christians were not to think. Rather, the point was that their reasoning had to agree with the Scriptures and be dependent upon biblical notions. In his polemics against Castellio, for example, Beza rebuked him for making an idol fashioned by his own reason out of God: "Philosophers freely confess, when it comes to God, that they are blind. But you, on the other hand, need no other teacher to attain to the knowledge of God than 'nature' and 'reason.' Certainly, when you act that way you conduct yourself like someone

---

in the finer points of philosophy, at least one time hiring a philosopher to assist him in the debate (Lewis, "Genevan Academy," 46; and Raitt, *Montbéliard*, 86-88).

97 Beza, *True and visible Markes*, A2r-A3v.
98 Ibid., n.p.
99 Beza, *Houshold Prayers*; in the prayer, "Upon the Symbol or Articles of Belief." In another prayer, Beza showed the limits of human reason. Only in heaven will all be revealed to Christians: "Nevertheless I do very well know, that the depth of these profound mysteries cannot be discovered to our senses, likewise that the treasures of your wisdom, of your counsel, and of your judgements, are a very bottomless gulf, and your ways impossible to be found out. . . . I do only with flexible heart embrace, and carefully in my cogitation, according to the measure of your gifts, meditate upon that secret of godliness, which I have received by the preaching of your gospel, and do in part know it. Attending, until being delivered from sin and corruption, I may see you face to face, and in presence behold that which now I see as it were in a very dark glass" (ibid., E5r-E5v).
100 Beza, *Houshold Prayers*, in the prayer "That we may well use afflictions."

who leaves the judgment of colors to only blind men."[101]

For Beza, the Scriptures were the source of revealed knowledge. Thus he encouraged his students to emulate the apostles and derive their doctrine from the Bible:

> Let us now add to that, that even though the disciples were thus disposed and changed in their understanding, they were sent back to the Scriptures. Because it is there where it is necessary to search of him for the knowledge of which we are disposed. And if those themselves who received the Holy Spirit were sent to the Scriptures, what will be of those fools and madmen who seek for a theology in a Plato or in an Aristotle, and in general in the discourses of their carnal follies, whether in whole or in part?[102]

The philosophers, Beza argued, were wrong, then, more often than not because they taught contrary to the Bible. For instance, philosophers called the clear teaching of Scripture that Jesus rose from the dead absurd. Beza's judgment was that this "makes it necessary to oppose in sum all the musings of the Philosophers, or rather of the madness or insanities of this world."[103] Even Aristotle, whom Beza liked the most of all philosophers, had to be critiqued by Scripture. When Aristotle was correct in ethical points, for instance, Beza argued that this was merely because the Peripatetic at that point was agreeing with the Bible:

> Let this therefore stand for an undoubted truth – both against profane men, who examine whatsoever they find in the Scriptures concerning these matters by their false grounds and deceivable axioms, and also against those smatterers, who in this respect make no account at all of these heavenly writings – that as all true religion is to be fetched only out of God's word, so also that the whole knowledge of natural things, which we find in profane philosophers . . . ought to be tried and leveled by the rule of the Scriptures, unless we will willfully depart and wander from the truth. . . . [For example, what James said of faith] that that only is a true and lively faith which shows itself by good works, must also be applied to all other virtues. Wherefore Aristotle in his first book of Ethics did herein very well (although otherwise he neither knew the chief virtues nor the true cause and the true effects of the rest) that he imagined the chief good not to consist in bare virtue by itself, but rather in the operation and action of virtue.[104]

In addition to intruding upon the authoritative place of the Scriptures,

---

101 Theodore Beza, *Responsio ad Sebastiani Castellionis Calumnias*, in *The Potter and the Clay: The Main Predestination Writings of Theodore Beza*, trans. Philip C. Holtrop (Grand Rapids: Calvin College, 1982), 148.
102 Beza, *Sermons sur la Resurrection*, 358.
103 Beza, *Sermons sur la Passion*, 958. See also Beza, *Canticles*, 107-08.
104 Beza, *Job*, on Job 1:1.

philosophy was unable to make persons holy, Beza claimed. He constantly made this complaint, comparing the impotence of philosophy with the sovereign power of the Spirit to change lives. "See then how far the violent and outrageous affections of our mind will soon carry us," Beza pointed out, "which the philosophers would have us to rule by reason, this remedy truly of theirs being not altogether unprofitable, but yet not of sufficient force, even in the least temptations, which the Spirit of God alone lightning our understanding does minister to us in our distress."[105] Instead, Christians needed both knowledge and holy affections, Beza urged. So, commenting on Psalm 39, Beza noted that "the prophet throughout this Psalm mixes prayers full of affections, that he might teach us that these things are not to be disputed coldly of us, as though we were in philosophers' schools. But we must use most vehement and earnest prayers, whereby we should ask of God both to have our affections eased and our faith continued."[106] The problem with the philosophers' emphasis on "virtue" was that it did not take into account the radical extent of human sinfulness. Only the sovereign Spirit could change persons internally.[107] And that inner change is the focus of pastoral concern. For this reason, Beza urged his students at the Academy, as they scanned "the false wisdom of the Philosophers" and noted "the corruption of the schools, to which the poor youngster is introduced as in a very stinking brothel," to "never separate your studies and humane letters (*bonnes lettres*) from the true science of salvation."[108] Since salvation was the ultimate goal, philosophy fell short. In his call for a chaste use of philosophy, Theodore Beza showed himself to be a pastoral theologian.

Conclusion

Methodologically, then, Theodore Beza was a humanist. He was concerned especially with the study of original sources and with persuasive rhetoric. But he was a Protestant humanist, one who believed and practiced *sola scriptura*, who thought that all religious truth necessary for persons to believe for salvation was given by divine revelation in the Bible. Beza thus concentrated his efforts on studying the Scriptures of the Old and New Testaments and on explaining their truth persuasively to his listeners and readers. He did not shy

---

105 Ibid., K4r.
106 Beza, *Psalmes*, 77.
107 Beza, *Job*, F4v. In his comments on Job 1:1, Beza explained in some detail the difference between "virtue" and hearts that had been renewed by the Holy Spirit. As good as some "virtue" was, it was never good enough, for since unregenerate persons opposed God they could never obtain the highest of all virtues, namely, doing all they did for God's glory (ibid., on Job 1:1).
108 Beza, *Sermons sur la Resurrection*, 416, 417, 418.

away from using more "scholastic" language when he was forced to in debates or when trying to explain truth from the Bible, but his overriding concern was to understand and explain the Bible. Beza's educational background provided him with extensive training in humanism. The whole corpus of his writings shows his continuing humanistic concern, and his years at the helm of the Genevan Academy solidified his humanistic identity. Supremely, Beza's belief in the spiritual battle raging around him drove him to the Bible as the source of comfort and support for weary pilgrims. Beza's humanism was thus a Christian humanism, a conviction that the Bible expressed truth that was essential to carry believers safely to heaven.

The Salvific Thrust of Beza's Systematic Theology

For Theodore Beza all theology was pastoral. We noted this in our exposition of his methodology above. Beza's four most systematic works also prove this point. First, we will note the historical setting of each work, showing the pastoral needs that Beza was attempting to meet in them. Then we will analyze the works in some detail, showing their structure, the relationship of their various parts, the method Beza employed in them, and his goal in writing them, if it can be determined. Although Beza was able to structure his theology differently in diverse situations, his goal was constant. Beza wrote these doctrinal treatises as a pastor to guide persons through the spiritual battle to heaven.

Confession de la foi Chrestienne *(1559)*

Beza's *Confession*, originally published in 1559, deserves special attention as a composite of Beza's pastoral systematic theology. Scholars are united in judging this Beza's most complete systematic work of theology. Jean Barnaud argued that the need for a work of moderate length explaining the Protestant faith was enormous in the late 1550s: Calvin's *Institutes* was too imposing for the ordinary Christian, while his *Catechism* was not developed enough to provide lay persons with a manual of theology.[109] Auguste Bernus agreed with this evaluation, as did Geisendorf.[110] The most recent proponent of this view was Michel Réveillaud who argued that the four fundamental works of sixteenth-century French Protestantism were Calvin's *Institutes*, Calvin's 1542

---

109 Jean Barnaud, "La Confession de Foi de Théodore de Bèze," *Société de l'Histoire du Protestantisme Français* 48 (1899): 620.
110 Bernus, *Théodore de Bèze a Lausanne*, 72; Geisendorf, *Théodore de Bèze*, 78-79. In Baird's opinion, the *Confession* "took a classical position and was recognised, both by friend and by foe, as an authoritative exposition of the Reformed belief" (Baird, *Theodore Beza*, 269).

Catechism, Beza's *Confession*, and the Confession of Faith adopted by the French churches in 1559. Each work, he argued, addressed a particular audience: the *Institutes* comprehensively addressed all the important matters of the Christian faith; the *Catechism* and the 1559 Confession were "content to recount briefly for believers or new converts the most important elements of the Christian faith"; Beza's *Confession* occupied an intermediate place between these extremes, for it is more complete than the *Catechism* and "a sort of popularization of the *Institutes*."[111] One indication of the *Confession*'s importance was the number of times it was reprinted, even during Beza's lifetime. The first French edition of 1559 was expanded and published that same year. The French editions were reprinted several times up to 1564, but no changes were made in the text. The revised 1559 French version was translated into Latin in 1560. This Latin edition was reprinted eleven times during Beza's lifetime, up to 1599.[112] Not only was the *Confession* reprinted, and translated very quickly into Italian, Dutch, and English,[113] but it was also apparently read, at least in France, well into the seventeenth century.[114]

The prefatory letter Beza composed for the French *Confession*, gives us insight into his theological method and the situation he was addressing in this treatise. We see, first of all, that Beza originally composed this to convince his father of the truthfulness of Protestantism.[115] When he later published it for a wider audience, he intended it as a manual of instruction for pastors and lay people. Pastors needed to know how to "feed their flock with the Word of Life," and church members had to "know and understand that which is proclaimed to them, in order to be nourished and consoled by it, and in order to be put on their guard against wolves and false prophets."[116] All Christians were to read the Bible for themselves, but he feared that without a concise handbook of biblical doctrine they would not be able to relate the parts together in a

---

111 Theodore Beza, "*La Confession de Foi du Chretien* par Théodore de Bèze," ed. Michel Réveillaud, *La Revue Réformée* 6 (1955): 2.

112 Gardy, *Bibliographie*, 62. Gardy (ibid., 69) qualified Barnaud's contention ("La Confession," 632-33). Raitt pointed out that the *Confession* was not revised after 1560 (Raitt, "Theodore Beza: 1519-1605," 94).

113 Gardy, *Bibliographie*, 62; Barnaud, "La Confession," 633. See appendix one.

114 Thus in 1685, eighty years after Beza's death and 126 years after the initial publication of Beza's *Confession*, the Archbishop of Paris condemned the *Confession* in particular and prohibited his flock from reading it (Baird, *Theodore Beza*, 270; Geisendorf, *Théodore de Bèze*, 79).

115 Beza, "*La Confession de Foi du Chretien* par Théodore de Bèze," 11. Beza clearly intended to convert his father to Protestantism. In the introduction to the Latin edition of 1560 he wrote, "J'ai composé à l'origine cette *Confession de foi* en français, pour satisfaire mon père . . . et aussi, si je le pouvais, pour le gagner à Christ dans sa vieillesse avancée" (ibid., 11 n 1).

116 Beza, *The Christian Faith*, iv.

coherent fashion: "having begun to read the Texts of Scripture, they have not some brief instruction which unclouds their mind and accustoms them to the language of the Holy Spirit in order to comprehend the true sense and relate all to His purpose."[117]

To this end, in the second place, Beza explicated his theological method. He meant this book to be an introduction to, and a help in understanding, the Bible. The Bible held pride of place in his treatise. Yet as a good humanist, he was concerned to present his work in good order, as well as to check his conclusions against scholars who preceded him. He claimed he had arranged the *Confession* "in the best order" composed of all "which I have learned in the Christian Religion through the reading of the Old and New Testament, with reference to the most faithful commentators."[118] His desire, he concluded, was "that all those who will read this 'Confession' compare it carefully with the Scriptures, which are the sole and true touchstone for proving the true doctrine."[119]

Third, Beza declared that the ultimate purpose of Christian theology was twofold: to lead persons to salvation in Christ and to strengthen Christians in their faith. People had to believe the truth "for their salvation."[120] "The Kingdom of God is not a Kingdom of ignorance," Beza lamented, with reference to Rome's insistence that persons trust in whatever the church believed, "but of faith, and, consequently, of knowledge; for it is beyond the ability of anyone to believe that which he is ignorant of."[121] Fueled by this concern for persons' salvation, Beza composed this short treatise of Christian doctrine. In the preface to the Latin version Beza lauded those "who compose short and perspicuous summaries" of biblical truth so that those who "apply themselves to the reading of the Sacred Scriptures may have certain heads ready at hand, to each of which they may afterwards refer and accommodate what they read."[122] Here Beza noted that Calvin treated the same subject matter "very copiously" (*copiosissime*) in his *Institutes* and "very briefly but very accurately" (*brevissime quidem sed a curatissime*) in his 1542 Catechism. "From these books also," he declared, "I profess to have derived the present work."[123] Yet he continued, "nothing forbids that the same feast be repeated with a slight change in the arrangement, to the great enjoyment of those who partake." Specifically, he praised "short and perspicuous (*breves et perspicuas*)

---

117 Ibid., v.
118 Ibid., iv.
119 Ibid., vi.
120 Ibid., iii.
121 Ibid., iv.
122 Theodore Beza, "Autobiographical Letter of Beza to Wolmar," in Baird, *Theodore Beza*, 367.
123 Beza, "Autobiographical Letter," in Baird, 366; Beza, "Epistola" of *Confessio Christianae fidei* in *Tractationum Theologicarum* 1:βiii.

summaries," in which category he placed his *Confession*.[124] According to Beza, then, his *Confession* taught the same doctrine as Calvin had promulgated, although he was intentionally more concise than his mentor.

Like Calvin in his *Institutes*, Beza used a trinitarian outline for the contents in his *Confession*.[125] The similarity of structure with Calvin's *Institutes* is remarkable. After the short first chapter on the Trinity, the next three elaborated the different persons of the Trinity and their respective roles. The second chapter dealt with "Dieu le Père," the third with "Jésus-Christ, Fils unique de Dieu," and the fourth with "le Saint-Esprit." Like Calvin, Beza then discussed the church, the subject matter of chapter five. A unique feature of the *Confession* is Beza's final two chapters which have no structural equivalent in the *Institutes*. Chapter six on "le jugement dernier" and the seventh titled "Brieve comparaison de la doctrine de la Papauté avec celle de l'Eglise chrestienne" do not contain contents foreign to Calvin's sentiments, though. What Beza included as his seventh part, Calvin did by means of scattered invectives against Catholicism throughout the book. Beza's concern both to provide a readable guide for Christians into scriptural truth and his desire to protect them from Catholic falsehoods led him to clarify the differences between Protestantism and Catholicism; hence his seventh chapter. Beza's pastoral concern shone through in chapter six. This was no mere academic tome; rather, the Confession contained an urgent message. Eternity was in the balance, and Beza wanted persons to flee to Christ and escape the final judgment.

Because of its length, the *Confession* affords us an in-depth view of Beza's theological method. To begin with, the book is filled with biblical quotations and allusions. Having begun the book by stating that "we believe there is only one divine essence, whom we call God," Beza then gave reasons for this belief: "Not only because the contemplation of natural things teaches us these things," he said, "but *much more* because the holy Scriptures teach it to us (Deut. 4:32; Eph. 4:6)."[126] Scripture then, according to Beza, was much surer than human reason or the light of nature. At the close of the treatise, he urged his readers to compare his words to Scripture. In so doing they would see that Beza had

---

124 Beza, "Autobiographical Letter," in Baird, 367; Beza, *Tractationum Theologicarum*, 1:βiii.
125 Letham, "Saving Faith and Assurance," 1:144. Parker noted the importance of the titles of the four books of Calvin's *Institues* (T. H. L. Parker, *Calvin: An Introduction to his Thought* [Louisville, KY: John Knox Press, 1995], 6-7). He noted that the "very form is used to declare the unity and the threefoldness of the Godhead. As the first three Books correspond to the creedal witness to Father, Son and Holy Spirit, so, but less obviously, the titles of these Books testify to the unity by speaking only of 'God' and not of 'Father', 'Son', or 'Holy Spirit'" (Parker, *Calvin*, 9). See also Muller, "Predestination and Christology," 219-27.
126 Beza, "*La Confession de Foi du Chretien* par Théodore de Bèze," 15; my italics.

faithfully represented the Bible's teaching and that thus it was consistent with the best thinking: "We have good hope that whoever has read carefully and attentively all that precedes will easily understand, in comparing our doctrine with the Word of God, and with the profanity of the Papacy, on which side is the truth of God, and that the calumnies hurled at us are contrary to all reason."[127] The Bible determined, he emphasized, the doctrines taught in the *Confession*, and they were confirmed by regenerated reason.

According to Beza, antiscriptural practices marred the Roman church. The practice of setting up an authoritative pope, even though Catholics could not "show this by the express word of God," must be eschewed.[128] Only God could tell the church what to do, and he instructed through the Bible.[129] Since God spoke in Scripture, Christians must listen for "the voice of Christ" when the Bible is preached.[130] Scripture was the final arbiter in religious matters, as opposed to human reason that was impaired and often wrong. "We confess," Beza said, "that we have no desire to be more wise than Jesus Christ, and that we leave to the flesh and to the world their wisdom."[131] So Beza implored his readers to consider his claims: "whoever has read carefully and attentively all that precedes will easily understand, in comparing our doctrine with the Word of God, and with the profanity of the Papacy, on which side is the truth of God, and that the calumnies hurled at us are contrary to all reason."[132] For Beza, then, the Bible determined theological truth since Christ spoke authoritatively in it.

Beza did not denigrate the history of the church, though. For him, as for the Protestant Reformers in general, church tradition was important, but not determinative. For example, ecclesiastical councils were right as far as they "decided according to the holy Scripture."[133] Throughout his treatise Beza referred to Augustine especially and to a few other fathers as authorities on his side in various debates. Beza referenced several church fathers to buttress his views, but usually by qualifying where exactly their authority lay. Thus, while attempting to set forth the doctrine that all persons' natures were corrupt and opposed to God in their natural state and having already marshaled his biblical support in favor of this, Beza said, "This is why St. Augustine said,

---

127 Beza, *The Christian Faith*, 121.
128 Beza, "*La Confession de Foi du Chretien* par Théodore de Bèze," 91 ("on ne saurait rien montrer de cela par la Parole expresse de Dieu").
129 Ibid., 109 ("c'est à un seul Dieu de declarer ce qui est péché contre lui, ou ce qui ne l'est pas, parce que c'est lui seul qui a la puissance sur notre conscience et sur notre foi").
130 Ibid., 120 ("il nous faut écouter la voix de Christ, même s'il nous parle par des mercenaires et des ministres de mouvaise vie").
131 Ibid., 104.
132 Ibid., 121.
133 Ibid., 15 ("l'Eglise en a décidé par la sainte Ecriture").

conformably to Scripture, that human nature was deprived of its liberty" since its will was vanquished by the corruption to which it yielded.[134] Augustine was authoritative as long as he spoke "according to Scripture."[135] Beza was loathe to pass over the wisdom of those who preceded him, but tradition possessed authority only when the church had spoken "by the Word of God."[136] Following this, Beza argued for the primacy of the Bible over tradition: "one must take this middle course: on the one hand, not to easily scorn the determination of the councils . . . on the other hand, not to be attached to them to the point of not always reserving to the Word of God its . . . entire authority; because, by itself, it is clear and fluent enough to found and prove the main points of religion."[137] For Beza, then, Scripture was perspicuous and authoritative.

Although Beza claimed to derive his doctrine from the Bible, he was logical in the presentation of that doctrine. Nowhere in the *Confession*, perhaps, is his logic shown more clearly than in his discussion of the character of God and the creation of man. Beza said first that God was perfectly righteous. "It follows" ("il s'ensuit") that he must punish injustice. But since God is also merciful, "il s'ensuit" that the good he does to men comes from grace. And since God's decrees are immutable, "il s'ensuit" that all that happens to persons was ordained by God eternally. But, Beza argued, this did not prevent the use of secondary causes; rather "it establishes secondary causes by which all these things happen," "because" God determined not only what would happen, but also what means he would use to make it happen. "Therefore," even though the causes themselves might be evil, God's decree is holy. Some will be saved and others damned, for God's glory ("as all the Scripture testifies"). "It follows therefore" that God eternally decreed to create persons to manifest his glory, in saving some by his grace and in judging others. "To execute this decree, it was necessary that God create man good and pure."[138] "It was also necessary" that humans should be created mutable and choose to sin, "because" if sin had not

---

134 Ibid., 22 ("C'est pourquoi saint Augustin disait, conformément à l'Ecriture. . .").
135 Ibid., 28 ("saint Augustin, suivant l'Ecriture, a très bien dit. . . ." In a similar fashion, Beza marshaled Bernard to his side when explicating his view of the importance of faith; but Bernard was an authority because his explanation of the centrality of faith was spoken "conformably to all of Scripture"). Cf., "saint Bernard disait conformément à toute l'Ecriture. . ." (ibid., 31).
136 Ibid., 29 ("l'Eglise a très bien decide, par la Parole de Dieu, contre Macédonius. . .").
137 Ibid., 106. Beza followed this assertion with two extended quotations from Augustine and one from Ambrose, who said, "tout ce qui ne provident pas de la doctrine des apôtres est plein de méchancetés et de malheureusetés" ("everything that does not spring from the apostles' doctrine is full of wickedness and disaster") (ibid., 108).
138 Ibid., 20.

entered into the world in this manner, God would not have been able to magnify his mercy in saving those who were guilty.[139] But fallen human reason was fallible. In another place, therefore, Beza maintained that human ratiocination was often wrong concerning the powers of the human will: "Accordingly Scripture defines what is good quite differently from human reason. For Scripture, the nature of unregenerate man (that is to say, of a man who is not restored and as recreated by grace) is not only damaged, it is also totally corrupted and voluntarily enslaved to sin." At this point, Beza quoted Augustine for confirmation of his view that the unbeliever "sins necessarily, but all the time voluntarily."[140] But Augustine merely agreed with the authoritative Scriptures in Beza's scheme. For Beza, therefore, reason and logic had a place, although he argued they must be subsumed under Scripture's clear teaching.[141]

Beza's humanistic methodology, with its biblical emphasis, served his pastoral intention. In the *Confession*, his most systematic treatise, Beza clearly set forth his eschatological view of reality. Satan and God were active in a spiritual battle, and heaven and hell were in the balance for his readers. For example, the Roman church, Beza claimed, was under the devil's control, for God "has not willed to loosen the reins of Satan" there.[142] In fact, Beza argued, all the false practices in the Catholic church "proceed from the spirit of the Devil," for "Satan can do no better than to pass off his synagogue for the true Church."[143] Related to Beza's methodological focus on Scripture, Satan was dangerous within the Roman fold because he had subverted the rule of the Bible there. This removed salvation from that church, for redemption was only found within the Bible. "The principal difference is," Beza averred, "concerning the substance of the doctrine wherein consists our salvation. . . . the black is not more contrary to the white, than the religion of the Papists is to this religion of the church of God. . . . their religion proceeded from the Prince

---

139 Ibid., 19-20.
140 Ibid., 8 ("Il pèche nécessairement, mais toutefois volontairement").
141 Beza showed this clearly in his discussion of the doctrine of eternal judgment. He complained about the wrongheadedness of those who speculated too much about both heaven and hell. Such speculations were beyond human understanding. Human speculations must be quiet before God's truth in Scripture: "les fantaisies enrages de ceux qui pensent pouvoir determiner quand ce jour viendra, les speculations de vieilles touchant l'Antéchrist, les joies du paradis et les peines de l'enfer . . . mais aussi que nous détestons de tout notre coeur. Car nous disons qu'il n'est pas permis de sonder les choses caches, et de mêler nos imaginations avec la vérité de Dieu. . . . Il nous suffit de savoir que la joie que nous espérons est incomprehensible (I Cor. 2:9), et que le tourment prepare à tous les infidels est eternel" (ibid., 120).
142 Ibid., 64.
143 Ibid., 89, 72.

of darkness" as is shown by the fact "that they will not have the word of God to be used and understood of all people, and also that they juggle forth all their mysteries for an unknown tongue."[144]

Beza's ultimate pastoral concern was that the treatise's readers experience salvation in Jesus Christ. This, indeed, explained his complaint with Rome, specifically the Catholic neglect of Scripture. Their denigration of the Bible's authority was awful, because if the apostles had ignored even "one thing that was necessary for salvation," who would be so impudent as to claim he knew what it was? Besides, Christ taught the opposite. Besides, "by what means would they [the apostles] have been saved themselves" if more was necessary for salvation than to believe the apostolic writings. Therefore, to be saved, persons must "confess that they [the apostles] knew and understood distinctly the whole doctrine of salvation."[145] Again he declared "let us doubt not that the apostles not only preached, but also left by their writings the whole Word of God necessary for salvation."[146] For Beza, then, the argument over the locus of authority in the church was not merely an issue of semantics; eternity was in the balance for persons within the church. In other words, according to Theodore Beza in his *Confession*, theology is of the utmost importance for it would usher persons into either heaven or hell. All theology is pastoral.

Altera brevis fidei confessio *(1559)*

To the earliest edition of his *Confession* in 1559 Beza appended *Autre Briefve Confession de Foy, de mesmes la precedente, & par le mesme autheur*.[147] We know almost nothing about the origin of the *Short Confession*.[148] We may surmise that Beza's concern was to state succinctly the contents of his longer

---

144 Theodore Beza, *A Briefe and Pithie Summe of Christian Faith, Made in Form of a Confession, with a Confutation of al Such Superstitious Errors, as are Contrairy Thereunto* (London: Roger Ward, 1589), 232.
145 Beza, "*La Confession de Foi du Chretien* par Théodore de Bèze," 85 ("si les apôtres ont ignore une chose qui soit exigée pour le salut, quel sera l'homme qui pourra dire, sans une impudence extreme, qu'il en a la connaissance? Et comment demeurera vrai ce que dit Christ qui affirme le contraire [Jean 14:26; 16:13]? Et, qui plus est, par quel moyen auraient-ils été sauvés eux-mêmes? Il reste donc nécessairement le devoir de confesser qu'ils ont connu et entendu distinctement toute la doctrine du salut").
146 Ibid., 73 ("Et ne doutons pas que les apôtres non seulement aient prêché, mais aussi qu'ils aient laissé par écrit tout ce qui est Parole de Dieu nécessaire au salut").
147 Theodore Beza, *Confession de la foi Chrestienne, faite par Theodore de Besze, contenant la confirmation, d'icelle, et la refutation des superstitions contraires: Reveue et augmentee de nouveau par lui, avec un abregé d'icille* (n.p.: Conrad Badius, 1559), 249-67.
148 See Gardy, *Bibliographie*, 72-73.

Confession, since he specifically said the *Short Confession* contained the same doctrine as that which preceded it. Here in thirty-four articles Beza outlined the doctrine which Christians should believe in order to be sustained and protected in the midst of the spiritual battle. Since this is the shortest comprehensive theological statement that Beza produced, we will spend some time delineating the logical flow of the *Short Confession*, and note what Beza emphasized and what he disregarded.[149]

The main point of the *Short Confession* was to show persons how they might obtain salvation through Jesus Christ. In his summary, Beza noted that his burden had been to clarify the doctrine of salvation and make clear that salvation was only found in the true church.

> Behold in sum what is the doctrine of our salvation through Jesus Christ only, by the means of our faith. And whosoever receives this doctrine, the which cannot be, but where there is faithfully preached, and the sacraments truly ministered, according to the order established by the word of God, is a member of the church of Jesus Christ, which is called catholic, that is to say universal, and out of that church is no salvation. Moreover, all congregations and assemblies whatsoever they be, which have not those marks, although they call themselves the church of Jesus Christ a thousand times, whatsoever place or succession they allege or show forth, can be no other but the synagogue of Satan, where there is but damnation. And therefore it is good and needful for all men to separate themselves, and depart from them according as St. Peter said, "Save yourselves from this perverse generation," speaking of Aaron's successors, and of the church of Jerusalem.[150]

To Beza, this discussion had eternal consequences, for one's eternal state depended on whether or not he was within the bounds of the true church. Beza was not being merely rhetorical when he condemned the false church as "the synagogue of Satan," for here Satan was active in opposing God's means of salvation. Consequently in this false church "there is but damnation."[151]

The structure of the treatise is quite simple. Salvation is its thrust. Beza began with the character of God and sinful humanity. He then discussed the efficacious nature of Christ's atonement and what trusting in Christ for salvation meant. Finally, after discussing the Spirit's role in bringing about faith, Beza explained ways a person's faith should increase. Beza's goal was salvation for his readers.

An overview of the movement of the *Short Confession* demonstrates Beza's salvific thrust throughout the treatise. He began, then, by showing the plight of sinners. Since "God is perfectly right, wise and just, and all men wholly and altogether sinners," in order for God to forgive sinners, he must either deny his

---

149 See also Muller, "Predestination and Christology," 198.
150 Beza, *Briefe and Pithie Summe*, 344-45.
151 Ibid.

perfect character or satisfy his eternal justice fully.[152] All persons should love God supremely, but their sinful natures cause them to despise him. Thus, Beza said, "it follows necessarily, that either all men without exception must be condemned, or else find someone that will pay their debts."[153] But no creature could serve this function.

Thus, in the second part of the treatise (articles seven through eleven), Beza explained why only Christ could be the savior from sins. The savior must be the God-man: "For if he is not mightier than any creature, that is to say, very God, he cannot bear the burden of the wrath and anger of God, but should himself be overwhelmed under it, then much less could he satisfy for others. And if he is but a man, how should he deliver man by his satisfaction? It is necessary then that a mediator be found who is God and man, and such a one is Jesus Christ."[154] Christ is fully God and fully man. Therefore he is the perfect mediator between God and man. Applying this truth to his readers, Beza exhorted them: "Therefore we may with good right conclude that we find only in Jesus Christ perfect remedies against all the evils that do or might frighten our conscience, or keep us from coming to the glory of God, or might cause us justly to be condemned to eternal death."[155]

However, Beza noted in the next six articles that knowing this true doctrine does one no good if one does not trust in Jesus Christ for salvation, "For as it profits not a sick person to have a good medicine except he use it, nor a hungry man to be at a table's end garnished with plenty of good meats, except he eat of them, likewise are the remedies of Jesus Christ against the wrath of God and eternal death set before us in vain, except we use them."[156] To partake of this remedy, first, persons must see how Jesus' death for sinners is of advantage to them; and, second, they must see how they can take hold of this salvation. Then Beza showed that the central idea taught throughout Old Testament history had been God's desire to save persons by the Savior to come. Satan hated this, however, and tried to suppress it. But God had the Old Testament written down so the truth would be known: "because God knew that the devil would move and stir up false prophets, who would spread forth their lies as the true commandments of God, he willed Moses and the prophets to write all that God revealed to them, to the end that the false prophets should not so easily deceive the people."[157] The Bible, then, was written to teach salvation in Jesus and to be ammunition for Christians in the spiritual battle with Satan. And God's revelation included the New Testament:

---

152 Ibid., 324.
153 Ibid., 325.
154 Ibid., 326.
155 Ibid., 328.
156 Ibid.
157 Ibid., 330.

Jesus Christ . . . willed his doctrine not only to be preached by the mouth of the apostles and evangelists, but also that their hands should unite in such wise, that the church should have to the end of the world one certain doctrine, upon which she might stay and rest, and also by it might separate most clearly the lies of the false prophets and antichrists from the only verity of God, which is comprehended wholly and perfectly in the books of the Old and New Testaments, so that it is not lawful to change anything, either add to it, or take from it.[158]

Biblical doctrine was a safeguard for the church—its "stay and rest"—against the schemes of Satan.

Yet biblical truth would avail nothing if the Holy Spirit did not work in the hearts of sinners to make them embrace it, Beza argued in the following seven articles. When pastors preach and exhort sinners, "it is as if they spoke unto insensible stones." Therefore, Beza continued, "we must know that as God works to the external senses by his word pronounced by his ministers, even so he works inwardly by his infinite power, that is to say, by his Holy Spirit."[159] First, the Holy Spirit convicted the ungodly of their sin before God. Then he applied the gospel to them by enlightening their understanding to comprehend the gospel and by granting them faith in Jesus. Third, the Spirit sanctified those who put their trust in Jesus: first, by enlightening the mind so that the believer likes what he previously thought was foolish; second, by transforming the Christian's will, making him hate sin and causing him to love righteousness.[160]

Then Beza explicated the two means the Holy Spirit used to grow Christians in their faith. First of all, he employed the Bible, for "as it is created in us by the Holy Ghost, through the means of the word of God, which is sown in our hearts, and for that cause is compared to seed, so likewise it is nourished and increased by the same word, when we hear it diligently and truly preached in the church of God, and also when we read it in our houses, and think upon it diligently, and meditate in it day and night, forsaking all human and worldly affections, which might turn us from God, and hold us in worldliness."[161] In the second place, the Holy Spirit used the two sacraments of baptism and the Lord's Supper to grow Christians in the faith:

> God aids and helps our debility and weakness in such sort, that being not content to declare unto us by his word with what love he loves us in his Son, Jesus Christ, but would also join to his word certain outward marks and signs, to which also he added certain ceremonies or manner of doings, representing (by a certain manner) to our eyes, and giving into our hands his Son, Jesus Christ, with all his goodness

---

158 Ibid., 331.
159 Ibid., 332.
160 Ibid., 335-36.
161 Ibid., 336-37.

and virtues . . . to the end that our faith being aided and supported by these helps, should be more confirmed in us, to draw us nearer to Jesus Christ.[162]

We should note several things about Beza's *Short Confession*. First of all, there are lacunae. Beza assumed, but did not defend, the authority of the Bible to his readers, for instance. Nor did he discuss predestination. In fact, he only hinted at it in the eighteenth article where he said that unless the Holy Spirit awakened sinners they would not hear or embrace the preaching of the gospel. In the second place, the *Short Confession*'s structure makes it clear that Beza was primarily concerned with presenting the doctrine of salvation for his readers. Written to counter the Roman Catholic idea that salvation was dispensed through the church's authority and its sacraments, Beza's work was no mere dry scholastic tome. It breathed his passion for the glory of God and for sinners to be reconciled to God by faith in Jesus. The *Short Confession* is thus a notable example of Beza's pastoral theology.

Quaestionum et responsionum *(1570)*

Nothing is known about the origin of the *Quaestionum et responsionum Christianarum libellus*.[163] The treatise consists of 214 theological questions put to Beza by an anonymous interrogator and Beza's often very detailed responses. The length of the responses is an indication that they were not meant to be memorized.[164] The questions, if not written by Beza, were at least arranged in a very well-defined structure to make his argument.[165] He was very

---

162 Ibid., 338.
163 See Geisendorf, *Théodore de Bèze*, 280. Bray argued that this treatise mirrored the structure of Calvin's thought: "One begins by considering the question of our knowledge of God and then moves on to our knowledge of man." He maintained this was especially clear from its first point where Beza "poses the precise questions with which Calvin began his Catechism of 1542/45," even though Beza changed the order (Bray, *Beza's Doctrine*, 76). Beza lauded Calvin's catechism, so it is not striking that he would follow Calvin's structure here.
164 Summers suggested that it was more akin to medieval and Renaissance theological expositions (Kirk M. Summers, "Questions and Responses," in Beza, *Little Book of Christian Questions and Responses*, 3).
165 An internal indication of this claim comes in question 192 where, in the midst of attempting to delineate the exact difference between "permission" and "will" in the doctrine of God's decree, Beza urged the questioner: "I wish that the chief points be brought up by you, so that I can respond to them individually" (Beza, *Little Book of Christian Questions and Responses*, 82). Additionally in question 107, after a long digression on the way corruption was spread through the human race and as a means to return to a discussion of the way of salvation through Christ, Beza's interlocutor said, "Therefore, now let us return to the remedy of that evil, which is

selective in the doctrines he treated. For instance, he did not examine the doctrine of the church at all. I contend that the *Quaestionum et responsionum* explicates his doctrine of salvation more than any of the other four systematic works of Beza.[166] I think Beza's intention in penning this detailed theological treatise was to show persons how they could be saved eternally.[167]

The treatise manifests Beza's salvific focus. Heinrich Heppe was wrong to judge this, along with his *Confession*, to be Beza's most complete work of theology.[168] In its most recent English translation, Beza devoted one page to the doctrine Scripture, two pages to the doctrine of God, fifty-eight pages to Jesus and salvation, and thirty-two pages to the relationship of God's sovereignty to salvation.[169] These internal factors suggest that Beza intended this to be a discourse on soteriology.

This soteriological focus is starker when one examines the logical structure of the work. Beza argued along the following lines. First, he said, God created humans so that he might receive glory in giving salvation to persons. But we can only learn of this through the Bible, when the Holy Spirit helps us to understand those things necessary for salvation. First of all, one must know that God is a Trinity of three persons, but this knowledge will not lead to salvation. Rather, one must know that God possesses perfect justice and perfect mercy. The death of the Son highlighted the Father's love. The efficacy of Christ's death for sin was verified by his resurrection and ascension. Now, Christ reigns in heaven and there he intercedes for the church; this intercession will continue until he consummates his Kingdom. At that time persons will either be consigned to eternal hell or be received into heaven for eternity. But the only way to attain this salvation is through placing faith in Christ. Christ's righteousness is imputed to believers; they then receive the benefits of wisdom, justification, sanctification, and redemption. Then Beza discussed how God's sovereignty related to individual salvation. First of all, God sovereignly ruled all that happened in the world; yet although God decreed evil, he was not culpable for it. At this point, persons need to submit to God's revelation in Scripture and not judge it by human reason; ultimately God's providence is a mystery. Next, God actively predestined those to whom he would give faith in Christ. Although God was sovereign even over the reprobate, they and not he

---

receiving Christ by faith alone" (ibid., 39-40). Beza was clearly moving the discussion along at this point.

166 I agree with Muller who maintained that "the treatise demonstrates a primarily soteriological concern" (Muller, "Predestination and Christology," 195).

167 Summers's contention that the *Quaestionum et responsionum* "certainly stands as the crowning achievement of Beza's career" is overstated (see Summers, "Questions and Responses," 3).

168 See Geisendorf, *Théodore de Bèze*, 280.

169 See Beza, *Little Book of Christian Questions and Responses*.

were the ones responsible for their damnation. In conclusion, Beza instructed believers about how they could find assurance of their salvation and exhorted them to persevere in their faith.

The *Quaestionum et responsionum* shows Beza's theological method in great detail. The work was structured very logically. Some of the answers were quite detailed and were clearly not derived from Scripture. Yet, according to Beza, the teachings of Scripture, even those which seemed to be contrary to human reason, were to be received humbly and authoritatively by persons. The Bible was the supreme authority in the formation of doctrine. At times its contents and ideas could be advanced through human logic, but on other occasions reason merely had to accept its teachings humbly.

Although Beza employed tight logic, his dialectic was buttressed by Scripture. For example, he employed the illustration of two counter-moving wheels to help explain the relationship of God's decree to evil.[170] Similarly, Beza argued that Scripture's teaching of differing degrees of punishment for the damned suggested conversely that there would be various levels of glory for the saved commensurate with their diligence in serving Christ, "for the rationale of contraries requires it" (*id poscit eadem contrariorum ratio*). He then noted his biblical support for such a notion: "what the apostle said, that those who have sown sparsely, will reap sparsely, does not seem to refer to temporal blessings only."[171] Finally, after referencing the dictum that "the end is the first intention of the doer," to show God's sovereignty over both election and reprobation, Beza quickly deferred to the Bible as the ultimate authority: "lest we seem to wander outside of our bounds, that is, to employ only arguments of consequence, first I say that all doctrines which strive against the analogy of faith . . . are shattered by the Scriptures. Then I say, that as often as the Scriptures make mention of the predestination of the elect . . . the rest must be understood to be predestined to death."[172]

Beza's theological method was driven by his doctrine of anthropology. The Bible was authoritative doctrinally because human reason opposed God. Human ratiocination, he averred, "always falls short, until it is regenerated; for first even when it knows and discerns the good, it nevertheless does not know and discern as it needs and ought, on account of the original corruption which the philosophers are not ever able to suspect. Then, in many even serious matters, not only does it not discern the truth, but also utterly and of set purpose fights the truth" because this reason was connected to the sinful human heart so

---

170 Ibid., 68-69. But even this illustration, which was suggested by his marginal reference to Ezekiel 1:5, was soon backed up with a lengthy exposition of Scripture's teaching on this doctrine (ibid., 69-71). The Bible was the supreme authority in theological argumentation.
171 Ibid., 62; Beza, *Tractationum Theologicarum* 1:675.
172 Beza, *Little Book of Christian Questions and Responses*, 85, 86.

that it is "both blind and stubborn."[173] So, Beza exclaimed, "Away with that reason which, not only is not initiated by the Word of God, but also is openly set against it!"[174] The human heart, tied as it was to fallen affections, was to blame. It was "not the fault of the Holy Scriptures, in which plainly and clearly enough the true dogmas of religion are explained."[175]

To counter fallen human reasoning, God had given the Bible that Christians must try to understand and submit to. The teaching of Scripture is the limit of our knowledge: "Those who investigate [the exact details of hell and heaven] do sin in vain, not only because the curiosity which drives us to seek out the things which the Lord has hidden from us must be condemned, but also because it is of extreme madness to want to comprehend that which you are not capable of comprehending." Instead of this fruitless speculation, Beza exhorted his readers: "let us acquiesce in those things which the Lord has revealed to us in His word concerning these matters, that the future happiness of the godly and the unhappiness of the ungodly will be so great that the manner and measure of neither is able to be comprehended."[176] So Beza condemned unchecked rationalism.[177]

Finally, Beza's pastoral vision was a prominent part of this treatise. Satan was active in the world, Beza asserted, especially in promoting heresy within the church. For instance, those who denied that Christ was a Mediator in both his human and divine natures were "an instrument of the Devil, united to impede the work of the Lord."[178] Responding to those who taught that original sin was not part of the core of the person, but merely rested "in accidents or qualities" (*in accidentibus sive qualitatibus*), Beza argued that the Devil's schemes and fallen persons' sin united to promote this heresy: "These are the thoughts of inept men," he said, "and likewise did Satan once deceive certain men, who wished to bend Christian dogmas to the norm of their own foolish reason."[179] In addition, Beza charged Satan with convincing people that they had to obtain salvation through their own efforts: "I do not, I think, perceive

---

173 Ibid., 55, 57.
174 Ibid., 23.
175 Ibid., 57. Additionally, disagreements among Christians could be explained by the fact that until they arrived in heaven all believers are only partly regenerated. Their hearts, therefore, still have dark and rebellious parts (ibid., 57).
176 Ibid., 28.
177 When speaking of the mystery the apostle Paul said existed when persons were united to Christ by faith, Beza commented: "Rightly, then, does one warn that we should instead labor to feel Christ living in us, than seek the rationale of this communication in us, which surpasses our capacity, although we know that it is spiritual and that it is done by the instrument of faith" (ibid., 42). Whatever these are, they are not the sentiments of a cold scholastic.
178 Ibid., 19.
179 Ibid., 31; Beza, *Tractationum Theologicarum* 1:664.

your craftiness," he commented to his interlocutor, "but that of Satan. For since he is not able to utterly take away the glory of our salvation from Christ, therefore he tries at least to tear away some small bit of it."[180]

Because of his eschatological vision, Beza had great pastoral concern that was evident throughout this treatise. The thrust of the work was to show persons how they could obtain salvation, by displaying the dangers of hell and the surpassing glory of heaven. So Beza spent most of his time explaining the value of the work of Christ, showing that Christ's death was able to save persons apart from any of their works. Finally, scattered throughout the treatise Beza pointed out the way in which readers might obtain assurance of their salvation. Beza's pastoral vision drove this "scholastic" dialogue, showing he was a humanist methodologically and a pastor at heart.

Petit Catéchisme *(1575)*

In 1575 Beza published his *Petit Catéchisme*. The history of this short primer is mysterious. Neither Geisendorf nor Clavier mentioned it, and Baird only noted it in passing.[181] Gardy noted that the catechism was not originally published separately, but was appended to Calvin's larger catechism.[182] The mystery behind this work lies in the question, Why did Beza publish a catechism since he held Calvin's catechism in such high regard?

In the preface to his 1559 French *Confession* Beza may have given some clues, though, about why he was led sixteen years later to compose his own catechism. The practice of the early church had been to instruct the faithful in the Apostles' Creed, he claimed. Since that time, he maintained, "When it pleased God to raise again the banner of his church which a long time had been thrown down, this custom, not only very laudable but also absolutely necessary, has been re-established in honor, and even commended more than ever."[183] Then Beza went on to praise Calvin's 1542 catechism, a work, he claimed, "which gives an abridged knowledge of all the Christian religion" better than any other work available.[184] Yet Beza did not think Calvin's catechism was sacrosanct. He confessed that he published his *Confession* because he wanted to treat in greater detail the topics Calvin had addressed. He did not think that he was disagreeing with any of Calvin's teachings, but that his treatise met a need which Calvin's shorter work did not, since "men use heavenly food as they use that which is for the nourishment of the body; the same food prepared will

---

180 Ibid., 58.
181 Baird, *Theodore Beza*, 271.
182 Gardy, *Bibliographie*, 167.
183 Beza, *"La Confession de Foi du Chretien* par Théodore de Bèze," 11-12.
184 Ibid., 12 ("un ouvrage donnant une connaissance abrégée de toute la religion chrétienne, tel que le 'catéchisme de cette église'").

please some when it is prepared in one fashion, but for others it must be prepared in another fashion."[185] This may at least hint to the direction that Beza felt years later to compose a simpler catechism than Calvin's, a catechism easier to memorize because of its brevity but which nonetheless expressed his predecessor's doctrine faithfully.

The focus of Beza's catechism is salvation.[186] In the first question Beza stated what the goal of the work was: he was concerned that his readers be in a right relationship with God and honor him in that sphere.[187] Thus he was concerned not with doctrinal knowledge for intellectual purposes alone. Wanting his readers to be in a relationship with God, Beza's pastoral concern was evident. Indeed, this salvific thrust was evident throughout the entire catechism. In the second section, Beza said he hoped to die in the Christian faith, apparently because in it alone could he have salvation.[188] The third section's content was Jesus Christ, who, Beza stated at length, became a man to die for persons' sins. He argued in section four that most refuse the salvation that is offered them in Christ; only those who are God's elect put their faith in the Savior.[189] Importantly, Beza mentioned God's election only here in the catechism to explain why it was that only some persons trusted in Christ; those who did not come to Christ for forgiveness were held responsible for their unbelief.[190] Sections five and six fleshed out the relationship between justification and sanctification. Although Beza spelled out some of the fruits that were necessary in order to assure one of salvation, his repeated emphasis was that these works did not save, but were indicators that the one performing them had already been saved.[191] The final four sections of the catechism explained the means that the Holy Spirit used to bring persons to salvation in Christ and keep them there. He usually employed preaching, prayer, and the use

---

185 Ibid. ("les homes usent des mets célestes, comme ils usent de ceux qui concernent la nourriture du corps; les mêmes mets plairont aux uns accommodés d'une façon, aux autres, accommodés d'une autre façon").
186 See Muller, "Predestination and Christology," 196-98.
187 "Qu. 1. Why has God placed us in this world? A. To know and serve him" (Beza, *A Little Catechisme*, A1r).
188 "Qu. 6. Do you then believe in one only God, the Father, the Son, and the Holy Ghost? A. Yes. And by God's goodness, will die in this faith" (ibid., A2v).
189 "Qu. 5. Does this faith come of ourselves? A. No, but from the only grace and goodness of God, who does freely give it to his elect and chosen ones" (ibid., n.p.).
190 "Qu. 1. Shall all the world be saved? A. No, for the greater part of the world refuse their salvation" (ibid., n.p.). This is the same logical place that Calvin's discussion of predestination occupied in his *Institutes* 3.21-24.
191 "Qu. 6. Good works then make us not God's children? A. No, for contrariwise, a man must first be the child of God before he can do good works. But this is a mark or badge whereby a man may know the children of God" (ibid., n.p.).

of the sacraments.[192] The overwhelming thrust of Beza's catechism, then, was to teach persons how they might experience salvation in Christ. A secondary emphasis, in the second half of the catechism, was to point out to believers how they could be assured of their salvation. Salvation and assurance were the key themes.

Several observations are relevant at this point. First of all, Beza's concern throughout the catechism was pastoral. This was not meant first and foremost to be a detailed doctrinal treatise, but rather a means of instructing persons about how they could obtain salvation in Christ and how they could be certain of that salvation. The final words in the catechism show this: "God give us all grace to go to it, to his honor and glory, and to our salvation. So be it."[193] God's glory and his readers' salvation were Beza's expressed reasons for composing this short work. Second, the catechetical form limited Beza's methodology. He did not include Scripture citations within the answers to the questions, nor did he include Bible references after them. His method was intentionally logical and didactic, but that does not mean that his method disregarded the authority of the Bible. Indeed, after stating the purpose of the catechism in the first question, Beza laid out to his readers, in the next six questions, where they could obtain the knowledge to know how they might know and serve God: it was found in the Bible alone, which comprised the Law and the Gospel. In the third place, the doctrine of God's predestination played little role in the catechism. Beza only mentioned it two times: in the fourth section to show why some believed in the Savior and others did not, as well as in the sixth section to draw out the fact that only those who have first been chosen by God can do any good works. Fourth, Beza strove to show the relationship of his catechism with the church's doctrine throughout the ages: the Apostles' Creed summarized Christian belief about God in section one and about Jesus in section three. Finally, Beza was very concerned to show his readers how to be assured of their salvation. To this end, he attempted to clarify the relationship between justification and sanctification at length and then showed the way in which the sacraments functioned to provide assurance of salvation for Christians.

Conclusion

This chapter has established that for Beza all theology, by definition, was pastoral. Beza's pastoral theology was built upon the foundation of his eschatological vision that noted a spiritual battle between God and Satan. In

---

192 "Qu. 1. The Holy Ghost then is he which makes us the children of God. But what instruments or means does he ordinarily and commonly use to bring us to that honor and keep us in the same? A. The preaching of the word, prayer, and the use of the sacraments" (ibid., n.p.).

193 Ibid., n.p.

light of this battle, persons needed to receive revelation from God. And they have, because God has spoken in his word, the Bible. This accounts for the word-centeredness of all of Beza's theology. Yet because persons are sinful they will not understand the word unless God by his Spirit gives them grace to receive and understand that word. This accounts for the pneumatological emphasis of Beza's theology. Still, persons must interpret God's word correctly, since God spoke through normal human language. This accounts for Beza's emphasis on correct biblical interpretation. That is why I termed Beza a pastoral humanist, one who was concerned to understand the Bible using proper interpretive techniques in order to hear from God in the midst of the spiritual battle.

I demonstrated this pastoral humanism in Beza's theology from a key sermon he preached as well as from several other of his pastoral writings. Then, from a careful examination of Beza's four most systematic theological productions, I showed that the ultimate point of all of these writings was to lead his readers to salvation in Jesus Christ. That is, these systematic works were soteriological. This demonstrates, I contend, that for Theodore Beza all theology is pastoral.

It remains to show the way in which Beza applied the doctrine of God's sovereignty to his parishioners in light of the ongoing spiritual battle. I will show that for Beza this doctrine, a theological position that often has been maligned as being esoteric, was intensely practical. In fact, it was vital for healthy Christian living during the earthly pilgrimage. It is to this task that we turn in the next chapter.

Chapter 4

God's Sovereignty for His People: Comfort in the Spiritual Battle

God's limitless sovereignty was an anchor for weary souls. Theodore Beza drew comfort from this truth throughout his life. Nowhere, perhaps, is this clearer than in his prayer "upon eternal death." Here we see Beza, the affectionate Christian, trusting in his Lord's control over all things:

> I will not, neither can I ascend higher than your word teaches me, to enquire wherefore you would not so establish the blessed being of this the greatest and chief of your visible works, that he might not fall. I have matter enough to occupy the strength of my soul, to meditate upon, to have in detestation, yes even before your majesty to accuse the pride of our nature, which thought not itself in honor sufficient, unless it were equal with your deity, freeing itself from all fear, and obedience unto you, and by that rash ingratitude cast himself headlong from innocence into sin, from life into temporal and eternal death. To you, O Lord, belongs righteousness, and to man confusion and shame. And you, after your good pleasure, show mercy to whom you will show mercy. The vain philosophy, and foolish curiosity, which is not content with the simplicity of Christian faith, retained within the limits of your sacred oracles, shall make much enquiry about this fall of Adam, to the end, if she could, to penetrate into your secret counsel, about the creation and end of your works. Yes even in that which touches the election and reprobation of mankind she dares in the bottomless pit to discourse of your infinite justice, and the argument of your incomprehensible glory . . . with her terrestrial conceits, for to declare in her imaginations, your grace to the elect, and your judgment against the reprobate, daring to plead their cause, as also she will resolve of their estate after this life, and of the quality of their punishment.
>
> But your children, O heavenly Father, instructed by your doctrine through the light of your Spirit, will in their hearts humbly reverence your decrees, which are always just, even in the first condemnation of all mankind, and will be content to magnify your goodness, for the grace that it has pleased you to bestow upon them in Jesus Christ, adopting them by him of your free mercy into your family. For they have learned in your school that the inaccessible brightness of your judgments dazzle the best sighted minds and spirits, yes wastes and consumes them when they presume to approach to enquire the secret causes. This do I know, neither will I know any more, that all things do work for the best of your elect, because that having known them before all ages, you have also predestinated them to be made conformable to the image of your Son, called and justified them to be glorified. The vessels of wrath prepared to perdition, do feel none of these free

mercies and celestial riches, whereof it comes, that when they think upon death, they see nothing but fearful, horrible, damnable, all intolerable pain, without diminution or end, an infernal devilish, and endless torment, a gnashing of teeth, with blasphemy and despair, a perpetual disquiet both in body and soul, an eternity to their woe and damnation; and which is worse, a most merciful God, whom they shall know to be in heaven, and yet not to be their God, but their adversary, and sovereign Judge, to be as severe and rigorous to them, as he shall be gentle and favorable to his children. This is in sum, all that the reprobate may expect or hope for in death. . . . these miserable men depart this their earthly habitation, with great grief and trembling, ... [T]he proof that they are going to make, of the eternal torments with the devils in the burning lake of fire and brimstone, which is never quenched, given to the soul presently upon the temporal death, and to both body and soul in the day of the resurrection of all flesh, I say in the second and eternal death, a death which continues without dying. . . . this pain is not the least to the damned . . . that they never have any motion of the Spirit to repent or convert unto you the only and true God.[1]

According to Theodore Beza, God's sovereignty was essential for Christians in the midst of the spiritual turmoil of this life. God's sovereignty was neither a philosophical doctrine of fatalism nor a misanthropic desire to consign the bulk of humanity to perdition. It was, rather, a necessity given the facts of demonic persecution and human weakness. Only the omnipotent Sovereign could uphold his people on earth during their pilgrimage to heaven.

For Beza the doctrine of God's complete sovereignty was intensely pastoral. Knowledge of God's supreme control over all aspects of life was a great need of Christians. Only such truth could comfort them in the midst of the numerous troubles of life. In order to develop this thesis in the present chapter, I will examine Beza's pastoral doctrines of providence and predestination. After briefly noting the contours of his doctrine of providence, I will specifically point out the way that Beza stressed this doctrine in various genres of treatises. Two of his works, the first on Job and the second on the plague, will offer fitting examples of his pastoral application of God's providence. Concerning God's sovereignty as it worked out in salvation (i.e., predestination), I will first of all demonstrate from Beza's own writings two often overlooked points. First of all, predestination was not an essential part of the gospel message. Second, an examination of several genres of the Bezan corpus will show that Beza believed the doctrine of monergistic salvation was salutary for believers. God's absolute sovereignty was essential to bring persons to Christ for salvation, to uphold them through the troubles of life, and to usher them safely into heaven. In other words, instruction about God's sovereignty was a pastoral necessity.

---

1 Beza, *Houshold Prayers*, in the prayer "Upon eternal death."

Beza's Political and Theological Context

First, though, we must recount the context in which Beza lived, pastored, and theologized. Theodore Beza lived in precarious times. We recounted in the first chapter Beza's very challenging context. Here we do well to remember William Monter's estimation of the guiding theme during which Beza served at the helm of Genevan life: "The principal theme of the history of the republic [of Geneva] from 1564 to 1603 was her search for political security."[2] The small, independent city-state seemed to be at the mercy of her neighbors, all of whom for one reason or the other had reason to oppose Geneva. To the south, Savoy had aspirations on conquering the choice spot on Lac Léman, along with its profitable industries. France was a massive, volatile, and Catholic, neighbor to the west. Lutherans, massed northward in Germany, were a constant barb in the side of the Reformed Protestants in Geneva.

Perhaps no single event so tried Beza's trust in God as the horrible massacre of Protestants in France that began on St. Bartholomew's Day in 1572. Until that time, Protestant hopes for their fortunes in France were bright. Robert Kingdon wrote that "the two years stretching from the Peace of St. Germain, signed in August of 1570, to the massacres of St. Bartholomew's, perpetrated in August of 1572, were probably the most halcyon in all of history for those French Protestants who looked to Geneva for guidance."[3] Beza's influence in France, in particular, was great. He traveled to La Rochelle in 1571, where he had acted as the chairman of the Reformed churches' synod there. He had also attended the synod at Nîmes the following year, though as a regular delegate this time.[4] The French Protestants were growing in number and influence, with Geneva functioning as their spiritual leader.[5] After the St. Bartholomew's slaughter of thousands of Protestants, including several leading Protestant noblemen, by Catholic mobs throughout France, Protestantism never regained its footing in the country. Geneva was concerned that the swell of anti-Protestant sentiment would invade its gates. Scott Manetsch recounted that

> refugees warned of Catholic plans to attack Geneve and kill Beza. The reformer was certain that the slaughter in France was the unfolding of a Catholic plot to impose the decrees of the Council of Trent by force and exterminate the Protestant religion once and for all. Overwhelmed by these rumors and threats, Beza shared his darkest thoughts with his friend Bullinger in Zurich: "This is perhaps the last letter I will ever write to you. For it is abundantly clear that these massacres are

---

2 Monter, *Calvin's Geneva*, 196.
3 Kingdon, *Geneva and Consolidation*, 193.
4 Ibid., 194, 197.
5 Manetsch, "Theodore Beza," 62-63.

the unfolding of a universal conspiracy. Assassins are seeking to kill me, and I contemplate death more than life."[6]

Beza was distraught.[7] "Beza struggled between hope and despair," according to Manetsch, "clinging anxiously to the reports delivered by the hundreds of refugees filling Geneva's streets. 'Daily I receive news from the farthest corners of France that those whom I thought safe have been killed; by contrast, I have been overjoyed to learn that some—but so very few—have survived whom I had given up for dead. O, how happy we would be if very soon we might be numbered among so many blessed martyrs!'"[8] Surely the sovereign God wanted the true church to shine forth with the gospel in France. Certainly he did not look upon his suffering servants happily. Was God's providence active in all things?

In addition to that political turmoil, Theodore Beza stressed God's sovereignty in history and in salvation because of his doctrinal context. That is to say, Beza emphasized this doctrine in treatises in which he was refuting false views of God's role in salvation. In this he followed Calvin.[9] In the same way,

---

6   Ibid., 55-56, quoting Theodore Beza, *Correspondance de Théodore de Bèze*, ed. H. Meylan, A. Dufour, C. Chimelli, and B. Nicollier (Geneva: Librarie Droz, 1988), 13:179.

7   For a helpful summary of Beza's attitude at this time, along with excerpts from his letters, see Geisendorf, *Théodore de Bèze*, 306-08.

8   Manetsch, "Theodore Beza," 58, quoting Beza, *Correspondance* 13:190. Writing to German Protestants 4 September 1572, Beza said, "One thing only consoles me, the hope that my future life will be but brief, so that I may soon draw nearer to my God" (Duke, Lewis, and Pettegree, eds. and trans., *Calvinism in Europe 1540-1610*, 113).

9   Calvin had written his *Congrégation [sur] l'élection éternelle de Dieu* (1551), *Consensus Genevensis* (1552), *A Brief Reply in Refutation of the Calumnies of a Certain Worthless Person* (1557), *On the Secret Providence of God* (1558), and *Treatise of the Eternal Predestination of God* (1560) to defend the doctrine of predestination, against Castellio, Pighius, Bolsec and perhaps others (Muller, "Use and Abuse," 40). See also François Wendel, *Calvin: Origins and Development of His Religious Thought*, trans. Philip Mairet (New York: Harper & Row, 1963), 90. Williston Walker's judgment of the importance Calvin placed on predestination comports with our understanding of Beza's reason for defending this doctrine. Bolsec's attack on God's sovereignty in election, Walker averred, "was the rejection not merely of what seemed to Calvin, however it may appear to the modern world, a plain teaching of Scripture, but of a doctrine of special comfort to the Christian life. In that light Calvin always viewed the dogma of predestination. . . . An attack upon a doctrine so important in itself, and so bound up with Calvin's own credit as a religious teacher, demanded his most strenuous resistance. While Bolsec might be the agent, the real author of the criticism, in Calvin's judgment, was Satan himself" (Williston Walker, *John Calvin: The Organizer of Reformed*

Beza penned his most strident articulations of the Genevan doctrine of predestination in the heat of controversy. His *Tabula Pradestinationis* (1555), *Ad Sebastiani Castellionis calumnias* (1558), and *Ad acta colloquii Montisbelgardensis* (1586-1587) were responses to opponents who had challenged the Genevan orthodoxy.[10] Although Beza's 1582 *De praedestinationis doctrina et vero usu tractatio absolutissima* is often labeled polemical, we should note its genesis in Beza's routine lectures at the Academy through biblical books. The fact, however, that he chose to publish his lectures on Romans 9 separately probably indicates the importance Beza continued to attach to the doctrine of predestination.[11] As we examine Beza's doctrines of providence and predestination, respectively, we need to remember the heated controversial tone of his day. We shall see that for Beza the debate was over far more than consistent logic. The heart of the controversy concerned persons' abilities to trust in God. Only the sovereign Lord, the one omnipotent both in providence and redemption, could uphold his people in the midst of the spiritual battle. Christians found comfort in the sovereign God alone.

The Providence of God Explained and Defended

The place to begin our examination of Beza's use of the doctrine of God's providence in the spiritual battle is quickly to notice the contours of the doctrine in Beza's writings.[12] First, we will examination Beza's use of the doctrine of providence in his systematic works. Next, we shall notice the way he elaborated on the doctrine in some of his polemical treatises. Then, we will carefully examine the way Beza expressed the doctrine in his pastoral treatises, especially two written during very trying times in his life at the helm of the reform in Geneva.

Providence in the Systematic Treatises

The remarkable thing about Theodore Beza's description of providence in his systematic treatises is the varied placement of the doctrine. We must remember that Beza penned each of these works to explicate the Christian doctrine of salvation. Thus, to the Reformer God's providence supported the truth of

---

Protestantism (1509-1564) [New York: G. P. Putnam's Sons, 1906; reprint, New York: Schocken Books, 1969], 316-17).

10 Gardy, *Bibliographie*, 47-53, 55-58, 197-99; Geisendorf, *Théodore de Bèze*, 68, 74-75, 351-56.
11 Gardy, *Bibliographie*, 187.
12 I do not intend to explicate Beza's doctrine fully. McPhee, especially, has done this well. See McPhee, "Conserver or Transformer of Calvin's Theology?," 223-88. See also Kickel, *Vernuft und Offenbarung*, 122-35.

God's Sovereignty for His People 139

Christian salvation. This is transparent in the *Confession* where Beza included providence as the third point of the entire treatise. Defining it, Beza said,

> Nothing happens by chance, and without a very righteous decree (*très juste ordonnance*) of God (Eph. 1:11; Matth. 10:29; Prov. 16:14). Nevertheless, God is in no wise the author or the one culpable for any evil which takes place. Because his power and his goodness (*sa puissance et sa bonté*) are so incomprehensible, that even when to do something he uses the devil or wicked men—whom he then punishes justly—he does not fail nevertheless to ordain and to do his holy work well and righteously (*d'ordonner et de faire bien et justement son oeuvre sainte*) (Act. 2:23; 4:27; Rom. 9:19-20).[13]

Beza, however, saved discussion of providence almost to the end of his *Quaestionum et responsionum Christianarum libellus*. Salvation, not God's sovereignty, was the keynote of this treatise. That is not to suggest, however, that providence was not an important element in this discussion. Towards the end of the treatise, Beza defined providence, saying, "Nothing at all happens without God's will or knowledge (that is, by chance or accident), but totally as God himself decreed it from eternity, disposing all the intermediate causes powerfully and efficaciously, so that they are necessarily brought to their destined end, in respect to His decree. Nevertheless, He is not the author or allower of any evil, since He always acts most righteously, with whatsoever instruments He executes His works."[14]

Providence in the Polemical Treatises

Beza's polemical treatises are replete with discussions of God's providence. Beza's detractors argued that the Genevan doctrine had a twofold error: first, it made God the author of sin; and, second, it denied persons their free wills. We will especially note Beza's discussion in one of his polemical treatises. In 1558 Beza responded to Sebastian Castellio's attempt to controvert the Genevan

---

13 Beza, "*La Confession de Foi du Chretien* par Theodore de Beza," 16. Neither Beza's *Short Confession*, appended to the *Confession*, nor his *Little Catechisme* contained any distinct discussion of providence.

14 Beza, *Little Book of Christian Questions and Responses*, 77-78. Note also the main points of the doctrine of providence set forth by John Cornelius, a ministerial student at the Geneva Academy, before Beza and Faius and published in a faithful summation of the Genevan theological position (Theodore Beza and Antoine de La Faye, *Propositions and Principles of Divinitie Propounded and Disputed in the Universities of Geneva, by Certaine Students of Divinitie there, under M. Theod. Beza, M. Anthonie Faius, Professors of Divinitie. Wherein is Contained a Methodicall Summarie, or Epitome of the Common Places of Divinitie* [Edinburgh: Robert Waldegrave, 1591], 17-19). On providence in the post-Reformation era, see Muller, *Dictionary of Latin and Greek Theological Terms*, 251-52.

doctrine of predestination.[15] Before looking at the doctrine of God's sovereignty as it related to salvation, Beza dealt with Castellio's attack on the sovereignty of God and its relationship to evil. To begin with, Beza defined providence. He urged that Scripture

> attests that all things, no matter what, are governed by God, including those that seem to be most fortuitous (*quae a Deo gubernari testatur quaecunque etiam maxime videntur fortuita*). It proclaims that even "tiny sparrows do not fall to the ground apart from the will of the Father," and that "all the hairs of our head are numbered." In fact, Satan cannot touch Job apart from God's decreeing (*nisi Deo ita decernente*), and accordingly "permitting him to do so." The demons could not even rage against the swine apart from seeking their power from Christ – which he granted them not unwillingly, at all, but willingly. So, we can only say that all things are done with God willing – and consequently, when we see anything come to pass, let us confess that it has not occurred apart from God's just, eternal, and immutable decree. But if someone exclaims here that we are introducing a "stoical necessity," I shall acknowledge with Augustine (or rather, with truth itself) that God's will is the necessity of things (*Dei voluntatem esse rerum necessitatem*) – but I deny that it is "stoical." Nor do we bind God to secondary causes, as Homer portrayed his Jupiter, who complained that when he wanted to resist fate he could not. We, I say, acknowledge no such fate; but we affirm that there is a sure and immutable outcome of all things, which the Lord has decided freely, wisely, and justly, from eternity. Yet we say that secondary causes are not compelled by God's decree (*Dei decreto non cogi causas secundas*) – except when he is pleased to restrain his adversaries – but are rather prone to be carried to the end determined by God (*sed pronas ad finem a Deo constitutum ferri*).[16]

In an effort to preempt Castellio from criticizing him for "obscurity," Beza related thirty-eight aphorisms which explained his views about God's ordination and its relation to evil.[17] These aphorisms about providence are significant in our discussion. On the one hand, their tone is quite "scholastic." On the other hand, Beza's motivation for defending this doctrine was pastoral. He was ultimately concerned about this matter because of his belief in an ongoing spiritual battle between God and Satan. Only the sovereign Lord could sustain his people.

The first seven aphorisms show that God effects all things according to his

---

15 Gardy, *Bibliographie*, 55-58.
16 Beza, *Responsio ad Sebastiani Castellionis Calumnias*, in *The Potter and the Clay*, 110-11; Theodore Beza, *Ad Sebastiani Castellionis Calumnias, in Tractationum Theologicarum, in quibus plerasque Christianae Religionis dogmata adversus haereses nostris temporibus renovatas solide ex Verbo Dei defenduntur* (Geneva: Vignon, 1582), 1:351.
17 Beza, *Responsio ad Sebastiani Castellionis Calumnias*, in *The Potter and the Clay*, 124-33.

eternal counsel. Beza concluded them by saying, "As it pleased him, God himself decreed from eternity all things to be, so that they also happen in his own time, by his own efficacy, as he desires."[18] The next ten aphorisms showed that God used "secondary causes and mediating instruments" to execute the counsel of his will.[19] This was absolutely essential to Beza in order to free God from the charge of being guilty of sin. Beza summarized such "blasphemies" as teaching "that God is the Author of sin, or delights in iniquity, or even wills it; that Satan or mankind obey God when they act in an evil way; or that whenever they act in an evil way they are doing what God wills and are therefore not guilty."[20] Instead, God "freely and powerfully forms, moves, and directs [secondary causes], as he pleases," while not being bound by them in any Stoical sense of necessity.[21] In addition, one must be careful not to misrepresent the worth of given actions. The value of any action is determined by its orientation towards God: "I call an action 'evil,'" Beza continued, "which does not have the revealed will of God as its goal. A 'good' action, on the other hand, is one that keeps that will in mind."[22] So an action may be ascribed to two different agents, one of whom is charged as guilty and the other of whom is said to be righteous. Here Beza illustrated his point: "if a magistrate delivers a guilty man to the executioner, there is no one who does not rightly praise that work. But if the executioner kills that man under the impulse of hatred, or avarice, or some other depraved desire, instead of respect for the judge's command, he certainly cannot escape the crime of homicide in the eyes of God."[23]

Beginning in the eighteenth aphorism, and running to the end, Beza applied these facts to the case of God. His controlling point is that since God is the definer of good and evil, and since he is good himself, no sin can be attributed to him: "Whatever God does is good, since no evil can flow forth from the Highest Good. And he effects all things. Therefore, all things are good inasmuch as God effects them – and that distinction of 'good' and 'evil' finds place at most in the instruments and those things concerning which we have spoken."[24] God uses both good and evil instruments. But even when he creates and impels evil instruments so "that through them he may do what he has decided," in this "God does rightly and without any injustice."[25] Nor do these evil instruments subjectively obey God, because "in view of their own plan and

---

18 Ibid., 125.
19 Ibid.
20 Ibid.
21 Ibid.
22 Ibid., 126.
23 Ibid., 127.
24 Ibid.
25 Ibid.

will, they do not do God's work but their own." Therefore God is not culpable of sin because "the term 'sin' applies only to a deficient quality that lies wholly within the acting instrument," and "the just work of God [through these sinful instruments] can be diametrically opposed to the unjust work of man."[26] The key to this dilemma, according to Beza, was that "God acts differently through good instruments than through evil ones." He continued this explanation, arguing that

> For apart from the fact that he does his work through good instruments, even good instruments do their own work by that power and efficacy that the Lord provides them – and the Lord finally does his own work through them, and he operates also in them, to "will and to do." But through evil persons (for example, through Satan, or men, inasmuch as they are unregenerated) as often as the Lord executes the just counsels and decrees of his eternal will, he demonstrates his power and efficacy in his work through those who are either unwitting or unwilling. But nonetheless, inasmuch as they do their own work, the Lord does not operate within them at all, but releases the reigns to Satan and gives over to his just judgment also the wicked who are to be stirred up and roused, that they might be borne along by his own and their own choice.[27]

Why did Beza compose this scholastic and polemical treatise? The answer is at the end of the treatise. God had to be sovereign, Beza contended, in order to be the anchor for his people through the many vicissitudes of life. Only a sovereign God, that is, one sovereign even over human sin, could console his people in the midst of the trials they faced:

> So now we understand that God's predestination and will were present in the afflictions of the saints. In another place Peter also discusses the cross of Christ (in Acts 2:23 – a text we have frequently cited already) and recalls the "determinate plan and foreknowledge of God." Elsewhere the whole church at Jerusalem recollects the "hand and counsel of God" (Acts 4:28). But does God approve the iniquity of those who persecute the church? He surely does not – but indeed the wicked who persecute the church shall also pay finally the rightful punishments. By that same act which he rightly punishes in his enemies, God tests his church and daily makes it perfect – and in this respect the will, counsel, fixed and definite decree, and finally the very action of the most just and most wise God intervenes no less in these activities than when he uses select and holy organs for accomplishing things that are most good and excellent in themselves. And certainly, if this consolation were taken away from us (as it assuredly is if we believe you, who dream I know not what idle "permission" apart from God's will and decree in such matters), then how shall we ever remain firm and constant? One does not solve all things when he thinks the outcome and the issue of all such

---

26 Ibid., 128.
27 Ibid., 128-29.

matters are governed by God. But we must be persuaded especially at this point: Satan and Satan's instruments cannot oppose us (no matter how little) unless this good Father of ours so decreed and purposes from eternity in our interest, in order that our consolation might be full and unshakeable (*ne tantillum quidem adversum nos moliri posse Satanam, aut Satanae instrumenta, quod non ab aeterno bonus ille noster Parens commodo nostro decreverit, ac proposverit, ut plena ac solida sit nostra consolatio*).[28]

The Reformed churches were suffering. Beza himself was suffering. Consolation could be found in God alone, that is, in the totally sovereign Lord who controlled all events and even Satan himself. The doctrine of providence was fundamentally a pastoral doctrine and an issue of personal security to Theodore Beza.

Application of Providence in the Spiritual Battle: *Treatise on the Plague* and *Lectures on Job*

Beza's life and times were tumultuous. Two treatises that he penned, especially, show the manner in which he found solace for himself and his listeners in the midst of the battles raging around them. God's sure control of all things, a providence that was often beyond human comprehension, was the fortress in which believers could take refuge.

De Peste Quaestiones duae Explicatae *(1579)*

In 1579 Beza wrote *A Shorte Learned and Pithie Treatize of the Plague* as a casuistic document. In it he attempted to answer the question, Should a Christian flee the plague or remain and trust God with the outcome?[29] This was no merely intellectual question. The Black Death had carried away about a third of the entire European population during the fourteenth century.[30] It continued. The plague struck Europe on average every ten years in the sixteenth century. For instance, eight years of pestilence struck Augsburg in the first part of the century, killing nearly 40,000 people, though the city's population rose to only 45,000 persons in this century. In London, 27 percent of the population died in 1563 and 18 percent in 1593 due to the plague, a total of approximately 40,000 persons. Similar horrendous death rates struck other European cities.[31] Contemporaries understood the plague to come in several forms, affecting different organs in the body. Bubonic attacked the lymph glands, pneumonic

---

28   Ibid., 136-37; Beza, *Tractationum Theologicarum* 1:377.
29   Gardy, *Bibliographie*, 178.
30   Timothy George, *Theology of the Reformers* (Nashville: Broadman, 1988), 23-24.
31   Richard Mackenney, *Sixteenth Century Europe: Expansion and Conflict* (New York: St. Martin's, 1993), 84.

the lungs, and septicaemic the blood. Additionally, syphilis came on the scene when sailors brought it home from their exploits in the New World.[32]

Geneva was not spared. During Calvin's tenure the plague struck twice, first from 1542 to 1544 and again in 1560.[33] So great was the concern, in fact, that the site of the Geneva Academy was partly selected because its location afforded a steady breeze which was thought to deter the spread of the disease.[34] Beza's stay in Geneva was also marred by onsets of the blight. The year of Calvin's death, 1564, the plague broke out. It showed up again in 1567-1568 as well as in 1570-1571.[35] The plague contributed to Beza's traumatic life in personal ways. His brother, Nicolas, fled to Geneva in 1570 but died of the pestilence shortly thereafter.[36] The plague's onset in 1571 resulted in a lack both of professors and of students at the Academy. In September of that year the magistrates almost closed the school, but Beza single-handedly kept it afloat. He was the sole lecturer at that time. In 1572 only four students enrolled in the *schola publica*, the upper school that also trained future ministers.[37] Thus Theodore Beza felt the sting of the plague in very personal and profound ways.

Beza's treatise on the plague is noteworthy for three reasons. First, in explicating his view of God's providence, Beza combated faulty ideas of God's governance of the world. Second, he gave practical advice to persons confronted with the plague. Finally, he applied the plague to his readers, showing them that the God behind the plague stood ready either to condemn or to receive them. In other words, for Theodore Beza the plague and God's providence displayed in it was fundamentally pastoral.

First of all, Beza noted that God was the supreme cause of all that came to pass. Thus he asserted thats "Almighty God governs and orders natural causes and their effects, as it pleases him."[38] Christ's death proved this.[39] To

---

32 Ibid., 23; George, *Theology of the Reformers*, 23-24. Beza classified syphilis with the plague in his treatise under consideration: "Let us speak," he urged, "of these pocks, whether it be the French, or the Spanish, and I would to God it were not also the Dutch. That it is a punishment set of God for whoredom, which in this time is counted for a play, I think there is no man which dares to deny, neither yet that it is indeed the hand, sword, and arrow of God which strikes whoremongers" (Theodore Beza, *A Shorte Learned and Pithie Treatize of the Plague*, trans. John Stockwood [London: Thomas Dawson, 1580], n.p.).
33 Geisendorf, *Théodore de Bèze*, 252.
34 Maag, *Seminary or University?*, 10.
35 Geisendorf, *Théodore de Bèze*, 252-54; Monter, *Calvin's Geneva*, 211.
36 Clavier, *Théodore de Bèze*, 51. Beza mourned his loss deeply. He wrote to Bullinger at this time, "My mourning is deep. . . . I would like you and your honored brothers, your colleagues, to sustain me by your prayers in the extreme exhaustion that I feel" (ibid., 52).
37 Maag, *Seminary or University?*, 31-32.
38 Beza, *Treatize of the Plague*, n.p.

accomplish his will, God used secondary causes.

Secondary causation, in fact, was the heart of Beza's conflict with his opponents. The subtitle to Beza's treatise showed that he was trying to answer two different questions, both of which revolved around the notion of second causes. The full title of the English translation of the treatise was *A Short Learned and Pithy treatise of the plague, wherein are handled these two questions: the one, whether the plague be infectious, or no: the other, whether and how far it may of Christians be shunned by going aside. A discourse very necessary for this our time, and country; to satisfy the doubtful consciences of a great number.*[40] Those whose opinions Beza was opposing asserted various erroneous views of providence. First of all, they argued that the plague was not infectious because God did not employ second causes to accomplish his will. They said, according to Beza, that "the plague is called 'the hand of God' (2 Sam. 24), 'the sword of God' (1 Chron. 21) and is also signified by the name of 'arrows' (Pss. 31 and 90). Therefore it comes not of infection, when as neither hand, nor sword, nor arrow wounded by infection." They went wrong, Beza asserted, because of their failure to interpret figurative parts of the Scripture appropriately. Thus, he rebutted, in Psalm 17, "David calls his enemies 'the hand of God,' who not withstanding by natural means assaulted him. And when as the hand of God is said to have made us, natural generation is not shut out." Surely, instead, we should understand some parts of the Bible metaphorically: "By those metaphorical terms of 'hand,' 'sword,' 'arrow,' is no more signified of what manner this disease is in itself, than what is hail, or the scab, when God is said with a stretched out hand too have stricken Egypt."[41] Although his detractors argued that the plague came about by the singular providence of God and denied that the Lord used secondary causation of any sort, Beza argued that the Almighty was the first cause who used second causes to accomplish his will. In this case, the spread of the plague by means of the air was an instance of God's employment of second causes. So his opponents' arguments, "unless I be fully deceived, make nothing at all to the taking away of the contagious air, the second cause of this sickness."[42]

A couple of illustrations proved that single causation was wrong, Beza argued. If one denies God's employment of second causes, he began, one

---

39   Christ died by chance, Beza averred, "if you stand upon the cause of his natural death, and yet he died of necessity, if you go to the unchangeable appointment of his Father, because his hour was come. And withall he died willingly, because he laid down his life for us. Thus far therefore is neither chance nor will repugnant unto the most certain decree of God" (ibid.).
40   The Latin title was *De Peste Quaestiones duae Explicatae: una sitne contagiosa: Altera, an et quatenus sit Christianis per secessionem vitanda.*
41   Beza, *Treatize of the Plague*, n.p.
42   Ibid., B4[r].

should not eat food or take medicine when one is sick either: "For why, if this reason be good, shall it not be lawful to affirm the same of all second causes of death. Go ahead then, let us neither eat, nor drink, nor seek any remedy against any diseases; let soldiers also go unarmed to battle, because death ordained by God cannot be avoided."[43] In fact, though, he averred that failing to use the means God had given us to avoid death was sin.[44] Besides, Scripture left us examples to follow, notably the examples of both Christ himself and the apostle Paul who strove to avoid death at times. "What should I say more?" he asked rhetorically, "when as Paul knew assuredly, that neither he himself, nor any of those which were with him should perish in the shipwreck, yet said he to the mariners preparing to flee out of the ship, 'You cannot be saved, unless these tarry.' Christ also, albeit he knew that his hour was not yet come, yet did he more than once withdraw himself, when he was sought for to be slain."[45]

His opponents' view of single causation had dire effects. Since the plague was not infectious, for God was the single cause of the disease in their opinion, Christians who went aside from the plague lacked faith.[46] But this was faulty reasoning according to Beza. First of all, it was not sound biblical interpretation. It failed to note that

> in the holy Scriptures is not set down what every one has done. In many the general rules of doctrine are sufficient to determine those things whereof we have no commandment, nor any particular example. It is without doubt that it is not set down how often the people have been visited with the plague, neither yet how every man behaved himself in the plague. . . .

---

43 Ibid., A5[r].
44 Ibid., A5[v].
45 Ibid., B5[v].
46 Beza argued that they derived their views either from Plato, who argued that it was foolish to fear death, or from biblical notions so that they rebuked those fleeing the plague because, in their words: "they think not well of the providence of God, by whose unchangeable decree the course of man's life especially is limited, that they distrust God, and chiefly believe not this promise, 'I will be your God and the God of your seed,' that they are void of all charity. . . that they tempt God after the example of the Israelites (Ex. 17.3 and Ps. 78.18), appointing God by what manner, place, time, and by what means he may save them. . . that they fear death too much, that they set themselves against the will of God, which is always good, that they think themselves stronger then God, and that they can escape his hand" (ibid., n.p.). Later, Beza put their assertions into syllogistic form: "There can nothing be sent of God, say they, but that which is good, no there is nothing good, but that which comes of God: but the plague is sent of God. Therefore it is good, if not of its own nature, yet in respect of the good end, namely, to punish our sins, to try our faith, to drive us to repentance, to bring forth hypocrites into the light. . . . Finally, they say, that as many as fly the plague, do that which no Christian ever did, when as there is no example thereof in the holy histories" (ibid., n.p.).

God's Sovereignty for His People

> But yet, say they, David did not flee very sore plague, whereof is mention made (2 Sam. 24).... I grant, but how many peculiar circumstances do forbid us to make of that a general conclusion? For he himself was the cause of this plague. ... Moreover, where, I pray, should he have fled, when the plague was whole in all his dominion.[47]

In the second place, Beza argued, God's decree does not "take away the ordinary and lawful means to save our life" so that we may "use these means, when as it is yet hid from us what God from everlasting has decreed concerning the prolonging or ending of our life."[48] The fear of death is not wrong, he argued. A desire to flee from the plague was not misplaced since "the fear of death, if it is grounded upon good reason and is moderate, is not only not to be condemned, but also to be allowed as a preserver of life grafted in us by God."[49] Contrary to his opponents, then, Beza argued that in his providence God used the plague as a second cause to spread disease. It was thus infectious. So believers should not be dissuaded from fleeing it since there was biblical warrant to flee death and since saving one's life might also be subsumed under God's decree.

How should a believer thus react when confronted with the plague? Although one might suspect, based on the above discussion, that Beza would encourage Christians to flee from the plague, he offered guarded advice to his readers on this issue. The issue was not black and white, in his opinion. Rather, one must trust God in all circumstances, and both staying and fleeing could manifest faith in the Almighty for different persons. Even though a person may "use going aside both well and ill," Beza argued that "they offend much less, who even when they might otherwise with a good conscience withdraw themselves had rather yet to tarry."[50] That is to say, everything else being equal, it was better to remain. In order to flee from the plague, one ought to have a good reason: "these offend much less than those which being carried away with too much distrust, or with immeasurable fear of death, foreseeing all duties of

---

47 Ibid., n.p.
48 Ibid., C2[r]. Later, in his lectures on Job, Beza made a similar point. After arguing from Job 2:7 that Job's boil was caused by a contagion in the air and that Satan was thus rightly called "the prince of the air" since he is the one who inflicts persons with diseases, Beza pointed out that the normal way that people get sick is not "by the means of wicked spirits. For most commonly they come of natural and ordinary causes." Following this, he urged "how necessary a thing it is for us, so to use natural medicines, that nevertheless we put not our trust in them, nor yet in the physician.... But ... the godly ought to seek for help nowhere else, but at God's hands, who only wounds and heals, who leads to the grave, and brings back again" (Beza, *Job*, I1v-I2r).
49 Beza, *Treatise of the Plague*, C3[r].
50 Ibid., n.p.

humanity."[51] In this point, then, Beza countered a wrong notion of providence by insisting that God stood behind the plague. One must view the disease Christianly, then. Whether fleeing the plague or staying, one must trust God.

Finally, in his concluding point Beza applied all that he had said previously to his readers. God's strong providence, he here argued, was so strong that it could strengthen one to trust the Lord with one's life, even while one was ministering to those afflicted with the plague. Whatever one did—and Beza reasserted that the Scriptures only provided guidelines for appropriate behavior on this point—he should commend "himself unto God," trusting him alone, and act with a clear conscience.[52] Surprisingly, though, the main point of Beza's exhortation was that his readers should use the occurrences of the plague and its deadly ramifications to remind themselves of the even more awful judgment to follow for all persons who did not trust Christ. Beza urged that everyone should "summon himself unto the judgment seat of God unto the plague as unto the coming of news of the wrath of God, condemning himself, that he may be acquitted by him, and that, besides, he weigh with himself that he is called forth to plead his cause, and that this rod cannot be avoided with change of places, but of manners, and that if he must die, that this is decreed for the good of them that die, forasmuch as they are blessed, which die in the Lord."[53] Christians could rest in God's sure providence. But all must be aware that eternity awaited them after their earthly life. Theodore Beza once again showed himself to be a pastor in his application of God's providence over the plague. Christians were

---

51 Ibid., n.p. This issue of whether it was right or not to turn away from the plague was a very tangible question for Beza. The Genevan authorities would not allow Calvin to minister to victims of the plague when it struck the city in 1542, 1545, and 1560 for fear that he would die from its effects. They denied him this service even when he desired to minister (Beza, *Life of John Calvin*, xlii, xlvi; Geisendorf, *Théodore de Bèze*, 252; cf. Monter who argued that unlike Beza, Calvin "accepted his exemption from this duty" [*Calvin's Geneva*, 211]). Beza argued vehemently that all pastors, himself included, should be in the lottery to choose who would minister to those afflicted by the plague. But he was denied this service the first time in 1564. When the pestilence hit again in 1568, he had been too sick to be considered. Finally, at the 1570 outbreak, he was included in the pool of pastors although he was not selected (Geisendorf, *Théodore de Bèze*, 253-54; Monter, *Calvin's* Geneva, 211; cf. Philip Edgcumbe Hughes, ed. and trans., *The Register of the Company of Pastors of Geneva in the Time of Calvin* [Grand Rapids: Eerdmans, 1966], 367-70). Conradt showed from one of Beza's letters to a Polish inquirer the effects of the plague on Beza's life. He apologized in 1568 for not replying sooner, explaining "that because of the plague he has had to leave his house and his books for a period" (Conradt, "John Calvin, Theodore Beza and the Reformation in Poland," 165).

52 Beza, *Treatize of the Plague*, D[r].

53 Ibid., n.p.

in the midst of turmoil in this life, sometimes manifesting itself even in dying from the pestilence, but God's sure hand would guide them to glory in heaven. The most important thing was to make sure that Christians arrived in heaven there to be acquitted before God's tribunal. God's providence over the plague should encourage them to trust in him now, and hope in his eternal salvation.

Jobus, Theodore Bezae partim Commentariis
partim Paraphrasi illustratus *(1589)*

Based on Theodore Beza's own testimony, this work more than any of his other treatises gives us a glimpse into his beliefs about God's providence. He wrote in the preface that the doctrine of providence was "nowhere in all my books of divinity more largely and fully disputed of, nowhere handled in a more manifest and certain application to a particular example, nowhere determined more plainly by the word of God."[54] For that reason, we will examine the doctrine Beza explicated therein.[55]

First, though, we must attempt to understand the context in which Beza first lectured in the Academy on Job and then wrote this treatise. Beza's *Job* was published after a period of intense trouble for the city-state of Geneva. Scott Manetsch well laid out the contours of the times for Beza. In the summer of 1586, Catholic Savoy's Charles-Emmanuel besieged Geneva

> with his powerful army, preventing the city from harvesting its crop or importing wheat. A Savoyard fleet on Lac Léman enforced the blockade. With the city treasury virtually empty and the Academy almost entirely vacated, the magistrates decreed in August 1586 the suspension of university courses and the temporary dismissal of the three professors other than Beza. On August 5, Beza and his two clerical colleagues, Jean Pinault and Jean Jacquemot, appeared before the Small Council to protest the decision. Their impassioned appeal was revealing: The Genevan Academy, they argued, was famous throughout the world. It had long been the "nursery" of Reformed ministers in France. Even now, students from far-off England were on their way to Geneva to prepare for the ministry. If the academy were closed, this would bring dishonor to the magistrates of Geneva and great harm to the churches. Beza and his colleagues further suggested that the closure would please their enemies and give a strong advantage to Catholic colleges. . . . the Genevan magistrates rescinded their decree and permitted the Academy to remain open. Three months later, however, with the treasury empty, they were forced to dismiss the professors of Greek, Hebrew, and philosophy. Beza alone was left. During the next eight months, he kept the academy "open" single-handedly, giving public lectures in theology three times a week. Appropriately, he chose to lecture on the book of Job. Finally, in the summer of

---

54 Beza, *Job*, A3v.
55 Raitt has offered the only study of this work of which I am aware. See Jill Raitt, "Lessons in Troubled Times," 21-45.

1587, the armies of Savoy, ravaged by the plague, were forced to loosen their grip on the city, allowing both students and professors to return to the Genevan Academy. Charles-Emmanuel's policy of aggression against Geneva remained unchanged, though temporarily thwarted.[56]

Indeed, Beza himself reflected on the difficult times that had led him to meditate on, study, and lecture on the book of Job. In the prefatory letter to his English translation of *Job*, addressed to England's Queen Elizabeth, he wrote that as he was confronted with Geneva's war with Savoy and the dangers involved therein,

> Most noble Queen, according to the charge which in this church is committed unto me, partly the renewed misery and calamity of a far more dangerous war, with which we now at this present are distressed. . . . the enemy hard at our gates scarcely suffered us to breath, that even at the very same time I expounded the history of Job in this school, as an argument most fit for these wretched times. . . . such things as came into my mind in expounding this part of Scripture, when I had first gathered them into brief notes and after more diligently perusing them, at the request of some of my hearers was intended to publish them. . . . it is clear, that you, beholding all those things which befell Job, in many of those oppressed exiles flying unto you for refuge, have in a manner so sensibly felt . . . all their afflictions. . . all which grievances you, treading in the steps of this our Job, have borne out with marvelous constancy and patience.[57]

---

56 Manetsch, "Theodore Beza," 190-91. On Geneva's troubled history with Savoy, see Monter, *Calvin's Geneva*, 196-207, and Geisendorf, *Théodore de Bèze*, 368-78.

57 Beza, *Job*, A3r-A3v. Beza's prefatory letter is significant in underlining his view of biblical authority, along with his self-conception as a humanist. He noted, first of all, the reasons Job had often not been handled well by previous commentators: its difficult theological matters; its ancient Hebrew (he claimed it was the oldest book in the canon); and its preponderance of rare words (ibid., A4r). Rome was wrong, he argued, to limit the study of the Bible merely to the Vulgate. Instead, he urged, "Those which are able, should have recourse to the original, and those which cannot, should betake them to commentaries, and diligently in the fear of God weigh the arguments and reasons of the different interpretation both of the old and new writers" (ibid., A4v). But his biblical work was much more than just the activity of a humanist. Beza argued that the importance of his activity derived from the authority of the Bible. One must understand Scripture in its context, he argued. He wanted to compile the best possible original, after comparing the best manuscripts, and translation of the Old Testament ,as he had done of the New Testament, but said "I was restrained by reason that I could not get any store of Hebrew copies to my mind. Nevertheless I endeavored to effect somewhat in two most hard and intricate books, namely, Ecclesiastes and the Psalms, the context of which books being here and there mended partly by inserting some few words into it, partly by examining every word diligently by itself and carefully observing the

He began the lectures in January of 1587, during the conflict with Savoy and later prepared them for publication.[58] Geneva's dire situation led Beza to reflect on God's providence, especially as it related to evil. This was anything but a mere academic tome.

The issue of providence was of paramount importance to Beza because of pastoral necessity. In their troubled times it would be easy for Christians to doubt God's care for them or his ability to take care of them. So he was discussing "that notable question of God's providence in ruling the whole world, in which is discussed how that partiality, which is commonly seen in the adversity of the godly and prosperity of the wicked, may be reconciled with God's justice, necessary to be known of all Christians."[59] God's providence alone could make sense of and provide comfort in the midst of Beza's troubled times. The doctrine of providence was also of paramount importance because of the spiritual battle in which Beza and other Christians were involved. Not only did God actively use Satan to accomplish his goals in the world (as Beza would argue later), but Satan was also the one who actively sought to overturn the doctrine of God's providential control of creation. By making mockers slander God as the author of evil, the devil actually made them into atheists. Thus the Reformer lamented that

> the wicked even at this day do upon [evil] build their manifest atheism and impiety. Verily all this doubt proceeded from that infectious poison of Satan, which he hid under the glorious name of the knowledge of good and evil. . . . Where do such pestilent cogitations creep into our minds, but that, being as it were utterly void of reason, we think that only to be right and good, the cause and reason whereof we ourselves do conceive and like, and go about to square the infinite wisdom and justice of God to the most crooked rule of our own weak and slender capacity? Such also at this day are the clamors of them who cry out that we make God the author of sin when we say that nothing is done rashly, nothing

---

> order of the whole discourse. I labored to expound by an accurate and plain paraphrase. All which I did for no other intent, than that I might hereby provoke and stir up the industry of more learned men than myself to the performance of that which is better. And now truly, behold, I have adventured the very same in this history of Job; yes, and somewhat more also. For I have written a full commentary upon the two first chapters thereof, wherein I have soundly and plainly so far as I could, unfolded and laid open many questions of no small importance, and specially that controversy of the providence of God. I have moreover set down before the beginnings of all the other chapters following, both the sum of those things which are handled in them, as also the manner how every argument therein contained, is disposed. The ignorance or rather contempt of such method, I dare be bold to say, has brought many both false and also foolish expositions, not only into this book of Job, but also into the writings of the prophets and apostles" (ibid., A5r).

58 Ibid., n.p.
59 Ibid., A3v.

beside his will and foreknowledge, but that whatsoever is thought, spoken or done, comes to pass, God having wisely and justly decreed the same, whether he uses good or evil instruments. In like manner their blasphemies, who take away God's eternal decree of reprobation, who accuse us for bringing in a Stoical necessity.[60]

Beza clearly viewed the doctrine of providence through the lenses of a spiritual battle. The Lord was punishing people for showing contempt for the gospel in Beza's day. In order to purify and try his children, God, "has, if ever at any time, now let loose the reins to the devil and his angels," Beza claimed.[61] Beza's troubled times, specifically the troubles of Geneva, were part of the spiritual battle raging between Satan and the Almighty. So Beza's point in preaching on God's providence and publishing the lectures was to encourage God's people to persevere. Satan and his hordes were actively attacking the church, even through the instrument of the Savoyard army at Geneva's gates. In a sense, the Christian church was in Job's situation, undergoing intense demonic opposition. Job stood firm, even though he did not know the hidden things, the issues discussed between God and Satan in the first two chapters. Now, though, Beza was burdened to exposit those chapters, letting God's children in on the hidden secrets of God's providence, as it were. Believers should be encouraged because of these truths, even if they had to undergo severe suffering now.[62] For Beza, then, even though the discussion of providence might be very technical, it was much more than just theoretical. Knowledge of God's providential control over all things was a pastoral necessity in the midst of the spiritual battle. Only God's providence would protect his people, comforting them in suffering now and ultimately bringing them to heaven. Thus, in his preface, Beza set the stage for his discussion: the doctrine of providence was essential in light of the spiritual battle. Providence was pastoral.

Beza's elaboration of the doctrine of providence in his lectures on Job 1 and 2 is significant for three reasons. First, it contains a rigorous defense of the doctrine. Second, Beza here argued that providence only made sense when one understood the spiritual forces involved, and when one knew that heaven was the final resting-place of Christians. Third, we shall finally note the many ways that Beza the pastor employed providence to encourage his listeners. Confidence in God's complete providence should lead his people to trust him in all the vicissitudes of life.

Beza's most extended discussion of providence came in his comments on Job 1:21. Here Job, upon learning of the confiscation of all his herds and the

---

60 Ibid., B1v.
61 Ibid., B3r.
62 Ibid.

deaths of all his sons and daughters in one calamitous day, confidently asserted "Naked came I out of my mother's womb and naked shall I return there. The Lord gave, and the Lord has taken away, blessed be the name of the Lord." Taking the middle of the verse—"the Lord gave, and the Lord has taken away"—as his starting point, Beza defined at the outset the question he would address. He wanted to know "whether it may be truly said, and whether we ought so to speak, that God both in respect of his will and of his actions which are always just, does bear any part, yes, and which is more, that he bears the chief and principal part in willing and working all those things and every of them, which are committed most unjustly and wickedly in the world."[63] Beza wanted to know if God was the prime mover behind the evil actions that occur in his creation. At the outset he said that he agreed with this statement because "it is very agreeable to true religion, and that it greatly stands with the glory of God. Others, on the contrary, do abhor it as a thing blasphemous and full of impiety."[64] God's greatness and glory demanded that one agree that all things—including evil—were under his providential command.

At this point Beza inserted nine points explaining his view of providence. His discussion was tightly argued.[65] He reasoned:

1. That God, as he is the maker of all things which are, both in general and in particular, without any exception, so he is the governor and ruler thereof.
2. Therefore, that nothing can be done, and that nothing can happen, either God being unwilling and striving against it (for then he should not be almighty) or else not knowing of it, or not caring whether it be done or no (for then he should not be a right and just ruler of the world.)
3. Therefore, that not only the event of things, but even all the second causes, are moved, ruled and directed to their ends by God, not being ignorant or idle, much less constrained and against his will, but by God decreeing and willing to have it so.
4. Therefore, all things and every one, are done by the decree, will and working of God (*Omnia igitur & singula decernente, volente & operante Deo fieri*).
5. That the will of the most just and most wise God is not to be esteemed, either by the state and condition in which his creatures are (for now some of them are good, and some evil) neither by the quality of the causes which he uses (for some of them do work rightly and well; some ill and naughtily; some neither well nor ill; some do not work, nor move themselves at all), but contrariwise, thus we must think of the will of God, that whatsoever he wills, moves or works, he wills, moves and works it always justly, that is, all things both in whole and in part, both universally and particularly

---

63 Ibid., on Job 1:21.
64 Ibid.
65 I will insert my interpretive aids, and numbers not enumerated in the original, in brackets. The parenthetical comments are from the original.

considered. He that denies these things, denies God. But you will say, by this means is taken away all difference between good and evil in our thoughts, sayings and actions; and so God himself (which is great blasphemy) is made the author of all evil and wickedness. God forbid. But again we will refute the falseness of this consequence, by these most certain axioms and grounds.

1. Although God does no more stand in need of any middle and second causes to rule all those things which he has made, and to direct them unto their proper ends, than he did want either matter or instruments, when he created all things of nothing, by the great and mighty power of his word, yet notwithstanding he has made and ordained causes, such and so many as he thought good, whose means he does use, not of any necessity (as the Stoics have fondly dreamed) but most freely, to effect whatsoever he will, even whenever, and however it pleases himself.

[2. God uses three kinds of instruments or means.] The instruments and means which God does use, are threefold. For some of them be altogether passive, that is, of themselves they cannot move themselves, nor do anything, unless they be moved either immediately of God, or else of some other secondary causes; and of this kind, be all creatures which are without life. There are other things which are moved outwardly, but so that they themselves do move also, by a certain natural appetite, being guided and directed by no understanding or reason, and therefore they cannot properly be said either to do well or ill. Of this sort are all brute beasts, in which are manifold degrees of motions, not needful now to be spoken of. Others yet are so outwardly moved, that they being endued with understanding and reason, have some parts of their own in working, whereby they do effect some work, which may truly and properly be called their own.

[3. Of the third sort are angels and men, created good, but mutable.] All these last kind of instruments . . . angels and men, have been good, and every one of them were so made from the beginning. Nevertheless, this goodness in them was subject to change and alteration, forasmuch as God only is absolutely and always good, without any mutation or change.

[4. These fell, by God's decree and by their free will.] Hereupon it came to pass, (and that not without the decree of God always doing justly, who then did open the way to declare and show forth both his just severity, which should ensue, and also his most bountiful mercy in Christ) hereupon, I say, it came to pass, that part of the angels, and all mankind in Adam did fall, and that through their own free will and inward motion.

[5. These remain in that state, so that their nature is fallen and they do evil.] That fall did neither quite destroy the nature of the angels, nor yet of mankind, but did only deprave and corrupt it: yet so, that their whole will and inward motion continuing in that state wherein it is now, cannot move and apply itself to do anything but sinfully:

and therefore it can do nothing, which may justly be accounted good; but all whatsoever it does, is always sinful and wicked.

6. This evil in those wicked angels, God has not as yet taken away, nor yet ever will, as the holy scripture teaches us. But he has, and does, and will more and more correct and amend it in those, whom, through his infinite mercy, he has chosen out of all mankind, and whom he has predestined to salvation in Christ and through Christ; who having their minds enlightened, and their will effectually sanctified by the Holy Ghost, as God works by them rightly, so do they also well and rightly move themselves; in so much that both the work of God moving them, and the work of them moving themselves, not according to the flesh but according to the spirit, is good and just.

7. But that we may make a difference between the just work of God, wrought by those instruments which also move themselves, and that other work or action, whether good or evil of the instruments themselves, in like manner moving themselves, the ancient father has taught us to distinguish God's action from his permission (*inter Dei Actionem & eiusdem Permissionem distinctio*), which distinction is as true and necessary if it be rightly understood and according to their meaning, as it is false and little less than blasphemous, as it is abused of the sophisters.

8. For they, who fearing lest God should be made the author of sin, do separate his permission from his will, by which all things, without exception, are that which they are, and who hold us in his hand, that those things which are wickedly done by evil and sinful instruments, are only foreseen, and not decreed. They, I say, do first of all very unwisely confound the works of God, which are always just, what instruments whatsoever he use, with the work of the instruments, which do not well and rightly move themselves. Again they exempt the far greatest part of the things which are done in this world, from the decree and ordinance of God, seeing they are infinitely more, which are done ill, than which are done well. And so they shut up into a very narrow room that power of God, by which he works and governs all things, and upon which not only the event and issue of every thing, but even the things themselves, together with all their actions, do depend. Moreover they deprive the godly, being afflicted by Satan and his instruments, of a most singular comfort (*potissimam hanc consolationem*), whereby we are persuaded out of the Scriptures, that Satan and his ministers are not able to take in hand, much less to do anything against us, unless the Lord both be willing and has decreed the same (*nisi sic Deo volente et decernente posse*). Lastly, I say it is manifest impiety, to think that anything, though never so final and contemptible, has ever been, or hereafter shall come to pass, which God (being always most perfectly good and just, who also is ignorant of nothing, who works all in all, and against whose will nothing can be done) has not freely and of his own will decreed from all eternity.

[9. God's decree is always done. Yet he acts differently in the just and the unjust.] Therefore as touching God himself and his proper or peculiar work, he always justly wills, decrees, and works whatsoever he does in this world, by whomever, whenever, and however he does it, that is, whatever is done, or whatever comes to pass in this world both in general and in particular. Now in respect of the middle instruments which are also moved of themselves, albeit always he well and rightly moves and uses them, yet properly is he said to work in good instruments, that is to say, which rightly move themselves, as namely in the good spirits, and in his regenerate, creating in them good motions, which he afterwards cherished and brings to good effect; so that the whole glory of that good work which is wrought by these lively and moving instruments, is to be given to God as the principal cause and author thereof. But as touching evil instruments, and such as do not well and rightly move themselves, namely the devils and all those who are not regenerate, yes, the very regenerate themselves so far as the flesh sins in them, God is not said to work in them, as one who puts not into them any inclination and will to do wickedly, but only not restraining that corruption which naturally he finds in them. He suffers and gives them leave to move themselves and to do according to their evil and naughty disposition. And yet God always uses well and to good and just purposes these evil and sinful instruments, either as a most just Judge setting the wicked together by the ears, to work one another's destruction, or as a loving Father chastening his children even by the hand of those wicked ones, and sometimes exercising them as he thinks best, for his own glory and their profit.[66]

Lest one charge Beza with being scholastic or making God the author of sin, Beza quickly followed these grounds by asserting that lest "any man find fault that all these grounds are taken from human reason, and not from the word of God, let him answer me, whether God himself may not properly and without blasphemy be said to have sent Joseph to Egypt (Gen. 45) to have raised up Pharaoh, upon whom hardening his own heart, he might show his power (Ex. 4.21)."[67] Although his points accorded with human reason, Beza was loath to deny Scripture its place of supremacy. The Bible taught God's absolute sovereignty and providence over his creation.

Having surveyed the contours of Beza's doctrine of God's providence, we should notice, in the second place, that this doctrine was only coherent within the eschatological framework he had. His vision of a spiritual battle informed his outlook on God's control of the world. His view of powerful demonic forces, including Satan himself, necessitated Beza's accentuated belief that God

---

66 Ibid., G1r-G2v.
67 Ibid., G2v. Beza continued, listing several Old and New Testament examples of the same sort. He concluded, "Both that opposition and contrariety between God's permission and his will, between his decree and his action, is confuted, and also the works of God which are always most righteous and just are truly discerned from the evil works of naughty and sinful instruments" (ibid., G2v-G3r). Just as God used evil instruments to afflict his people in the old covenant, "So likewise the godly are afflicted by the will and foreappointment of God," Beza asserted (ibid., G2v).

was completely sovereign both in determining and in guiding all that took place within his creation. Only the sovereign God could control the devil. Only God could protect his children on earth. Only God could safely bring his children to be with him in heaven.

Beza's integration of God's providence with his spiritual vision came out time and again in his exposition of Job. In Job 2:5, Satan, angry at Job's constancy in the face of severe trials, implored the Almighty, "But, I pray you, now stretch out your hand, and touch him to his bones, and to his flesh, lest he blaspheme you to your face." Beza observed the reality, but also the limitations, of Satan. Satan here confessed that he had no power in and of himself to harm Job. It had to be given him from God. Yet in this, God did it for good, whereas Satan did it for evil. So, concluded Pastor Beza, "Job's temptation is of Satan, but his trial and invincible constancy is of God the Lord."[68]

Similarly, in his preface to the third chapter, in which Job finally spoke after suffering terribly, Beza commented on the reason Christians suffer. "It is for their good and profit," he told his suffering listeners, "whether by this means it pleases God to chastise them with his fatherly rod, or else to exercise and train them up, partly that they be weaned from the things of this world, and partly that his virtue and power may be seen in their infirmity, who in the end crowns his victorious champions with eternal happiness."[69] God, then, may have a multitude of different reasons for the trials of his people, including discipline, growth, death to the world, and his own glory, since he would be shown to be strong in upholding his weak people in the midst of their hardships. The ultimate goal of them all according to Beza, however, was heaven. There God would vindicate the saints by giving them eternal happiness because of their perseverance in the midst of trials. Indeed, Beza thought Christians' heavenly goal was the ultimate answer to the trials they suffered in this life. Thus he continued by asserting that the final antidote to Christians' sufferings was heaven. "Death is more beneficial to them than life and rather to be desired, not because they are weary of the troubles and discommodities of this life," the Reformer taught, "nor yet because they directly seek their own good and profit . . . but partly, that they may once for all, wholly be set free from so miserable bondage of sin. . . partly also that they may behold him as it were face to face, yes and more rightly serve and honor him, whom all their lifetime they have most earnestly sought."[70] Since they had sought God through the turmoil of life, God would transport them safely into his presence after they had suffered. This was assured due to God's absolute providence for his people.

Finally, then, Beza the pastor applied his doctrine of God's providence to his listeners during Geneva's troubled times in the late 1580s. When reading

---

68 Ibid., on Job 2:5.
69 Ibid., on Job 3.
70 Ibid.

Beza's exposition of Job, one is struck by the multiplicity of incidences where Beza sought to comfort and edify his listeners by his exposition of God's providence in light of the spiritual battle. In Beza's mind God's providence—even his decree of evil—was salutary to Christians who were going through difficulties.

Thus, in Job 1:6 Beza said the author "set down what the Lord decreed about these things in heaven." Foolish men – not just philosophers, but even some "in the school of God" – taught the notion that if God was indeed sovereign over all events he must be the cause of evil. In countering this false idea, Beza had a very pastoral concern, for he said that Satan tried to overthrow the faith of the church by making Christians doubt God's goodness in this life. "This is one of Satan's chief stratagems and practices against us," he lectured, "seeking either out of hand and at once to overthrow the foundation of our faith and hope, or else by little and little to shake and weaken it, that he may bring us to despair."[71] Discussion of God's providence, and his relationship to evil, was not merely a quarrel over words, then. It concerned the very foundation of the faith, for it concerned the character and power of God. It dealt with the good of God's people.

Was God, then, responsible for evil? To this Beza answered, in sum, "that nothing is done here upon the earth, whether it go well with the godly or ill with the wicked, or to the contrary, which God has not most justly and wisely decreed from all eternity for his own glory, and both for the profit of the godly and the just vengeance of the wicked."[72] Does this call God's holy character into question? No, answered Beza. Rather we see "that God, whether he use good or bad instruments, always deals justly" and that if we wait on him to work out his plan we will eventually be able to acknowledge "that he is a lover of righteousness, which he blesses, and a hater of iniquity."[73] In fact, rather than making believers doubt God's character, his providential rule over evil should give them hope in the midst of the battle raging around them. Indeed, "the fury both of Satan and of all the wicked, wherewith they are carried against the children of God, is so bridled by the power and will of God, that they cannot go about, much less effect anything, but only so far forth as God gives them leave."[74] God controls Satan and his demons and all evil so that the Lord ultimately controls how much harm they can perform. This should comfort his people in the midst of their trials and temptations.

Beza noted in Job 1:6 that Satan was drawn into God's presence against his will because the devil is under "God's authority and jurisdiction." So Satan can only do the harm God allows him to commit. In using Satan, though, God

---

71 Ibid., on Job 1:6.
72 Ibid., Div.
73 Ibid.
74 Ibid.

remained holy, because "In accomplishing the will of God herein, so often as Satan with his imps does as it were put to their helping hands, they are not to be thought to do it of any dutiful and obedient mind, but that they are delighted with that destroying power, that God gives them, to hurt and annoy his creatures."[75] This should not cause consternation among believers. It should rather encourage them through their earthly pilgrimage. "This doctrine is full of excellent comfort," Beza continued, "For thereby we understand that by the power of our God the rage of that hungry lion is abated and bridled, and that God will never suffer him to do anything against his children, which shall not be to their good and profit, as the apostle tells us (Rom. 8.28) and also teaches us by his own example (2 Cor. 12.17)."[76] Rather than causing Christians to question him, God's absolute sovereignty actually was the anchor for his troubled children in times of hardship.

Believers would have no comfort in the face of suffering if they could not be certain of God's control over evil, Beza argued in another place.

> God therefore is not the author of sin, although he is said not simply to suffer or permit, but even of his own will and purpose to work by an evil instrument, which unless we acknowledge, where shall we lay the foundation of our comfort in tribulation? And how shall that saying of Peter stand, that the will of God is so, that we should suffer for well doing (1 Pet. 3.17)? But this certainly is true, that the evil will of an evil instrument comes not of God, but proceeds wholly from the voluntary motion of the wicked, which notwithstanding God directs to his right end, fetching light even out of darkness, as it appears by Satan's words. For God puts not these things in his mind, but he is his own prompter, through that old cankered malice which is in him. And yet in this case one and the same manner of dealing is not always seen.[77]

"Where shall we lay the foundation of our comfort in tribulation?" Beza urged on his listeners. Only God's sovereign providence was strong and sure enough to uphold them.

In conclusion, we should note Beza's summation of Job 1, especially drawing on verse 21, "the Lord gives and the Lord takes away." Job, according to the Reformer, was a type for Christians who should follow him in his confident trust in the Lord during hardship. Should his listeners want comfort,

---

75 Ibid., on Job 1:6.
76 Ibid. Reflecting on Job 2:10, Beza again made the point that knowing Rom 8:28 should give Christians strength to follow Job's example of seeing God's hand in their suffering: "This is the issue of all Satan's practices against the elect, to whom, seeing all things fall out for the best, as the apostle tells us (Rom. 8). and daily experience also teaches, so often as the Lord deals with us, as here he does with Job. Why do we not rather than that we should expostulate and reason the matter with God?" (ibid., on Job 2:10).
77 Ibid., E2v.

they must emulate Job's quiet confidence in his Lord: "They that are rightly persuaded of the providence of God, and by the example of Job do acknowledge God to be the most just and wise governor of all things, not only in general, but in particular, they of all others do find out that most quiet and safe haven, wherein, having been tossed with never so violent storms of afflictions, they do quietly remain."[78] In a long application Beza asserted that Christians cannot know true assurance if they do not trust in a completely sovereign Lord:

> Effectual vocation [i.e., calling] . . . begins in the elect faith, hope, and charity, upon which follows justification by faith, and finally glorification. For these are always inseparably united. And unless we be certainly persuaded of this, we shall never enjoy any true peace of conscience. For otherwise it must of necessity follow, either that God is changeable, with whose will it may stand to have him condemned, whom before he would have saved, or else the condition of faith annexed to the promise of the gospel shall depend not upon God's immutable decree, but upon the will of man. The former cannot be said without blasphemy; and this is lumped with the heresy of the Pelagians. . . . Two things are in this argument especially to be observed. For this steadfastness and immutability takes place both in every one of the elect, and in the church, properly so called, that is, in the whole company of the elect and true believers, and not in these or those particular churches, nations, people, cities or families, not yet in the church, being so generally or universally taken, as in it are contained not only the elect and true believers, but hypocrites also and castaways. . . . Secondly we must know that among those principal gifts of the Spirit, there are some which in the faithful end together with this life, and others, which are only begun in this life, and shall be made perfect in us in the life to come. Of the first sort are faith and hope, not as though their nature were flitting and inconstant, but because – all those things being now finished and come to pass, which the elect in this life partly as being already past, and partly as yet to come, believed and hoped for – there shall then no longer be any place for faith and hope. But the knowledge of God by which while we live in this world, we know him only in part, shall be made perfect in the world to come, when we shall stand in God's presence, and see him as it were face to face; and charity, by which we love God and our brethren in this life very coldly, by reason of that fight which is between the flesh and the spirit, shall after a wonderful manner, such as no tongue is able to express, unite and join us with God and his blessed saints. . . . [Those teaching otherwise overthrow] that true and sure foundation of our faith and hope, by which we are upheld in most grievous temptations.[79]

Believers could have joy, even in the face of persecution, because their

---

78 Ibid., on Job 1:21.
79 Ibid. Although this anticipates my discussion of Beza's doctrine of assurance in chapter five, it is appropriate to notice it here in the context of his discussion of God's providence.

heavenly Father sovereignly ruled his creation. God's total providential care of them in this life and the life to come was the only route to "true peace of conscience."

The Pastoral Application of God's Providence

An examination of Theodore Beza's other pastoral treatises shows that he consistently emphasized the same themes he had developed in his treatise on the plague and his lectures on Job. One cannot read these works without noticing the emphasis he placed on Christians' suffering and on God's providence in the midst of their trials. This emphasis made sense given Beza's context. For instance, Manetsch pointed out that the picture on the title page of *Histoire ecclésiastiques* (1580) "aptly captured his [Beza's] resolute confidence in divine providence. Despite satanic opposition and intense suffering, he believed that the true church of God would survive and continue to proclaim the gospel until the return of Jesus Christ."[80] Beza had said as much in his treatment of Job. There he applied Job 1:4 to the contemporary situation in Europe, emphasizing the role Satan played in the consternation there:

> Verily this is the time, if ever, in which we have but small cause to rejoice. God has brought horrible famine, war and pestilence in a manner upon the whole earth; especially upon France and the Low Countries, we see the churches well nigh oppressed by the adversaries. Antichrist rages and leaves no treachery nor force unattempted against England and that most gracious Queen, which has been a refuge and as it were a sanctuary to a number of poor and miserable exiles. In Helvetia the spirit of discord waxes rank. Finally those bloody Jebusites strike up the alarm throughout all Christendom.[81]

---

80 Manetsch, "Theodore Beza," 130-31.
81 Beza, *Job*, C4r-C4v. Note his long application on Job 1:6, where he pointed out God's sovereignty even over the evil in Europe in the 1580s: "Neither is it to be doubted, but that as God hertofore defended his church by angels, in that miserable slavery, from infinite dangers (Dan. 10.20 and 11.1) so now also he defends us miraculously from Antichrist and the conspiracy of the whole world, sometime by confounding their language, other times by overthrowing tyrants, sometimes from heaven laughing our enemies to scorn, sometimes by blessing godly kings and princes, yes, and miraculously preserving queens, nursing mothers of the church; whereof if ever there was a manifest example, now it is to be seen in that thrice excellent princess Queen Elizabeth of England, whom God's singular providence has delivered from the infinite entrappings of Satan, Antichrist and the pope of Rome, even in our age, and whom we truly may call the common sanctuary and refuge of the afflicted church. And I pray you since the first civil wars stirred up in France by those chosen instruments of the devil, who can doubt but that those worthy men, protectors of the French churches, were assisted and guarded by the

Beza's providential reading of history extended beyond his exposition of Job. When reflecting on Psalm 94, he mentioned that the activity of Satan opposing God in the biblical account was typological of the way in which the devil acted in his own day. "This most excellent Psalm," he wrote, "is a displaying of the tyranny of Satan, by whose furies the most mighty princes of the world being stirred up, do violate all the laws of God and man, especially when they rise up against the godly, even as though there were no God, or that he had no providence at all, of which horrible rage and wickedness the chief kingdoms of Europe give us an example at this day."[82] Even more poignantly, Beza referred to his own troubled times in his paraphrase of Psalm 137. There he wrote,

> The Holy Ghost would have this excellent psalm to be extant that he might teach us very notable things, and necessary to our comfort, namely, that there is a time of silence under the cross, when the power of darkness has his time, notwithstanding that we must retain always our constancy, not only in faith, but also in zeal, lest we betray the truth with our silence, or forsake our duty for fear of men. . . . The oppressors of the church shall never carry away their wickedness unpunished, and chiefly they which do inflame the cruelty of the mighty men against the innocent.[83]

Indeed this "time of silence under the cross" was a reality for many Protestants in western Europe in Beza's lifetime. This was not rhetorical flourish but stark reality. Yet Beza was unwilling to limit God's sovereignty over the hardships of the church during his day. Although he was not culpable of committing sin, God ordained and controlled all that came to pass, even evil. Again, Beza's treatises were filled with these very sentiments. Thus in his commentary on Ecclesiastes 8:17 Beza defined providence as that "whereby almighty God governs all and everything." His providence, however, was incomprehensible to persons, moving beyond "all capacity and understanding of men."[84]

God's providence was boundless. It included such apparently minor

---

angels? Neither surely may we think that they were then forsaken of them, when as in the last conflict being taken into heaven they departed. And truly at this time no human force, but plain heavenly and extraordinary, does keep safe this heroical and worthy King of Navarre, the safeguard of the French Church; and the noble Prince of Condé, against those wicked cutthraots, conspirators and enemies both to the church and kingdom of France" (ibid., D2v-D3r).

82 Beza, *Psalmes*, 221.
83 Ibid., 331.
84 Beza, *Ecclesiastes*, D1[r].

God's Sovereignty for His People 163

blessings as giving persons a sound night's sleep.[85] It also included men's very wills and actions, as Beza explained in his exposition of Ecclesiastes 3:14:

> For whatever men purpose, discuss, determine, and take in hand, yet shall that always stand whatever God has determined should be done in times past, or shall be done in time to come. Whose unchangeable will, it were very unadvised and even wicked to think, that anything might or ought to be added unto, or taken from. For God at his own pleasure, though not always to be discerned of us, yet always justly, rules and guides all things to compel men even against their wills to appear before him and to reverence his Majesty.[86]

God's active governance extended to activities of Satan, as Beza prayed while reflecting on "And lead us not into temptation, but deliver us from evil" in the Lord's prayer: "as through your mercy, you suffer not Satan (the author of all temptations) to reduce your children, neither sin to overcome them, so when you will punish man in your justice, they remain deprived of your protection, and under the power of the devil to be subject to his tyranny, and to live in a reprobate sense, here do we therefore reap this singular consolation, that this great adversary of our salvation can do nothing against us, unless you give him leave."[87] The Sovereign controlled everything that happened.

Thus God decreed and controlled all that transpired. But he often used others to do his bidding. Beza again explicated his view of the manner in which God used secondary causes to accomplish his ordained end. His comments on Psalm 107 are noteworthy in this regard:

> This psalm, than the which nothing can be spoken more truly, nor more eloquently, neither yet more divinely, affirms the providence of God, both general and particular, to be most just and also most merciful, bringing forth and most elegantly describing very good examples of those things which come to pass, both by sea and by land, that of necessity we must grant, their causes and effects wholly to be governed by God – either against the wicked, which deny God utterly, or remove him from the government of the world, as do the Epicureans, or who think that he regards the things that he has made only generally, as do the Peripatetians, or who bind him to second causes as do the Stoics, and also against superstitious persons, confessing the truth indeed, but attributing to their feigned gods that which belongs to the most mighty and merciful God alone. At whose lies being worthily condemned, the prophet admonishes the godly and them that are truly wise that they should learn rather to have the works of God in

---

85 "I acknowledge of your providence and benignity, that having passed this night under your guard and protection, I may yet see the light of the day" (Beza, *Houshold Prayers*; in the prayer, "For the Morning").
86 Beza, *Ecclesiastes*, B4[r].
87 Beza, *Houshold Prayers*, in the prayer "Upon the Lord's Prayer."

admiration, and to praise both his most excellent wisdom and moderation in them, than to call them in to doubtful question, and be foolish with the wicked.[88]

Beza's refrain for his listeners and readers throughout his treatises was that they must trust God. As the sovereign ruler, God was preeminently trustworthy. "Falling down before the majesty of God, which we cannot comprehend," Beza urged his listeners to "rest wholly in his will."[89] Trust should work out into fervent petitions to the Almighty as Beza related in his reflections on Psalm 57: "we may gather, that it lies in the hand of God, not only with how great, but with how long miseries – yes, even by wicked men – he will exercise his servants, and therefore that we must pray continually, as well for the gifts of constancy, and perseverance, as for the gift of faith."[90]

As a pastor, though, Beza was not naïve enough to tell his listeners that it would be easy for them to trust God's providence with their hardships. It was not simple to place trust in the Lord when, for example, evil persons prospered while the righteous suffered at their hands. Reflecting on Ecclesiastes 5:8, Beza exhorted his readers:

Let it not cause you to forego your godliness, and to give over the duty of a man that fears God, because you see some oppressed who ought to have been relieved, or because you see in some places that laws are broken under color of right, therefore to begin to doubt of that providence of God. For however these things seem to be tossed up and down, as if the world had no governor, yet be sure there is one above all these, that abuse the honor whereunto they are advanced, who has also standing by him innumerable and most mighty ministers, whom in due time he may set a work to execute his decrees upon these proud men.[91]

What should weary and wounded persons do when the evil prospered? As

---

88 Beza, *Psalmes*, 256. Beza's comments on Psalm 73 are also pertinent in this regard because of his critique of the manner in which philosophers attempted to deal with evil and implicated God for it. The "chiefest of all" things taught in this psalm is "that it shall never go well with the evil men, and that by their own fault. Contrariwise, that it shall never go evil with the good, and that by the singular mercy of God. For unto the evil men, good things are turned to evil, and on the contrary, unto the good men, even evil things turn to good. This is a very precious doctrine, which is handled oftentimes both in other psalms, and in divers places of the scripture, especially in Job, and the prophet Habbakuk, but above all in this psalme . . . whereas bare, slender, and sometimes foolish things are taught in the schools, of the difference of good and evil things, and of the virtues, and of their causes and effects, even among those philosophers, which did count virtue their only mead, and did judge only the wise man to be always blessed" (ibid., 163).

89 Beza, *Ecclesiastes*, C5[r].

90 Beza, *Psalmes*, 125.

91 Beza, *Ecclesiastes*, on Eccl. 5:8.

we noted above, Beza called on them to place their trust in God. During their earthly pilgrimage that would be difficult at times, Beza acknowledged. But there was an answer to the dilemma. Heaven was the ultimate goal of God's providence for the believer. In fact, Beza's pastoral treatises constantly reproduce his eschatological vision as the key to hoping in God's providence in this life. He did not shy from pointing his listeners to heaven as the resting place where they would be free from the spiritual (and earthly) warfare of this life. Because of God's providence for his people, Beza encouraged his readers that "shortly, instead of this misery you shall receive the true peace which the world can neither give, nor take away, and the true repose of conscience, even the very anchor and earnest payment of that durable blessedness to follow."[92] In his exposition of Psalm 4, Beza repeated the same refrain, urging his readers that in the midst of suffering their greatest assurance came from the hope that was laid up for believers in heaven:

> This psalm teaches the whole church, and every member of the same, that when the wicked rage we ought not only not to despair or be discouraged, but rather boldly to reprove our adversaries, resting upon the power of God, whereof we have had so oft experience, and trusting to the goodness of our cause, and chiefly to the most assured promises of the life to come, upon which we must always have our eyes bent, and never depend upon the transitory commodities of this world.[93]

The sovereign Lord would take care of his children—now and forever.

Once again, Theodore Beza's prayers are a spotlight into his soul, in this instance into the manner in which his eschatological vision led him to see the outworking of God's providence for his people ultimately in their residence in heaven. For example, Beza addressed his prayer "For obtaining the virtue of patience" to the "God of patience, and of all consolation, the just dispenser both of calamities and benefits, and that all to one end, evermore happy to those whom you love in your eternal Son, our Lord Jesus Christ." There he prayed to his heavenly Father, "as there is nothing in your word but serves to our learning and to the guiding of our temporal life as a means to obtain the possession of heavenly joys, so does it principally insist in this, to lift up our hearts to an

---

92 Beza, *Christian Meditations*, on Ps 32:7. Beza's eschatological vision expressed here is more poignant given the circumstances that called forth this work from Beza's pen. According to Raitt, in the troubled 1580s when Geneva feared Savoy would persuade her Spanish allies to attack Geneva, fasts were often proclaimed. "Beza's book of *Christian Meditations*," she noted, "was composed to assist the faithful in these exercises and consists in prayers drawn from the seven penitential psalms. They are intended for private devotional use" (Raitt, "Beza, Guide," 97-98).

93 Beza, *Psalmes*, 5.

earnest meditation and firm expectation of eternal life."[94] Repeating this future-hoping theme later, Beza prayed, "The present sorrow of your children is unto them the watch of some future joy at hand, and that all adventures, the last of their most painful days, is the first of their eternal rest, in the second life."[95]

But Beza's prayer "That we may well use afflictions" demonstrates his eschatological hope in God's providence for his people most lucidly. One of the keys to dealing with troubles in this life, according to Pastor Beza, was to have a heaven-perspective and to realize that since they made believers like Christ these tribulations actually prepared Christians to be with Jesus in heaven. Thus he asked the Lord to strengthen his people "to bear out the afflictions and miseries of this life, wherein it pleases you especially to exercise yourself, upon diverse good considerations, namely, to make them conformable to the image of your Son, to the end that suffering with him, they may also reign in his glory."[96] So, at the end of the prayer, he asked:

> Especially grant, O Lord, that I may attain to this reason of true wisdom, always to be content with your will, the sovereign and just cause of all things; namely, in that it pleases you, that the livery of your household should consist in carrying their cross after your Son, to the end that I should never but be seasoned to drink the wholesome myrrh which purges the soul from the lusts of the flesh and replenishes the same with the desires of eternal life. Also that I learn in whatever my estate, cheerfully to submit myself to the conduct of your providence, being well assured that whatever I suffer, all the crosses of my life shall be unto me so many blessings and helps from you my Father to make me go the right way into your kingdom, and increase unto me the price of glory in the same.[97]

According to Theodore Beza, then, God's providence should be a comfort for Christians. Certainly God's ways were often perplexing. The spiritual battle was raging. Satan and his fiends actively opposed the church. Their efforts included using earthly powers to persecute and kill believers. All of this occurred, Beza vigorously maintained, only at the behest of the Lord. Yet in the midst of these evils, Beza urged believers to trust in God's goodness and power, and to pray fervently to him for his help. Their hope, he repeated on several occasions, was in God's promise, especially his assurance that he would work all things in their lives for good. But Beza was a realist. Ultimately Christians' outward lot in this life might never be better. Their supreme hope was that God would bring them out of this tumultuous life to heaven. God's supreme providence assured them that they would indeed arrive there safely.

---

94 Beza, *Houshold Prayers*, K5v.
95 Ibid., in the prayer "For obtaining the Virtue of Patience."
96 Ibid., in the prayer "That we may well use afflictions."
97 Ibid., K3v-K4v.

The Doctrine of Predestination Explained and Defended

Just as Theodore Beza believed God to be sovereign over all the events of life, he believed the Lord was absolutely sovereign in the salvation of Christians. In this sense, the doctrine of predestination was a sub category of the doctrine of providence to the Reformer. Like providence, predestination was essential given the spiritual realities, Beza averred. Predestination was a comforting doctrine for God's children.

This alone explains, I contend, the pains Theodore Beza went to in order to defend this doctrine and, indeed, to use it as a comfort to Christians. This simple fact controverts much of the Bezan historiography. I will therefore attempt quickly to counter the reigning consensus that predestination was the *sine qua non* of Beza's theology. This will comprise two steps: first, showing that when Beza defined the Christian gospel, he did not include the doctrine of predestination; and, second, noticing that Beza employed the doctrine of predestination differently in varied genres. Depending upon his purpose in writing, he emphasized God's sovereignty in election or downplayed its importance. Next I will explicate the use Beza made of the doctrine of predestination pastorally. Beza believed God's sovereign hand was absolutely necessary to uphold his people in the midst of the raging spiritual battle. Predestination was a pastoral *sine qua non*, but it was anti-speculative with a vengeance.

The Sum of the Gospel According to Beza

Beza's primary concern was salvation in Christ.[98] The gospel, in Beza's mind, centered upon God's gracious activity of rescuing sinful persons through the redeeming work of Jesus Christ. Since this is a fact that is often overlooked in Bezan studies, I will note those places from two of his pastoral treatises where Beza explicitly said he was going to explicate the gospel. Fortunately, in several places in these pastoral works Beza summarized what he thought were the major components of the Christian gospel. Here, that is, he concisely taught the central truths of the Christian faith. In none of his explications did he include predestination.

In his paraphrase on the Psalms, Beza summarized the gospel in several places. When dealing with Psalm 110, he included a long exposition of what he thought were the most central aspects of the Christian gospel:

> I think that this most excellent and most precious psalm may aptly be called an epitome of the gospel promised, wherein truly – although the Jews, which were given up into a reprobate sense, go about to cover light with darkness – these chief points of our salvation are declared, both with a great perspicuity and a marvelous

---

[98] See my discussion of Beza's pastoral systematic theology in chapter three.

brevity. First, the divinity of Christ, verse 1, as Christ himself does interpret it (Mat. 22.42, etc.). For the very enemies of Christ did not doubt but he was man and that of the stock of David. Secondly, his humanity with his everlasting power and kingdom, both in heaven and in earth, and also with the name which is above all names, the very Godhead being excepted, and therefore the unity of the person in both natures, besides that presence of his divine majesty, which Eutyches affirmed, is in the same verse, in these words, "Sit at my right hand" as the apostle interprets it (Heb. 1.12). Thirdly, the battles of the same king, and his victories against all his enemies, visible and invisible, in the last part of the same verse as the apostles interpret it (1 Cor. 15.24. and so forth, and Heb. 10.13). Fourthly, from what time this king began his kingdom, verse 2, as Isa. interprets it (Isa. 2.3) and by the thief hanging upon the cross (Luke 23.42), whereunto Pilate himself though he thought no such thing subscribed it in three languages. Fifthly, a plain description of the true church, that is to say, of them that are set up against the enemies of this king, in the second verse. First, that they are a people which obey willingly and without dissimulation. Furthermore, as soldiers are known by their liveries or other cognizance, under whose standards they fight, even so the armies of this most holy king are known by holiness. And this holiness without all doubt before God, is Christ himself, who is made unto us wisdom, justice, sanctification, and redemption, and in whom we are without spot or blot. But before men, the very fruits of faith are the cognizance, which the prophet declares, borrowing the manner of his speech, of the ornaments of the priests and Levites, in which chiefly at their solemn feasts they came forth every one in their order. Thirdly, he signifies that this beauty now lies hid under the cross and miseries unto which the church is subject but that which we are (as is written in 1 John 3.2) shall appear in that day of the restoring of the church, whereof Peter speaks (Acts 3.21) and Paul (1 Cor. 15.28). In the fourth place, he compares the assembly of the godly, how miserable soever it is, with the army of most chosen young men, that we may know that the power of God is made perfect in our infirmity, which power chiefly appeared in the first infancy of the Christian church being new born, even with the great shame of those that succeeded afterward. Finally, all these things, namely, both the church itself, and all the gifts wherewith it is adorned; he says, by a most excellent and apt similitude, that it is a dew falling down from heaven, as out of the womb of the morning. That is to say, it is the mere and only gift of the free goodness of the heavenly Father. Sixthly, a description most perfect of another office of Christ, that is to say, of his eternal priesthood, confirmed by an oath, repeating also under the figure of Melchizedek the conjunction of both the natures into one subject (verse 4) of which thing, how many and how great mysteries there are, it is declared in the seventh chapter of the Epistle to the Hebrews throughout. Seventhly (in verses 5, 6, 7) the battles chiefly of Christ himself, and afterward even of the church which shall follow, from the beginning of the revelation of the gospel unto the second coming of Christ, against all the most mighty princes, and chiefly against Satan, the tyrant of this world – unless by the monarch, whereof he specially makes mention in the sixth verse, we had rather understand the Roman empire, and his image, even Antichrist. Which thing

Daniel did expound more plainly afterward (Dan. 2.44) and John in the Revelation, when the triumph shall be so much more glorious, both of the captain, and also of the soldiers, as the battle has more sorely and longer continued.[99]

Similarly, in his treatment of Psalm 97 Beza developed the chief points of the gospel:

> This psalm verily is most worthy for all the godly to meditate most diligently, as a most divine and brief summary of all the mysteries of the gospel, and these are the chief places thereof. First, the divinity of Christ, by the repeating of the name Jehovah six times, and by attributing all glory and power unto him (verse 2, 5, 6, 9, 10) finally, by worshipping the very angels, verse 7, it is most manifestly confirmed, as the apostle does interpret it (Heb. 1.6). Secondly, his humanity, as the same apostle interprets it. Which thing is also proved hereby, that here it is treated of that kingdom as it were first then to be begun (verse 1, 2, 6, 9) whereby it is plain that it cannot be referred only to his Godhead, but that it appertained necessarily unto the King that should be born of the stock of David which should so be God, that he should also be man, and so also man, that he should be very God. Thirdly, a plain prophecy of the spreading of the spiritual kingdom throughout the whole world (verse 1, 5, 6.) whereunto Christ himself had regard (Jn. 5.22; Mat. 28.18). Fourthly, the rebellion of very many, unto whom the gospel should be, and now is, the savor of death unto death (verse 2, 3, 4, 5) whereunto Christ had respect (Luke 12.49). For I had rather interpret these things thus, than to apply them to the preaching of the law. Fifthly, that incredible power of the Spirit of God, which should declare itself in the ministry of the apostles (verse 1, 6, 7, 9), which Christ also foretold before (John 12.32 and 14.12). Sixthly, the exaltation of the very person of Christ (verse 9) whereunto the apostle manifestly alluded (Eph. 4.10 and Philip. 2.9). Seventhly, faith by hearing the word in the elect, and the unspeakable joy of the conscience that shall follow thereof, verse 8. Eighthly, the office of those that are justified and sanctified, verse 10. Ninthly, the cross is like a certain apparatus attending upon the promises of the gospel, which yet shall have a most joyful end, verse 11 and 12. Whereunto the apostle most manifestly alluded (Philip. 4.4).[100]

The Reformer's treatment of Psalm 32 demonstrates that Beza was in the mainstream of the Reformation in his emphasis on the doctrine of justification by faith alone. According to Theodore Beza, justification, not predestination, was the heartbeat of Christianity:

> This most precious psalm teaches the chief and principal article of the Christian faith, as the apostle testifies, and interprets it (Rom. 4.6), that is to say, that all our blessedness consist in the free forgiveness of our sins. For all other religions deceive men in this point chiefly, that they teach them to seek salvation at their

---

99 Beza, *Psalmes*, 267-69.
100 Ibid., 227-28.

own righteousness, which can nowhere be found. But in the gospel only, Christ our only mediator is declared unto us to be made righteousness of God his Father. The prophet also teaches in this psalm that this doctrine does not bring in a foolish and careless security, as the papists falsely slander it, as though the free imputation of the justice of Christ should abolish the care and endeavor to do good works. For he, on the contrary, declares that the Spirit of regeneration is always annexed with the gift of righteousness by imputation, which is received by faith, which kindles in the hearts of them that are justified an earnest loathing of sin, hope, true obedience, and other virtues. Whereof this follows, that the conscience being pacified, enjoys a true and perpetual joy, whatever storms do arise. Therefore this psalm differs from the first, because it shows the chief effects, whereby a man may be known to be blessed. But this declares the cause of that blessedness, and also of the effects, and by this consideration may Paul and James be reconciled.[101]

Finally, Beza summarized the gospel of reconciliation in his sermons on Canticles in this fashion. Again predestination is conspicuously absent:

In sum, these few words, "Come your way," ought to serve us for a summary abridgement of the whole doctrine of salvation, consisting in these two points—that during this life, we should continually aspire on high, unto a far better life; and that to come thereunto, turning ourselves from all the enticements and allurements which stay us here below, and using this world so, as if we were not at all in it (1 Cor. 7.31 and Gal. 6.14) every of us take our way right unto God according unto his vocation, practicing and putting in use his commandments. And not, when he says "Come your way," seeking after excuses such as are mentioned (Luk. 14.18) for unto such it shall not be said, "Come you my well beloved," but "go you cursed." The Lord grant us to hear that so happy word, and preserve us from this other so fearful and so horrible.[102]

Several comments are in order. First, the gospel, according to Beza, did not equal predestination. But, second, the gospel was intensely Christocentric.[103] It was grounded upon Christ's person, both his divinity and his humanity. This God-man was the only one capable of mediating between the holy God and sinful persons, by being the righteousness of God for them and imputing it to them. Third, the gospel was armor for Christians for battle. Beza emphasized warfare terminology as he described the manner in which the church was attacked. Christ was victorious over all his enemies, and the church would ultimately be victorious as well. However, earthly princes and tyrants, and

---

101 Ibid., 54.
102 Beza, *Canticles*, 256.
103 In his sermons on Christ's death, Beza similarly asserted that the title hung on the cross above Jesus ("This is the King of the Jews") "comprised all the mystery of the salvation of his people" (Beza, *Sermons sur la Passion*, 168).

especially Satan sought to oppose the progress of the church at all turns. This spiritual battle would color the history of the church until Christ's victorious second coming. Although the church's future was magnificent, its beauty often lay buried under crosses and miseries in this life. The fact of this battle led to Beza's next emphasis. Fourth, the gospel, according to Beza, was intensely pastoral. It alone could relieve guilty consciences. It also could fill persons with joy as they contemplated their forgiven state in Christ. It only could support them amid the storms which were sure to vex them as they made their pilgrimage to heaven. Finally, the gospel, according to Beza, was grounded in God's sovereignty. Although the gospel did not equal predestination, it rested on the sure foundation of God's omnipotence. The benefits of the gospel were granted the church as a gift because of God's sovereign goodness. The Spirit of God was powerful, strong enough to create faith in God's chosen ones when they heard the gospel preached. The gospel, then, was a sure promise, grounded upon God's power and love. Although the church was attacked on all sides now, God's people would surely arrive safely in heaven because of his goodness and care for his children.

God's sovereignty was not the gospel, then, although without it there would be no good news. For instance, in his *De praedestinationis doctrina* of 1582 Beza clearly used the doctrine of predestination to buttress the gospel. This treatise devoted to the doctrine of predestination came from Beza's lectures at the Academy on Paul's letter to the Romans, when Beza reached the ninth chapter of the epistle. Significantly, though, Beza attempted to place his discussion of predestination in the flow of the entire letter. He began his summary by noting the way in which Paul elaborated the gospel. "The sum of it is," he declared, "as follows: We are graciously saved in the one Lord Jesus Christ, who is apprehended by faith."[104] That, in sum, is the gospel, according to the Genevan Reformer. We note again that the doctrine of predestination had no place in his summation of the cardinal doctrine of Christianity.

Although the gospel was not predestination, predestination was essential to the gospel. In fact, Beza continued his exposition by grounding one's ability to trust in the gospel in the certainty of God's sovereignty:

> If Paul had not laid out a foundation for this treatment on which our very faith could be supported, and opened up the source from which it emanates, and if he had not explained the means by which it comes to us from a certain impulse through the Holy Spirit, his foregoing discussion [in Rom 1-8] would be completely deficient and useless. For why then would we stand firm in any temptations (of even the slightest sort), endowed with faith, and equipped with that security and that most certain trust that he described at the end of the

---

104 Theodore Beza, *De Praedestinationis Doctrina*, in *The Potter and the Clay: The Main Predestination Writings of Theodore Beza*, trans. Philip C. Holtrop (Grand Rapids: Calvin College, 1982), 296.

preceding chapter [Rom 8]? Why, if it depended on some strength that lies in or within ourselves?

Foreseeing this in the last chapter [Rom 8], the Apostle therefore rose to faith from the love by which we love God and from the effect of faith that is necessary and perceptible to our senses. So too now, he brings us forth from faith to calling, and from calling to predestination, and at last from predestination to the eternal and unshaken purpose of God. Finally, at that point—when the anchor of our faith and hope is firmly fixed—we may easily overcome all storms. Moreover, he now begins at last to expound explicitly, in its aspects, that mystery that he proposed in a few words and in an abbreviated form at the end of the preceding chapter.[105]

For Theodore Beza, therefore, predestination was not the *sine qua non* of Christian doctrine. The doctrine of predestination was the "anchor of our faith and hope" (*anchora Fidei speique nostre*) that enabled believers to "easily overcome all storms."[106] Predestination was intensely pastoral according to Beza. God's sovereignty alone assured troubled Christians that when they faced the vast temptations the apostle elaborated in Romans 8:31-39, they would stand firm. In the midst of the spiritual battle, the battle for their very souls that surrounded the gospel, God would certainly uphold them by his sovereign tender care.

Predestination and Genre

As a pastor and teacher Beza expressed himself differently in different contexts. Genre is one of the keys to understanding Beza's doctrine of predestination aright. Beza was quite able to express the doctrine of predestination differently in varied genres. If one merely reads his *Tabula*—or just looks at the table prefixed to it!—one will likely form a slanted opinion of Beza's doctrine of predestination. Here we shall briefly examine the place that predestination occupied in three different genres of Beza's treatises: systematic, polemical, and pastoral.

SYSTEMATIC WORKS

The most remarkable thing about Beza's treatment of predestination in his systematic works is that doctrine's inconspicuousness.[107] We can begin our

---

105 Ibid., 296-97.
106 Theodore Beza, *De Praedestinationis Doctrina, in Tractationum Theologicarum, in quibus plerasque Christianae Religionis dogmata adversus haereses nostris temporibus renovatas solide ex Verbo Dei defenduntur* (Geneva: Vignon, 1582), 3:413.
107 See my treatment of the structure of Beza's four systematic treatises in chapter three. Since I dealt with these structures there, I will be brief in my treatment of the entire treatises here.

investigation by looking at Beza's 1559 *Confession*. The *Confession*—which, based on the number of times Beza edited and republished it, was his equivalent to Calvin's *Institutes*—remarkably never even deals with the doctrine of predestination outright. Beza's *Autre Briefve Confession de Foy* made hardly any mention of predestination. In fact, it only hinted at the significance of God's sovereignty in salvation in article eighteen which stressed the Spirit's role in regeneration. His *Quaestionum et responsionum Christianarum libellus* certainly dealt at length with predestination. Questions 195 to 208 explicated this doctrine specifically.[108] Yet, their placement towards the end of the treatise and the purpose of the work shows that Beza intended to stress the doctrine of salvation, not eternal predestination, here. Finally, in his *Petit Catéchisme* Beza only mentioned predestination twice: the first time showing why only certain persons believed and the second accounting for those who do good works. Like the summation of the gospel we previously noted, Beza's systematic theological treatises emphasized the gospel of salvation in Jesus Christ, not God's hidden decree of election.

POLEMICAL WORKS

As we noted earlier in our discussion of Theodore Beza's context, several of his occasional and polemical treatises dealt extensively with the doctrine of predestination. We will limit our discussion here to two of these polemical productions, since the other two, *Ad Sebastioni Castellionis* and *Ad Acta Colloquii Montisbelligartensis*, were both structured around Beza's opponents' arguments.

Beza's *De praedestinationis doctrina* arose from Beza's lectures through the epistle of St. Paul to the Romans. It consists, for the most part, of Beza's detailed exposition of Romans 9:1-23. At the end of the published lectures, though, Beza included several theses. Introducing them, he said, "It seems good to us now to arrange this entire discussion in the following theses, as seen in their proper order. Thus the whole method of the dogmatical sections of this epistle [Romans] may be cast before our eyes, as it were, from the sixteenth verse of chapter one to the end of chapter 11. In a most inspiring and (at the same time) a most erudite way, that embraces the highest teaching of the Christian religion."[109] The first thirteen theses, "On Justification," covered Paul's teaching in Romans 1:18 to 8:39. Only after he recounted the themes of Romans 1-8 did Beza address election in his six theses "On Predestination," which summarize Romans 9:6-23. There, Beza argued that, first, God's covenant of eternal life is certain. Second, from eternity and merely according to his will, God from eternity chose certain persons and nations to belong to him; the others he hated. Third, nevertheless God is not unjust, for he did not

---

108 See Beza, *Little Book of Christian Questions and Responses*, 83-96.
109 Beza, *De Praedestinationis Doctrina*, in *The Potter and the Clay*, 382.

decree to reprobate apart from the actual sinfulness of the wicked. Fourth, since God's decree is immutable, he rightly rages against the reprobate. Fifth, as Creator, God has absolute authority over everything created by him. Sixth, God is supremely just in reprobating the wicked, but he is supremely merciful in saving the elect.[110] Even in one of his most mature treatments of predestination, then, Beza thought he was deriving his opinions from the mind of St. Paul in Romans.

Beza's 1555 *Tabula Pradestinationis* interests us because the aphorisms Beza included as explanations to his "table" lucidly explicate his doctrine.[111] We shall merely summarize the aphorisms, as Beza arranged them in their eight chapters. In the first chapter, "That the question of God his everlasting Predestination, is neither curious, nor unneedful in the church of God," Beza asserted that Augustine had dealt with the doctrine of predestination in several places. From Augustine's handling of the doctrine, the church should learn two things: first, that predestination must be discussed and debated from God's word, and, second, that it must be handled for the purpose of edifying the saints. Chapter two, "Of the everlasting counsell of God, hid in him selfe, whiche notwithstanding is in the ende understoode by the effectes," expounded God's eternal decree concerning salvation. From eternity, God decreed to create two sorts of men—the elect and the reprobate. His decree came from his good pleasure alone, not from their foreseen works or faith. It is therefore inscrutable, but, in order to confirm God's people in their hope, the Bible shows Christians how to find assurance. It begins with the proof of the second causes (works) and goes to those causes themselves (faith and calling to salvation). From there the quest for assurance of salvation proceeds to Christ, in whom believers were elected, and finally rises to God's eternal purpose. The

---

110 Ibid., 384-86.
111 The text of Beza's aphorisms are included as appendix three. Muller noted the importance of Beza's intentional arrangement of his material. Numerous Scripture citations were interspersed between the often lengthy aphorisms, a fact which was obscured by the first English translator (Muller, "Use and Abuse," 46). I have appended the aphorisms from the later, and more correct, English translation. Additionally, some scholars have incorrectly reprinted Beza's "table" without any of his aphorisms. This has wrongly suggested that the chart could be understood without the biblical proofs or Beza's explanations. See, for example, Heinrich Heppe, *Reformed Dogmatics: Set Out and Illustrated from the Sources*, trans. G. T. Thomson, rev. and ed. Ernst Bizer (London: George Allen & Unwin, 1950), 147-48, and, recently, Paul F. M. Zahl, *A Short Systematic Theology* (Grand Rapids: Eerdmans, 2000). Zahl began his entire work by stating that Beza "said that the whole of Christian theology could be condensed on a single sheet of paper. He did this, and it remains an epigrammatic touchstone for all who come after him." He included Beza's "table," without any explanation, as an appendix titled "A Summary of the Entire Christian Faith" (ibid., 1, 96-97).

reprobate are guilty in themselves since they choose to sin, even though their sin is willed by God.

In chapter three, "Of the execution or fulfilling of the everlasting counsel, in that which is common both to the elect or chosen, and also to the reprobate or off-casts," Beza argued that God did not create persons sinful. Had he done so, God would be the author of sin. But the Lord created Adam and Eve pure and with a free will; they proceeded to sin. This fall into sin, though, was not outside of God's providence. It occurred by the "will" or "decree" of God, not just his bare "permission."

Chapter four was titled "By what order of causes God hath opened the way to declare his election, and in some part to execute or perform it." Here Beza recounted the biblical scheme of salvation. Human beings were so sinful that they could not save themselves. Therefore, the Father sent his Son, the God-man, as a priest to die for them. Certain steps must occur in order for them to become united to Christ. The Holy Spirit must convict them of sin and draw them to Christ. The only condition presented in the gospel is "believe in Christ." For them to do so, however, the Holy Spirit must regenerate them, because their free will is dead in sin. Real Christians will persevere by God's grace.

In chapter five, "In what order the Lord does begin to execute or fulfill, and indeed effectually to declare his counsel or reprobation or off-casting," Beza argued that God fulfilled his purpose in the reprobate. God willed from eternity that they should be damned, but he also decreed the causes of their damnation. So, for instance, the reprobate refused to believe the gospel when it was preached to them. Although necessary (because decreed by God), their stubbornness was also of their own free will and therefore spontaneous. They were responsible for their destruction.

Beza labeled chapter six "Of the last and full execution or performing of the counsel of God, both in the chosen, and also in the off-casts." Here Beza argued that God worked differently in the elect than in the reprobate. He gave the elect faith in Christ, united them with Christ now, and would certainly bring them to heaven in the future. On the other hand, he left the reprobate in their sins. So the Lord would show himself to be supremely merciful to the elect, and just in his dealings with the damned. Chapter seven, "What way this doctrine may profitably be openly set forth and taught," and chapter eight, "How every several person may apply with some profit this general doctrine to himself," were the applications of the foregoing discussion. We will discuss these final two chapters of the *Tabula* later.

Several brief comments are in order.[112] Although this was an extended and sometimes complex treatment of the doctrines of election and reprobation, Beza

---

112 See Muller, "Use and Abuse," 47-61, for an exposition of the *Tabula*.

wrote it as a response to Bolsec's attempt to counter Genevan orthodoxy.[113] Second, Beza's predestinarianism was very Christocentric. The focus of God's electing work was to unite his children to Christ by faith. Third, apparently following his own admonition at the end of chapter one, Beza intended this work to be edifying to his readers. He interspersed pastoral applications throughout the first six chapters and included the final two chapters to show his readers how they might apply the doctrine of eternal predestination to themselves. These final two chapters comprise almost one-third of the text of the aphorisms. Richard Muller's estimation seems correct: "Beza's fundamental intention is to demonstrate how such a doctrine [predestination] belongs to Christian instruction and is a support of piety. In short, the intention of the Tabula is to show that the doctrine of the decree and its execution, as presented through the collation of biblical texts, is a source of consolation and strength—in this particular context, against the claims of Bolsec that the doctrine was not based on a simple reading of Scripture and was a monstrous distortion of the gospel."[114] Finally, Beza again followed his own exhortation from chapter one and tried to be intentionally biblical in his exposition. For instance, in his aphorisms Beza footnoted about five hundred and seventy-six different biblical references. Between the aphorisms he wrote out the Scripture references so that the Bible texts comprise a larger part of the *Tabula* than do the aphorisms.

PASTORAL WORKS

Following Armand Dückert's 1891 study of Beza the preacher, most researchers emphasize that Theodore Beza did not stress the doctrine of predestination in his pastoral works. Dückert briefly noted some of the places that Beza discussed the doctrine in his sermons, but then he expressed some initial puzzlement at Beza's reticence to discuss a doctrine he spent a great deal of time on in other places. Dückert concluded that the particular doctrine of predestination would not have been appropriate given the topics with which Beza dealt in his homilies. He also claimed that Beza did not think the role of the preacher included expositing doctrine.[115] However, I find it no more startling that Theodore Beza emphasized themes other than predestination in his sermons than I do that he barely dealt with it in his systematic treatises, as I previously argued.[116]

That is not to say, however, that Beza did not teach on predestination at all in his pastoral treatises. For example, in his thirty-first sermon dealing with the

---

113 Ibid., 35-46.
114 Ibid., 35.
115 Dückert, *Théodore de Bèze*, 43; cf. 33-36, where Dückert treated Beza's doctrine of predestination.
116 See chapter three.

death of Christ, Beza dealt at length with the doctrine of predestination.[117] We note here merely Beza's exhortation at the head of the sermon. He noted two reasons for discussing predestination in this context. First, many misunderstand it; second, it encourages believers. Thus, since predestination was clearly set forth in Scripture it must be taught and believed:

> We must deduce this matter longer, since this passage requires it, and since it is also very badly understood by many persons, who are scandalized by their error in it, instead of being edified by it (*au lieu d'en estre edifiés*). But whatever those say who find this doctrine so strange—since the holy Scriptures not only testify that there is a Paradise and a Hell, that there will be some who are saved and some damned, that there is in God mercy and judgment, but also that there are some elect (*esleus*) and some reprobate (*reprouvés*), and some vessels destined (*destinés*) to dishoner and some to honor, and some vessels of wrath appointed (*appareillés*) to perdition and some vessels of mercy who are prepared (*preparés*) for glory—we must hold this doctrine as the pure truth of God (*pure verité de Dieu*), and we must be charmed by his understanding. But we must examine it very well and be resolved in it by the same Scriptures.[118]

The doctrine of predestination was important since it was found in God's word and was therefore "the pure truth of God." Predestination was not foreign to Theodore Beza's pastoral work, as we shall note below.

Predestination: Anchor in the Battle

Predestination was vital pastorally. God's sovereignty in saving his people—rescuing them powerfully and certainly from the consequences of their sin—was an anchor for them to hold on to throughout the trials of this life. For Beza, the doctrine of predestination was a comforting truth.

Beza's pastoral and devotional works are replete with applications of predestination for his listeners. We shall note the numerous ways from these writings the ways that Pastor Beza urged his listeners to find comfort in their heavenly Father's care for them. First, though, we should note the pastoral application of predestination that Beza set forth in one of his most strident defenses of the doctrine of God's sovereignty in salvation.

As we noted previously, the final two chapters of Beza's *Tabula* consist of Beza's application of predestination to his readers.[119] Chapter seven consisted of sage advice about the manner in which the doctrine of predestination should be taught. Beza urged here that anyone teaching on predestination must force

---

117 Beza, *Sermons sur la Passion*, 820-56. Beza dealt extensively with predestination and its effects in believers in the second part of the sermon (ibid., 842-50).
118 Ibid., 842.
119 See appendix three.

himself to be biblical in his presentation. The Bible, not idle speculation, must guide the presentation of this most important doctrine. This being said, the best way to proceed was like Paul in the epistle to the Romans to move from the law to forgiveness in Christ; only then should the higher doctrine of predestination be addressed. Finally, Beza urged his readers to know their audience when discussing this doctrine. They must be gentle with those who are immature in the faith and not waste their time philosophizing with those who oppose predestination.[120] The eighth chapter, in particular, displayed Beza's pastoral acumen. Here he discussed the issues of perseverance and assurance at length, since these issues naturally arose after talking about predestination and reprobation.[121] Beza stressed throughout that predestination, though it humbled persons by stressing God's absolute sovereignty, should strengthen Christians. Thus in the fourth aphorism he pointed out that

> When we see that the doctrine of the gospel is not only ignored by almost the whole world but is even treated very crudely, what will strengthen us more than if we affirm that nothing happens by chance; that God knows his own; and that finally those who commit such errors (unless they are given to repent) are predestined, not accidently but by the sure, eternal counsel of God, in order that in them (as in a mirror) God's just wrath and power might shine forth?[122]

Earlier in the *Tabula* Beza had pointed out the utility of predestination for Christians. He said,

> Each of these executions of God's justice – the former as well as the latter – is finally accomplished in three stages. We have already explained the first one. As far as the elect are concerned, in that very moment in which they received the gift of faith they "passed over" in some sense from "death to life." Of this they have a sure pledge. But this life of theirs is completely hidden in Christ until their first death promotes them one stage. Through that death the soul, which is freed from the chains of the body, enters the "joy of its Lord."
>
> Finally, on that day appointed for the "judgment of the living and the dead," when this corruptible shall have "put on immortality" and God shall be "all in all" – at that time, and only then, will they gaze openly on his majesty and enjoy to the full and "inexpressible joy" predestined them from eternity, because of that reward that is owed to the justice and holiness of Christ. He was "delivered up for their sins" and was "raised from the dead for their justification." As will be

---

120 Francis Turretin echoed very similar advice to his students in the next century. See Francis Turretin, *Institutes of Elenctic Theology*, trans. George Musgrave Giger, ed. James T. Dennison (Phillipsburg, NJ: Presbyterian and Reformed, 1992-1997), 1: 331.
121 See the discussion of these in chapter five.
122 Beza, *Tabula*, in *The Potter and the Clay*, 88.

God's Sovereignty for His People 179

evident from their entire living, they have walked "from faith to faith" by his power and spirit.[123]

Christ was the sure pledge of a Christian's salvation. Since he had been raised to new life and since they were united to him by faith, they would also be raised to be with him in heaven. This was certain because of God's sovereignty on behalf of his people. God's sovereignty in salvation was a pastoral comfort to his people, according to Theodore Beza.

As we turn to Beza's pastoral treatises, we will see clearly that for Beza predestination was meant to be a comforting doctrine for Christians. It was the anchor for their souls in the raging sea of this life. God's sovereignty should give them certainty in this life and hope of a better life to come.

The *Houshold Prayers* afford us a fitting place to begin looking at the pastoral exposition of his doctrine of predestination. In his prayers more than any other single place we see Beza the Christian who exuded passion for his gracious God. He was affectionate towards his heavenly Father, first of all, because in his prayers Beza acknowledged on several occasions that he was by nature a sinner who deserved nothing but God's wrath and who was unable to save himself. But in his mercy, God had saved Beza. Thus, while reflecting on the part of the Lord's Prayer that states, "Your will be done on earth as it is in heaven," Beza prayed, "My will, O Lord, is altogether perverse and depraved, unless it is formed by you, wherein rests and consists all my good. Create in me this holy will, and give me grace to fulfill it."[124] Sin was serious, he noted later in the same prayer: "Our sins as debts do bind us to death – which is their reward – and to hell – which is their grave. They are as a strong bar, to keep us from coming to you, O most holy God. Yes, which is more, they are as a cloud that shadows your eyes, from looking favorably upon us."[125] In another prayer, Beza's confession of his own sin exposes the weakness he felt in himself. He was a sinner deserving death and unable to do anything to save himself. Thus he prayed,

> We confess ourselves, in your presence, to be so great sinners that our unworthiness will not suffer us to look up unto heaven without fear that you should, in your just wrath, thunder upon us. Neither can we cast our eyes upon the earth, but we shall see as it were hell open for the reward of our wickedness. For we are, not only as the children of Adam, conceived and born in sin, worthy of your curse, but also, by our own faults, lusts, uncleanness, bad thoughts, and wicked works, whereunto through our corruption and frailty we do daily fall,

---

123 Ibid., 71.
124 Beza, *Houshold Prayers*, C4r.
125 Ibid., in the prayer "Upon the Lord's Prayer."

which also in consciences are so many witnesses to condemn us, and as it were heralds that do denounce unto us death and hell.[126]

That was not the final word, though. Beza went on to note that God's grace was stronger than his sin. "But, O Lord," he remarked, "your mercies do infinitely exceed our malice, and your eternal compassions, are upon sinners that convert and turn unto you."[127] In fact, throughout his prayers Beza delighted to thank God for his grace towards him. This particular grace of God, shown only to his elect, did not lead to despair. Rather, it gave Beza confidence in God's benevolence amid the turmoils of life. "O Sovereign Father of all things," he prayed, "and by a singular privilege, Father of the children whom it has pleased you to adopt in our Lord Jesus Christ, to be co-heirs with him in the celestial life, I learn in your word, that this inheritance and blessed estate is a contemplation of the glory of this great Savior of the elect."[128] Not only would God protect him now, but Beza knew that the final result of God's predestining activity was the joy of heaven.

This eternal confidence rang out in other prayers of Beza. He thanked God that "you are my Father." Because of that he prayed,

> I cannot but expect a happy end of all my estates having already received of your mercy the assured pledge of salvation, forgiveness of sins. But, Lord, grant especially that this your grace in Jesus Christ, may be unto me a comfort, and light all the days of my life, especially in the darkness of my death, to retain and hold me fast in the hope of my salvation. . . . so that full of peace, by the effects of your Spirit, I may cheerfully leave my body to the earth, assured of the resurrection, and that my soul may, by the angels, be guided to the rest of the blessed.[129]

The mercy he had already received from God's hand led Beza confidently to trust that his Father would provide for him in this life and would certainly guide him "to the rest of the blessed" in heaven. His omnipotent Father would usher Beza into glory. Beza's prayers demonstrate that for him predestination was

---

126 Ibid., O1r.

127 Ibid.

128 Ibid., M4r.

129 Ibid., in the prayer "For the Morning." Similarly, in another place after he had discussed the righteousness of God in both election and reprobation, Beza asserted that Christians have great confidence in God because of his electing activity: "I beseech you therefore, O Lord, that as you have given me grace to believe that by your grace I am made a vessel of mercy, I may live in the life of the righteous, sanctified by the Spirit of Christ, to depart happily in him, and so to ascend unto you into your new Zion, and there to receive the price of the victorious crown, which this great Savior of the elect has purchased for the perfection of their glory" (ibid., N3v-N4r).

preeminently a comforting doctrine for believers.[130]

Beza's sermons on Song of Songs also showed his pastoral application of eternal predestination. First of all, he noted, all persons were sinful by nature and therefore unable to save themselves. Explaining what was meant by original sin, Beza said it consisted in "the corruption of the whole man, which is, as it were, the essence of this sin." Continuing, he argued that it "makes us guilty, and children of wrath worthy of the curse of God from our conception (Psal. 51.7; Rom. 5.14,18; Eph. 2.3). There are afterwards the fruits proceeding from this cursed root, which bind us specially unto eternal death."[131] Because of human sin, no one will come to Christ unless God first worked in that person, according to Beza. Thus, he repeated throughout his sermons that everything good in a Christian's life was due to the grace of Almighty God. Preaching on Song of Songs 1:4, "Draw me, we will run after you," Beza commented that God must save persons because "there is in our nature nothing but most desperate and most obstinate rebellion, until the Spirit of God drives away, first, the darkness of our understanding, which cannot, nor will not of itself, so much as think upon the things of God (2 Cor. 3.5) and that secondly it correct the forwardness of our will, which is an enemy of God, and of whatsoever is truly good (Rom. 5.10 and 8.7). And this is the cause why the apostle (Ephes. 2.1) says not simply, that we are wounded, but that we are naturally dead in our sins and offences."[132] God must sovereignly save sinners or no one will be

---

130 Beza's prayers also show that he thought that sinful persons were responsible to come to Jesus, even though only the sovereign God could effect their salvation. Note, for instance, this prayer: "It has pleased you, according to the decree of your unsearchable counsel, that man, formed after your image, and falling through mistrust and curiosity, should, by faith, be restored to the excellency of his nature; and as he sought knowledge above your commandment, and so strayed from you, and wandered out of your kingdom, so he should be reunited and reduced into the path of salvation, by believing only your word in the promised Messiah, bending the power of his soul, to the knowledge of you, in embracing the preaching of the cross. . . . But because we all are born blind, and corrupt in our understanding and will. . . . [W]e of ourselves are not capable, so much as of any good thought, until you that know how to draw light out of darkness returns to re-create us, and by your Spirit to shine in the firmament of our souls, to the end to frame us to every faithful disposition, and obedience, and so to make us believe in the gospel of your grace" (ibid., in the prayer "Upon the Symbol or Articles of Belief").
131 Beza, *Canticles*, 420-21.
132 Ibid., 56. Later in his sermons on the Canticles, and again using Eph. 2, Beza asserted that "we must do God this honor, to confess that it is he, who according to his infinite goodness, as he has destinated us to salvation in his Son before the foundation of the world, so does he in his time prevent us, seeking after us all when we are strayed, and finding us when we are fled from him, and bringing us into his house, which is also the dwelling place and habitation of our good and holy mother. But this is after such a manner notwithstanding, that we are not all this while like

saved, Beza argued.

In giving new life to dead persons, God had not acted towards them as if they were insentient, Beza remarked. Rather,

> [God's] voice must also be heard and received by his grace, who opens the heart to hear well (Act. 16.14) as this spouse in this place witnesses, showing that she is the true church, according unto the saying of Jesus Christ, that his sheep hear his voice, and not the voice of a stranger (Joh. 10.3, 5). In a word, therefore, we would never come unto him, no never so much as think to go unto him, if he came not first unto us, to warn us thereof, and to form in us the desire of going unto him. And which is more, if he accompanied not this grace of going unto him, with a second grace of blessing and effecting in us this desire of going unto him to the end that that might be accomplished in us which he says by his prophet, I have made myself to be found of them who sought not after me (Isa. 65.1).[133]

The elect must respond to God's wooing in faith. Because of God's grace they

---

blocks and trunks, which a man finds and carries wherever he will, without any feeling or motion in themselves. God then seeks after us, forming in us the desire to seek after him. He finds us, giving us the means and the power to find him. We take hold of him and embrace him meeting with him, because he creates in us the faith which takes hold of him. He brings us into the house of our mother, bestowing on us the grace of desiring to join ourselves unto the company of the true church never to stir or depart from it. These two things then agree very well together, provided that we add this, that as God produces in us natural effects by natural causes which he has created in us, so, if the question be of these graces which are merely supernatural – seeing flesh and blood reveal not these things unto us (Matth. 16.17), no our natural wisdom is enmity to God (Rom. 8) – we must vouch and confess that the purity of understanding and uprightnesse of will are the mere free gifts and graces of him who enlightens the eyes of our understanding (Ephes. 1.8) and creates in us both to will and to do (Philip. 2.13). So that if this proposition and sentence be true, when we speak of the creation of the world, that it made not itself, and that a dead body raises not himself. So is it as true, the question being of the light of the soul, be it in the understanding or uprightness of will, that we are truly the workmanship of God by his mere and only grace (Ephes. 2.1,5,10)." (ibid., 341-42).

133 Ibid., 243. Earlier Beza had made the point that unless "the spouse [Christ] spoke first in this place, as coveting and desiring her beloved, . . . notwithstanding we must take diligent heed how we think, that this desire of hers which opened the mouth, began from her. It is then the bridegroom which has spoken first unto her, and prepared her within to seek and search after him as it is said. . . . Which St. Paul plainly and without figure expounds unto us (Ephes. 2.5), calling us poor and wretched carrions, dead in sin. And this is it which the most just of us all must avouch and confess, that it is the Lord which has loved us first, and therefore has washed us (Rev. 1.5; 1 John 4.10), and elected and chosen us, not in ourselves, no more than he has made us by ourselves (Psal. 95), but in his well-beloved" (ibid., 15).

certainly would.

In his *Vie de Calvin* Beza implicated Satan as the one who had stirred up controversy concerning predestination. God, though, turned Satan's designs on their head. Satan had moved Bolsec to dispute the doctrine, but Calvin's devastating rebuttal meant that "All that Satan gained by these dissensions was, that this article of the Christian religion, which was formerly most obscure, became clear and transparent to all not disposed to be contentious."[134] Thus Beza warned the listeners to his Song of Songs sermons that the alternative to trusting in God's doctrine of predestination revealed in Scripture was to follow Satan's schemes, including Pelagianism and semi-Pelagianism.[135] Those like them who "utterly take away the supernatural grace of God, which is the first ground and foundation of our salvation" are heretics. They have been "heretofore rightly condemned and detested."[136] Such heretics, he claimed, charged that Beza and the Genevans

> transform men into blocks and stones, depriving them utterly of understanding and will, which conclusion they falsely draw from our doctrine. For we know well enough, God be thanked, that the fall of the first man has not deprived him of understanding and will, by which faculties man yet differs from brute beasts. So far we are from transforming him into wood or stone, although the scripture calls the heart of the man unregenerate, a heart of stone, opposed to a heart of flesh, that is to say, made soft and tender by the grace of God (Ezek. 36.26). But we say that in that which concerns the knowledge of the true God unto salvation, that is to say, touching the doctrine of the gospel, which is the power of God to salvation to all that believe (Rom. 1.16), flesh and blood reveal it not unto us, neither in whole nor in part (Mat. 16.17). But the Son of God must reveal it unto us (Joh. 1.18), not as if we had eyes and there needed nothing else but to present the truth unto them to make us to see, but giving us first eyes, that is to say in the language of the apostle (Eph. 1.18), enlightening the eyes of our mind, which were before clean put out in respect of this knowledge of our salvation. The same is to be said of the will utterly out of rule, and repugnant to that of God.[137]

However, Beza urged that Christians "ought to avouch and confess, that it is the mere and only grace and mercy of God, not which aids our nature being weakened, but which changes it altogether in quality, bringing us out of darkness into light . . . and from death unto life . . . and he which knows not this grace and that so far too as this point reaches, knows not what the gospel means, or the words of the Lord (Jn. 6.44)."[138] For comfort's sake, one must hold firmly to the doctrine of predestination. Failing to trust in God's

---

134 Beza, *Life of John Calvin*, lviii.
135 Beza, *Canticles*, 188.
136 Ibid., 57.
137 Ibid.
138 Ibid.

sovereignty as revealed in Scripture ultimately robbed one of comfort and assurance in this troubled life, because it made salvation dependent not on Christ but on oneself. If one did not rest in God's sovereignty in salvation, Beza lamented,

> What shall become of Jesus Christ? He shall give us only the means to become saviors of ourselves, if not in whole, yet in part. His bloodshed mingled with our works shall make them available unto salvation, being himself alone no more sufficient, than our works by themselves without him. And which is worse, this point being once won and gained by Satan, then he began to show his horns openly. For thereupon men began to forge meritorious works at their pleasure. . . . Finally to leave nothing to Jesus Christ but a phantasm and shadow of merit and satisfaction, purgatory was devised and set up to warrant and bring the dead from their sins, by certain merits and deserts of the living.[139]

No, a Christian's hope rested in the fact that "only the grace and favor of God therefore has elected us, called us to salvation, and is the cause of our salvation, from the beginning unto the ending. For, that faith created in us by grace apprehends and takes hold of Jesus Christ, and of life in him. It is because it has pleased God so to ordain and appoint the causes, by the which he executes his eternal counsel touching our election and salvation."[140] God's gracious election made salvation sure.

In his sermons on Song of Songs Beza taught God's total sovereignty. God's decree determined all that came to pass, including whom he would save and whom he would reprobate. Believers "cannot" and "ought not," he exhorted, "but by very uncertain presumptions discern those, which he has designated or not designated unto this favor." They must, therefore, leave "unto God his secret judgments."[141] For his children, though, God's complete sovereignty should not be a source of fear. Rather, it must encourage them to trust in God's care for them and to love him who first loved them. Thus Beza told his listeners, "You see then my brethren what the love and dilection of the bridegroom is towards his bride, from which proceeds our salvation. You see on the other side how we ought reciprocally to love him who has loved us so much, wherein consists the testimony of our election and salvation (1 Joh. 4.12)."[142] In another place he explained at great length the way in which God's salvation of his people should lead them to love him, trust him, and wait patiently to be with him in heaven for eternity. Pastor Beza explained

---

139 Ibid., 189.
140 Ibid., 190.
141 Ibid., 41.
142 Ibid., 43.

that before the foundation of the world he [God] provided for [salvation by uniting] man so near unto himself, that he and the eternal Son of God are but one person, man-God, and God-man. And what moved God to do this admirable work? Certainly nothing but his infinite goodness and love, as the prophet writes (Psal. 8.5 and 144.3). And who can say the contrary? This counsel of his being once determined, what induced this great God to execute and perform it by so rare, so strange, so admirable a means, that the angels themselves . . . yet desire to comprehend it more and more (Exod. 25.10 and 1 Pet. 1.12). Certainly this cannot have proceeded but from the same fountain of his unspeakable dilection and love, through which he had accepted of us in his Son (Ephes. 1.6 and Joh. 3.16). And what moved this bridegroom, the eternal of God, to choose unto himself this polluted maiden to make her his spouse? To bear with her for so many her adulteries (Jer. 3.1)? What more? To make himself subject unto the curse of the Father (Gal. 3.13), to give his life for her (Ephes. 5.25), to carry her sins even upon the tree of his cross (1 Pet. 2.24; Phil. 2.8). Certainly this love and good will of his, the depth whereof no man is able to sound, or measure the height, breadth, or length thereof (Eph. 3.18). And what is the ground and foundation of our faith, but this assurance, that we are loved with an invariable and unchangeable dilection (Rom 8.38)? And how could we hope in him, and how call upon him without the testimony of the Holy Ghost, who teaches us and seals it us in our hearts that he loves us (Rom. 8.15; Gal. 4.6; 1 Cor. 2.12; Jam. 1.6)? This is it therefore in a word which the spouse would say in this place, that nothing else invites her to retire herself unto God, and to have her refuge unto him, nothing assures and ascertains her, nothing else distinguishes and makes her different from the world, but the love which her bridegroom bears her, whereunto as unto her ensign she keeps herself, to be covered therewith and as it were wrapped in it. Neither may we think it strange that the name of dilection or love is given unto this standard, seeing that yet more significantly the name of love or dilection is attributed unto God himself, because he is the fountain thereof from whence it flows upon us being his nature to love man, yes, such as he has chosen, whom he justifies and sanctifies, and will finally glorify. And this love engenders back again another love in us, being given us to love him, who has loved us so much as is to be seen by this whole canticle.[143]

To Theodore Beza, the doctrine of predestination, since it displayed the immense love and faithfulness of God for his children, was a doctrine meant to comfort Christians in the midst of the spiritual and physical turmoil of this life.

Conclusion

We have seen in this chapter that for Theodore Beza the doctrine of God's sovereignty was a comforting doctrine. God's complete control of all events and of the whole course of history assured his people of their Sovereign's care for them, even when their outward situations looked bleak. They could rest,

---

143 Ibid., 225-26.

even presently "under the cross," in God now, knowing that because of his care for them he would bring them out of the struggles of this life to be with him in heaven. Similarly, Beza stressed that God's sovereignty in the salvation of his children was a comfort to them in this life. Although the doctrine of predestination did not sum up the Christian gospel, it supported the gospel. Because of God's omnipotence in salvation, his people could be certain that their Father would care for them in Christ now, and for eternity. Nothing – neither the fickleness of their own souls nor the schemes of the devil – could wrench them out of God's hand. In light of his eschatological vision, Theodore Beza used the doctrine of God's sovereignty pastorally.

Some of the few autobiographical words from the pen of Beza offer a fitting conclusion to this chapter. In Psalm 91 the psalmist overflows with trust in Almighty God. In 1580 Beza reflected on this psalm and wrote the following exhortation to his readers. God's omnipotent and omnibenevolent care should comfort them in the midst of the spiritual battle and lead them to trust in him:

> whereas God has scourged many countries about us within these few years with the pestilence, and seems still to threaten the same plague, I would desire that our divines should not take in hand that disputation, which ought to be sent unto the schools of physicians, whether the pestilence be contagious or not. But rather to beat into the minds of men the doctrine which is so necessary and so well set forth in this psalm, namely, not only the general providence of God, but also the most particular, which governs all the second causes most justly and most orderly, who watches also for the safety of his, is set forth to be seen so lively, and is ratified with so many, and so plain sentences, even the person of God being brought in to speak to them, that nothing seems more to be desired in this point. And truly, I will not think much to declare unto the glory of God, what I have proved certainly by experience. This is the thirty-first year since, by the goodness of God, I have willingly forsaken my country, and all that I had, that I might freely serve Christ. And it came to pass, at my first entry into the public assembly of the Christians, that the company did sing this psalm, by the singing whereof, as though I had heard God himself calling me particularly, I felt myself so comforted that I have kept it since that time most dearly graven in my heart. And I may truly witness this before God that I have received marvelous comforts by it, both in sickness and in sorrow, not only by meditating on it when I was also smitten with the pestilence, and the same plague had infected my family, even four times, but also in other most grievous temptations.[144]

According to Theodore Beza, God's sovereignty provided the only sure hope for troubled pilgrims.

---

144 Beza, *Psalmes*, 214-15.

CHAPTER 5

Pastoral Implications of God's Sovereignty: Assurance in the Spiritual Battle

Assurance in Context

Jakob Andreae plagued Theodore Beza. Not only was Andreae a formidable theological thinker and a very able debater, but he also had the edge politically.[1] Since the Peace of Augsburg in 1555, the Lutherans generally had maintained the upper hand against the Calvinists in debates since the Lutherans had the certainty of peace with Catholics in the vast expanse of Germany. The Calvinists, on the other hand, were often in danger politically and militarily.[2] When Beza traveled to Montbéliard in 1586 to debate Andreae, the subject of consideration was supposed to be the Lord's Supper. But Andreae and Count Frederick decided to add Christology, baptism, the use of images, and eternal election to the agenda for disputation. Predestination was their trump card. They knew that the people of Montbéliard had sided with Bern for single predestination against Calvin's and Beza's notion of double predestination. Surely Andreae would be able to show the horrendous implications of Beza's stress on divine sovereignty and so win Montbéliard to the Wurttenberg persuasion of Lutheranism.[3]

Although Andreae regarded the doctrine of predestination as the weak link in Beza's doctrinal position, Beza thought it was essential to a Christian's comfort. The Lutheran asserted that assurance was located in baptism. When one doubted his standing with God, one merely needed to recollect his baptism into the faith and his reception into the church. That initiation into faith was not preparatory, but held within it the promise of God's grace. Beza, conversely, claimed that baptism was not the *locus* of assurance for a doubting Christian. Certainty of salvation was located in the gracious activity of God for his

---

1   See Robert Kolb, "Jakob Andreae," in *Shapers of Religious Traditions in Germany, Switzerland, and Poland, 1560-1600*, ed. Jill Raitt (New Haven: Yale University Press, 1981), 53-68.
2   See, for example, W. Stanford Reid, "The Battle Hymns of the Lord: Calvinist Psalmody of the Sixteenth Century," *Sixteenth Century Journal* 2 (1971): 36-37.
3   Raitt, "French Reformed Theological Response," 180-82; idem, *Montbéliard*, 23, 134-35.

children.⁴ Pastor Beza grounded assurance in the character and power of God.

At the first stage of his argument, Beza repudiated Andreae's premise that regeneration was always united with baptism. The Lutheran's position was a misinterpretation of several biblical passages, combined with numerous instances of faulty reasoning.⁵ For those who followed Andreae's advice, therefore, the ultimate end would be despair:

> suppose I have been baptized, and [have been] adopted [as] the son of God. Yet seeing you teach that the grace of God is not so sure but that I may fall from the same, as indeed I feel that I have grievously fallen, what do you now else but lift me up with one hand to heaven, and with the other cast me down into hell? What mean you therefore to teach me those things which are so far from easing me, as that contrarily they do more and more lay out unto me my abominable and ungrateful heart? See now what sure consolation, consciences [that are] grievously afflicted may reap by this doctrine of their comforter, D. Andreas.⁶

Instead of this faulty method, Beza proceeded to demonstrate what was "grounded upon a sure foundation, and which I myself have often found to be true in my own experience."⁷ First he rebutted Andreae's charge that Beza grounded Christian assurance in the eternal decree of God. Not the decree, but the invitation of God to sinners was the basis of certainty, Beza countered: "We teach, contrarily to that which D. Andreas does most falsely object against us, that the eternal decree, or as Paul speaks, the purpose of God, must not be sought in the bottomless counsel of God, but rather in the manifestation of it, namely, in his vocation, by the word and sacraments. This I speak of such as are of years of discretion, as they must needs be whom we seek to comfort in this place."⁸ Although this external call of God to sinners was for all persons generally, Beza next went on to apply the "comfortable and restorative medicine, which is taken from God's effectual vocation, as it were out of an apothecary's box" to Christians suffering from troubled consciences.⁹

So, Beza explained his view of Christian assurance. To begin with, he noted that there are different kinds of persons who have troubled consciences. First, there are unbelievers concerned about their salvation; second, there are

---

4   See Raitt, "*Probably* They Are God's Children," 156-70.
5   Theodore Beza, *An Excellent Treatise of Comforting Such, as are Troubled about Their Predestination. Taken Out of the Second Answer of M. Beza, to D. Andreas, in the Acte of Their Colloquie at Mompelgart*, in *A Golden Chaine, or, The Description of Theologie . . . by that man of God, Mr. William Perkins*, trans. Robert Hill (London: John Legatt, 1621), 563-67.
6   Ibid., 568.
7   Ibid.
8   Ibid.
9   Ibid., 569.

Christians struggling with assurance. First, then, there are those who either never heard the gospel or did not respond in faith when they did hear it. Such persons might reason incorrectly, prompted by Satan, that they will never be saved. However, in this case "Satan plays the sophister" because this is not necessarily true. Such thinking proceeds "as if a man looking at midnight, and seeing that the sun is not then risen, should therefore affirm that it would never rise."[10] Beza responded to such unbiblical reasoning by asserting that the external call of the gospel is enough to thwart the devil's assaults against persons' consciences, since those who hear the gospel summons are in a much better situation than those who never hear the good news of Jesus. Those who do not respond to God's call in the gospel have only themselves to blame since they have kept themselves from coming to God: "I tell him," Beza reasoned, "that they who never had external nor internal calling, they, if we regard an ordinary calling, must perish. But whoever is once called, he has set, as it were, his foot in the first entry into the kingdom of heaven. And, unless it be by his own default, he shall come afterwards into the courts of God, and so by degrees into his Majesty's palace. And for the confirmation of this, I use divers ways."[11]

Continuing his counsel to these unbelievers, Beza urged them not to worry about their consciences but to come to Christ immediately. First, he argued, the fact that they have heard the gospel from one of God's messengers already shows that the Almighty has been good to them. "For why, say I, do you doubt of his good will towards you, who in mercy has sent me, a minister, to call you unto him? You have no cause, unless you allege the number of your sins."[12] If persons are still troubled by the magnitude of their sins, Beza urged them to receive the mercy of God expressed in the forgiveness that was in Christ: "Oppose the infinite greatness of God's mercy against your sins, who has sent me to bring you unto him. The Lord vouchsafes to bring you into the way of the elect. Why are you a stumbling block unto yourself and refuse to follow him?"[13] If the troubled persons did not feel like they could come to Christ now, Beza urged that they pray for that desire: "If you feel not as yet inwardly yourself to be stirred forward, pray that you may be."[14] Finally, Beza showed his pastoral acumen by diagnosing the desire troubled persons have for forgiveness as a sign of God's prior gracious work in their lives. "Know this for a most sure truth," he exhorted, "that this desire in you is a pledge of God's fatherly good will towards you. He neither can, nor will, be wanting to this which he has stirred up in you."[15] They have no need to fear, even if they are

---

10 Ibid.
11 Ibid., 570.
12 Ibid.
13 Ibid.
14 Ibid.
15 Ibid., 570-71.

aged, for God has countless numbers of times called persons to himself "at the eleventh hour." Such, then, were the steps Beza used to counsel those who had never received the gospel. He testified of this process's great usefulness over the years: "These and other remedies I used, of which I never remember that it repented me."[16]

The second class of persons Beza counseled were Christians who were struggling with assurance, especially those who had committed grievous sins or had failed to be diligent in church attendance. Such persons, Beza claimed, were often "very good and godly." While they lamented their standing with God, Beza did not: "they are so altogether busily conversant in reprehending and judging themselves that they for a while forget the mercy of God."[17] Beza followed a methodical regimen in counseling these troubled believers.

First of all, he attempted to ascertain what exactly was troubling them. His pastoral concern was evident when he related that he took "special care of this, that they being already overmuch cast down, that I then, by the severe denunciation of the Law, do not quite overturn them. Yet so, as that I do not altogether withdraw them either from condemning their former sins, or the meditation of God's judgment. And so, as much as I can, I temper the words of consolation, so that I [in] nothing cloak God's anger against them for their sins."[18]

Second, having diagnosed the reason for their fear, Beza then showed how he would continue with such persons. Have they always been in such a state? No, they usually replied, because "the time was, when I was in great joy and peace of conscience. I served the Lord. Then was I a happy person, full of faith, full of hope." But, they now said they had lost their first love, "and there is nothing vexing me more than to remember those times past."[19] At this point, Beza questioned them: "whether consideration is more grievous to you of the apprehension of God's judgments or the dislike of yourself that you should offend so gracious and so loving a Father?" They usually responded that both troubled them, but especially the latter. "Therefore, say I, does sin also displease you in that it is sin, namely, because it is evil, and God who is goodness itself, is offended with it?" They agreed, generally expressing shame that they should be so bold as to come into the presence of a merciful God. But, Pastor Beza pointed out, such reasoning showed they were in a state of soul opposite to what they assumed: "Then I tell them, that no man is offended, but rather is glad when he can injure one whom he hates."[20] In other words, their disquieted state was evidence of their love for God. After this interchange,

---

16 Ibid., 571.
17 Ibid.
18 Ibid., 572.
19 Ibid.
20 Ibid., 572-73.

Beza concluded by exhorting such troubled persons to cease their fearing and to put their hope in God's salvation, rejoicing that they are included in his family. Beza's final exhortation is full of pastoral wisdom:

> Be of good comfort, my dear brother, you are in good case. For who can love God, especially when he is wounded by him? Who can bewail the loss of his friendship? Who can desire to come again into his favor, but he whom God still loves, although for a time he is angry with him? Except perhaps you have not learned thus much, that the knowledge of our salvation comes not from flesh and blood, but from God himself, who first promised to instruct us, and from Christ Jesus, manifesting the Father unto us. And that it is God's blessing that we love God, who loved us first when we were his enemies. You have therefore, my good brother, just cause, why you should be greatly displeased with many things past, but there is no cause why you should despair. Briefly, you have inwardly and, as it were, dwelling with you, evident testimonies of your future reconciliation with God; especially if you cease not to pray to him earnestly, who has laid the foundation of repentance in you, namely, a dislike of sin, and a desire to be reconciled to him. The sheep which wandered out of the fold ceased not to be a sheep, albeit it went astray for a time. You now are that sheep, to whom that faithful shepherd of all those sheep, which the Father has committed to him, leaving those ninety and nine, does not so much by my ministry, declare that he seeks you, as having already sought you – though you, not seeking him – has indeed found you. Knock, says he, and it shall be opened unto you. And have you now forgotten those promises, which were so often made to them that repent, and also which they had experience of, who in the sight of the world were in a desperate case? But I, says he, again feel no motions of the comforter; I have now no sense of faith, or hope. But I feel all the contrary. No, say I, you deceive yourself, as I told you before. For it is the comforter alone, who teaches you to hate sin, not so much for the punishment, as because it is evil and dislikes God, albeit he shows not himself so fully at the first, because you had so many ways grievously offended him, so that he seemed for a while quite to forsake you. And, that you have not quite lost him, but that he is yet in some secret corner of your soul, from where at your instant prayers he will show himself unto you, this will plainly declare unto you, which I now admonish you of the second time. But let us grant as much as you say, yet, sure it is that your faith was not dead: but only possessed with a spiritual lethargy. You lived in the womb of your mother, and there were ignorant of your life. A drunken man, although he lose for a time the use of reason, and also of his limbs, yet he never loses reason itself. You would think that in winter the trees were dead, but they spring again in the summer season. At night the sun sets, but in the next morning it rises again. And how often see we by experience, that he who at one time took the foil in a combat, at another did win the prize?[21]

Beza's written response to Andreae's attacks displays a level of pastoral

---

21 Ibid., 573-75.

sensitivity unsurpassed in the Bezan corpus. His response is noteworthy for five reasons. In the first place, Beza's pastoral heart was clearly exhibited here. Second, he maintained that assurance was a component of the on-going spiritual battle. As a traveler through the spiritual battlefields, Beza himself struggled with assurance, he said, and so would all believers. Next, Beza here laid out step-by-step instructions on the best means of obtaining assurance, dependent on the varying situations confronting a person. In the fourth place, here Beza grounded assurance neither in the eternal decree of predestination nor in the so-called "practical syllogism." Instead, Beza used a process of pastoral reasoning. Drawing on the troubled person's knowledge of God's character and the fullness of Christ's satisfaction on the cross, he demonstrated that the fact the person was troubled about his salvation at all, meant the person was a believer. Last of all, Beza acknowledged God's sovereignty in the entire process of assurance. Even when God might withdraw from a person to punish him or her for sin for a time, salvation was not in doubt. The sovereign God would save his own.

Assurance in Light of the Previous Discussion

This chapter is the fitting conclusion to what I have previously argued. My discussion in this chapter makes sense only in light of the previous chapters. And the issues dealt with here are the logical pastoral implications of what we have learned of Theodore Beza in the previous pages.

In chapter one I set forth the vision that I argued drove Beza in all that he did as a Christian, a pastor, and a trainer of pastors. This eschatological vision consisted of the reality of God and Satan and their on-going opposition to each other, as well as the certainty of an eternal heaven and hell for all persons. Beza viewed reality through this lens. His goal was to get himself and his charges through the pilgrimage of this life safely to their eternal rest in heaven. In the third chapter I argued that above all Beza was a pastor, concerned with taking care of his flock, not with dissecting fine points of scholastic theology. And in chapter four I argued that Beza found the doctrine of God's complete sovereignty, his complete sovereignty in ruling creation and in saving sinners, a comfort in the midst of the trials of life. God's sovereignty, indeed, was the one thing that comforted believers as they struggled through hard times here. God's omnipotent care for them assured them of their final resting place in heaven.

We have already seen in his interchange with Jakob Andreae the way in which Beza showed himself to be a thoughtful pastor. Beza saw himself as a minister in the church who had been given the charge of preparing persons for heaven, and of helping them to discern in the midst of the trials of life whether or not they were indeed believers. Assurance of salvation, along with its corollaries perseverance in salvation and the necessity of sanctification, was a pressing pastoral reality with which Beza was very familiar. Given Beza's eschatological vision, the need for Christian assurance was great. Christians' lives here were not their final homes. They were on a pilgrimage here; heaven was their true, eternal rest. But until they arrived in heaven, they would experience troubles, and occasional doubts about their standing with God. More than in any of our previous discussion, in this chapter we see that Beza was supremely a thoughtful and caring pastor.

Given the fact of the spiritual battle, as a wise pastor Beza knew that struggling Christians needed assurance of their future life in heaven. They needed this encouragement to keep waging the war necessary in their pilgrimage on their way to their eternal resting place. This explains, I think, the numerous *loci* of assurance that Beza delineated in his writings. As we shall see, he encouraged his flock to seek for certainty of their salvation in a variety of places. The weary pilgrims needed the solace of numerous means of finding assurance so that they would be strengthened to persevere. Ultimately, though, Beza knew that Christians would not have complete, final assurance until they were ushered safely into God's presence. Satan's wiles were too crafty, and their own indwelling sin was too powerful to allow them to have complete lasting assurance until they went to be with their Lord forever. Beza's eschatological vision thus informed his belief in the urgency, as well as the imperfection, of Christian assurance in this life.

Since the devil's schemes were wicked and Christians were fickle, where were they to find comfort in the midst of the battle? Their holiness did not meet the requirements God had for them. They knew from Scripture that Satan's plots to shipwreck their faith were crafty, and powerful. Beza found the ultimate anchor for the souls of tried and troubled Christians in God's sovereignty. Because God was powerful, he would protect his children— whatever befell them here. And because God was good, he would remain faithful to his many covenant promises. Beza did not find God's total sovereignty problematic to Christian assurance and comfort, as Andreae had suggested. God's sovereignty was rather the ultimate solace for weary souls as they made their way to heaven.

The discussion to follow will develop these points. First, we will look at the way in which Beza placed the issue of Christian assurance squarely in the context of the on-going spiritual battle. We will notice this primarily from his handling of assurance in his *Confession*, but we will also note how his eschatological vision of reality permeated his other writings. The ultimate answer to the on-going battle and to the doubts it caused for sensitive Christians was that their heavenly Father was sovereign and that he was faithful to his covenant promises. Having shown the reality of the spiritual battle, we will next demonstrate from the sweep of Beza's treatises the numerous different ways that he argued believers could find assurance of their salvation. I will argue that Beza found such a multiform scheme necessary in light of the eschatological battle. Since the war was so brutal and since believers were so easily injured in the fight, he set forth numerous *loci* of assurance for the good of his readers. He thus showed himself to be a pastor of souls, concerned for his fellow-believers' well-being. In light of this, we will briefly critique those who argue that Beza primarily used the practical syllogism when discussing assurance. In the final sections of the chapter we will briefly notice the way in which the Reformer dealt with pastoral issues of perseverance in salvation and the need for sanctification. Since these will have been discussed at length in the section on assurance, however, these two sections will be relatively brief.

Assurance and God's Sovereignty in the Spiritual Battle
The Confession

Beza expounded the relationship of the spiritual battle to Christian assurance at great length in his 1558 *Confession*. We have already noted the character and popularity of this summary of his thought.[22] The fact that in his summation of Christian truth, which we noted was originally written to persuade his father of Protestantism and later was meant to summarize the Protestant faith for the reading public of Europe, Beza assumed the powerful role of Satan and demonic forces shows once again that his eschatological vision of reality informed his view of the Christian life, and of Christian theology. Assurance was a concern for Christians because they were assaulted by demonic forces as they made their way to their final home in heaven.

In the fourth chapter of the *Confession*, "le Saint-Esprit," Beza dealt at length with the doctrine of Christian assurance. The greatest cause of the need for assurance was Satan and his assaults on Christians. In the tenth section Beza alerted his readers to the spiritual nature of the question of certainty of salvation. The heading of that section was "The remedy which faith finds in Jesus Christ alone against the first assault of the first temptation—the multitude of our sins."[23] The devil worked in concert with troubled consciences to assault Christians and make them doubt their salvation. To Beza's mind, Satan was the agent behind troubled consciences. That is to say, lack of assurance could be traced back to the devil. Thus "all the temptations of Satan and all the troubles of our conscience" or "Satan and our conscience" were the twin enemies of assurance. The answer to Satan's accusations, Beza argued, was in Christ alone: "in Jesus Christ alone, we find sure remedies against" Satan's wiles.[24]

Satan attacked by raising three questions to the troubled Christian, Beza said. First, the devil tried to persuade believers that they were "truly unworthy

---

22 See chapter three.
23 Beza, "*La Confession de Foi du Chretien* par Theodore de Beza," 33. The title of this section is "Le remède que la foi trouve en Jésus-Christ seul contre le premier assaut de la première tentation: la multitude de nos péchés."
24 Beza, *The Christian Faith*, 19. We must note here the Christocentric focus of Beza's doctrine of assurance. He said at the outset that in Jesus Christ was located the answer to the problem of doubting Christians.

of being saved and very worthy of perishing." So he made them consider that God is "perfectly righteous," the one "who is the great Enemy and Avenger of all iniquity."[25] Beza responded to this accusation in the form of direct address to the devil. The Adversary had only noticed half of the story:

> You say, Satan, that God is perfectly righteous and the Avenger of all iniquity.—I confess it; but I add another property of His righteousness which you have left aside: since He is righteous, He is satisfied with having been paid once. You say next that I have infinite iniquities which deserve eternal death.—I confess it; but I add what you have maliciously omitted: the iniquities which are in me have been very amply avenged and punished in Jesus Christ who has borne the judgment of God in my place (Rom 3:25; 1 Pet 2:24). That is why I come to a conclusion quite different from yours. Since God is righteous (Rom 3:26) and does not demand payment twice, since Jesus Christ, God and man (2 Cor 5:19), has satisfied by infinite obedience (Rom 5:19; Phil 2:8) the infinite majesty of God (Rom 8:33), it follows that my iniquities can no longer bring me to ruin (Coloss 2:14); they are already blotted out and washed out of my account by the blood of Jesus Christ who was made a curse for me (Gal 3:13), and who righteous, died for the unrighteous (1 Pet 2:24).[26]

Jesus Christ, specifically his complete work of atonement for his people, was the answer to Satan's charges.

But the devil was not done. His second weapon was the perfect standard of God's law. Satan charged, reported Beza, that "it is not sufficient to have no sin, or to have satisfied for sins. But more is necessary; that man should fulfill all the Law, that is to say, that he love God perfectly and his neighbor as himself (Deut 17:26; Gal 3:10-12; Matt 22:37-40). Bring therefore this righteousness, Satan will say to our poor conscience, or know well that you cannot escape the wrath and curse of God."[27] The defense against this attack was again found in Christ, Beza responded. "Now, against this assault, what will all men profit us except Christ alone? For it is a question of perfect obedience which is never found in any save in Jesus Christ alone. Let us learn therefore here to appropriate to ourselves once more, by faith, another treasure

---

25 Ibid.
26 Ibid., 21. Compare Beza's words in a later sermon: "The more our Savior suffered injuries, the more are we assured that he paid for our sins up to the last . . . because we recognize so much more in this strange spectacle—it was the terrible wrath (*la terrible fureur*) of God against our sins . . . [therefore, let us] consider and meditate on this infinite mercy and clemency of this great heavenly Father, not having spared his Son in any way in order to reconcile himself to us, and the infinite love (*charite*) of this great and only Son of God, stooping so low, for his enemies. This obedience of the Son therefore was a deed of our brother, by which he introduced us into this heavenly heritage" (Beza, *Sermons sur la Passion*, 381).
27 Beza, *The Christian Faith*, 22.

of Jesus Christ: His righteousness." Jesus, apprehended by the believer's faith, was the answer, for in grasping Christ in trust the Christian was given his Lord's perfect righteousness. "On [the basis of] this point," Beza concluded, "Satan must of necessity close his mouth, provided we have the faith to receive Jesus Christ and all the benefits He possesses in order to communicate them to those who believe in Him (Rom 8:33)."[28]

The Adversary was not done, though. He had still one more arrow to use to fell Christians. Christians were still sinful and corrupt by nature. "How, then," he censured believers, "will you dare to appear before the majesty of God who is the Enemy of all pollution (Ps 5:5), and who sees the depths of the heart (Ps 44:21; Jer 17:10)?"[29] Once again, Beza rebutted this blistering charge with Christ. Trusting in Jesus Christ not only resulted in justification, Beza argued, but also in sanctification. This answered Satan's charge: "Inasmuch as we have faith, we are united (1 Cor 6:17), embodied (Eph 4:16; Coloss 2:19), rooted (Coloss 2:7), ingrafted in Jesus Christ (Rom 6:5). In Him, from the first moment of His conception in the womb of the virgin Mary (Matt 1:20; Luke 1:35), our nature was more fully restored and sanctified (Heb 2:10, 11)." Even this holiness of life did not result from human effort, but from trust, though. "This sanctification of human nature in Jesus Christ is reckoned as ours, through faith."[30]

Christ then was the answer to the assaults of the devil. In Christ alone was salvation, Beza argued in good Reformation fashion, and he was appropriated by faith alone. The believer who clung to Christ in faith need not fear Satan's charges for three reasons: Christ had paid the penalty for his sins, Christ's righteousness was imputed to him, and the Christian would inevitably be sanctified since he was justified.

In light of this Satanic attack, Pastor Beza now tried to make sure his readers could determine whether or not they had put their faith in Christ. How could one know for certain he had trusted in Christ alone for salvation? Beza provided a two-pronged answer: both an internal and an external testimony for the questioning Christian. These testimonies, Beza argued, were essential in order that the Christian might know that by trusting in Christ he had "repulsed Satan." So Beza urged that

> The means [to be sure one had placed one's faith in Christ] is to return from the effects to the cause which produces them. Now, the effects which Jesus Christ produces in us, when we have taken hold of Him by faith, are two (*les effets que Jésus-Christ produit en nous, quand nous l'avons saisi par la foi, sont doubles*). In the first place, there is the testimony which the Holy Spirit gives to our spirit that we are children of God, and enables us to cry with assurance, "Abba, Father."

---

28 Ibid.
29 Ibid., 23.
30 Ibid.

(Rom 8:16; Gal 4:6). In the second place, we must understand that when we apply to ourselves Jesus Christ by faith, this is not by some silly and vain fancy and imagining, but really and in fact, though spiritually (Rom 6:14; 1 John 1:6; 2:5; 3:7). In the same way as the soul produces its effects when it is naturally united to the body, so, when, by faith, Jesus Christ dwells in us in a spiritual manner, His power produces there and reveals there His graces. These are described in Scripture by the words "regeneration" and "sanctification", and they make us new creatures with regard to the qualities that we can have (John 3:3; Eph 4:21-24).[31]

The Spirit thus internally assured believers they were children of God, while he worked externally to exhibit the life of Christ in Christians. Based on this two-fold criteria, Beza argued, persons could conclude certainly if they were believers in Christ. "These are therefore the two effects that Jesus Christ produces in us," he summarized. "If we experience them, the conclusion is infallible: we have faith, and, consequently, as we have said, we have in us Jesus Christ living eternally."[32]

Beza elaborated on these two criteria later in the *Confession*, specifically attempting to answer questions that Christians might have about their election to salvation in Christ. First, he reiterated the supreme value of Christ for his people. He argued that "whoever takes hold of Him by faith, possesses Him eternally . . . thus, His righteousness is also made ours; it is imputed to us. To this alone we hold, on this alone we totally rely, for it alone is perfect."[33] Second, though, Beza urged that "good works" necessarily followed when one had been ingrafted to Christ by faith. But sanctification had to be evaluated carefully. In the first place, good works "give us more and more assurance of our salvation; not because they are the causes of it, but as testimonies and effects of the instrumental cause through which we obtain salvation, that is to say, our faith."[34] In the second place, until heaven no Christian will be perfect, so we must remember that "the goodness of God is so great that He regards his adopted children, not in themselves, but in Jesus Christ, His beloved Son, to whom they are united by this singular bond of faith."[35] It was only at this point that one might rightly think about God's eternal election, Beza asserted. He reasoned in this manner: "As good works are for us sure testimonies of our faith, it follows that they make us equally sure of our eternal election. For faith depends necessarily on election." Faith, he urged, "is nothing other than that by

---

31 Ibid., 24; Beza, "*La Confession de Foi du Chretien* par Theodore de Beza," 38.
32 Ibid., 25. Pastor Beza urged the Christian based on this to "watch above all to maintain, by continual supplication, this aforementioned testimony which the Spirit of God gives to His own" and to "develop, by a continual exercise of good works to which his vocation calls him, the gift of regeneration which he has received" (ibid.).
33 Ibid., 33.
34 Ibid., 34.
35 Ibid.

which we are sure of possessing eternal life; by it, we know that before the foundation of the world, God has predestinated us to possess, through Christ, so great salvation and such excellent glory."[36]

This was much more than just good logic, however. This line of reasoning was essential to combat the wiles of the devil:

> When Satan casts a doubt before our eyes concerning our particular election, it is not necessary to first approach the eternal Counsel of God to know what was purposed there (*lorsque Satan met en doute à nos yeux notre election particulière, il ne faut pas s'approcher tout d'abord du Conseil eternal de Dieu pour chercher à connaître ce qui y fut résolu*); His majesty would dazzle us. But, on the contrary, we must begin lower down, with the sanctification which is begun in ourselves and the effects of which we feel, and, from there, to climb higher. Our sanctification, from which proceed all the good desires and the good works, of which we have spoken above, is a sure effect of faith, or rather of Jesus Christ who dwells in us through faith (Rom 8:5-9); on the other side, whoever is united to Jesus Christ is also necessarily effectually called, he is thus predestinated to salvation; finally, the Providence of God cannot make mistakes, and consequently none of the elect perish (John 6:37). It follows that sanctification is as the first step by which we begin to climb up the knowledge of the first cause of our salvation—our free and eternal election. For, whoever says that he believes, and yet his life is not led by the Spirit of God, shows clearly that he is a liar and is deceiving himself (Rom 6:2; 1 John 2:3-6). That is why St. Peter exhorts us to confirm our calling and election by good works (2 Pet 1:10); not that they are the cause or the foundation or our calling and election—for St. Paul expressly declares the contrary (Rom 4:2)—, but because good works render a sure testimony to our conscience that Jesus Christ dwells in us (1 Pet 3:21), and that, consequently, having been elected to salvation, we cannot perish (John 6:39).[37]

Thus, the internal testimony of the Holy Spirit and the external witness of good works were Beza's two-pronged method of finding assurance in the midst of the spiritual battle.

In his application of this method to his readers Beza showed himself to be a wise pastor. The internal and external witnesses of salvation should buttress each other and work together to assure Christians of their standing with God: "the two effects of faith are as two anchors to hold us secure from two sides; when the one fails us, we must lean the more strongly on the other, until we have recovered our strength from the two sides."[38] In light of Beza's

---

36 Ibid., 35.
37 Ibid., 35-36; Beza, "*La Confession de Foi du Chretien* par Théodore de Bèze," 51.
38 Ibid., 36-37. Here Beza used as examples David and Peter, whose sins certainly caused "the effects of their regeneration and sanctification" to become feeble. "But, in the temptation which urged them to despair, they leaned on the other anchor, that

eschatological vision, neither of these two buttresses would be perfect until heaven. Beza reasoned in the following pastoral manner:

> to partake of Jesus Christ, it is not required that we have a perfect faith (*une foi parfaite*), but only a true faith (*une foi vraie*). Now, faith does not cease to be true even if it is very little and weak, to the point of sometimes being as if totally buried. Thus, a sole spark of faith, and, consequently, a little movement of the effects which it produces, provided that they are true, that is to say, provided that they proceed from the true Source of faith, are sufficient to assure us of our salvation (*une seule étincelle de foi, et, par consequent, un petit mouvement des effets qu'elle produit, pourvu qu'ils soient vrais, c'est-à-dire pourvu qu'ils partent de la vraie source de la foi, sont suffisants pour nous assurer de notre salut*). In reality, our salvation does not properly depend on our faith, although without faith no-one can be saved, but on Him who is taken hold of by faith, that is to say, on Jesus Christ. And faith is of such power that, following the promise of God, a sole grain of faith, as small as it may be, takes hold of Jesus Christ entirely (Matt 17:20). However, the greater is our faith the greater is its efficacy to bind us more and more to Jesus Christ and to graft us more closely to Him. And if we slide back instead of going forward, that must displease us greatly. But the Devil has not won his case on the pretext that we have slidden back, provided that the issue shows that it was to our final benefit (*Mais le Diable n'a pas gagné son procès sous prétexte que nous avons reculé, pourvu que l'issue montre que ce fut pour mieux sauter*).[39]

The two marks of assurance – the internal testimony of the Spirit and the external witness of good works – were supports in the midst of the spiritual battle during the attacks of Satan. Assurance, then, was necessitated by the spiritual battle and the devil's effort to keep doubting Christians from persevering in the faith. Ultimately, though, these two criteria were not the grounds of salvation. They pointed to the ultimate ground of believers' certainty: Jesus Christ. Because of God's sovereign and gracious appointment, Jesus Christ was the anchor sufficient to support struggling pilgrims on their way to heaven.

The Bezan Corpus

Theodore Beza's eschatological vision, along with its implications for Christian assurance, permeated his other writings. We have already noted this from one of Beza's systematic treatises, the *Confession*. By looking at one of Beza's biblical works, a polemical treatise, and his published prayers, we shall notice the manner in which Beza viewed assurance through the lens of the spiritual

---

    is to say, on the testimony which the Spirit of God gave to their conscience" (ibid., 37).
39 Ibid., 37; Beza, "*La Confession de Foi du Chretien* par Théodore de Bèze," 52-53.

battle in three other types of writing.

In his paraphrase of the twenty-seventh psalm, Beza showed his readers that Christians' foes, that is, their spiritual "enemies," made assurance necessary. Although Beza here emphasized the necessity of the correct use of "means" for obtaining salvation, he also located all of the means *extra nos*:

> Here are opened unto us, even when all things seem most desperate, three lively, and never failing fountains, whence we may draw assured comfort. One is, to take hold of the power of God by true faith, and oppose it against all the boastings of the enemies. The second, a continual desire always of the glory of God, keeping evermore a safe conscience, and using diligently the means whereby our faith may be confirmed, that is to say, the hearing of the word preached and the use of the sacraments – if so be that we may have them; if not, yet must we have a continual meditation of them. The third is, earnest prayer, with faith and patience.[40]

Although Beza did not elaborate on the identity of the enemies, he did argue that the adversaries' attacks made the situation desperate for believers. In light of the attacks, Christians needed to find assured comfort. Right use of these means assured one of success against the assaults of the enemy.

Additionally, in the *Tabula*, his polemical treatise defending Calvin's view of predestination, Beza noted that assurance was made necessary because of the realities of spiritual opposition. After he had explicated the doctrine of predestination, Beza labored in the final chapter to show "How Individuals, with Some Profit, Can Apply This General Doctrine to Each Other."[41] We noted in chapter four that these points of application in this treatise were significantly longer than the other portions of the treatise. Here we should note two other factors about Beza's application, in particular. First, assurance was necessitated by the spiritual battle. Second, Beza reiterated the two-pronged basis of assurance he had outlined in the *Confession*: the internal testimony of the Holy Spirit to the Christian and the external witness of a changed life resulting in good works. Beza's pastoral advice, since it was elaborated in this polemical and doctrinal context, is remarkable:

> So then, do you wish (whoever you are) to be assured of your predestination, and therefore the salvation you await, against all the attacks of Satan? I say, do you want to be assured, not by doubts and conjectures that assail the human mind, but as certainly and surely as if you ascended to heaven itself and understood that secret decree from the very mouth of God? Take care, and be diligent that you do not begin at the highest stage, for otherwise you will not endure the immense light of God. Therefore, begin at the lowest stages; and when you hear God's voice resounding in your ears and heart and calling you to Christ, the only Mediator, consider step by step, and inquire carefully if you are justified and sanctified by

---

40   Beza, *Psalmes*, 44
41   Beza, *Tabula*, in *The Potter and the Clay*, 80.

faith in Christ. For these are the effects, and from them we understand that faith is the cause.

You will know this partly from the Spirit of adoption who inwardly cries "Abba, Father," and partly from the power and efficacy of that same Spirit within you – if, that is, you experience and also demonstrate in reality that sin, though it "dwells" in you, does not "reign" in you. But what then? Is it not the Holy Spirit who causes us spontaneously not to give free reign to our wicked and depraved desires, as those are wont to do whose eyes the Prince of this world has blinded? Who else "exhorts us to prayers," no matter how cold and sluggish we are? Who arouses in us those "inexpressible sighs"? Who implants in us after we have sinned (sometimes intentionally and knowingly) that hatred for the sins that we commit – not because we fear punishment but because we offend our most merciful Father? Who, I say, bears witness to us that our sighs are heard? Who urges us even to dare entreat God, our God, and still our Father, even after we have offended him? Is it not the Spirit, and he alone, whom "freely we received," as "freely he is given" for a sure pledge of our adoption? But if we can infer faith from these effects, we can only conclude that we are efficaciously called and drawn, and that from this calling in turn (which we have shown is peculiar to God's children) we comprehend entirely what we are seeking. We therefore were given to the Son, since we were predestined by God's eternal counsel, which he proposed in himself, to be adopted in the Son. From this it follows, in short, that since we were predestined by that most unshakable will of God, which depends on itself alone, and since "no one can snatch us from the hand of the Son," and since perseverance in faith is necessary for salvation, we have a sure expectation of our perseverance, and consequently our salvation. And therefore it is wicked to have any more doubts concerning that matter.

Consequently, it is totally wrong to say that this doctrine renders us negligent or dissolute. It is so wrong that, on the contrary, it alone gives us access to examine and even understand, by means of his Spirit, the very "depths" of God. We only know those "depths" in part as long as we sojourn here, and therefore we must daily do battle with the "heavenly weapons" against despair. . . . Furthermore, how can anyone remain firm and constant to that end, against so many dangerous internal and external temptations, and so many "strokes of chance," as the world likes to say, if he has not first established in his mind what is utterly true: that God does all things according to his good will, no matter what, or whatever instruments he uses, in the interest of his own, and that the man who is set in such a plight may number himself among "those in his book"?[42]

This long quotation from a treatise defending predestination against Bolsec's attacks demonstrates again that for Theodore Beza assurance was necessary because of eschatological reality. Knowing the proper means by which to arrive at assurance strengthened the Christian "against all the attacks of Satan." Such knowledge strengthened the believer to "daily do battle with the 'heavenly weapons' against despair." Assurance was requisite because of the spiritual

---

42 Ibid., 80-82.

battle.

Finally, in his published prayers Beza reiterated how the spiritual battle made assurance both necessary and difficult to obtain. In the preface to his *Houshold Prayers*, Beza noted that prayer itself was often difficult for believers because of Satanic opposition. Since God wanted prayers to be fueled by affection for him, Beza urged his readers that "we must, praying carefully, lift up our hearts with a true zeal to God, banishing out all other thoughts, abandoning Satan with all his baits, opening our hearts, that our heavenly Father may thereunto infuse and pour down his blessings."[43] Later, Beza remarked that not only did a believer's indwelling corruption hinder prayerfulness, but in addition, "the devil does at all times lie in wait to seduce us. So does he, especially, at such times, seek to creep into our minds, to divert our thoughts elsewhere, that they may be polluted with many blemishes, notwithstanding that they of themselves sufficiently go astray. Yes our vanity, imperfection, and coldness, does many ways betray itself, that we may well say in one word: no man prays rightly, but he, whose mouth and mind Christ directs with his Spirit."[44] Satanic opposition was real. Prayer was a spiritual weapon to be wielded by believers against the devil.

The *Houshold Prayers* also noted the means of protection in the battle. In the fight against the devil for assurance, Christians must lean on the love and perfect character of their Heavenly Father. In one place, for example, Beza prayed, "Strengthen us likewise with your virtue, O almighty God, against the temptations and assaults of Satan, delivering us victoriously, preserving us also from such dangers and miseries, as everywhere follow us at the heels in this life . . . because we are of the number of your children."[45] In another prayer, Beza rejoiced that though Satan's schemes were bad, God's grace was more powerful: "Satan, the prince of darkness, lies always in wait to hurt us, seeking principally to make a breach into our hearts when we stand least upon our guard. But, O Almighty God, in your presence also are the thousands of angels, to watch those whom you have called to the inheritance of your salvation, of which number we believe ourselves to be, through the mercy which it has pleased you to show us. Give us grace therefore to be delivered from the temptations of the devil."[46]

Thus, this survey of various genres from his pen shows that for Theodore Beza assurance of salvation was necessitated by the spiritual battle raging around Christians as they made their pilgrimage to heaven. The devil made believers question their standing with God. As a pastor sensitive to the spiritual predicaments of his parishioners, Beza encouraged his listeners to seek

---

43 Beza, *Houshold Prayers*, B5v.
44 Ibid., B6r-B6v.
45 Ibid., O3r-O3v.
46 Ibid., P3r-P3v.

assurance in Jesus Christ. The Holy Spirit would testify to them internally of their salvation, and the good works they produced in response to their salvation would serve as external proofs of the same. Their hope resided thus in God's character and the grace he had shown them and promised to continue to pour out on them for eternity. But until believers reached their final resting place in heaven, they would not have complete assurance due to the trials that inevitably attended this life.

The *Loci* of Assurance for Weary Christians

Were we to end our discussion of Beza's doctrine of assurance here, we would conclude the following. As we saw in his remarks to Andreae, Beza was a seasoned pastor, adept at counseling doubting souls. To Andreae, he emphasized God's perfect character and his sovereignty as helps in obtaining assurance. In the *Confession*, he emphasized a two-pronged approach to assurance: the internal testimony of the Holy Spirit and the external proof of works. In the *Confession* as well, though, Beza put Christ forward as the answer to the devil's attempts to make Christians doubt their salvation. And, finally, the spiritual battle made assurance both necessary and often difficult to obtain.

Already we see, then, that Beza had a pastoral, and a broad, approach to the issue of Christian assurance. He knew that demonic attack coupled with indwelling sin in Christians made assurance difficult to obtain during their earthly pilgrimage. Spiritual reality was such that they needed as many means of finding comfort for their standing with their heavenly Father as was possible. For these reasons, Pastor Beza delineated several *loci* of assurance. He pointed out even more means than those we have already noted, as a way of aiding weary pilgrims to continue on their journey.

Beza taught that in order to have assurance during their pilgrimage Christians needed to scan the horizon from eternity past to eternity future. God's eternal purposes for his people were one *locus* of assurance for doubting Christians, as was God's glorious future for his people in heaven. And between these two poles the Lord had given his people several means of attaining certainty of their salvation.[47] We note seven distinct *loci*.

---

47 In a similar fashion, Reformed dogmaticians typically noted several ways for Christians to arrive at certainty of their salvation, including the "practical syllogism," but ultimately resting on God's love for them expressed in Christ and their faith in him as their foundation of hope. See Heppe, *Reformed Dogmatics*, 176-78, 585-89.

God's Character and Promises

The place to begin was God's perfect character, specifically the Lord's infinite love for his children as shown in his promises to them. God's love was of great comfort to Christians as they sought assurance, Beza often repeated. God's love was the fortress that protected his people from the attacks of the devil. Thus Beza petitioned, "Strengthen us likewise with your virtue, O almighty God, against the temptations and assaults of Satan . . . because we are of the number of your children."[48] When he reflected on Psalm 6:2 ("Have mercy on me, O Lord, for I am weak. O Lord heal me, for my bones are vexed"), Beza found encouragement in the character of God: "what emboldens me then after this sort. Your goodness, your pity, your compassion, which is so much the greater as it stretches itself upon the unworthy, and there most abounds where there is most sin."[49] In his reflections on Psalm 148, Beza showed that God's sovereignty and his grace, shown especially in the covenant he had made with his people, was the ultimate ground of comfort for them in times of trouble:

> I am of that number of those to whom you have bound yourself, not, alas, for any merit of mine but only your free mercy. I am, I say, one of those by your grace, namely, of those who hope for that which you have promised and given them grace to believe. Without this I would not [know] where to become, nor which way to turn myself. And therefore, O high God, I prepare myself to you, that you might teach me which way to hold. You see how my enemies hem me in. Deliver me, O eternal, who alone can and will do it, for so much as I have no refuge but under your cover.[50]

God's compassionate character was one *locus* of assurance, one that should strengthen believers in the midst of spiritual opposition.

Significantly, though, Beza not only asserted that God's love for Christians was their stronghold in the tumults of life. He also asked the Lord to increase his awareness of God's love for him and to keep him safely in his love so that he would persevere in the faith until the end. He prayed that since

> you are my Father, I cannot but expect a happy end of all my estates, having already received of your mercy the assured pledge of salvation, that is, forgiveness of sins. But Lord, grant especially that your grace in Jesus Christ may

---

48 Beza, *Houshold Prayers*, O3r-O3v. In the first prayer of this collection Beza expressed the same idea when he prayed, "I believe that I am of the number of your children, through your mercy, which it has pleased you to vouchsafe me. And therefore, O my God, I cannot see doubt hereof, but that you lovingly hear me, and are inclined to help me, and to relieve me in all my necessities" (ibid., in the prayer "Upon the Lord's Prayer").
49 Beza, *Christian Meditations*, Ciiv.
50 Ibid., on Ps 143:8.

be to me a comfort, and light all the days of my life, especially in the darkness of my death, to retain and hold me fast in the hope of my salvation .... [S]o that full of peace, by the effects of your Spirit, I may cheerfully leave my body to the earth, assured of the resurrection and that my soul may, by the angels, be guided to the rest of the blessed. . . . Likewise, my God, increase in me faith working every good work, and give me grace constantly to persevere, and thereof to make confession even to my last gasp . . . . Thus your grace, O my God and Father, be with me, and your blessing [be] upon all the works of my hands. So be it.[51]

A final example, this one from Beza's sermons on the Song of Songs, demonstrates that Beza grounded assurance in the love of God for his people. In this place, Beza asked what moved the Lord from eternity to elect certain people to be his own?

And what moved God to do this admirable work? Certainly nothing but his infinite goodness and love, as the prophet writes (Psal. 8.5 and 144.3). . . . And what moved this bridegroom, the eternal of God, to choose to himself this polluted maiden to make her his spouse? To bear with her for so many her adulteries (Jer. 3.1)? What more? To make himself subject unto the curse of the Father (Gal. 3.13), to give his life for her (Ephes. 5.25), to carry her sins even upon the tree of his cross (1 Pet. 2.24; Phil. 2.8). Certainly this love and good will of his, the depth whereof no man is able to sound, or measure the height, breadth, or length thereof (Eph. 3.18). And what is the ground and foundation of our faith, but this assurance, that we are loved with an invariable and unchangeable dilection (Rom 8.38)? And how could we hope in him, and how call upon him without the testimony of the Holy Ghost, which teaches us and seals it thus in our hearts that he loves us (Rom. 8.15; Gal. 4.6; 1 Cor. 2.12: Jam. 1.6)?[52]

The foundation of believers' faith, Beza maintained, was their sovereign Father.

Jesus Christ

God's love was concrete, not nebulous. Theodore Beza located divine love especially in the death of Christ on the cross for sinners. When he was counseling troubled believers about where to look to find certainty of God's love and of their salvation, Beza directed them over and over again to Jesus Christ. Christ and his work was the second *locus* of assurance for Beza. We see this, for example, in Beza's sermons on the Song of Songs. There he made it clear that assurance was found in Christ: "a holy assurance grounded on him which is our peace (Ephes. 2.1, 4)."[53] In another place, Beza elaborated on

---

51 Beza, *Houshold Prayers*, in the prayer "For the Morning."
52 Beza, *Canticles*, 225-26.
53 Beza, *Canticles*, 17. Beza continued, "As his Spirit bears us witnes in our hearts (Gal. 4.6)," showing the role of the Holy Spirit in Christian assurance as we will

Christ's work as a means of assurance in the midst of spiritual attacks:

> Let us therefore hearken unto this spouse [Christ], or let us be rather this spouse, which says, "My beloved is mine, and I am his." What shall Satan then be able to do against us, seeing this bridegroom, together with all that he has, is ours? Why should our sins appall and astonish us, seeing he has carried them upon the wood of his cross (1 Pet. 2.24), seeing he is the lamb that takes away the sins of the world, and that which he has suffered for us, is ours? Shall the lack of righteousness, and the perfect accomplishment of all the Law of God which we ought to perform daunt us? Why? He has accomplished the whole Law for us, and he is ours with all his obedience (Gal. 4.4 and Rom. 5.19). Shall our natural corruption affright and terrify us? Why? He, in whom it is fully and entirely repaired for us, is ours with all his integrity and holiness (Rom. 8.3) besides that this corruption begins already to die in us, so that we are no longer in subjection unto it (Rom. 7.18). Shall death hold us still chained and fettered with his bands? Why? He who is the life, and he that has overcome death for us by his own death, is ours. What thing then is able to trouble our repose or abate our assurance?[54]

Satan had no claim on the one who possessed Christ by faith.

Recognizing that sometimes believers would not possess certainty of their salvation, Beza directed them to Christ's work for them. This Christocentric pastoral advice is evident in Beza's prayer for a person near death:

> If notwithstanding in the infirmity of my flesh, the fearful image of death troubles me in the straits of my departure. If the world that always too much bewitches us, makes my thoughts then bow to his will. If Satan pitches his assaults, and snare, and upon the remembrance of my sins, sets hell before my face. Moreover, if my own perturbations keep me from apprehending your eternal consolations. In such most necessary extremities, promise, my good God and Father, in these anguishes, to approach unto me, to save me from the running and swift stream of such brooks, that they may not carry me away to perdition. Illuminate my thoughts with your Spirit. Waken my soul out of the sleep of death. Renew my heart by the virtue of your Spirit. And put into my hands the staff of your assured conduct, to bring me out from the laboring of this sorrowful passage, causing me, with the eyes of my faith, to behold my righteousness upon the cross of my Savior, the discharge of my debts in his sacrifice, my victory in his combats, my life in his death, my glory and joy in his resurrection. That so replenished with peace, I may cheerfully resign my body to the earth, as assured that it will rise again, and my

---

note next (ibid.). Note, as well, Beza's exhortation to "let the worthiness and perfume of Jesus Christ alone suffice us, in whom we are fully complete (Col. 2.10), although of mere grace and mercy it pleases him to accept of and to crown the fruits of his Spirit in us" (ibid., 51).

54   Ibid., 296-97.

Pastoral Implications of God's Sovereignty

soul to heaven, with these last words of Christ, "Into your hands, O Father, I commit my spirit."[55]

Christ's death, according to Beza, was the focal point of God's benevolent actions for his people. Through Christ, God made an eternal covenant with his people, a covenant that had its roots in eternity, but which also assured believers of their eternal resting place with God. Beza's reflections on Psalm 102 manifest his covenantal focus:

> And for so much as I am stayed upon this your permanent power, and unchangeable good will, assured, I say, upon that throne, whereof your Son, my redeemer, has taken possession, to make me his co-heir through the mercy, integrity, obedience, satisfaction and merit with which he purchased for me the celestial kingdom. I am certainly resolved, that this staidness will uphold me, and that through all the tempests, by which it pleases you to lead me for the manifestation of your bounty and power in conservation of them, I shall yet arrive in that eternal haven, wherein all we, whom you allow for your servants, though never so unprofitable, being born age after age, and whom you shall acknowledge for true children of Abraham, Isaac, and Jacob, with whom you contracted the covenant of eternal life, shall have our dwelling world without end. Amen.[56]

Christ's salvific work continued therefore to be a cornerstone of Theodore Beza's doctrine of assurance.

As their Priest, Christ saved his people from their sin. But as their King, he continued to protect them in the midst of the spiritual battle. Only Christ could protect Christians from Satan. Thus Beza noted very poignantly,

> Does Satan amaze you? He has vanquished him for you. Does the corruption of your nature astonish you? The Son of God making himself man has fully sanctified it for you. Do your sins, which are fruits of this corruption, make you

---

55   Beza, *Houshold Prayers*, M1v-M3r. Note once again the doubts that Satan raised which required assurance. This was, in fact, a constant refrain in Beza when dealing with those who lacked assurance. He encouraged them to look to Christ's work for them, as, for example, when he prayed for sick Christians: "Be his shield, against the assaults and terrors of death, especially if his conscience troubles and accuses him for his inward and hidden sins, which are open in your sight. Then let the Holy Ghost, the perpetual comforter of all faithful souls, vouchsafe to represent unto him for his defence the passion and sacrifice of our Lorde Jesus, who has himself borne upon the cross all our iniquities, that so he might absolve and discharge us, before your judicial throne." Later in the same prayer, he said, "even to his last gasp, never fearing the temptations of Satan, of death, or of hell, as being assured, that Christ has overcome them, and led them in triumph, breaking their bonds, so that he may, in all Christian confidence, cry out with your apostle, 'O death, where is your sting? O hell, where is your victory?'" (ibid., Q2r-Q3v).
56   Beza, *Christian Meditations*, Giiiir-Giiiiv.

afraid? He has borne them all upon the tree, and has paid for your discharge. Which is more, his righteousness is yours, he himself is yours. Are you afraid of men [who] say God is for you? Does death frighten you? It is vanquished and turned into an entry of life. Behold then all your enemies scattered, behold quite under foot all such as afflicted you within and without, because the Lord allows you for one of his servants and household.[57]

Thus Christ, as well as the covenant God made with his people in Christ, was a second *locus* of assurance in the spiritual battle.

Faith

According to Pastor Beza faith, the means by which a believer grasped hold of Christ, was a third *locus* of assurance in the spiritual battle. In perhaps his most succinct definition of "faith," Beza said it was "A certain persuasion and assurance, which every true Christian man ought to have, that God the Father loves him, for Jesus Christ his Son's sake."[58] Beza believed that those who had grasped Christ by faith had all the blessings of being Christians. Thus he prayed that "they who lodge him [Christ] in their hearts, have you, O God, truly present and enjoy you and your benefits."[59] In the same prayer, Beza lauded the joy that came from knowing Jesus: "we are unable to know you, or to feel the efficacy of your love towards us, but only in the same Christ."[60] Jesus Christ was the focal point of Christianity, and of Christian comfort, and he was grasped by faith.

In a different prayer, Beza again noted that part of the essence of faith was having a sense of assurance – here he identified it as a feeling of "peace and joy" – that one was accepted by God in Christ:

> So great is the vanity, ignorance, and infirmity of our nature, that if you, O most merciful God, work not that in us which you command us to do, if you do not teach us that we may know, if you do not convert us that we may cleave to your word, if you do not give us to your Son that he may keep us yours, if he bring us not clothed in his righteousness to the throne of your grace, and if your Spirit leads us not in the paths of your kingdom, holding us fast in the effects of his gifts upon the way of your truth, we cannot hearken to this voice of the Shepherd of our souls, neither in our hearts conceive such and so lively a faith, that all

---

57 Ibid., on Ps 143:12.
58 Beza, *Little Catechisme*, section 4, question 3.
59 Beza, *Houshold Prayers*, in the prayer "For the obtaining of the knowledge of God in Jesus Christ."
60 Ibid., E3v-Er4.

uncertainty might be banished, and the same sealed with his own efficacy. Much less can we feel the peace and joy that true faith brings with it.[61]

True belief reaped a sense of joy and peace before God in the soul of the one who had faith. Therefore one could know if he had true faith by sensing the joy that accompanied acceptance with God. Again, then, assurance was of the essence of faith, according to Beza.

The Holy Spirit

Beza showed his trinitarianism by stressing that assurance of salvation flowed from the Holy Spirit as well as from God's love and Christ's death. The Spirit's role was different than either the Father's or the Son's, though, since his work in assuring believers was to bring to mind and apply to them the truths of the Father and the Son. He pointed struggling Christians to the character and work of God for them. He developed Christian character in believers, changing lives and so bringing them certainty of their salvation. He also bestowed joy to them as a pledge of their adoption as God's children. In this sense, the Spirit was the fourth *locus* of Christian assurance.

Thus in a prayer when someone "feels his death at hand," Beza prayed that Christ's "sacrifice gives me peace with you. His blood cleanses me. His obedience absolves me. His wounds cure me. In his torments my soul finds her rest. For of all these benefits I feel your promise sealed in my heart by your Spirit, which makes me cry unto you, Abba Father, and assures me that you will of your free mercy, in the name of your Son, and for his sake, give me remission of my sins, and eternal life."[62] He also asked the Lord, "that by the efficacy of your Holy Spirit, I may obtain the true and firm consolation of the faithful soul, the height of his joy, of his quiet and content, and the infallible direction to his perfection, namely, the assurance that you, my heavenly Father, have adopted me into the number of your children."[63]

The Holy Spirit, according to Beza, applied Christ to Christians. As we have already noted, he did this through the instrument of the believer's faith. Thus Beza noted that there is

> but one means to be joined and united with Jesus Christ in order to have salvation in him. It is faith, which is an assurance that all Christians ought to have of their election and salvation, only by the grace and goodness of God, in Jesus Christ. Faith and assurance is created, and daily increased by the virtue of the Holy Ghost, within the hearts of the elect, by the means of preaching the word of God,

---

61   Ibid., in the prayer "To obtain the gift of Faith."
62   Ibid., in the prayer "For him that feels his death at hand."
63   Ibid., F2r-F2v.

and the ministration of the sacraments. . . . So this faith is as the hand, which only receives and apprehends Jesus Christ to the salvation of him that believes.[64]

In his *Tabula* Beza defined this faith more exactly, showing the Spirit's role in creating and maintaining faith in Christians.

> This Spirit causes the elect to be truly impressed by a sense of their calamity; and in the second place, he creates faith in them, that they may be able to meet the condition connected with the preaching of the Gospel. Moreover, this faith, in a certain sense, is twofold. On the one hand, it is that by which Christ is known generally and universally, or that by which we give assent to the history of Christ and the prophecies written concerning him – a faith that is granted, on occasion, even to the reprobate themselves. On the other hand, it is that which belongs to the elect in particular and is posited in our applying to ourselves, as our very own, the Christ offered universally and for all men, and our being rendered individually more certain of our election, which formerly was hidden in God's secret but was later revealed to us. It is revealed partly by the internal witness of conscience through God's Spirit, conjoined with external preaching, and partly by the power and efficacy of that same Spirit who leads his individual elect, emancipated from the slavery of sin, to freedom, that they may begin to will and do the things that are of God.[65]

The Spirit had still other effects in the lives of true believers. In the first place, the Holy Spirit eased troubled consciences and created peace and joy in his people. In the *Confession* Beza said "it is easy to see why the Holy Spirit is called the Comforter. . . . For, since His office is to apply Jesus Christ to us by faith. . . . it follows that, by Him alone, our consciences have such peace that we have this to give us joy in our afflictions (Rom 5:1-3; James 1:2)."[66] Again, while commenting on Psalm 51:11, Beza emphasized the importance of the sense of joy that the Spirit gave to God's children:

> but, my God, reject me not, neither deprive me of all that feeling which you had once given me, and whereof you did never as yet wholly bereave me. For I know and believe myself to be of the number of those whom you will not lose, though I have deserved to be quite cut off. Rather, my God, instead of taking quite from me all that residue which your goodness has yet left me, restore to me again that of

---

64 Beza, *Briefe and Pithie Summe*, 246-47.
65 Beza, *Tabula*, in *The Potter and the Clay*, 54-55.
66 Beza, *The Christian Faith*, 68. In another place, Beza argued that the primary goal of the Christian life was to have a peaceful conscience before God: "to obey you with a quiet conscience, the same being the chiefest, the highest, and the most perfect degree of love . . . to be brief, it is that which in the secret of our hearts, gives us a sweet feeling of your peace, which surmounts all the reason of our understanding" (Beza, *Houshold Prayers*, in the prayer "To obtain the virtue of Love").

which my sins have spoiled me, and settle me once more in the assurance of my salvation, that most unspeakable pleasure and joy which you bestow upon your children.[67]

In the second place, the Spirit caused his people to do good works. For example, in his late lectures on Romans 9, in a section titled "On the Use of the Doctrine of Predestination as it Refers to Ministers of the Word and to Some who Pass Judgment on Others," Beza pointed to the connection between the Spirit and the evidence of good works in Christians:

> Since we must judge a tree "according to its fruits," we must certainly support and constantly exhort, and even confirm more and more in the witness of their election those whom we have recognized, from their own words and deeds, to be "good trees." They are the trees that are planted, as it were, by God's hand, and watered by his Spirit. But we must do this in such a way that we always urge them to perseverance and constancy in repentance, and warn them energetically that what is "outside" of them must correspond to what is "inside." Otherwise, we could stray at this point – or rather, they could deceive themselves. For we cannot determine (except only probably) the personal election of other people.[68]

No where do we see Beza's multifaceted approach to Christian assurance more than in the role he assigned to the Spirit in granting assurance. The Holy Spirit produced both objective (e.g., changed lives) and subjective (e.g., joy and peace) signs of believers' adoption into God's family. All the Spirit's activities, though, were grounded in God's love as manifested in Christ's death for his people.

---

67 Beza, *Christian Meditations*, on Ps 51:11-12. Later, on Ps 143:6 ("I stretch forth my hands unto thee. My soul desires after the thirsty land"), Beza again emphasized assurance and experience: "This encouraged me, my God, to stretch forth my hands to you. This, I say, strengthened my poor conscience to address itselfe to you, yes with more burning desire, than ever the most parched ground gaped for the moisture of your rain" (ibid., Hiiv).

68 Beza, *De Praedestinationis Doctrina*, in *The Potter and the Clay*, 379. In his prayers, Beza noted that all the good works Christians perform flow only from the appreciation they have towards God who loved them: "we love you, because you first loved us, and like as also through your grace you make yourself and your benefits known to us. The more therefore that we find ourselves disposed to love you, the more should we believe that you make yourself to be felt in the inward parts of our souls, to be our God and our Father, and that therefore we have the greater cause to confirm and comfort ourselves in the love you bear us" (Beza, *Houshold Prayers*, in the prayer "To obtain the virtue of Love").

The Church

In Beza's thought the church was a fifth *locus* of assurance. The church, he prayed, was like an ark which keeps Christians safe during times of evil: "you will always preserve from all calamities and miseries those who stand fast in the ark of your Church, grounded upon your word in the gospel of reconciliation to the Lord Jesus, and depart in his faith."[69] Specifically, the sacraments of the church were a means of assuring Christians, Beza maintained. In answer to the question, "why has God ordained these signs [of the two sacraments] to his promises?" Beza gave the answer "to make us so much the more assured of the certainty of them."[70] The eucharist, specifically, was meant to assure God's people. "To what end [is the Supper given]?" Beza queried. His answer again stressed assurance: "To testify unto me and to assure me that even as this bread and this wine are ordained for the maintenance and nourishment of this life, so our Lord Jesus Christ has given his body and his blood for me, and given himself to me, to the end that from him, as from a fountain, there may flow unto me eternal life."[71]

Specifically, the Lord's Supper was meant to increase Christians' faith and comfort in this life. Beza explained "that this great benefit [Christ's death for his people] might still be present to our perpetual comfort, and for the increase and support of our faith, that his body risen again in glory for our righteousness and perfection, ascended into heaven, and sitting at your right hand, should also be communicated unto us here beneath in your church, in the mystery of the eucharist, to be our food and nourishment unto holy and eternal life."[72] The eucharist increased the comfort of believers by being a precursor of the fellowship they would have with God for eternity: "Oh happy are we already, who in Christ, in the communion of the faithful, do taste the sweetness of this celestial banquet, wherein we shall see you, and face to face contemplate one only and true God, being filled with your glory in endless peace."[73] One of Beza's aphorisms in his *Tabula* made this point as well:

---

69 Beza, *Houshold Prayers*, in the prayer "That we may not depart from the Church."
70 Beza, *Little Catechisme*, section 8, question 2.
71 Ibid., section 9, question 3. Beza reiterated this later when he asked, "Why has the Lord ordained and instituted two signs in his holy supper, seeing that in baptism there is but one only?" and answered "To assure us that he does not feed us to the halves but wholly, being not only our meat but also our drink" (ibid., section 10, question 1).
72 Beza, *Houshold Prayers*, in the prayer "For the Communion in the holy Eucharist."
73 Ibid., H1r. Additionally, Beza stressed that as the Supper brought assurance it also acted as a means of keeping Christians in the faith; it helped them to persevere: "grant that in true efficacy I may participate in this sacrament of his body to increase in faith and love, and all other your gifts, that I may never abandon your holy covenant" (ibid., in the prayer "For thanksgiving after the Communion").

These, then, are the stages by which the Lord is pleased to create freely, within his elect, that precious and peculiar gift of faith by which they lay hold on their salvation in Christ. But since faith in us is still too imperfect for us to be able not only to persevere (which is surely necessary) but also to make progress in it, we are initiated, for that reason, first of all, to the sacrament of baptism. Next, this faith is again sealed within us, not only by the hearing of the Word but also by the sacrament of the Lord's Supper. For surely, the main end of these sacraments is that there be definite and efficacious seals, or even attestations, of the communion of the faithful with Christ, that he may become, for them, "wisdom, justice, sanctification, and redemption." Therefore, Paul very frequently emphasizes that we "have peace," once we are "justified by faith."[74]

How, then, could Christians gain assurance of their salvation? One means Pastor Beza stressed was to remain within the bounds of the church and receive God's blessing there.

Prayer

Prayer, according to Theodore Beza, was a sixth *locus* of assurance. How could one have certainty of his salvation? Through prayer, Beza averred. No where does Beza explain this more than in his preface to the *Houshold Prayers*. Beza's premise throughout the preface was that prayer was a means to shore up Christians in their pilgrimage to heaven. Not only was it a means the Lord had instituted to help believers attain their salvation, but it was also a precursor to the fuller relationship they would have there with God. This demonstrates once again that Beza's eschatological vision affected his entire life, and his pastoral ministry. In this regard, Beza noted that "in the miseries of this life, we comfort ourselves, by looking for the benefits of the kingdom of God" through prayer. It does this by refreshing "us through the remembrance of his gracious promises, which confirm us in the same, and of the blessings already received at his hands, which move us in our necessities to hope for the like, and wait for it with all patience. It augments in us a desire to be conjoined with him through our Lord Jesus Christ in whom all our good does consist."[75] Supremely, then, prayer was proof of a Christian's relationship with Christ.

Given the reality of Satan and his schemes against Christians, Beza noted that one of the things for which Christians should pray was assurance:

> To present ourselves before God, to offer unto him our vows, and to beseech his fatherly love, or dilection, for guiding us, by his good Spirit, unto the light of his truth, to increase in our hearts faith, love, constancy, humility, and other of his heavenly gifts, to forgive us our debts, to mortify the corruptions of our nature, to

---

74 Beza, *Tabula*, in *The Potter and the Clay*, 56-57.
75 Beza, *Houshold Prayers*, B3r-B3v.

clothe us with his spiritual armor against the assaults of the devil, the world and the flesh, to provide for our necessities, to preserve us from infinite dangers, which compass us round about. To be short, to grant us his Holy Spirit, to guide the whole course of our life, to the glory of his name, and the peace and salvation of our own souls.[76]

In fact, he noted, one of the chief benefits of prayer is that it lifted Christians, as it were, up to heaven, which was their true home: "By prayer we bless God for his goodness, power, wisdom, justice, and mercy towards us. Because of our prayers, he blesses us in doing us good and distributing his benefits amongst us. It is unto us as the soul of our souls. For prayer quickens our affections, and lifts up our hearts unto heaven who otherwise would be dead in sins and trespasses, by following the vanities of this wicked world."[77] In a sense, then, Beza thought that prayer allowed believers to experience their future salvation now. The activity of communing with God in prayer in the present assured them of their future with him.

Heaven

The final *locus*, heaven, may be the most surprising one that Beza offered. This was a natural teaching, though, when we remember the eschatological view of reality that undergirded Beza's life. All that he did as a Christian, a scholar, and a pastor was informed by the fact that he was cognizant of a spiritual battle raging around him. And Christians would be subjected to the mayhem of this warfare, including Satan's assaults on their assurance, until they arrived safely in paradise. We see this, for example, in Beza's reflections on Psalm 130, where he argued: "Who has charged himself with all our sins, not one except? Who was obedient for his poor Israel, that is to say, his elect, even to that death of the cross? I embrace you with both my arms, O Jesus Christ, who has reconciled me to the Father, assuring me by your Spirit of the comfort of my salvation in you. And so fast embracing you, I receive the pledges of life and everlasting bliss."[78] Assurance was located *extra nos*, in Christ. More than that, certainty of salvation was centered on eternity, not the present. To Beza, assurance was ultimately found in the sure hope of heaven which was made certain by Christ's death for his people in the past and their holding on to him by faith in the present. By embracing Christ now, Christians received a sure pledge of eternity. But the fullness of the certainty was yet to come.

"Shortly, instead of this misery," Beza likewise noted, "you shall receive the true peace which the world can neither give, nor take away, and the true repose

---

76 Ibid., B1v-B2r.
77 Ibid., B2v-B3r.
78 Beza, *Christian Meditations*, on Ps 130:8.

of conscience, even the very anchor and earnest payment of that durable blessedness to follow."[79] In another place, having noted the importance for Christians constantly to feed upon Scripture in this life, Beza noted how different heaven would be from the present existence. There all of believers' joys would be complete. He said that at that time, "Lord, being wholly changed, I shall not hear your word for fashion's sake, but I shall therein take all my pleasure. I shall eat, I say, with a good appetite of this quickening food, for I shall find a good snack in it. I shall digest it, and never think myself satisfied with it. Day and night I shall not cease to apply all my understanding thereunto, that more and more I may be nourished and sustained in the full enjoying of that true, absolute, and eternal felicity."[80] Heaven would be the ultimate source of certainty. Believers would experience everlasting joy there.

Beza's prayer "For heavenly life" clarifies the manner in which he understood the hope of heaven to result in assured trust in the present. He began by noting that the essence of heaven is knowledge of God: "In sum, a life which by the full view that we shall have of your eternal deity, O almighty God, shall make us know you, as you have known us, and as you are in Trinity of persons – Father, Word, Spirit – and in unity of essence. Likewise to love you according to the excellence of your nature with our whole hearts and thoughts, and our whole strength and might, and in this love to obtain our perfect and full contentment."[81] In heaven alone would believers have joy that was without defect or delinquency. Given this fact, Beza prayed:

> I beseech you therefore, O Lord, to give me grace, that withdrawing my affection more and more from the dark cloisters of the earth, sprinkled with tears, I may lift up my desires to the bright habitation of your deity, where the treasures and incomparable joys of your paradise remain in an eternal life . . . comforting myself incessantly night and day, in that the promise is made unto me through my savior Jesus Christ, to the end, that in my last hour – come out of my misery and entered into my felicity – I may with a happy flight go take my rest above in your peace, O my God, which surmounts all understanding, and for to sing psalms of thanksgiving to you without end.[82]

Heaven would be the ultimate experience of assurance. But by withdrawing one's love from the world and placing it in the hope of heaven a Christian could be comforted now in the certainty of his "happy flight" to paradise soon.

Beza's prayer "To demand the virtue of hope" sums up the role heaven played as the locus of assurance in his thought. Beza began by addressing the issue of sanctification. Just as God worked regeneration in the elect, so he also

---

79 Ibid., on Ps 32:7.
80 Ibid., on Ps 1:2.
81 Beza, *Houshold Prayers*, in the prayer "For heavenly life."
82 Ibid.

sanctified them, by planting within them "virtue, making it bring forth fruit, furthering thereby daily the rooting out of sin and increase of the gifts of your grace."[83] This thought immediately led Beza to pray to God for assurance of his salvation, a sort of supernatural sense of hope in God: "I beseech you, O Lord, that as it has pleased you freely to justify me by the singular gift of faith in our Savior Jesus Christ, granting me peace with your Majesty through his sacrifice, so you would promise to illuminate the eyes of my soul, to make me know, to the sanctification of your name, what the hope of those is whom you have called to the incorruptible inheritance of your glory."[84] Being spurred on by this certain hope, the saints should meditate on it regularly. However, Beza pointed out that they would not know this assurance fully until they arrived in their eternal rest. Thus he prayed that he would be "supported with an assured expectation one day, and forever, to obtain the celestial riches . . . . Finally, there to be fully united to Christ, and by him, to you, O Father, the fountain of eternal life, and so to possess the sovereign good eternally. Let this holy meditation, and the hope to enjoy that full and perfect contentment, so occupy my senses that it may be my thought, my pleasure, my labor, my habitation, and my most ordinary vocation."[85] Heaven then would be the ultimate *locus* of assurance for weary Christians since there they would be with their God and Father for eternity free from the spiritual battle and from the sin that plagued them here below. In paradise, they would be fully assured of their acceptance with God. By God's grace, they could have certainty of their future now.

Conclusion

In sum, then, Beza offered varied *loci* of assurance because of his eschatological vision. While on their earthly pilgrimage, believers in the midst of the spiritual battle could find certainty of their salvation in a number of different places. These ranged from eternity past (God's love for them from eternity) to their eternal future in heaven, with a number of other *loci* besides. But all these were grounded in God's love for believers, Beza averred:

Therefore, whenever Scripture wants to confirm the children of God in a sure hope, it is not content with the witnesses of secondary causes – that is, the fruits of faith – nor with secondary and proximate causes themselves – namely, faith and calling. Rather, it rises to Christ himself, in whom nonetheless, as our Head, we are really elected and adopted; and it mounts from there all the way up to that eternal purpose that God has set forth in no one else than himself alone.[86]

---

83   Ibid., I1v-I2r.
84   Ibid., I2r-I2v.
85   Ibid., I3r-I3v.
86   Beza, *Tabula*, in *The Potter and the Clay*, 34.

And they were all given to Christians by the grace of God for believers' strengthening and encouragement until they arrived in heaven: "O heavenly Father, it pleases you to give us here below in the following of our course, a convenient leisure to meditate upon the most wonderful effects of your Spirit in us, the singular work of our new birth, the progress of our faith, the fruits of our love, the feeling of our peace in the hope of our salvation to come, when we shall, by Christ, be wholly united to you alone."[87] As helpful as the various *loci* were in the midst of the spiritual battle, and Theodore Beza argued that they were absolutely essential for Christian comfort, they were proleptic. That is to say, believers now only tasted of the full assurance that they would ultimately have in heaven. Though it was certain in the present, assurance's full realization waited for its fulfillment in paradise.

The "Practical Syllogism"

No where has one *locus* of assurance in Beza's thinking been exaggerated to the neglect of others more than in the emphasis that several scholars have placed upon Beza's use of the *syllogismus practicus* or "practical syllogism." Joel Beeke defined this pastoral issue of assurance succinctly:

> A "practical syllogism" (*syllogismus practicus*) is a conclusion drawn from an action. The basic form of the syllogism when it pertains to salvation is as follows: Major premise: Those only who do "x" are saved. Minor premise (practical): But I do "x". Conclusion: Therefore I am saved.[88]

Broadly speaking, there are two schools of interpretation of Beza regarding the practical syllogism. John Bray and R. T. Kendall represent the first. Bray trumpeted that "for Beza the rock of assurance was not to be found in the person and work of Christ, as it had been for Calvin. Nor did he intend to base assurance upon an apprehension of the divine elective decree. In his search for a means whereby the believer could gain assurance Beza eventually seized upon an application of the *syllogismus practicus*."[89] Similarly, Kendall asserted that Beza's use of the practical syllogism was a radical departure from Calvin's

---

87 Beza, *Houshold Prayers*, L5v.
88 Beeke, *Assurance of Faith*, 97 n. 153. Johannes Wollebius expressed it this way: "In exploring our election we must advance by the analytic method from the means of execution to the decree, beginning with our sanctification, with a syllogism like this: Whoever feels in himself the gift of sanctification, by which we die to sin and live unto righteousness, is justified, called or presented with true faith and elect. But I feel this by the grace of God. Therefore I am justified, called and elect" (Heppe, *Reformed Dogmatics*, 176).
89 John S. Bray, "The Value of Works in the Theology of Calvin and Beza," *Sixteenth Century Journal* 4 (1973): 82

biblical view. After he pointed out four problems with Beza's doctrine of assurance, Kendall summed up his conclusion about Beza by arguing that "Beza's doctrine requires the use of the practical syllogism in order for one to be persuaded he is one of those for whom Christ died."[90]

Robert Letham and Richard Muller represent the second school. This group of scholars asserts that Beza did indeed employ the practical syllogism, indeed perhaps more stridently than Calvin had, but they insist that Beza did not abuse this method of finding assurance. Letham, for instance, claimed that Beza gave "a prominent place to sanctification as a means of assurance of election." He continued, however, to argue that Beza's "attempt at making election Christocentric enables him to focus assurance on Christ."[91] Both Letham and Muller noted an increased use of the practical syllogism by Beza in his later years. Letham pointed especially to Beza's 1599 *Eximia tractatio de consolandis qui circa praedestinationem tentatur* (which he failed to note had originally been part of Beza's 1586 *Acta*) and his 1588 *De remediis adversus praecipuos insultus Satanae, tractatio*.[92] Then—with no contextual support, but merely based on an appeal to the "very titles of these works and the problems with which they are concerned"—Letham asserted that in this work Beza "makes pervasive use of the practical syllogism and introspection as the solution [to those doubting their election]. There is a marked absence of Christocentricity. At no time in the work is Christ seen as the basis of assurance."[93]

Muller's conclusions were more qualified, but he nonetheless saw progression in Beza's thought. In his 1555 *Tabula*, Beza "clearly, had no concern to press toward the *syllogismus practicus*."[94] The following years showed a change, though. By the time of Beza's 1570 *Quaestionum et responsionum*, he showed "a tendency toward the adoption of an analytic

---

90 Kendall, *Calvin and English Calvinism*, 29. Kendall argued that, unlike Calvin's proper view, Beza's doctrine of limited atonement "(1) inhibits the believer from looking directly to Christ's death for assurance; (2) precipitates an implicit distinction between faith and assurance; (3) tends to put repentance before faith in the *ordo salutis*; and (4) plants the seed of voluntarism in the doctrine of faith" (ibid.).
91 Letham, "Saving Faith and Assurance," 1:153.
92 I have not been able to locate this work.
93 Letham, "Saving Faith and Assurance," 1:154. Letham's statement that "there appears to be evidence that in later years Beza's scholasticism and rationalism may have hardened. Certainly, there seems to be an element of change in some of his writings published towards the end of his life" (ibid.) is unwarranted. Based on other late works of Beza's—such as his sermons—and Letham's failure to notice different genres, I maintain that Beza was not tied to the practical syllogism, nor was it an inherently scholastic method.
94 Muller, *Christ and the Decree*, 80.

method in discussing predestination, a more speculative, *a posteriori*, argument than witnessed by his earlier thought leading within five years to the *syllogismus practicus* of the *Catechismus compendarius*."[95] Yet Muller proceeded to qualify this statement. Beza, he asserted, employed the practical syllogism "as, at most, a partial solution to the problem of assurance," also referring regularly to the internal witness of the Holy Spirit. "But," Muller continued, "when Beza asks the question of the Christian life that results from faith, justification, and sanctification, proceeding, that is, from the divine cause to its human effects, he more pointedly even than Calvin, demands that good work follow."[96] Then, referring to Bray as an authority, Muller postulated that in Beza there is "hardly a trace of Calvin's teaching concerning Christ as the ground of assurance.... Beza allows more of a separation to occur between the *munus Christi* and the *ordo salutis* than does Calvin."[97] Both of these schools of thought, then, stress that Beza used the *syllogismus practicus* more than Calvin had. And this, they asserted, was a negative development.[98]

I shall offer three responses. First, although I cannot here enter into the discussion of whether or not Beza did in fact deviate from Calvin's doctrine of Christian assurance, I think that Calvin's methodology in the *Institutes* mirrored his hand-picked successor's. Calvin defined faith as "a firm and certain knowledge of God's benevolence toward us, founded upon the truth of the freely given promise in Christ, both revealed to our minds and sealed upon our hearts through the Holy Spirit."[99] Later, Calvin asserted that the essence of faith was certainty: "As faith is not content with a doubtful and changeable opinion, so is it not content with an obscure and confused conception."[100] Similarly, he made the blanket statement that "he alone is truly a believer who, convinced by a firm conviction that God is a kindly and well-disposed Father toward him, promises himself all things on the basis of his generosity; who, relying upon the promises of divine benevolence toward him, lays hold on an undoubted expectation of salvation."[101] If this were all the information Calvin left us, we should have to conclude that assurance was of the essence of faith since he

---

95 Ibid., 85.
96 Ibid.
97 Ibid. Muller proceeded to warn—as Niesel had done before—about the harmful effects of using Beza's syllogism in conjunction with the question of divine election (ibid.).
98 In addition to our critique, see Marvin Anderson's criticism—concurring with Roland Bainton's—of those who argue that Beza stressed the value of works above the Word or sacraments in arriving at assurance ("Theodore Beza," 327-28).
99 John Calvin, *Institutes of the Christian Religion*, ed. John T. McNeill, trans. Ford Lewis Battles, Library of Christian Classics, vols. 20-21 (Philadelphia: Westminster, 1960), 3.2.7.
100 Ibid., 3.2.15.
101 Ibid., 3.2.16.

stressed the Spirit's role in revealing and sealing the truth to the Christian. Where there was faith, there was *by definition* assurance.

This, however, was not the whole picture for Calvin. Soon after these spectacular statements of faith's certainty he qualified his exuberance. "Surely, while we teach that faith ought to be certain and assured," he resumed, "we cannot imagine any certainty that is not tinged with doubt, or any assurance that is not assailed by some anxiety. On the other hand, we say that believers are in perpetual conflict with their own unbelief."[102] So, Calvin qualified his insistence upon assurance. The Word and the Spirit worked in believers in order to seal the promises of God in their hearts, he said.[103] Yet, he reiterated, "Faith is tossed about by various doubts, so that the minds of the godly are rarely at peace—at least they do not always enjoy a peaceful state."[104] And even though he had previously lucidly stated that the final resting place of faith—and hence the *locus* of assurance—was Christ, not oneself,[105] Calvin did not shy from continuing his discussion in the next chapter by emphasizing the necessity of repentance in the lives of Christians.[106] So, for Calvin, the place of assurance, though ultimately it consisted of Word-induced faith in Christ, could be cloudy for Christians in this life. Assurance was of the essence of faith. Yet assurance was almost never free from doubt in this life. Faith was central, but works were important as well.

Beeke's conclusion about Calvin's doctrine of assurance is apropos at this point in our discussion. Beeke had previously noted the manner in which Calvin, on the one hand, stressed that assurance was of the essence of true faith, but, on the other hand, taught that "though faith *ought* to be assuring, no *perfect* assurance exists in this life."[107] Beeke attempted to make sense of these "apparent contradictions" in Calvin's thought. He concluded that "By insisting that the Spirit's *primary mode* of bringing assurance is to direct the believer to embrace the promises of God in Christ, Calvin rejects any confidence being placed in the believer as he is in himself. Nevertheless, Calvin does not deny that a *subordinate means* to bolster assurance is realized by the Spirit on the

---

102 Ibid., 3.2.17.
103 "The Spirit accordingly serves as a seal, to seal up in our hearts those very promises the certainty of which it has previously impressed upon our minds; and takes the place of a guarantee to confirm and establish them" (ibid., 3.2.36).
104 Ibid., 3.2.37.
105 Calvin said, for instance, that "if you contemplate yourself, that is sure damnation. But since Christ has been so imputed to you with all his benefits that all this things are made yours, that you are made a member of him, indeed one with him, his righteousness overwhelms your sins; his salvation wipes out your condemnation; with his worthiness he intercedes that your unworthiness may not come before God's sight" (ibid., 3.2.24).
106 Ibid., 3.3.
107 Beeke, *Assurance of Faith*, 52; cf., 50-51.

Pastoral Implications of God's Sovereignty 221

basis of His own work with the believer which bears fruit in good works and various marks of grace."[108] What then of the "practical syllogism" in Calvin's thought? "Calvin did not use the *syllogismus practicus* in a *formal sense*," Beeke concluded, "for the formal usage of syllogisms to glean assurance belongs to a later date. But Calvin did utilize the principles of the syllogism in a *practical* sense."[109] This appears to me to be a very competent evaluation of the matter. Beza's use of the practical syllogism was not, then, so far beyond Calvin's as is often assumed.

Second, we have already seen numerous *loci* of assurance that Beza highlighted for his listeners. One must look at the composite teaching of Beza and not characterize him as one-dimensional. Bray and Kendall for some reason excluded the other avenues Beza pointed out for finding certainty of Christian salvation and stressed his use of the *syllogismus practicus*. We have seen, however, that in his *Confession* Beza stressed the twin themes of the internal testimony of the Holy Spirit and the external witness of good works as the proper means to finding assurance. If this were all that Beza had written on the subject—and we have seen that he had much more to say—even here we would have to judge that Beza's presentation of assurance was not monolithic. As a seasoned pastor, Beza offered numerous ways to find certainty of forgiveness with God to his listeners, ways adapted to the needs of his listeners.[110]

Third, there are internal clues in Beza's "syllogistic" works that he saw the *syllogismus practicus* as just one means of finding assurance. Muller particularly noted Beza's *Quaestionum et responsionum* as well as his *Petit Catéchisme*—the first because it displayed increased analytic reasoning on Beza's part, the second because it showed his bold use of the syllogism. Is this a correct assessment?

The *Quaestionum et responsionum* indeed appears to be a "scholastic" treatise. Yet, as we explained in chapter three, Beza's purpose in writing this work, clouded as it is in mystery, was soteriological. He wanted to explain to persons how they might become Christians. Beza actually showed himself a Christian pastor in his treatment of assurance here.

If we start our examination with Beza's definition of faith, his pastoral emphasis on assurance becomes manifest. "What is faith?" Beza asked. It was more than intellectual agreement, he said. It was, instead, "a firm assent of one's mind accompanying that recognition of the facts, whereby it happens that each man applies particularly to himself the promise of eternal life in Christ Jesus, just as if he already were actually a possessor of it."[111] Later, in the midst

---

108 Ibid., 72.
109 Ibid.
110 See the discussion of Beza's response to Andreae above.
111 Beza, *Little Book of Christian Questions and Responses*, 29.

of his discussion of sanctification, he included another pastoral application. Beza answered a question of God's delay in making his children holy by asserting that instead of asking the question Christians should "marvel at His goodness, in that He instills any little drop of regenerating grace in man. Yet why He defers the full sanctification of us into another age, there are many reasons, and chiefly two. One, because we are of little faith, and therefore, as much as is in us, we impede the inworking of the Holy Spirit. The second, so that, as we are saved by grace alone, and not by works, he who glories, should glory only in God."[112]

Yet, Beza continued, those sanctified must be active in doing righteousness, "For true sanctification is not able to be idle; and of what kind a fruitbearing tree is, so also is the fruit of that tree. Therefore, since our intellect is partly illumined with the knowledge of the true God, we also know in part; since we partly assent to the promise of God, and apply it to ourselves, therefore we believe in part; since our will is partly unchanged, therefore we will and do rightly only in part."[113] Later he clarified what he meant in answer to the question, "you say that good works are necessary to salvation?" He responded that "if faith is necessary to salvation, and works necessarily flow out of true faith, (as that which cannot be idle), certainly also it follows, that good works are necessary to salvation, yet not as the cause of salvation (for we are justified, and thus live, by faith alone in Christ), but as something necessarily attached to true faith."[114] But it was in his discussion of predestination that Beza showed his pastoral acumen most decisively in speaking about assurance. The interlocutor put forth the query, "in the perilous temptation of particular election, where should I flee for succor?" Beza's delineation of assurance encompassed three *loci* of assurance: the fruits of sanctification, the testimony of the Holy Spirit, and Christ. Troubled persons should run

> To the effects whereby the spiritual life is rightly discerned. . . . Therefore, that I am elect, is first perceived from sanctification begun in me, that is, by my hating of sin and my loving of righteousness. To this I will add the testimony of the Spirit, comforting my conscience as David said: "Why are thou cast down, O my soul? And why art thou disquieted within me? Hope thou in God; for I shall yet praise him, who is the health of my countenance, and my God." . . . From this sanctification and comfort of the Spirit we gather faith. And therefore we rise to Christ, to whom whosoever is given, is necessarily elect from all eternity in Him, and will never be ejected from the doors.[115]

Even with this tri-fold approach to assurance, Beza knew that because of

---

112 Ibid., 53.
113 Ibid.
114 Ibid., 61.
115 Ibid., 96-97.

demonic attacks assurance would not be perfect until heaven; indeed, the testimonies of assurance would often be "faint." "Yet still our minds must not be despondent," Beza counseled, "but must be strengthened by those indefinite promises, and again throw darts at our adversary. For although the struggle of our flesh against our spirit (especially as often as the Spirit seems to fall apart and be quenched) does bring great doubts to our consciences concerning the truth of our faith, still it is certain that this spirit which truly (although faintly) opposes the assaults of the flesh, is the spirit of adoption, whose gift is not to be repented of."[116] Finally, in a rhetorical and pastoral flourish Beza noted that perseverance, although it was certainly made difficult by the devil's schemes, was certain for believers. They could be assured of their final salvation:

> I confess that the Spirit is now and then interrupted in severe temptations, and that the testimonies of Him who dwell in us are so made unconscious, that for a time He seems to be utterly departed from us. Nevertheless, I say that He is never taken away, since the decree of God to save His own must be firm, and therefore, at the right time, finally the clouds of the flesh are chased away, and the happiness of the salvation of the Lord always returns, and shines as the sun into the troubled consciences of the elect. . . . those who have the Spirit of adoption have a sure pledge of eternal life. Therefore, in this most perilous struggle, the very thing by which Satan assaults us, can and must hold forth certain victory for us. For unless the Spirit of adoption (who also is the Spirit of sanctification, justification, life, and faith) is present in us, there would be no struggle, and the reign of sin would be peaceful in us.[117]

This brief exposition demonstrates, I think, that Beza's *Quaestionum et responsionum* is much more than analytic in its teaching about assurance of salvation. Indeed in one of his arguably most "scholastic" treatises, Beza showed himself to be very pastoral while speaking of assurance, sanctification, and perseverance.

This is also the case with Beza's later *Petit Catéchisme*. Again, I think that a close examination of Beza's teaching on assurance in this work contradicts the characterization of him as a promoter of introspection. Beza certainly did emphasize the value of works in assurance here. Answering the question, "But how may a man know whether he has faith or not?," Beza simply said, "By good works."[118] If that were all Beza said, he might justly be accused of emphasizing the *syllogismus practicus*. But that is not all Beza said. In fact, right before this question Beza explained quite a bit about assurance, specifically stating that one gained assurance first of all by looking in faith to Christ, and then also by trusting in God's grace. This section is worth noting in

---

116 Ibid., 97.
117 Ibid., 98.
118 Beza, *Little Catechisme*, section 5, question 1.

full:

Qu. 1. Shall all the world be saved?
A. No, for the greater part of the world refuse their salvation.

Qu. 2. Who then are they which shall be saved?
A. They that have faith and believe.

Qu. 3. And what is faith?
A. A certain persuasion and assurance, which every true Christian man ought to have, that God the Father loves him, for Jesus Christ his Son's sake.

Qu. 4. Why do you say for Jesus Christ's sake?
A. Because we being altogether corrupted and wholly perverse in ourselves, God could not love us, but in respect of him only, who is man altogether just and perfect, that is to say, Jesus Christ his Son.

Qu. 5. Does this faith come from ourselves?
A. No, but only from the grace and goodness of God, who freely gives it to his elect and chosen ones.

Qu. 6. And they which have this faith are they saved?
A. Yes of necessity, for God has given his Son to the end that everyone who believes in him, should have life everlasting. And he is not a liar.[119]

To begin with, Beza here noted that certainty was of the essence of faith. Every Christian "ought" to have this assurance. The assurance was strengthened as persons looked to Christ, the holy and just one, and also as they meditated on God's grace which he freely gave to his children. These, then, according to Beza, were the foundations of Christian assurance. Faith, he said, was grounded in the fact of Christ's perfect nature and in God's grace. These were what made faith possible. And, according to Beza, the Father sent his Son "to the end that everyone who believes in him, should have life everlasting. And he is not a liar."[120] That is to say, faith – since it grasped Christ and since it was supported by the promise of God – saved persons. Nothing else was necessary for salvation. Then, and only then, did Beza introduce works. Works, he argued, were merely secondary in nature, for they were proof that one had salvation. Yet since Beza had previously taught that faith, by definition, included assurance, we need to understand his use of the practical syllogism in context. What Beza did not say here, but did explain in several other treatises, was that although the essence of faith included assurance, sometimes Christians lacked assurance. In this case, he seemed to say, works had importance as

---

119 Ibid., section four.
120 Ibid., section four, question six.

assurance of one's salvation.

Later in the *Petit Catéchisme* Beza explained his view of assurance more clearly. Good works were necessary, he taught, but they did not save; only God's grace could save a person. However, the fruits of a changed life were "marks" by which one might know who the elect were, Beza urged. The order, though, was God's grace followed necessarily by a life change:

> Qu. 6. Good works then make us not God's children?
> A. No, for on the contrary, a man must first be the child of God before he can do good works. But this is a mark or badge whereby a man may know the children of God.
>
> Qu. 7. What then makes us the children and sons of God?
> A. Only the grace and mercy of God, by his Holy Spirit, because he has elected and chosen us from before all everlastingness, according to his good pleasure.[121]

Later, Beza urged that God gave the church sacraments for assurance. This is clear in the first two questions on the sacraments:

> Qu. 1. And what is a sacrament?
> A. It is a thing which God sets before men's eyes in his church, to signify to us for our salvation, another thing which men see not.
>
> Qu. 2. And why has God ordained these signs to his promises?
> A. To make us so much the more assured of the certainty of them.[122]

Thus later he averred that the eucharist was instituted, in part, "To testify to me and to assure me that even as this bread and this wine are ordained for the maintenance and nourishment of this life, so our Lord Jesus Christ has given his body and his blood for me, and gives himself to me, to the end that from him, as from a fountain, there may flow unto me eternal life."[123]

Beza's exposition of assurance in his *Petit Catéchisme* was thus multiform. He presented for his listeners several means whereby Christians might obtain certainty of salvation. They were all grounded in the sovereign work of God for his people. They all centered on the sufficient work of Christ on the cross for his people.[124] They were nourished by the Lord's Supper. And they were known by the "marks" of good works, by which persons might finally discern that they were truly believers

---

121 Ibid., section six, questions 6-7.
122 Ibid., section eight, questions 1-2.
123 Ibid., section nine, question 2.
124 These facts make the contention that Beza's doctrine of assurance was distinctly not focused on Christ untenable. See our discussion above about the *loci* of assurance.

Perseverance and Sanctification in the Battle

Assurance of salvation is not the only aspect of the Christian life which is affected by a strong doctrine of God's sovereignty. Sanctification and perseverance in the faith are also concerns for Christians who teach monergism and rely on God's omnipotence in the Christian life. In conclusion, then, we should briefly note Theodore Beza's exposition of these elements of the Christian faith.

Our exposition will be brief for three reasons. First, we have already touched on these doctrines in our exposition of Beza's doctrine of assurance. Questions about persevering in the faith until heaven, and of being made holy by the Spirit of God are, of course, paramount in discussions of assurance of salvation.[125] Second, others have touched on these issues before. But, third, no one to my knowledge has looked at them specifically to see the way in which Beza's emphasis on the absolute sovereignty of God functioned in the areas of sanctification and perseverance. That is my concern in the following exposition, specifically in light of Beza's eschatological vision of reality.

Sanctification

According to Theodore Beza, sanctification had a Trinitarian structure.[126] It was

---

125 Beza himself noted this, arguing that assurance of salvation should lead to perseverance: "we must observe and note after what maner of fashion these kisses are desired, namely with a most full and lively affection of a most assured faith, and with so ardent a zeal and desire, as none can be greater. And this shows the fruit which the Spirit of God brings forth in us, by this repentance of which I spoke, I mean a true assurance of conscience thoroughly pacified and quieted. Then, when by the grace and favor of God apprehended by a true and lively faith, we are resolved of the love of God, by the testimony and witness of his Spirit of adoption, teaching us what God has determined of us (1 Cor. 2.16) the which gift of God is such, that it is never altered or changed (Rom. 11.22) so that we can never be separated or removed from this love (Rom. 8.35). And thence is framed in us that ardent desire, which making us to forget all other things, without looking back at all behind us, furnishes us with forces to strive and go on with all our power in this race, according to the example of the apostle, without staying anything at all in the way, until we come to the end of the list, where the bridegroom waits for us" (*Canticles*, 23-24).

126 In his late work defending the Reformation understanding of justification, Beza included "Articles drawn up by the common consent of the pastors of the Swiss churches, at the general synod held at Berne" April 23, 1588. These consisted of ten theses on justification and six theses on sanctification, especially its relationship to justification. See Theodore Beza, *Response de Theodore de Beze Pour la Justification par l'imputation gratuite de la Justice de Jesus Christ apprehendé par la suele foi* (Geneva: n.p., 1592), 229-40.

based on the perfect work of Christ for his people; it was applied by the Holy Spirit to the elect; and it was possible only because of God's omnipotence. First, it flowed out of Christ's sacrifice. Thus exhorting his listeners from the text, "Draw me, we will run after you," Pastor Beza exhorted his readers: "we may not forget these words, 'After you.' For it is not enough to run, but we must first run in the right way, and secondly we must run right, without straying either to the right or to the left hand, and thirdly we must tend and go forward to the mark to which we ought to tend, if we will not have our pains to be frustrated and lost. All these things are given us in Jesus Christ solely and alone."[127] Second, the Holy Spirit had to work in God's people or they could not become holy. In his prayer "For obtaining the gift of the Holy Ghost," Beza asked the Spirit to do six things: illumine him, change his affections, give him zeal for God's glory, ease his conscience, refresh his soul, and give him an upright spirit that he might produce good fruits.[128] The Spirit alone could apply Christ to believers and make them holy. Third, sanctification was only possible because of God's sovereignty. Such a monumental task required the hand of the almighty Lord to accomplish it.[129] Thus Beza prayed:

> Promise so to augment in me this faith, that by the degrees of the perfection thereof, it may appear in all her fruits, causing me to worship, invocate, and serve you as you command . . . . so that daily increasing in this all spiritual virtue, I may attain to some portion of your sovereign wisdom, and perfect righteousness, to the end, that when my soul shall forsake this fleshly habitation, the same faith may be as wings to transport into your bosom, to the celestial rest of the angels and saints, there to possess the fullness of her peace, and of all joy.[130]

Indeed, God's sovereignty in sanctification led Beza to ask the Lord to sanctify him. For instance, he begged, "I beseech you . . . to change in me all that I have of myself, even my rocky and stony heart, and to make it pliable, and flexible, unto the voice of my Redeemer . . . to the end, that with a full and lively faith I may cleave to his eternal truth."[131]

---

127 Beza, *Canticles*, 64.
128 Beza asked the Spirit "to scatter the darkness of my understanding, and with the property of his fire, to purify my perverse affections, with his celestial lamp to kindle in my heart the true zeal of his glory, with his holy ointment, to enbalm my conscience with his sacred oil to rejoice and refresh my bowels, and with his virtue to renew in me an upright spirit, to the end that my soul thus cleansed from the dead works of the flesh, may be replenished with faith working all righteousnesse" (*Houshold Prayers*, F1v-F2r).
129 See Beza, *Canticles*, 36-37, 39, 232-34, 301, for example.
130 Beza, *Houshold Prayers*, in the prayer "To obtain the gift of Faith."
131 Ibid., in the prayer "Upon the Symbol or Articles of Belief." See Beza, *Canticles*, 303.

Sanctification was difficult for Christians because their enemy, the devil, assaulted them throughout their pilgrimages. Satan tried to make them abandon Christ and embrace sin. Thus Beza pointed out that

> whoever he is that will have part in this conjunction which is here understood by these kisses, in which our assured and everlasting felicity consists, he must cleave unto the Lord to be one spirit with him (1 Cor. 6.17), renouncing the prince of this world, and himself, and every other thing whatever, which may turn him never so little from this holy affection. . . . For, to attain to this conjunction, we are not to keep ourselves from all such thoughts, words, and deeds, by which the Holy Spirit, who teaches us to sigh after this bridegroom, is manifestly made sad and grieved, and in the end chased and driven out of the midst of us, whereby it comes to pass, that the later estate is made worse than the first (Matt. 12.45), as alas we see too many examples thereof at this day before our eyes. But we must stand also diligently upon our guard, to take heed that these kisses do follow one upon another in continual tenor and train, after God of his grace has begun once to be working in us. For our enemy is crafty and subtle, and can, to surprise and snare us, serve his turn even with those graces and blessings which God bestows on us, to make them so many instruments to our ruin and destruction. For who is he, who having said or done anything but something well, is not incontinently tempted with an opinion of himself? You see then how soon all is marred, if we stand not carefully upon our guard. . . . But behold Satan in his scout watch, who stirs himself so well, that amidst this faith, he sows so great impatience.[132]

The wiles of the devil made sanctification difficult for weary Christians. For this reason, God's total sovereignty was an asset, not a hindrance, to their holiness. Only he could protect them from the devil's traps. Only he could bring them safely to himself in heaven.

Perseverance

Theodore Beza's stress on the necessity of Christians' persevering in the faith is clear in one of the aphorisms from his *Tabula*. There Beza said

> He who has obtained the gift of true faith and has trusted in that same goodness of God must also be concerned about his perseverance. Yet he should not doubt, but should rather call on God in every kind of temptation and affliction, with the sure hope of attaining what he asks, at least as far as it is expedient, since he knows himself a child of God, who cannot fail him. Besides, he never strays from the right way without returning finally to that path, by the aid of that same grace. For though faith in the elect is occasionally buried for a time and may even seem entirely lost, to make them recognize their weakness, it still never recedes so far that the love of God and one's neighbor is entirely ripped from their minds.

---

132 Beza, *Canticles*, 24-26.

> Surely, no one is justified in Christ unless he is also sanctified in him and, in that way, is equipped for good works, which God "prepared beforehand, that we should walk in them."[133]

Beza was at his most pastoral here. Believers, he said, must persevere. They were responsible to remain in the faith. God alone, though, could keep them there, so their ultimate certainty of keeping the faith—even after times of seeming apostasy—rested in God's sovereign goodness.

Beza emphasized God's love and power as the bedrock of Christian perseverance. In his sermons on the Song of Songs, for example, he exhorted his listeners to trust in God's love for them:

> Now says our good God amidst so many tempests, which have overwhelmed and destroyed the world, and which have within these few years borne and beaten down so many good churches – the mother and her children being so cruelly driven forth – has promised us so great and singular a benefit, to preserve unto us this little cabin, assaulted with so many wild and cruel beasts, shall we always condemn so great a grace and blessing and so long a patience of his? God forbid, my brethren. But let us beseech him he would rather heat such as are cold, thrust forward those who recoil, hasten the slow, fortify the weak, and in general give us the grace that his word may dwell plentifully among us, according to the exhortation of the apostle (Col. 3.26), and that we may be fair and fruitful trees in his courts, to depart from this house here below, unto that everlasting palace where we shall reign eternally with him.[134]

Beza's comments on Psalm 86 also demonstrate his reliance on God's sovereignty as the support of Christians' persevering. David prayed in the psalm, declared Beza, because he knew "that God should not suffer him, being broken with the greatness of the dangers, to fall away, as it happens sometimes even to them that are most strong, unless God, by the power of his Spirit, strengthens our wavering faith."[135] Only the sovereign God could preserve his people.[136]

Beza's eschatological vision necessitated his stress upon perseverance. Satan and his schemes were real now. But heaven was also real, and it would be

---

133 Beza, *Tabula*, in *The Potter and the Clay*, 58.
134 Beza, *Canticles*, 344. Note, however, that the Lord's care for his children did not negate their responsibility. It rather should spur them on to ask him to aid them in their pilgrimage to the heavenly city.
135 Beza, *Psalmes*, 197-98.
136 Beza also stressed the priority of God's sovereignty in the spiritual health of his people in his exposition of the Song of Songs. He argued that as God first regenerated the Christian so God must continually keep the believer close to him. Without God's continual drawing of the believer to himself, sure damnation would result. See Beza, *Canticles*, 58-59.

glorious. Beza taught that belief in eternal rest in heaven should encourage a believer to persevere through the present battle. He thus prayed that he and his flock would "learn to desire heaven, and patiently to take all human crosses, and whatever may seem to us most grievous to the flesh, knowing that all things shall turn to our good, always provided that constantly we persevere in your service, for so shall we live and die with Christ, that we may enter into his joys in heaven, there to behold his glory."[137] Again, he exhorted his listeners that only God's sovereignty could protect them from the attacks of the evil one. God's loving power should encourage his people to persevere until they reached their full enjoyment of God in heaven:

> Where then is our stronghold, where we are at all times to flee and retire ourselves? Verily in the strength of the bridegroom . . . . This is he, then, who is the strong and mighty one, on whose side we must keep ourselves. For even those who die in this combat are of all others the most victorious. Now it may please the Lord who has drawn us out of darkness into this light of his truth, and has placed and preserved us most miraculously here in this holy rest and peace of conscience, waiting for the full accomplishment of his promises, to settle and engrave in our minds this holy assurance of his mighty power in good will towards us, that we be never astounded by the assaults of Satan, and of such of his adherents as he employs and uses against us. But that, on the contrary, we persevere and continue in this holy profession of his truth, as well by mouth as also by a holy and Christian life, until we come to the real enjoying of all that which he has made us to believe and hope for, according to his most holy and most assured promises. Conformably unto which doctrine acknowledging our over great negligence hereunto and laziness in our duty, with other infinite faults and offences of ours, we will crave mercy at his hands.[138]

Indeed, Beza urged Christians to trust in God's promises to them and to call out for his aid as they struggled to persevere to heaven. He therefore prayed that "through a steadfast faith in your promises, depending upon an assured hope, and true love, I do more and more draw upon myself the savor of your holy blessings. To the end that . . . I likewise may here below have this felicity, to finish my course in singing your praises, and so leaving this terrestrial life to join myself altogether to the celestial . . . to sing with them without end this song of perfect joy."[139] Similarly he exhorted his listeners that "seeing that God has bestowed this grace upon us, my brethren . . . and to have received us into it as it were out of all the countries of the world, let us be heedful to behave ourselves as it becomes us, that we be never cast out of it, and to pray unto God with David (Ps. 23.6 and 27.4) that we may continue in it all the time of our

---

137 Beza, *Houshold Prayers*, O4r-O4v.
138 Beza, *Canticles*, 358.
139 Beza, *Houshold Prayers*, E2r-E2v.

life, and that he will there entertain us with his favor, until that latter day in which we shall be carried up on high, there to reign with him eternally."[140] To Beza, then, perseverance was essential since life consisted of a pilgrimage to heaven. Believers had to remain in the faith through the entire journey, battling the assaults of Satan. Their only hope—and it was a sure one—was their Sovereign.

Conclusion

This chapter has shown that as a pastor who cared for his parishioners, Theodore Beza was very concerned that they have assurance of their salvation in Christ. The twin themes of our study converged in this pastoral function of counseling believers about assurance. Beza's eschatological vision, on the one hand, informed his view of the tenor of the times. Christians' lives on earth would undoubtedly be plagued by trials and tribulations because of the spiritual battle that was raging around them. God and Satan were fighting a war and the ramifications of that fighting for Christians were serious. The devil, their adversary, attempted to keep believers from having a sense of certainty of their salvation. On the other hand, Beza was convinced of God's sovereignty, his complete control over everything that happened. God's sovereignty extended from eternity past to the eternal future. It included even God's total control over all of Satan's schemes against Christians. Putting these two together, then, Beza argued that because of the spiritual reality of their times believers would often be plagued by doubts about their standing with the holy God. Yet in his love and sovereignty God gave his people many means by which they could be assured of their salvation. The variety of *loci* of assurance was necessary because of the evil times. Assurance for weary pilgrims was ultimately founded upon the character of their heavenly Father who had promised to be their God, now and forever. Although their hearts would often be heavy with the burden of their sinfulness and because of satanic opposition during their trek to heaven, they could find assurance that would encourage them to persevere. Ultimately, their assurance would be realized when they were transported into heaven, there to be with God forever, free from all sin and all worries. They could be assured of their future in heaven because God's promises were true. God's sovereignty, for Beza, was intensely pastoral. Without it, none would be saved. Without it, none could have confidence in his salvation. Rather than raising doubts about God's love and veracity, God's total sovereignty—his loving and truthful sovereignty—was the anchor for weary Christians, now and forever.

---

140 Beza, *Canticles*, 385-86.

Conclusion

My thesis was that Beza's pastoral concern based on his eschatological view of reality explains his activities as a pastor, the content of his writings, and his work as a professor for some fifty years. I maintained that Beza's pastoral vision was fueled by his belief in two eschatological realities: first, that all persons would spend eternity either in heaven or in hell; second, that a Christian's time on earth was a pilgrimage on the way to heaven marked by fierce spiritual conflict between God and Satan. Hence Beza's main concern in life was to make certain that he, his parishioners, and his students stood firm in the midst of the spiritual battle raging around them and arrived safely in their eternal bliss. The fact of this eschatological reality drove Beza to passionate pastoral dealing with his parishioners. I painted a picture of Beza's pastoral, or eschatological, vision as well as the manner in which his tumultuous times led him to conceive of such an otherworldly perspective. I argued that Beza's outlook on life was intensely pastoral.

The second chapter was important in order to locate my research in the history of Bezan interpretation. Much research has been done on Beza, and some of it is very good. I tried to point out in this chapter, however, the manner in which much of the previous Bezan research was faulty. Many scholars limited themselves to a few of Beza's works in their research. Others paid little attention to the context in which Beza wrote his various treatises. I argued that this was faulty historiographical technique. Instead, I maintained that genre and context were two essential factors to consider when studying Beza's thought. He wrote to address particular needs, and he did so in particular kinds of writings. Since scholars for the most part had failed to see these twin themes, for the most part they had not seen the true Beza, Beza the passionate Christian who was concerned with eternal realities.

In the third chapter I argued that for Theodore Beza all of theology was pastoral. I did this, in the first place, by surveying Beza's theological method. I argued that Beza was a humanist, given his emphasis on Scripture and the importance of understanding the Bible aright. He was a biblical humanist because the spiritual realities of his day forced him to look for truth from God. Satan actively promoted falsehood. Persons' sin and dullness hindered them from grasping eternal truths. Only God could convey truth to his people, and

Conclusion

Beza argued that he had done this in the Christian Scriptures. I then showed how all of Beza's systematic theological treatises were pastoral at the core. Even the most scholastic of them was primarily meant to lead persons to salvation in Christ. In both his theological method and his theological productions, therefore, Beza was above all else a pastor.

In the fourth chapter, I argued that Beza's emphasis on God's sovereignty in two of its key aspects, God's providence as well as his sovereignty in salvation, made sense in light of Beza's eschatological vision. Given their precarious situations, Christians were unable to save themselves or to protect themselves. Therefore, predestination and providence were both necessary. I maintained, then, that for Theodore Beza God's complete sovereignty was a comforting doctrine. Beza employed God's sovereignty throughout his corpus to encourage God's children to trust in their Father and, ultimately, to wait on him to bring them to heaven, as he had promised to do.

The fifth chapter continued to argue that, for Beza, God's sovereignty was emphatically pastoral. His stress on God's activity in salvation and the preservation of his children led to other pastoral issues that pastor Beza had to address. Thus questions about the perseverance of Christians, their sanctification, and especially their assurance of salvation during their earthly pilgrimage were in a sense derived from Beza's intense monergism. Only God could save them. But Beza's eschatological vision also led him to assert that assurance was often fleeting given the fact that Christians would suffer from demonic opposition during their earthly pilgrimage. Heaven ultimately would be their source of assurance. And the certainty of eternal rest in heaven, like all the other *loci* of assurance Beza produced, was founded on God's sovereignty. Thus to pastor Beza, God's sovereignty was the answer to the difficulties raised by the eschatological vision.

Throughout this study I intentionally attempted to right a wrong I noticed in the Bezan historiography, namely, the tendency on many scholars' parts to create a "canon within a canon" of Beza's writings. Many looked, sometimes not too carefully, at his polemical treatises dealing with predestination as if these were all that Beza penned during his long career as a Reformer. I took an opposite approach. After looking at the bulk of Beza's writings, I detected an underlying "eschatological vision of reality" that informed all of Beza's outlook concerning God, himself, his parishioners and students, and events in his troubled world. This eschatological, or pastoral, vision looms large in Beza's more personal works, especially his published prayers. But it is present in and informs his thought in his systematic and polemical treatises, as well. I attempted to draw out the implications of this pastoral vision from a variety of genres of Beza's writings. Thus I tried to correct the error I had noticed in much of the historiography.

The conclusions of my research are in general agreement with the growing number of scholars who maintain that there is not a sharp divide between the thought of Calvin and later Protestant Scholasticism. Once again, I think that the twin themes of context and genre are essential in this ongoing discussion. One must seek to understand the context that called forth the works of both Calvin and Beza, for instance. Then one should try to compare similar genres of writings to each other. Although I have not been able to delve into the pastoral theology of John Calvin in this study, I believe that if a rigorous study of Calvin's and Beza's pastoral theologies were undertaken the resulting pictures of their thought would show that they were quite alike. Perhaps my research will encourage other scholars to see if I am correct. Thus, my study is merely an embryonic attempt at understanding the pastoral theology of Theodore Beza. Much more research needs to be done on this significant topic in order to understand Beza's thought in this area. If I spur other researchers on to investigate this most fascinating and edifying of Christians and pastors, I will be satisfied.

Appendix One

Tables of Beza's Works

Table 1. Beza's Works by Year of Publication and Category

Year	Title	Category	Reprinted	Translated
1548	*Poemata*	humanistic	69, 97, 98, 99[1]	
1549	*Zographia*	polemical		
1550	*Tragedie Françoise du Sacrifice d'Abraham*	humanistic	53, 61, 65, 76, 80, 82, 92, 94, 95, 98	97, 99 (LT)[2] 95 (GT) 77 (ET) 72 (IT)
1552	*La Perfection des Chrétiens* [trans.]	doctrinal		
1554	*Réponse a la Confession du Duc de Northumberland*	polemical		
1554	*Alphabetum Graecum*	humanistic		
1554	*De Haereticis*	polemical		59 (FT) 1601 (DT)
1555	*Tabula Pradestinationis*	doctrinal		56, 75, 76, 81 (ET) 60 (FT) 71 (DT)
1556	*Novum D.N. Jesus Christi testamentum [Annotationes]*	biblical	65, 82, 89, 98	
1558	*Ad Sebastiani*	polemical	59	78 (ET)

---

1 To conserve space, unless otherwise noted, all dates given are from the sixteenth century. Thus I have written "65" not "1565." If the date is in the seventeenth century, I have written the complete date.

2 The abbreviations used are as follows: DT is Dutch; ET is English; FT is French; GT is German; HT is Hungarian; IT is Italian; LT is Latin.

Year	Title	Category	Reprinted	Translated
	Castellionis calumnies			
1559	*De Coena Domini*	polemical		
1559	*Confession de la foi chrétienne*	doctrinal	61, 62, 63, 64	60, 63, 70, 73, 75, 77, 81, 87, 95 (LT) 63, 65, 72, 85, 89 (ET) 61 (DT) 60 (IT)
1560	*[Deux sonnets en Latin]* [untitled]	humanistic		
1561	*Kreophagia, sive Cyclops*	polemical	72	64, 65 (FT)
1561	*Harangues prononcées a Poissy*	polemical		61, 62 (ET) 62 (GT)
1563	*Ad Francisci Balduini*	polemical	65	
1563	*Responsio ad defensiones et reprehensiones Sebastiani Castellionis*	polemical		
1564	*Vie de Calvin*	historical	1st ed.: 65 2nd ed.: 65, 96, 97, 98 3rd ed.: 75, 76	1st ed.: 64 (LT) 65 (GT) 78 (ET) 3rd ed.: 74 (HT) 1601 (DT)
1565	*Ad Brentii Argumenta*	polemical		
1565	*Tractatus tres*	polemical	67	
1566	*La Confession Helvétique Postérieure* [trans.]	doctrinal		
1566	*De pace christianarum*	doctrinal		
1566	*Psalmorum Davidis et aliorum prophetarum*	biblical	80, 81, 90, 93, 94	
1567	*Apologia ad libellum sorbonici theologastri F. Claudii de Xaintes*	polemical		
1568	*Graecae grammatices*	humanistic		
1568	*De polygamia*	polemical	71, 73, 87,	

Tables of Beza's Works 237

Year	Title	Category	Reprinted	Translated
			91	
1569	*De divortiis*	polemical	73, 87, 91	95 (DT)
1570	*Athanasii Dialogi V, de sancta Trinitate*	polemical		
1570 - 1582	*Tractationes theologicae*, 3 vols.	doctrinal polemical		
1570	*Quaestionum et responsionum christianarum libellus, pt. 1*	doctrinal	71, 73, 77, 80, 83, 84, 87, 1601	72, 84 (FT) 74, 78, 81, 86 (ET) 87 (GT)
1571	*Ad D. Nicolai Selnecceri*	polemical	72, 73, 78	
1572	*Épitaphe de Coligny*	humanistic		
1573	*Epistolarum theologicarum*	doctrinal polemical	75, 97	
1574	*Du Droit des magistrates*	polemical	75, 78, 81	80, 89, 95, 99, 1600, 1604 (LT)
1574	*Adversus Sacramentariorum Errorem*	polemical		88 (ET)
1575	*Petit Catéchisme*	pastoral	82	78 (ET)
1575	*Apologia...ad Acta Conventus...Torgae*	polemical		
1576	*Quaestionum et responsionum christianarum libellus, pt. 2*	polemical	77, 81, 87, 1600	80 (ET) 84 (FT)
1576	[trans. of Théodore de Raithou]	polemical		
1577	*Ad repetitionem primam F. Claudii de Sainctes*	polemical		
1577	*Lex Dei*	doctrinal	1603	
1579	*De hypostatica duarum in Christo naturarum unione*	polemical		
1579	*De veris et visibilibus ecclesiae Catholicae notis*	polemical		82 (ET) 92 (FT)
1579	*De peste*	pastoral	80	80 (ET)

Year	Title	Category	Reprinted	Translated
1580	*De Coena Domini, adversus Iodoci Harchii*	polemical		
1580	*Icones*	historical		81 (FT)
1580	*Histoire ecclésiastique* [ed.]	historical		
1581	*Harmonia confessionum fidei* [ed.]	doctrinal		
1581	*Pro Corporis Christi veritate*	polemical		
1582	*Chrestiennes meditations*	pastoral	83	82 (ET)
1582	*De praedestinationis doctrina et vero usu tractatio absolutissima*	doctrinal	83	
1583	*Épitaphe de Zacharias Ursinus*	humanistic		
1584	*De Francicae linguae recta pronutiatione*	humanistic		
1584	*Responsio ad quaestionum et responsionum Danielis Hofmanni, pt. 1*	polemical		
1584	*Canticum Canticorum Solomonis, latinis versibus expressum*	biblical		
1585	*Responsio ad quaestionum et responsionum Danielis Hofmanni, pt. 2*	polemical		
1586	*Ad Danielis Hofmanni demonstrationes ad oculum*	polemical		
1586	*Ad Gilberti Genebrardi accusationem*	polemical		
1586	*Response aux cinq premieres et principales demandes de F. Jean Hay*	polemical		
1586	*Sermons sur les trois premiers chapitres du cantique des Cantiques*	pastoral		87 (LT) 87 (ET) 1600 (DT)

Tables of Beza's Works 239

Year	Title	Category	Reprinted	Translated
1586	Theses theologicae in Schola Genevensi [ed.]	doctrinal	91	91, 94 (ET)
1587	Ad acta colloquii Montisbelgardensis, pt. 1	polemical	88, 89	87 (FT)
1588	Ad acta colloquii Montisbelgardensis, pt. 2	polemical		88 (GT)
1588	Ecclesiastes	pastoral	98	1600? (ET)
1588	Ad serenissimam Elizabetham Angliae Reginam	humanistic		
1589	Iobus	biblical		89 (ET)
1589	Expositio verissima juxta et succincta	historical		
1590	Tractatus pius et moderatus de vera Excommunicatione	doctrinal		
1592	Apologia pro justificatione	polemical		92 (FT)
1592	Sermons sur l'histoire de la passion	pastoral	98	92, 98 (LT)
1593	Sermons sur l'histoire de la resurrection	pastoral		93, 1601 (LT)
1593	De controversies in Coena Domini	polemical	94	
1597	Theodori Bezae ad Ioan. Guil. Stuckium	polemical		97 (GT) 98 (DT)
1598	Response à la letter d'un gentilhomme savoisien	polemical		
1603	Maister Beza's Houshold Prayers	pastoral		

Table 2. Types of Beza's Works Classified by Original Date of Publication

Year	Humanistic	Polemical	Doctrinal	Biblical	Historical	Pastoral
1548	I					
1549		I				
1550	I					
1551						

Year	Humanistic	Polemical	Doctrinal	Biblical	Historical	Pastoral
1552			I			
1553						
1554	I		II			
1555			I			
1556				I		
1557						
1558		I				
1559		I	I			
1560	I					
1561		II				
1562				I		
1563		II				
1564					I	
1565		II				
1566			II	I		
1567		I				
1568	I	I				
1569		I				
1570		I	I			
1571		I				
1572	I					
1573		I	I			
1574		II				
1575		I				I
1576		II				
1577		I	I			
1578						
1579		II				I
1580		I			II	
1581		I	I			
1582		I	II			I
1583	I					
1584	I	I		I		
1585		I				
1586		III	I			I
1587		I				
1588	I	I				I
1589				I	I	
1590			I			
1591						

Tables of Beza's Works 241

Year	Humanistic	Polemical	Doctrinal	Biblical	Historical	Pastoral
1592		I				I
1593		I				I
1594						
1595						
1596						
1597		I				
1598		I				
1599						
1600						
1601						
1602						
1603						I

Table 3. Types of Beza's Works Classified by Original Date of Publication, Date of Republication and Date of Translation into Other Languages

Year	Humanistic	Polemical	Doctrinal	Biblical	Historical	Pastoral
1548	I					
1549		I				
1550	I					
1551						
1552			I			
1553	I					
1554	I		II			
1555			I			
1556			I	I		
1557						
1558		I				
1559		III	I			
1560	I		III			
1561	I	III	II			
1562		II	I	I		
1563		II	III			
1564		I	I		II	
1565	I	IIII	I	I	III	
1566			II	I		
1567		II				
1568	I	I				
1569	I	I				
1570		I	II			

Year	Humanistic	Polemical	Doctrinal	Biblical	Historical	Pastoral
1571		II	II			
1572	II	II	II			
1573		IIII	III			
1574		II	I		I	
1575		III	III		I	I
1576	I	II	I		I	
1577	I	II	III			
1578		III	I		I	I
1579		II				I
1580	I	III	I	I	II	II
1581		III	IIII	I	I	
1582	I	II	II	I		III
1583	I		II			I
1584	I	II	II	I		
1585		I	I			
1586		III	II			I
1587		IIIII	III			II
1588	I	IIII				I
1589		II	I	III	I	
1590			I	I		
1591		II	II			
1592	I	III				II
1593		I		I		II
1594	I	I	I	I		
1595	II	II	I			
1596					I	
1597	II	III	I		I	
1598	II	II		I	I	III
1599	II	I				
1600		II				II
1601		I	I		I	I
1602						
1603			I			I
1604		I				

Appendix Two

Sermons sur l'Histoire de la Resurrection: Sermon 9[1]

(22) Yea, and certaine women among us made us astonished, which came early unto the sepulcher. (23) And when they found not his bodie, they came, saying, that they had also seene a vision of Angels, which said, that he was alive. (24) Therefore certaine of them which were with us, went to the sepulchre, and found it even so as the women had said, but him they saw not. (25) Then hee sayde unto them, O fooles, and slowe of heart to beleeve all that the Prophets have spoken! (26) Ought not Christ to have suffered these things, and to enter into his glory? (27) And he began at Moses, and at all the Prophets, and interpreted unto them in all the Scriptures the things which were written of him. (28) And they drewe neere unto the towne, which they went to, but he made as though hee would have gone farther.[2]

Luke 24:22-28

CONTINUATION OF THE ACCOUNT[3]

[240][4] We have understood up to here by the response of Cleopas—his and his companions—what was their double perplexity founded on two false presuppositions which today still deceive many. But what he now adds shows that they would have been from that time nonetheless on the point of being convinced if they had had more certain and more evident testimony of the resurrection of the Lord. Because what he says shows that they left the city before either Mary Magdalene, who was the first to see the Lord in person (Mark 16.9), or the women to whom the Lord showed himself on their return (Matt. 28.9), had made their report to the disciples. They therefore had gone out

---

1   Theodore Beza, *Sermons sur l'Histoire de la Resurrection de nostre Seigneur Jesus Christ* (Geneva: Jean le Preux, 1593), 240-72.
2   Theodore Beza, *The Newe Testament of Our Lord Iesus Christ*, translated out of Greeke by Theod. Beza. Whereunto are Adioned Briefe Summaries of Doctrine upon the Evangelists and Actes of the Apostles, together with the methode of the Epistles of the Apostles, by the said Theod. Beza. And also Short Expositions on the Phrases and Hard Places, taken out of the large Annotations of the foresaid Author and Ioach. Camerarius, by P. Loseler, Villerius, trans. L. Tomson (London: Robert Barker, 1601), on Luke 24:22-28.
3   I am including the original marginal section summaries as bold headings.
4   I am including the original page numbers in bold brackets.

at once after **[241]** some of the women, who had been more hurried than those to whom the Lord appeared on the road, returned and after them Peter and John: which is important to note to understand well the rest of the narrative.

HUMAN REASON—THAT OF COMMON MEN AND WISE MEN—LEADS US TO DISBELIEVE THE DOCTRINE OF OUR SALVATION

It is very true, however, that that does not excuse the unbelief of these two disciples, whatever reasons they may have had to believe or not believe that which was reported to them. Because the sensible and palpable vision and the testimony of angels, should rightly have enough authority to believe in this report. But on account of the fact that it was women who had reported this, and that they spoke of visions and that they spoke of angels, that is why these disciples, beside which this resurrection was of itself unbelievable to them, presumed that if Jesus Christ had come to life again, he would not have failed to show himself rather in some magnificence in order to triumph over all his confused enemies, and by this means to set up on the earth this glorious and great kingdom promised for his people by the Messiah. And thus too often, instead of simply trusting what has been well attested to us by Scripture, the simplicity of which the Holy Spirit uses, and which simplicity instead of edifying us—considering who is speaking—becomes a problem and even an irremediable drawing back. **[242]** It is also why the preaching of the gospel, which is the very powerful instrument of God in the salvation of all who believe (Rom. 1.16) has seemed a folly to the wise men of this age, who hold as false and ridiculous everything which does not accord with their folly, which they call wisdom (I Cor. 1.23). This happened to the Apostle in Athens (Acts 17.32) so much so that the profane authors called the true religion dictated by God to his people a superstition and mad folly. And still that is what the world calls "reason" and "wisdom." But let us hold to what the Son of God declared, who here calls Cleopas and his companion and all who resemble them "foolish," or at least destitute of sense. Because the same folly still endures, and indeed has not ceased to increase since, even though the Apostle had from so long a time so expressly—and indeed so harshly—reproached those "glorious" Corinthians. Since they were disgusted with the very holy simplicity of the language of the Apostle, they delighted so much in a gospel made up with profane rhetoric flourishing in Greece. And moreover, with regard to principle, he had warned the Colossians so clearly of not allowing themselves to be entrapped by the philosophy—falsely called "science"—of the Colossians (Col. 2.8).

And it would have pleased God for this plague to be **[243]** banished from the church. But instead this great evil is nevertheless continuing by getting worse. Because here and elsewhere in these stories, we have some examples of these who were mistaken solely in their naturally-depraved reasoning. But this reason already of itself so deceivable presents itself now made up with all sorts of artifices and prostitution. Because ever since it pleased God in this age we are in to restore the knowledge of languages and of the humane sciences [*bonnes sciences*], we have so much abused this gift of God, that today if it concerns religion, there are only too many who pollute this divine purity by a thousand human speculations fetched up from the mire of the Philosophers. They read the writings of the Philosophers, not to aid themselves in several things which are of usefulness for the present life, nor to persuade rebels because of common sense itself—and that which was the natural light in these great human sages could teach the truth in several points from the example of the apostle, and from the prophets themselves in several places. But on the contrary they mix together among the wine so pure, drawn from the spouse (Cant. 2.5), water fetched up from cisterns not refilled with rain from heaven, but with speculations and discourses. Speaking of these, the apostle rightly said that these great **[244]** sages demonstrated by this that they had become fools (Rom. 1.21-22) for not having taken measure, or for having wanted to understand, and even to determine, what neither flesh nor blood could teach, so much that a very learned ancient rightly said that philosophers were the patriarchs of heretics.

THE GREAT PROFANING OF THE HOLY DOCTRINE WHICH IS COMMITTED TODAY BY SEVERAL IN THE WAY THEY USE LANGUAGE AND TREAT HOLY THINGS

And with regard to the very simple and common language which Jesus Christ himself used, are we not in a time in which one sometimes does not set more of a difference between a babble affected by lawyers, or of some orator of this age? Or of some pleasing chatterer, and the manner of preaching the word of God in the way of the prophets, and indeed of Jesus Christ himself and of the apostles, according to the express rule that he gives (II Tim. 1.13) and the protest that he makes to these glorious Corinthians (I Cor. 2.1)? Because when all that such men babble is gathered, it is only words there, which the hearers delight in, being as wise as their preachers. And what I say is not to criticize the elegance (or grace) of arranging one's words in an orderly manner, and of using proper and significant words and terms—whether it is in teaching, in exhorting, or in reproving or speaking. But whatever the case, one must learn this holy rhetoric not from the precepts of orators, **[245]** to whom one must leave the affairs of this world, but from the examples of the writings of the prophets and apostles, where will not be found either pretense in sentences nor flowering in the arrangements of words, but a heaviness, a gravity, a vehemence which demonstrates to the eyes of those who have sound judgment, that it does not proceed from any human observation. But rather it is from an inspiration truly divine, which neither the wisdom nor the eloquence of the world could withstand. Yet they were constrained to yield to it (John 7.46; Acts 26.24).

IT IS NOT ENOUGH TO TEACH THE DOCTRINE, BUT IT MUST BE APPLIED AND CONFIDENTLY USED TO REPROVE HOWEVER THE NECESSITY REQUIRES IT

To return to my point, it is necessary that we consider the reason which moved the Lord to use a reproof, which could otherwise seem much too rough. Because like I said, these two were not of the number of those who are rightly called "infidels" and "unbelievers," but were only still in doubt, joined to the fact that he still had not declared to them who he was. Therefore the reason that he advances is twofold. The first, because they were so tardy to believe that which they ought to believe without making difficulty. In this we see that the Lord, although he employed a very harsh word, nevertheless was not excessive, as if he had consigned them among the totally unbelieving. The second reason is the structure of the first. It is as if Jesus Christ had employed **[246]** these words, "I reprove you of this lateness," not that I want to say that one must believe lightly everything which is said. But having regard of the matter of which we speak, which was so clearly and from so long a time predicted by the prophets, that you have not had any occasion to cancel them in doubt. For you see yourselves that if this were false, he of whom you are speaking would not be the Christ promised by the mouth of the prophets.

Therefore this is the summary of this reprehension that is full of a very great and very precious doctrine, a doctrine the Holy Spirit wants to engrave well on the heart of each one. Firstly, therefore, let us learn here that to preach the gospel is not simply to explain his text and settle some questions of doctrine, as several would like to shut the mouth of their pastors, when they pass these limits. Rather, pastors must apply medicine to their patients, which otherwise would be without fruit. And it is here anew that these same persons stumble, who will tolerate well that with the exposition of the text are joined sweet consolations, that the great goodness and mercy of God are commended, even that one uses exhortations to do well. (Indeed the pastor also must not at all omit these in their time and place, the same Holy Spirit having taken this so sweet surname of Comforter). **[247]** But if we come to reproofs, these ones and certainly those who are the most culpable, will take these as insults, and if need be they will endure rather to deprive themselves of good and faithful pastors than to endure their reproofs. Others not being able to do what they want, will gnash their teeth, and as a result will do so much the worse. Others will weigh these reproofs in the balance, and they will always find the reproofs to be excessive. Briefly, they have become so touchy, that they would not dare to touch the sick without drawing back, rather than enduring the test.

And what will a faithful pastor do about that? If he wants to please men, he is no longer a servant of God (Gal. 1.10). Therefore after knowledge he will ask God first for a spirit of discretion not to reprove anything lightly without knowing and understanding the fact that he is reproving. Next he will ask for the true use of the language of God, not just to speak, but to speak frankly as one must speak (Eph. 6.20). And closing his ear to threats and all respect for persons, he should listen to the Lord who is admonishing him in the manner of Isaiah, "Proclaim it with a full voice, do not spare yourself, raise up your voice like a horn and declare their trespasses to my people, and declare their sins to the house of Jacob." He will hear, I say, the trumpet of the apostle summoning him **[248]** by these words, "Preach the word, insist in time and outside of time, argue and scold" (II Tim. 4.2).

THE FAITHFUL PREACHER DOES NOT WASTE HIS PAIN, EVEN THOUGH ONE DOES NOT RECEIVE HIS WORD

And you must not at this time fail to do well, alleging that you are wasting your effort. Because Isaiah did not fail to preach (indeed for about sixty years or more) to rebellious and contradicting people; neither did Jesus Christ fail to preach to the priests and Pharisees who finally crucified him. Added to that, experience shows us very often that the seed sprouts in those that we have under our care, and who were for a time as unyielding as rocks. And on the contrary it is lost in those whom we had occasion to estimate to be a good and fertile land. It is therefore our responsibility to sow, to plant and to water, to obey him who sends us, and to leave the growth to his holy providence and power.

DOCTRINE MUST BE NECESSARILY DRAWN FROM HOLY SCRIPTURE. WHY AND HOW JESUS CHRIST USED THE TESTIMONY OF THE PROPHETS: WHAT ONE MUST DO STILL TODAY

Secondly, let us learn here to keep ourselves from being found rash under the pretext that he enjoined us to speak boldly and frankly. And let us consider, to keep from doing that, how our Lord Jesus Christ who well ought to have this credence of being heard without any replies, nevertheless founded his reproofs on the sayings of the prophets, as much in this passage as much as in everything he taught during his life. It is not that the prophets were above him, **[249]** since it is he himself who inspired and made the prophets speak and write (I Pet. 1.11), but in order that this confirmation of divine predictions with the understanding of it should shut of the mouth of the most unbelieving. What should they therefore do today who by the mouth of the Lord are ordained to teach, to console, to reprove, to reproach in his church? Will it be licit for them to fetch up from elsewhere that which they have to say than from this same source? The apostle is not of this opinion, even pronouncing a curse against the angels of heaven if there should be found among them any who announce anything contrary to that which he himself had preached (Gal. 1.8). And one should not now preclude from this testimony of the truth the writings of the prophets under the pretext that their predictions have been accomplished. Because besides the fact that there are some of which we are still waiting for the fulfillment—not with regard to this that the Lord must bear and do for us (because in this regard he has accomplished everything [John 19.30]) but with regard to the government of his church, and with regard to the full power of what we believe and hoped—besides the fact that, I say, the verification of the evangelical doctrine confirmed by the confirmation of accomplished prophecies, ought still today to produce confusion among the Epicureans and mockers **[250]** of God, with whom the whole world is filled, and on the contrary confirm the belief in this truth which God made known to them.

IT IS NECESSARY TO HOLD FAST TO THE CANONICAL BOOKS, IN ORDER TO BE ASSURED OF THE FAITH

Thirdly, the Lord is not speaking here of all the prophets. Because there have always been some false prophets in the church of God, as still today the whole world is full of them. But he speaks of the sacred canonical books and of the authority of which the synagogue itself does not doubt, even though those in the synagogue had a veil on their eyes which blinded them so that they could not see even a little there (II Cor. 3.14). It is therefore these books which we must ponder, there adjoining the apostolical writings in the fashion of those of whom it is spoken in Acts 17.11. And because Satan again recently thrust a large body of false writings in the middle of the apostolic preaching and writings—which testifies of the complaint which the apostle made in II Thess. 2.2—it is necessary to hold again to the canon of the Christian church, verified by the confirmation of the Jewish canon. Both are irrefragable, so it has not ever been allowable—not to any angel itself from heaven—to add to it or to subtract from it.

IT IS ALSO NECESSARY TO GUARD ONESELF FROM FALSE INTERPRETATIONS AS FROM FALSE TEXTS

And one must note that this addition or diminution not only regards the books, which by the grace of God were expressly disavowed in **[251]** the ancient church, and which, this notwithstanding, some ones today do not have any shame to take up again to the point of having (i.e., false writings) printed. But also this same falsity is committed in all interpretations of true texts, fetched up from elsewhere than from the Scriptures themselves.

A VERY EASY AND VERY CERTAIN MANNER OF DISCERNING ALL FALSE EXPOSITIONS

And if one wants very easily to understand these false expositions, one need do no other thing than compare them with the articles of our faith contained in our apostolic symbol,[5] divinely drawn up from the time of the primitive church for this reason. So if the objection of the adversaries of this truth came about—that is, that the obscurity of the Scripture requires some interpretation from elsewhere (which then they later attribute under the name and title of Catholic Church)—what would be the foundation of the conclusion stated here by the Lord? Because should they dare to say that the preaching of the apostles was more obscure than that of the prophets? and the shadows of the law more clear than the light of the gospel? and that their gospel—that is to say, that which they have added, to gnaw away at or change the Scripture—is more certain than

---

5   That is, the Apostles' Creed.

the writings of the prophets and apostles? Maybe they will indeed dare to say it, and if they do not say it overtly, the fact remains that they presuppose it. But who will believe them, except those who want to be deceived?

THE SCRIPTURES MUST BE KNOWN BY ALL CHRISTIANS

[252] Beyond all that, if it is not permitted for all Christians to read the writings of the prophets and apostles to discern the false from the true, why are these here sent back to the prophets? And why do all Christians today return to the word of the Lord, as the incorruptible seed of the church in general and of each member of the church in particular (I Pet. 1.23)?

IF THE SLOWNESS TO BELIEVE IS WORTHY OF HARSH REPREHENSION, HOW MUCH MORE SO THE ENTIRE DESPISING OF THE DOCTRINE? AND FROM WHERE THESE ERRORS PROCEEDED

Fourthly, if those there are really lacking sense, as the Lord speaks here, who are slow to believe in the Scriptures, what will be of those who never inquire of it? who forbid those whom they call the simple people from inquiring of it? of those who come to this school not in order to learn, but bringing their conclusion all made and their minds, filled with human discourse, that is to say bringing a poor flaming candle, with regard to that which is good, in order to lighten the Sun? Therefore this is what our natural sense, which is flesh and blood and which only serves to render us inexcusable, can introduce to us in this truth. So on the contrary there are not any more foolish than these "sages" there. Because what greater craziness can there be than to make the darkness judge the light? Therefore let us note diligently this description of Christians which consists in renouncing to oneself that which is not only nor principally meant of our lusts and **[253]** brutal affections. But note especially this "beautiful" reason and blind intelligence where rests the main evil which, if you let it govern, will certainly undo the gospel which is the unique doctrine of salvation, turning it to a scandal, instead of lifting us up, or scorning the true wisdom of God as folly, instead of accepting it to eternal life.

REMEDY AGAINST THESE EVILS

And when will it be recognized by the world? When it knows it is blind, that is to say, "never," as evidenced by those to whom the Lord spoke (John 9.41). But we, my brothers, who are of the number of those to whom God gave the grace of calling them from darkness into so admirable a light (I Pet. 2.9), and whom he placed as a show of his goodness and of his special providence, both near and far, let us learn to ask our God for an increase of this true sense of his light. And for this result, let us recognize more and more that we do not have in ourselves, neither the eyes to see, nor ears to hear, nor feet to walk. And let us recognize that what we have will soon vanish, if in place of walking from faith to faith, and from light to light, we collect and prepare the house for seven despicable spirits, worse than the one came from it. As I see some to my very deepest regret. I see great beginnings of this evil in a part of ourselves, without looking any further.

[254] STRANGE MEANS THAT MEN FORGE TO REMAIN IN THEIR UNBELIEF SHOWING MORE AND MORE THEIR INGRATITUDE AND THEIR STUPIDITY

In the fifth place, let us consider the conclusion of these two men who however were not at all off the path, and, may it please God, to whom many would be similar in their simplicity and docility. In sum, trustworthy women had told them that they had had visions, and two from among the apostles had given an account to them of that which they had seen in the grave, conforming in that to the account of the women. Therefore why is it that they do not believe in the resurrection of the Lord? Because no one would have told them that they had seen him. And how? Therefore this will not be enough that the Lord humbles himself as far as to teach us spiritual things by some of our senses (which is already like resigning his grandeur). But it will also be necessary that he is seen, that he is touched, that he is touched, that he is smelled, that he is heard with one's own ears. And when all this is done, still in order to know him it will be necessary that the mind absorb it and come to a conclusion, even against all that our senses tell us. Because to see with his eyes Jesus Christ risen, was still not to know him, nor the fruit of his resurrection. But beyond that here is still an evil worse than that what precedes it; it is that the natural mind when it is convinced by the senses, of something which [255] surpasses its capacity, instead of making it its profit, it mocks everything which it apprehends by its senses, or remains without understanding and lost without making up its mind.

And it is not necessary to search outside of this narrative for a more certain testimony of this than that which will be recited to us here after concerning the apostles themselves, when the Lord made them see and feel himself. Alas! and therefore how miserable is man since the best instrument which the Lord gave him to know Him—and knowing him to be very happy—is so far reversed, that this is what is contrary the most to this truth. And who can submit the least (Rom. 8.7) so that instead of the sophists who are persuaded that our reason, which we are using, needs only to be warned and helped? We must ask the Lord that he change and correct it, even as dead as it is with regard to that truth (Eph. 2.1), he gives us life, by giving us movement and affection from the beginning until the end. And this is what we ought to ask the Lord today as much as ever, in this completely inexcusable rebellion of the world, since we have the Lord, in addition to this narrative filled with so many testimonies of his resurrection and of his reign in heaven, and indeed palpable and sensible for the duration of forty [256] days, and recorded in order to be read and heard until the end of the world, sent in our time maybe more witnesses than ever since the time of the apostles, of what we must believe and hope from Him. But who has eyes to see and ears to hear these things? Alas there are very few. And among those even who see them, the ones seeing the most clearly are bleary-eyed or completely one-eyed. So we must see him here in order to see him on

Sermons sur l'Histoire de la Resurrection

high—and this with eyes of faith, which God wants very much to give to those who do not have them, and very much to sharpen those who received, like it was represented to us in the healing of the blind man, of which it is spoken in Mark 8.4.

IN THE TRUE FAITH, THE INNER AND OUTER MAN COME TOGETHER AND ALWAYS AGREE

In the sixth place, we should remember that the Lord does not want only that we believe, but he wants us to believe from the heart. This is directed not only against those for whom there is nothing but hypocrisy in order to deceive others. It is also directed against those who by falling asleep in their conscience are deceiving themselves, making themselves believe that, under the guise that God requires most of all the inside, they can clearly do what they want with the outside, doing that which pleases them among indifferent things. Let such hypocrites know that God who made the whole, outside and in, wants to have all or nothing, and that never was **[257]** nor will a man be recognized as a Christian before God, unless he believes inwardly and shows it clearly on the outside. And if those do no want to believe the one who will even be their judge, and who gave the judgment (Matt. 10.32 & Luke 12.8), they will feel to their own cost, when instead of going to school they will have to appear before the tribunal from which there is no appeal.

BELIEF IN THE PROPHETS AND EVEN SO MORE STILL IN THE PROPHECIES PRESUPPOSES THE KNOWLEDGE OF THE THINGS GOD DECLARES BY THEM

In the seventh place, let us notice that the Lord does not only want one indefinitely to believe the prophets, but he wants one to believe all the things that the prophets pronounced, and accordingly that God has still more clearly manifested by the apostles. Therefore where is this faith disguised, or rather of all things void, with which the great Catholics of today put to sleep the poor world? And how will this be the true church in which one only speaks in an unknown language, in which one poisons souls with a word not written, and in which all the worship of God is changed into songs and twisted things?

TRUE FAITH NEITHER ADDS NOR SUBTRACTS NOR CHANGES ANYTHING IN SCRIPTURE

Finally, for what reason will they be reckoned among believers who subtract from this knowledge as long as it displeases their natural sense, and who rely on this false philosophy, that is to say "artificial folly," of which the apostle speaks in Colossians 2.8? Or why are they counted believers who reject what displeases their minds as completely **[258]** fantastic, who are reappearing today in great troops so much more than ever? Let us oppose to all that, my brothers, true humility of spirit, and let us be aware of pulling out just a little of the Scriptures. Instead, let us search there for our principles and our conclusions far away from all profane curiosity, and especially this counterfeit humility which is the most superb arrogance, by the ruse of which Satan has slipped into the church so far that one is not able still to expel him from there today, notwithstanding the so-express warning of the apostle in Colossians 2.23.

THE VERITY OF THE SCRIPTURES IS PROPERLY FOUNDED ON THE AUTHORITY OF GOD. BUT THIS DOES NOT PREVENT ONE FROM BEING ABLE TO CONVINCE REBELS AND AFFIRM BELIEVERS BY TRUE REASONS JOINED TO THE SCRIPTURES

Finally the Lord goes on more. Because speaking of what he had suffered, and as much of his resurrection as of his ascension, and of the perpetual glory which would follow, "Should it not be," he said, "that the Christ must suffer these things, and that he should enter in this way into his glory?" First, what is the point of this question if it is not enough to cite the Scriptures without adding another reason except the holy will of God declared through his word, instead of it seeming that Jesus Christ wanted to show here some reason on which the contents of the Scriptures were founded? And we see that from the time of the ancient Fathers, and several learned men still today, in order to confound mockers, confirm themselves in our religion by many good and very visible reasons. **[259]** To which I respond firstly that really the only will of God being testified to us by his holy word, is the only true and immutable support of the true faith, seeing that it is the only rule of all true reason. And in fact this word, "must," takes us there, because the Lord was not missing other means that would have been satisfactory to him in order to save his people. But since he had so ordained, what he had already declared by his prophets, this could not nor should be done otherwise, and he even added there all the second causes and circumstances of times and persons, through which it was necessary that all of it happen in that manner. And if we do not lay down this foundation of the providence of God down to very small things, we take away as much from what belongs to him as is proper to him, that is, his infinite power and wisdom in this very just government of all which he created. And it would be necessary instead of calling on God to turn either to natural causes without any sovereign or governor, or to that abominable idol of Fortune without, because of this infallible providence in this event. It is necessary to envelop the Lord in any thing badly spoken, or badly done, since the Lord is always the enemy and avenger of all iniquity. But that does not prevent us, as much as **[260]** can and should be done – and certainly without wanting to subjugate the wisdom of God to our reason, and provided that one reverences the wisdom of God – from putting forward this little which remains of the light of reason in men, to shut the mouth, as much as possible, of the more impudent and shameless adversaries of the truth of God. Thus St. Paul, writing to the Romans, although they had already received the gospel with great testimony of faith, fights and contradicts every idolatry and superstition and the foolish musing of the Jews in the prerogative over other nations only by natural reason, which cannot be blotted out of the mind of men. He did likewise when he disputed in Athens against the philosophers (Acts 17). And from there originate so many very beautiful and truthful sayings, as much about divine things as human, sown among several other foolish and ridiculous opinions of profane writers of all sorts.

THE WEAKNESS OF HUMAN DISCOURSE IS NOT THE PLACE OF OUR PRINCIPAL POINT OF SALVATION

But what? That can only serve to render such men more inexcusable because such knowledge did not make them better nor more just. But when it is a question of the knowledge of the true God, who is an essence in three persons, and of the means of being reconciled to him, and saved, it is there which our mind not only does not see anything. **[261]** But what is more, it is so doggedly resistant, that it is necessary that God gives a person the grace of knowing his folly, and of illuminating another wisdom that flesh and blood do not teach, but God himself in his Son by the Holy Spirit, to those whom he is pleased to illuminate and draw to himself.

HOW THE ARTICLES OF OUR FAITH ARE NOT FOUNDED ON NATURAL HUMAN DISCOURSE (YET THERE ARE NONE OF THEM WHICH AFTERWARDS DO NOT PROVE THEMSELVES TO BE REASONABLE) BY NATURAL PRINCIPLES

But I rightly said again that while this knowledge of God is learned by faith, and not by human discourse, there is no article of faith, which cannot be proved by good and certain principles. To comprise a reasonably-founded doctrine there are certain principles that to speak against would be great impudence. Witness what the ancient very learned Christian philosophers taught against idolaters and pagans, which would deserve a very long and ample discourse.

PROOF OF THIS ABOVE IN THE ARTICLE TOUCHING OUR REDEMPTOR AND WHAT HE DID AND SUFFERED FOR US

But leaving the other articles, I will pause at that of which it is spoken here, that is, that men could be saved only by a Savior such as is taught us by the Scriptures—that is, the true God, and yet man, and indeed man passible, as the apostle disputed before King Agrippa in Acts 26.22, full of suffering, despised and rejected like it says in Isaiah 53.3. And then by the resurrection from the dead **[262]** he was raised to the sovereign degree of glory in order to conduct others there. All that, I say, can be proven and showed to have had to be true, or otherwise all men must perish, or God should not be God (which are tremendous absurdities) granting only that God is sovereignly righteous, and sovereignly merciful, and that all men are sinners. And man could not deny this unless he lost his sense. And here is how: God must, since he is perfectly righteous, avenge the sins of men as God, that is, the punishment corresponding to his infinite majesty. In so doing, if he struck all men, since every man is a sinner, he would not give mercy to anyone. And the result would be that all men are lost one by one. If he also gave mercy to all, that would deprive him of his perfect, indeed infinite, justice and as a consequence he would no longer be

God, except in the fashion of men. The same thing follows if he gives mercy only to one without having punished and struck him as God. And how should he (the one saved) be saved and lose all together?

It remains therefore that God himself finds and makes himself payer, in which he brings his sovereign righteousness and his sovereign mercy all together, constituting himself the surety and solvent to all the others to whom he was pleased to show mercy. And **[263]** what must this one himself be? True man, since it is human nature which offended and which must pay. And which man? One without any blemish. Because otherwise he himself would need another Savior, and God could not appease himself by an unclean and soiled payment. Therefore he must be true man, with regard to his substance, and true son of Adam the first man. Because if he were a man of another human nature, the nature which owes would not be paid in this surety. And in order to be thus of all man without guilt or any blemish, but on the contrary really sound and whole, he must be conceived and born in a way other than sinful men are born of sinful fathers. And who will do this? The power of the Most High. And to what must this surety satisfy? To the punishment corresponding to the majesty of the offended God, nevertheless so that the payer should not be crushed by this burden. Because living under this indignation of God as a surety, how should the principal debtors be acquitted? And who will be able to sustain this combat and to emerge victorious in it, if it is not God himself? Because to whom will we make the Sovereign equal except to himself? Therefore this surety must be as much true God as true man, in order to sustain this human nature until exhausting all the wrath of God, and yet that the **[264]** person who strikes might be distinguished not separately (because there is only one God in essence) from the person who is struck in this humanity, and who having accomplished this payment brings from it the crown of glory for himself and for those whom he purchased. And this cannot be done if he is not alive again, and ascends as a glorious one to this glorious immortality which is the summit of sovereign mercy, bringing there with him those for whom he shall have pledged himself and atoned (Heb. 2.10).

Let us now join together all these conclusions out of the aforesaid presupposition, that in order to save those whom God had destined to salvation, the Savior had to be God, different in person than he who struck him, which is the Son. And he had to be still a true son of Adam in unity of person, and by consequence conceived by the virtue of the Holy Spirit, who carried in his body and in his soul all the punishment owed to our sins, dying as the just one who was pledged for the unjust, and who after he abolished death by his resurrection took possession of eternal glory for himself and for his own. And all this had to occur by a sovereign mercy of God, having ordained and given us such a Savior, as he had promised by the prophets. Behold then how in spite of that which is secret and concerning what was ordained, and with regard to its execution it must be founded on this wisdom, **[265]** power, and goodness of God which surpasses all our capacity, and which must be the true and only foundation of our faith. Nevertheless there are too many apparent reasons left in man, either to bring the ones who contradict to too large and persistent absurdities, or else to give glory to God, or to remain confused.

IT IS NOTHING TO QUOTE THE SCRIPTURES IF BY AND BY ONE DOES NOT SHOW WHERE ONE'S BELIEFS COME FROM

It follows in our text that the Lord, after having spoken thus in general of the authority of the writings of the prophets, told them in detail that beginning with Moses, and next coming to the other prophets who were filled with such testimonies, as much of this great humbling as of the glorious victory of the Messiah. The Rabbis and false teachers of the Jews are not able to deny these testimonies, and cannot meanwhile accord in only one man these two qualities so contrary. And because they do not want to recognize the deity of this one, they are constrained from one Messiah to make two, that is, the one thus humbled, and the other so highly exalted. So that in wanting to have two, they do not have one. But, more, let us learn here that Jesus Christ did not do as the false teachers, boasting all the time of the name of God and of his word, and of the authority of our mother the holy church. But if, concerning that, one questions coming to the testimonies of the Scriptures, there are still the unwritten words [266], their traditions, antiquity, and the mask of councils put forward—God knows to what signs—when one must critique their evidence and their beautiful conclusions and test them on the touchstone. One must remember at the least a little of what some of the more ancient and admissible Fathers left behind by their writings a long time ago. That is, they taught that what is put forward without Scripture, may be as easily rejected as cited as an authority.

CURIOSITY OF THOSE WHO WOULD LIKE FOR THESE EXPOSITIONS OF ALL THE PROPHETS, PUT FORWARD BY CHRIST, TO HAVE BEEN RECORDED

Moreover some here desire that these allegations, which it must not be doubted that the Master had exposed very simply and very divinely—as say also these persons next after verse 32—had been recorded by the evangelist, with great profit to the whole church. But let us be satisfied with what the well-loved disciple declared about this, John 20.30, 31 and 21.25: the Holy Spirit omitted nothing which might be necessary in this place. And in fact I do not know if those who would like to have some more writings, would become more careful of reading them and profiting by them. The reading and meditation on what we have in the Bible is so despised, that men are accustomed to despise what they have and to ask for what they do not have.

THE DIFFERENCE THERE IS BETWEEN LYING AND SIMULATION AND DISSIMULATION. AND WHEN AND HOW THESE LAST TWO ACTS ARE ALLOWED

Finally, it is written in our text that [267] these words were continued until the town, where these two meant to stop. The Lord, pretending to leave them there and to go on more, thereupon he raised a question, a question of very great consequence. He asked if it is proper or not to speak or to do something contrary to what one has at heart, always presupposing that the thought is good and right. Because if it is bad, that is, if it is something contrary to the will of God or to the edification of neighbors, beyond doubt then one must not speak evil nor do evil either overtly or covertly. That then presupposed, I say that we must keep ourselves in this place of being neither too scrupulous, nor not conscientious enough. I call too scrupulous those who think that the outside must show what is on the inside, whether by word or by sign of their countenance. I call not very conscientious those who allow themselves to lie, whether for pleasure or to aid their neighbor, doing harm to the truth, and wounding their conscience. And all the time seeing that between the vicious extremities some are farther from the mediocrity in which virtue lies than the others, like lavishness is less far from liberality than greed. Consequently the defect of one too scrupulous is **[268]** without comparison more excusable than that of the one not conscientious enough. But it is necessary that the Holy Spirit and well-ordered love teach us the measure that we must possess between the two.

And to get there I say, first, that we must carefully avoid all occasions that can bring us to this channel of being tempted to counterfeit ourselves whether in word or in deed. Next after I say that not to say or not to represent all that one thinks, or not to say or represent a thing of the way that one thinks, is another thing than to lie, either by words or by actions. For example, the Lord wanted Isaiah to announce to Hezekiah the decree of his death, and for Jonah to announce to the Ninevites their overthrow in forty days—even though he had not decreed, and resolved this. Because if he had decreed it, he would necessarily have executed it. Nonetheless he did not lie, neither did he make his prophets lie. Because he is the truth itself. But knowing that the stupid ones feel nothing if they are not pushed forward, and that the dull ones hear nothing knowingly, if one does not speak too loudly, he did not want to say all that he had decreed. Therefore he kept silent the condition that he had opposed to his decree, to know if Hezekiah and if the Ninevites would convert. Neither Isaiah then, nor Jonah, and much less again the Lord, lied, **[269]** especially since Isaiah and Jonah themselves had not known this decree of God, given that it was conditional. They just knew it by experience. And this fact, which the legal experts call a great "fraud," was the salvation of Hezekiah and the Ninevites. This thus was working according to the Lord's will. Thus the Lord spoke to Moses not only by countenance but by expressed words (Exod. 32.10). "Leave me alone, and my wrath will flame up against this people, and I will consume them." He was thus saying otherwise than he was thinking and otherwise than he wanted to do. In this it can be said, truly all the time and holily, that he acted towards Moses and the people, in this deed, not by lying (which cannot be done, except with very abominable blasphemy, and really make the Lord be terribly angry) but by "pretence" and "double-dealing." Not with vice, but by a very great mercy. Of "pretence," in that he pretended that he boldly wanted to consume the people. Of "double-dealing," in that he concealed what he meant, that is, to move Moses so much to pray for this people so much more ardently—moving him also to the consideration of the greatness of the fault of this people. As a result, after this Moses acted towards the Israelites with the rigor that he should, and **[270]** made them so much more understand the greatness of their fault.

In the same way we do not say that Joshua was reprehensible, but that he did the actions of a great captain, having pretended to be afraid, and fleeing to catch the inhabitants of the city of Ai (Joshua 8.5). And such strategies of war are laudable when it is just, and provided that either perjury or illicit practices does not enter in, understood as practices against the first or second table of the Law or against all of both of them. But those who will have such a charge as spying and discovering the secrets of the enemy should pray well of God that he guide them little by little, given that it is very difficult that one not mix there some falsehood. And this would spoil everything, if the Lord should not excuse the fault, having regard for the good and right intention of the work like we see happened to the wise women of Egypt (Ex. 1.19), to Rahab (Josh. 2.5), to Hushai (2 Sam. 2.16 & 18), and to the woman who saved the two spies of David (2 Samuel 17.20). Thus we will not censure David for counterfeiting insanity to save his life (1 Sam. 2.13), since he had not lied or done wrong to anyone. Because it is another thing to make or conceal one's counsel, when one must say nothing of it for the glory of God, or for the well-being of neighbors, or himself, in order to avoid evil, than to lie knowingly with the intention **[271]** of permitting what is false.

Therefore the Lord used this countenance, pretending to go on further, although his intention was the other. He wanted by this means to move the hearts of those whom he had met in the road to ask him to stay with them, and to make them as such more near and burning to listen to him. He did not want by this deed to excuse the liars, hypocrites, or disguised and cunning, either in their words, or in their way of doing things. If that happened, we should not be able to have simplicity, or hold the truth in great enough esteem.

GOD HIMSELF MAKES OUR FAULTS SERVE SOME GREAT PURPOSE

In conclusion, my brothers, we have here a lot to learn of all sorts, firstly how the Lord teaches us to use our great faults for our own profit, provided that one remains submissive to his spirit. For if the disciples had not been so tardy to believe, the church would not have had such certain testimonies of the resurrection of the Lord. But to receive this fruit, one must know the true cause of the malady and comply with the physician. This malady is our natural sense wanting to make itself the critic and judge of the wisdom of God, which is made known in his holy Word. The Holy Spirit is the only doctor, having here spoken by the lips of the Master, as he speaks in his church by the lips of his faithful servants, not **[272]** only to instruct, but also to reprove and reproach, and advise; and we must leave the judgment to the doctor and not to the patients concerning what punishment the fault merits. And because there are many poisonous ones who are called doctors of the conscience, this same passage shows us which drugs are used by the true doctors, that is, of those who grow and originate in the field of the Scriptures of the prophets and apostles. Indeed, there are not only cited and put forward, but also well and duly explained and mixed by the comparison of passages that should provide the text and the gloss, everything being brought back to the articles of faith by the example which Jesus Christ himself showed the use and practice of here. Finally let us learn to ask God for a spirit of discretion, in order to keep ourselves from contravening in anything this simplicity and truth so recommended to Christians, not being, however, for that reason forbidden from adapting ourselves to the sick ones. But let us act according to licit means and not contravene in anything the integrity of conscience, and hold to good paths, if one cannot straight ahead hold on to the "great" path, to mutual edification. Amen.

Appendix 3

The Treasure of Truth

CH. 1: THE QUESTION OF GOD'S EVERLASTING PREDESTINATION IS NEITHER CURIOUS NOR UNNEEDFULL IN THE CHURCH OF GOD.

In his book *The Good Gift of Perseverance or Continuance unto the End* (ch. 14) Augustine says, "They say that the doctrine of predestination is an enemy to preaching, that it should be no good. As though it had been an enemy to the apostle's preaching. Has not that excellent teacher of the Gentiles so often commended predestination, and yet ceased not to preach the word of God?

"Also, as he which has received the gift does truly exhort and preach, even so he which has received the gift does obediently hear him that exhorts and preaches, etc. Therefore we exhort and preach. But they which have ears to hear obediently hear us. They which have not, that thing comes to pass in them which is written, so that hearing they should not hear. Hearing with the sense of their body, they should not hear with the assent of their body. But why the one has ears to hear, and the other has not, that is to say, why it is given to the one of the Father to come to the Son and is not given to the other, who has known the mind of the Lord? Must that which is manifest be therefore denied, because that which is hidden cannot be comprehended or known?"

Also in chapter 15: "Whether, if when this is heard some are turned unto a sluggish heaviness and slowness, and being readily bent to fall from labor to wantonness, go after their lusts, must therefore that be thought false which is said of the foreknowledge of God? And will not we also speak that which – the Scripture being witness – is lawful to speak? Likely we are afraid lest he should be offended who cannot take it. And are we not afraid lest we hold our tongues and he which can take the truth should be deceived with falsehood?"

Also in chapter 20: "If the apostles and the teachers of the church which followed them, did both, that they might entreat the godly of the eternal election of God, and might keep the faithful under the government of a godly life, what is it that these men are shut up with the invincible force of the truth think that they say well that predestination is not to be preached to the people, although it is true? No, it must utterly be preached, that he who has ears to hear, may hear. And who has ears to hear, if he has not received of him which promises that he will give? Verily, let him that receives not, refuse, yet so that he who desires, take and drink, drink and live. For as godliness is to be preached, that God may be duly worshipped, so also is predestination, so that he who has ears to hear, may glory in the grace of God—in God, not in himself."

This is the mind of that most excellent man, who notwithstanding puts two conditions: (1) one is, these matters should be reasoned of according to the rule of the word of God; (2) the other, if the same which the scripture declares as touching these matters be expounded aptly and unto edifying (of both these points we have purposed to speak in few words) first must be the doctrine itself and then of the use and applying of it.

CH. 2: OF THE EVERLASTING COUNSEL OF GOD, HID IN HIMSELF, WHICH NOTWITHSTANDING IS IN THE END UNDERSTOOD BY THE EFFECTS.

1st Aphorism

The ways of almighty God are unsearchable, without whose eternal and unchangeable decree nothing is done anywhere by any man, neither generally nor particularly. Not even those things are not to be excepted, which—albeit not in respect they are decreed of God, being always good and just, but in respect they are done by Satan and other evil instruments—are evil and therefore to be detested, and abhorred.[1]

2nd Aphorism

The same God from everlasting has purposed and decreed in himself, to create all things at their seasons to his glory. But man, and that after two sorts altogether divers the one to the other, namely, in such manner that some whom it pleases him according to his secret will, he makes through mercy partakers of his glory. These out of the word of God we call "vessels of honor," "elect,"

---

1   Under the heading, "Proofs out of the word of God," Beza included lengthy biblical citations after most of his aphorisms to ground his assertions in Scripture. He did not just cite the verses; rather, he wrote out each passage to show that he was duplicating the Bible in his theological exposition. As I argued above this was because Pastor Beza was trying to be biblical in his pastoral theology. Space will not permit me to include the text of Beza's citations. Rather, I will include the references to the biblical text in footnotes throughout.

Proofs out of the word of God: Rom. 11:33; Rom. 9:20; Job 9:10-12; Gen. 27:20; Eph. 1:11; Exod. 21:13; Prov. 16:33; Prov. 20:24; Prov. 21:1; Isa. 14:27; Jer. 10:23; Dan. 4:32; Matt. 10:29; Eph. 2:1-2; 1 Sam. 16:14; 2 Tim. 2:26; Gen. 45:8; Gen. 50:20; Exod. 4:21; Exod. 7:3; Exod. 9:11; Exod. 10:1, 20; Exod. 11:10; Exod. 14:4, 17; Deut. 2:30; Josh. 11:19-20; 2 Sam. 2:25; 2 Sam. 12:11; 2 Sam. 24:1; 1 Kings 12:15; 1 Kings 22:23; 2 Kings 18:25; 2 Chron. 11:4; 2 Chron. 22:7; 2 Chron. 25:20; Neh. 9:36-37; Job 1:21; Job 34:30; Psa. 105:25; Isa. 10:15; Isa. 54:16; Isa. 63:17; John 12:40 and Isa. 6:10; Jer. 48:10; Acts 2:23; Acts 4:27-28; Rom. 9:18-19; Rom. 11:32; Gal. 3:22; 1 Thess. 3:3; Rom. 8:29; 1 Pet. 3:17; 1 Pet. 4:19.

"sons of the promise," and "predestinate or foreordained to salvation." And another, whom also it pleases him to store up to that end, he shows his wrath and his power, that in them also he might be glorified, whom likewise we call "vessels of dishonor and wrath," and "unapt to every good work."[2]

3rd Aphorism
This election and choosing, or predestination and foreordaining to salvation being considered in the purpose of God itself, that is to say, the decree itself and purpose of electing and choosing, is the first fountain of the salvation of the sons of God, and does not spring as some would have it, from the foreknowledge either of their faith or works, but rather of that only which is in the good pleasure of God itself, from which afterward both election or choosing spring, and also faith and all good works.[3]

4th Aphorism
Therefore the Scripture as often as it will strengthen the sons of God with assured hope, stays not either in the testimonies or witnesses of the second causes, that is to say, in the fruits of faith, nor yet in the second and next causes themselves, namely, faith and vocation (or calling) but ascends or climbs up to Christ himself, in whom notwithstanding as in the head, we are indeed elect and adopted. And afterward it goes up even to that everlasting purpose which God has purposed in no other than in himself.[4]

5th Aphorism
Also when the Bible speaks of the destruction of the reprobates, albeit the whole fault remains within themselves, yet some times – as often as it is so needful – the Spirit of God to make known the riches of his glory upon the vessels of mercy, and his excellent power and also gentleness the better by comparison, lifts us up even to that high mystery, which in order goes before all the causes of their damnation. Of which secret, doubtless there is no other cause known to men besides God's righteous will, which we ought reverently to receive, as coming undoubtedly from him who is naturally just and can no other way be conceived of men, nor of any other.[5]

---

2 *Proofs out of the word of God*: Prov. 16:4; Isa. 43:6-7; Eph. 1:5-6; Rom. 9:23; 8:29; 9:7-8, 21; 1 Cor. 2:7; Eph. 1:4; 2 Thess. 2:13; 1 Pet. 1:2; Exod. 9:16; Rom. 9:22.
3 *Proofs out of the word of God*: Deut. 4:37; 7:7-8; Josh. 24:2; Ps. 44:3; John 15:16; Acts 13:48; 22:14; Rom. 5:6; 9:11-16, 18, 25; 11:7, 35; 1 Cor. 4:7; Eph. 1:4-5, 11; 2:10; Col. 1:12; 2 Tim. 1:9.
4 *Proofs out of the word of God*: Matt. 25:3; John 6:40; Acts 13:48; Rom. 8:29; 9:8, 11, 16, 23; Eph. 1:4-5, 9, 11; 2 Tim. 2:19; 1 Cor. 2:7, 10; 1 Pet. 1:19-20.
5 *Proofs out of the word of God*: Hos. 13:9; John 3:19; Rom. 9:23; Exod. 9:16; Ps. 33:15; Prov. 16:4; Rom. 9:11, 13; Isa. 54:16; John 6:44; 10:26; 12:39-40 and Isa. 6:10; 1 Pet. 2:8; Jude 1:4.

6th Aphorism
For we must make a difference between the purpose of reprobating, and between reprobation itself. For God would have the mystery or secret of it hidden from us. But of this, and of the destruction also that depends or hangs on it, we have causes expressed in the word of God, namely, the corruption, unbelief and sin (which are necessary, or must be in respect of the falling out of them) of the vessels made to dishonor.[6]

7th Aphorism
So about the question of the sorting of the causes of salvation into degrees, and placing of them, as it were, in a certain row or order in the salvation of the elect, we distinguish or make a difference between the purpose of electing or choosing, which God has decreed in himself, and the election or choosing itself, which is ordained in Christ, so that this purpose of God in the row and order of causes goes before this election and all other things which follow after.[7]

CH. 3: OF THE EXECUTION OR FULFILLING OF THE EVERLASTING COUNSEL, IN THAT WHICH IS COMMON BOTH TO THE ELECT, AND ALSO TO THE REPROBATE.

1st Aphorism
The Lord, to the end he might execute or fulfill that everlasting counsel to his glory, prepared himself a way according to his infinite or endless wisdom, which is common both to them which were to be chosen, and also to them which were to cast off. For when he had determined to show forth a notable example of his mercy in the salvation of the chosen, and also to make manifest his just judgment in condemning the reprobate, it was necessary that he should shut up both of them under disobedience and sin, that he might have mercy on all the believers, that is, on the elect (for faith is a gift of God peculiar or proper to the elect), and contrariwise, that he might find matter of just damnation in those to whom it is given neither to believe, nor yet to know the mysteries or secrets of God.[8]

2nd Aphorism
This therefore he did with such wisdom that the whole fault of the reprobates' damnation rests in themselves, and the whole praise of the salvation of the elect is wholly to be referred to his mercy. For he did not create man in sin – for so, which God forbid, should he himself have been the author of sin, and in his

---

6   *Proofs out of the word of God*: 2 Thess. 2:9-12; Rom. 11:20; 2 Cor. 4:3-4; Heb. 12:16-17.
7   *Proofs out of the word of God*: Rom. 8:30; Eph. 1:4-5.
8   *Proofs out of the word of God*: Rom. 11:32; Gal. 3:22; Acts 13:48; Eph. 2:8; 2 Thess. 3:2; Tit. 1:1-2; Phil. 1:29; Matt. 13:11; John 12:37-40.

justice he might not punish it – but rather he made him after his own image, that is, in cleanness and holiness.⁹

3rd Aphorism
The man afterwards, constrained by none at all and driven also by no necessity of concupiscence or lust as concerning his will (for as yet it was not bound to sin) of his own accord, and freely rebelling against God, bequeathed himself to sin, and to both deaths, that is, of body and soul.¹⁰

4th Aphorism
Yet we must confess that this fall of man happened not by chance, since the providence of God is stretched forth even to the very smallest things. Neither can any thing be said to come to pass, God not knowing of it, or else altogether winking at it, for so thinking (the which God forbid) we must be of the opinion of the Epicureans.¹¹

5th Aphorism
Neither yet did it happen by any bare and idle permission or suffering, which is severed from his will and decree, for as he has ordained the end it must be also that he has appointed the causes leading to that end. Unless we will affirm that the same end came to pass either at all adventures, or else by causes ordained by some other god, after the opinion of the Manichees. Moreover, it cannot be once so much as thought, that any thing comes to pass against the will of God, but that with great ungodliness we must deny him to be almighty, which thing Augustine also *lib. De correp et grat.* (ch. 104) has plainly noted: "It therefore remains that this fall did in such sort issue from the willing motion or stirring of Adam, as that yet it happened not against the will of God, whom after a certain wonderful and inconceivable manner it pleases that even the same thing, which he does not allow in that it is sin, comes not to pass without his will. And that, as we have said before, that he should show the riches of his glory upon the vessels of mercy, and declare his wrath and power in those vessels which he has made therefore, that he might set forth his glory by their just damnation. For neither is the salvation of the elect, nor yet the damnation of the reprobates, the last end of the counsels of God, but the setting forth of his glory, as well in saving them of mercy, as in condemning these by his just judgment."¹²

---

9   *Proofs out of the word of God*: Gen. 1:27; Eph. 4:24.
10 *Proofs out of the word of God*: Gen. 2:17; Rom. 7:20; 5:12.
11 *Proofs out of the word of God*: Matt. 10:29, 50; Prov. 16:33.
12 *Proofs out of the word of God*: Rom. 9:21-22; 1 Pet. 2:8; Exod. 9:16; Prov. 16:4; Isa. 54:16; Rom. 9:11, 13, 17-18.

6th Aphorism

Therefore that we may avoid these blasphemies into which the weakness of man's wit draws us, let us confess that the corruption of the chief workmanship made by God came to pass neither by chance, nor yet without his will, who of his incomprehensible or inconceivable wisdom makes and orders all things to his glory. Let us nevertheless grant, albeit that the judgment of man wrestle never so much against it, which in the beginning was both compassed about with certain bounders and was also afterward miserably corrupted or made ill, that the whole fault of destruction rests in man, because between that secret and inconceivable will of God and the same corruption of mankind which properly is the true and the first original or beginning of the destruction of the reprobates, the will of that first man comes in. This will, whereas it was created good, of man's own accord depraved or made itself naught, and therefore made open an entry to the just judgment of God to destroy all those to whom he will not promise to show his mercy. Now if these pleading again object that they could not be against this will of God, well, let us let them alone to their own destruction to reason against him who will easily defend his own righteousness against their foolish quarrellings. Let us rather reverence that thing which is above the reach of our wit, and turn all the conceits and imaginations of our mind to the setting forth of his mercy, which of his own sole goodness has saved us, being no less wicked and worthy of any kind of punishment than they are.[13]

CH. 4: BY WHAT ORDER OF CAUSES GOD HAS OPENED THE WAY TO DECLARE HIS ELECTION, AND IN SOME PART TO EXECUTE OR PERFORM IT.

1st Aphorism

Now when God had determined those former things with himself, as we have said, afterwards in the next and yet eternal or everlasting row of causes (as all things are present unto him), he severally ordained all those degrees or steps, by which he would lift up into his kingdom those of his which were to be chosen. Therefore because he is in such wise merciful, that in the meanwhile he neither ought nor can forget his justice, first of all there must have been some one ordained to be a mediator, by whom man might be wholly restored into his former estate, and that of free mercy which should appear in the salvation of his people. But man – besides that he is more weak than that he can sustain or bear the force of God's wrath – does also so please himself in his most miserable blindness (that he does not see) being wholly brought into slavery and bondage to the kingdom of sin, so much that the law of God turns to death to him. So far off is it that he is not able there to set himself at liberty, or else to satisfy or

---

13 *Proofs out of the word of God*: Rom. 9:13-15, 19-20.

make answer to the law of God, even in the very least point.[14]

2nd Aphorism
God therefore, the most gentle Father of the elect and chosen, tempering his justice with infinite or endless mercy, appointed his only Son of the same substance with him, and also God everlasting, who at the time appointed should be made a very, or true, man.[15]

3rd Aphorism
First, he appointed that the two natures be joined together into one Jesus Christ that the whole corruption of man might be wholly repaired and amended in one man.[16]

4th Aphorism
Secondly, he appointed that he might fulfill all righteousness, and might be both able enough to sustain or bear the judgment of his Father, and also be a high priest, worthy enough to pacify his heavenly Father, dying as the righteous for the unrighteousness, and by his obedience doing away the stubbornness of Adam, and cleansing all the iniquities of us all, being laid upon his shoulders.[17]

5th Aphorism
Finally, he appointed that with one oblation or offering of himself, he might sanctify or make holy all them that were to be chosen, destroying and burying sin in them, by the communicating or imparting of his death and burial with them, and quickening them into a new life by his resurrection, or rising again, insomuch that they also find more in Christ than they lost in Adam.[18]

6th Aphorism
And lest this remedy should be void and of no effect the Lord further decreed to give his Son to them, whom, as we have said, he ordained from everlasting to salvation. And in like manner he decreed to give them to his Son so that when he shall be in them, and they in him, they might be made perfect into one, by those degrees or steps which do hereafter follow.[19]

---

14 *Proofs out of the word of God*: John 9:41; Rom. 1:18, 24; 7:14; Eph. 2:3; 1 Cor. 2:14; 2 Cor. 3:7, 9; Rom. 7:10.
15 *Proofs out of the word of God*: Matt. 1:20; Luke 1:35; John 1:14; Gal. 4:4; 1 John 1:1-4; 2 Cor. 5:19; Phil. 2:6-7; Col. 2:9.
16 *Proofs out of the word of God*: Rom. 8:3.
17 *Proofs out of the word of God*: Matt. 3:15; 5:17; Rom. 5:18; 1 Cor. 1:30.
18 *Proofs out of the word of God*: Isa. 53:4-5, 11; Rom. 3:25; Acts 20:28; Col. 1:20-22; Rom. 5:19; 1 Pet. 2:24; 3:18; 2 Cor. 5:21; Rom. 6:3-5; Col. 3:1; 2:12; John 17:7, 19; Heb. 9:13-14; 10:14; Rom. 5:11, 16-17, 20.
19 *Proofs out of the word of God*: Rom. 8:32; John 3:19; 17:2, 9, 11-12, 23.

7th Aphorism
For first at what time it pleases him to reveal and open that secret that he ordained from everlasting, at that time, I say, in which they think not of these things (as men that are very blind, and yet, notwithstanding, they think that they most sharply see, whereupon assured destruction hangs over their heads), behold suddenly he sets before their eyes the great danger that they are in. And that they may be the more pierced for a witness to their conscience, lying as it were buried and numbed, he joins to it the preaching of his law, adding examples of his judgments, that they should be afraid and tremble at the remembrance of their sins. Yet he does not do this with the intent that they should remain in this fear and trembling, but rather that turning to behold the greatness of the danger that surrounds them, they should fly to the only mediator, Jesus Christ.[20]

8th Aphorism
Therefore after that severe or sharp preaching of the law, he sets forth to them the grace and gentleness of the gospel. Yet he adds this condition: if they believe in Christ, who alone can deliver them from condemnation and give to them the power and right to obtain the heavenly inheritance.[21]

9th Aphorism
And because all these things should be done in vain if God set forth these secrets unto men only by the outward preaching of his word written and openly published in the church of God – which notwithstanding is the ordinary and specially necessary instrument by which Jesus Christ is communicated or imparted to us – therefore when he has to do with his elect and chosen, together with the outward preaching or the word, he joins the inward power of the Holy Spirit, which does not, as sophisters suppose, repair or renew the remnants of their "free will" (for whatever "free will" is left to us, it consists or lies in this, that we sin willingly, shunning God, hate him, yes, and moreover can neither hear him, nor believe him, nor acknowledge the gift of God, nor so much as think any good thing. To be short, that we are wholly subject to wrath and the curse). But contrariwise, he rather turns their stony hearts into fleshy ones, draws, teaches, enlightens their eyes, opens their sense, heart, ears, and

---

20 *Proofs out of the word of God*: Gen. 3:15; 22:18; Rom. 3:25; 16:25-26; 1 Cor. 2:7; Gal. 4:4; Eph. 1:9-10; Col. 1:26; 2 Tim. 1:9-10; Tit. 1:2-3; 1 Pet. 1:18, 20; Josh. 24:2-3; Ezek. 16:8; Isa. 65:1; Eph. 2:3-5, 11-13; Rom. 5:10; 1 Pet. 2:10; John 9:41; 3:19; Rom. 1:18; 2:15; Acts 14:17; Rom. 2:14; Acts 14:17; Rom. 7:7; 1 Tim. 2:5; 2 Tim. 2:25, 19; Acts 2:37-38; 1 John 2:1.
21 *Proofs out of the word of God*: John 1:12; 3:16; Rom. 1:19; 8:1; 1 John 2:1; John 1:12; 3:16: Rom. 1:16; 5:1.

understanding.[22]

10th Aphorism
And first this Spirit in the elect causes them to be touched indeed with the feeling of their calamity or misery. Secondly he creates faith in them, so that they may be able to perform the condition annexed or knit unto the preaching of the gospel. Now this faith is after a manner twofold. The one, by which Christ is generally and universally known, namely, by which we assent to the history of Christ, and to the prophecy written of him, which faith is also sometimes granted to the very reprobates. Another, which is proper and peculiar to the elect stands in this, that we apply to ourselves as our own Christ universally and indifferently offered to all men, and be every one of us made assured of our election, which indeed before time from everlasting was hidden in the secret of God, but was afterwards declared to us, partly by the inward testimony or witness of our conscience through the Spirit of God being joined to the external or outward preaching, and partly also by the power and efficacy or virtue of the same Spirit, which brings to this point every one of the elect, being set at liberty from the bondage of sin so that they begin to will and to do the things which are of God.[23]

11th Aphorism
These are therefore the degrees or steps by which it pleases the Lord freely to create in his elect that precious and peculiar gift of faith by which they may lay hold of their salvation in Christ. But because faith is only begun in us to the end that we may be able not only to persevere or continue in it, but also to profit (which is altogether necessary) for this cause first of all we are initiated or entered as it were into religion by the sacrament of baptism. Moreover, besides the hearing of the word, that faith is again sealed in us by the sacrament of the Lord's Supper. Of these sacraments this truly is the chief end, that they are certain and effectual seals and also charters of the faithful communicating or partaking with Christ who is made unto them wisdom, righteousness, sanctification, and redemption. Therefore it is very often rehearsed in Paul, that

---

22 *Proofs out of the word of God*: Rom. 10:8, 17; 2 Cor. 5:18-19; Jam. 1:18; 1 Pet. 1:23, 25; Acts 16:14; Eph. 1:9; Col. 1:27; Rom. 6:20; John 6:44, 65; Gen. 3:8; Rom. 5:10; Rom. 8:7; John 8:47; Isa. 53:1; John 12:36, 40; Matt. 13:13, 11: John 3:3; 4:10; 1 Cor. 2:14; 2 Cor. 3:5; Eph. 2:1-3; Ezek. 11:19; Ps. 51:12; John 6:44-45; Ps. 119:130; Eph. 1:17-18; Isa. 50:5; Ps. 119:18, 73, 130; Col. 1:9.

23 *Proofs out of the word of God*: Jer. 31:19; Luke 24:45; Acts 16:14; 1 Cor. 2:10-12, 16; Col. 1:26-27; Eph. 1:16-18; 1 John 3:24; 5:20; Rom. 8:15-16; Gal. 4:6; Rom. 8:14; 1 John 3:10; 4:13-14; Phil. 2:13; Rom. 6:18.

we who have been justified or made righteous by faith have peace.[24]

12th Aphorism
For whoever has obtained the gift of true faith, the same also trusting the like liberality of God ought indeed to be careful to persevere or continue to the end, but not to stand in doubt of the same. But rather in all kinds of temptations and afflictions he should call upon God with assured hope to obtain that which he asks, so far as is expedient or meet, forasmuch as he knows himself to be the son of God, who cannot deceive him. Furthermore, he never goes so far astray out of the right way, but that through the benefit of the same grace, at length he comes into the way again. But sometimes faith lies buried in the chosen for a season, insomuch that it may seem to be wholly extinguished or quenched, to wit, that thereby they may know their own imbecility or weakness. Yet it never goes so far away, that the love of God and their neighbor is utterly plucked out of their minds. For no man is justified, or made righteous in Christ, but he is also sanctified or made holy in him, yes, and moreover is created for good works, which the Lord has ordained, that we should walk in them.[25]

13th Aphorism
This therefore is the way by which God ordains his elect unto the full execution or performance of his counsels, whom it pleases him to bring up amongst men until they grow up to full age. But as touching those whom he calls out of his kingdom, being yet scarce born or in their first years, the way is more compendious or shorter. For when he comprehends in his free covenant, of which Christ is the mediator, not only the faithful but also their posterity unto a thousand generations so that he plainly pronounces it to be holy, there is no doubt but that he has given the children of holy men, which pertain to his election (whom he alone knows) to his Son, who surely will not also cast these forth.[26]

---

24 *Proofs out of the word of God*: Mk. 16:16; Acts 2:38; Rom. 6:3-4; Gal. 3:27; Rom. 4:11; Col. 2:12; Eph. 5:25-26; 1 Pet. 3:21; 1 Cor. 10:16; 1:30; Rom. 3:21-22, 24-25; Rom. 4:2; 5:1.
25 *Proofs out of the word of God*: Num. 23:19; Pss. 23:6; 27:1, 3; John 6:7; 17:5; 10:28-29; Rom. 5:2-5; 11:20; 1 Cor. 2:12, 16; 10:12; Eph. 1:9; Phil. 1:6; 1 Thess. 5:24; 2 Cor. 1:21; Heb. 4:16; 10:22-23; Jam. 1:6; 1 John 5:14-15; 1:8, 10; Luke 22:32; 1 John 3:9-10; Rom. 6:1-2; 1 John 4:20; 2 Pet. 1:5-9; Eph. 1:4; 2:10.
26 *Proofs out of the word of God*: Gen. 17:7; Exod. 20:6; 1 Cor. 7:14; John 6:37.

CH. 5: IN WHAT ORDER THE LORD BEGINS TO EXECUTE OR FULFILL, AND INDEED EFFECTUALLY TO DECLARE, HIS COUNSEL OF REPROBATION.

1st Aphorism
It may easily be understood by those things that we have said before how the Lord brings to pass that they may go to their own place whom he has created, that he might be glorified in their just condemnation. For as Christ the second Adam from heaven is the foundation and whole substance of the salvation of the elect, so also the first Adam from the earth, because he fell, is therefore the first cause of hatred and destruction, which shall come upon the reprobates.[27]

2nd Aphorism
For when the Lord, being moved thereto with such causes as he alone knew, had purposed to create them to this end (that is, that he might show forth his wrath and power in them), he ordained, as it were, high degrees and steps, those causes by which it should come to pass that the whole blame of their destruction should lie in themselves, according as we have shown before. Man therefore falling willingly and of his own accord into that miserable estate, the Lord who worthily hates the reprobates, for so much as they are corrupt, shows forth his just anger upon some of them as soon as they are born.[28]

3rd Aphorism
But in them that are grown to full age he observes or uses two other ways, altogether diverse and contrary to one another. For he promises some not even this much savor as to hear anything at all of Christ (in whom alone is salvation), but he lets them go their own ways and to make haste unto assured destruction. For such testimonies or witnesses of his Godhead, as he has left to them, are of force only thus far, that they have nothing to pretend or allege for their excuse. But it is through their own fault, since this ignorance and sluggishness they are in is a punishment of that same corruption in which they were born. And truly whatever they can see in matters touching God, y this light, or rather darkness, of nature, although they did not faint in the middle of the race, yet it is such as it can by no means be sufficient to salvation. For it is necessary to salvation that we know God not only as God, but also as a Father in Christ. And this secret flesh and blood does not reveal or open, but the Son himself only to those whom he has received from his Father.[29]

---

27 *Proofs out of the word of God*: Acts 1:25; Rom. 9:22: Matt. 25:41; Rom. 5:18; 1 Cor. 15:21-22.
28 *Proofs out of the word of God*: Rom. 9:17, 22; Exod. 20:5; Eph. 2:3; Rom. 5:14.
29 *Proofs out of the word of God*: Matt. 1:21; Acts 4:12; 14:16; Rom. 1:24; Eph. 2:11-12; Rom. 1:19; Acts 14:17; 17:27; Rom. 1:20; 2:12; 1:21-22: John 17:3; 3:36; Matt. 11:17; 16:17; John 1:13.

4th Aphorism
But of some the fall is greater, namely, of them whom he vouchsafes indeed to have the external or outward preaching of the word. But they being called neither will nor can answer because they so please themselves in their blindness that they say they see. To them also it is not given to embrace the Spirit of truth and to believe. Therefore, although their stubbornness is necessary, yet it is willing (or, of their own accord). Therefore it comes to pass that being hidden to the feast they refuse to come insomuch that the word of life is foolishness to them and a stumbling block, yes finally a deadly savor of death.[30]

5th Aphorism
There are others besides these, whose understanding he stirs up to perceive and believe the things which they hear. But what is wrought is that "general faith" with which all the devils also being endued notwithstanding tremble.[31]

6th and 7th Aphorisms
Last of all, those who are of all men most unhappy, also climb the higher that they may have the greater fall. For by the benefit of a certain grace they are entered thus far, that they are also somewhat moved to taste of the heavenly gift, insomuch that for a time, having received the seed, they seem to be planted in the church of God, and also show others the way to salvation. But it is certain that the Spirit of adoption, whom we said to be proper to them who are never cast out and who are written among the secret of the people of God, was never communicated or imparted to them, for if they were among the elect they should doubtless remain with the elect.

All these therefore, because necessarily but yet voluntarily (or willingly, as they who are under the kingdom of sin) turn again to their vomit, and fall from faith, and are therefore pulled up by the root to be cast into the fire. They are forsaken, I say, of God who is moved with his own will, which no man can withstand. And their corruption and wickedness notwithstanding, he hardens them, makes their heart fat, stops their ears, finally blinds their eyes, and for the performance of this thing uses partly their own evil lusts (unto which he gives them up to be governed), partly that same spirit of lying (which keeps them bound in chains because of their corruption out of which, as out of a certain spring, there issues out a continual stream of infidelity or unbelief, ignorance, and iniquity). Therefore it comes to pass that because they have made shipwreck their faith they can never escape the day appointed for their

---

30 *Proofs out of the word of God*: Luke 12:47; Matt. 22:14; Luke 13:34; 19:42; Jer. 7:28; Prov. 1:24; John 9:41; 14:17; 12:39-40; 2 Thess. 3:2; Matt. 13:11; 22:2; Luke 14:16; 1 Cor. 1:18, 23; 2 Cor. 2:15-16.
31 *Proofs out of the word of God*: Jam. 2:19.

destruction, that God may be glorified in their just damnation.[32]

CH. 6: OF THE LAST AND FULL EXECUTION OR PERFORMING OF THE COUNSEL OF GOD, BOTH IN THE CHOSEN, AND ALSO IN THE REPROBATE.

1st Aphorism
Forasmuch as God is very righteousness itself, it is fitting that he should save the righteous, and condemn the unrighteous. But they only among men are righteous who being united and grafted in Christ by faith, yes, and also rooted in him, and being made one body with him, are in him and by him justified and sanctified, that is, made righteous and holy. By this it is proved that the life to which they are ordained to the glory of God by a certain right appertains only to them.[33]

2nd Aphorism
And contrariwise those who remain in the pollution or filthiness and death of Adam are worthily hated by God, that they may be damned by him. They are not so much as once accepted who have died before they could sin after the likeness of Adam, that is to say, in act or deed.[34]

3rd Aphorism
Both these executions or performings of the judgments of God are brought to pass by three degrees, as well in the one as in the other, of which the first has been by us declared already. For as touching the elect the very same moment that they have received the gift of faith, they have passed from death to life, a sure pledge of which they have. But their life is altogether hidden in Christ – until such time as that first death set them one degree forward, by which death, the soul being loosed from the chains of the body, enters into the joy of his Lord. Finally at the day appointed for the judgment of the living and the dead, when this corruptible shall put on immortality, and God shall be all in all, then shall they at length in presence see his majesty. And they shall be in unspeakable joy which was prepared for them from everlasting – that is, a reward due to the righteousness and holiness of Christ who was delivered for

---

32 *Proofs out of the word of God*: Heb. 6:4-6; Acts 8:13; Matt. 13:24; Acts 1:16-17; John 6:37; Ezek. 13:9; 1 John 2:19; John 8:34; Rom. 5:12; 6:20; 7:14; 8:7; 2 Pet. 2:22; 1 Tim. 4:1; Matt. 12:43; Rom. 9:19; 2 Thess. 2:6, 10-11; John 3:19; Isa. 63:17; Exod. 4:21. ("There are also more places which we have rehearsed above": Isa. 6:10; Rom. 11:31; Exod.8:32; Ps. 95:8; Acts 7:42; Rom. 1:29; 2 Kings 22:23; John 13:2; 2 Cor. 4:3-4; 2 Tim. 2:26; 1 Tim. 1:19; Prov. 16:4; Exod. 9:16; Rom. 9:21-22.)
33 *Proofs out of the word of God*: John 17:21; Rom. 9:5; Col. 2:7; 1 Cor. 10:16: Rom. 8:30; 1 Cor. 1:30; 2 Cor. 5:5; Rom. 6:23; 3:25, 29; Eph. 1:5-6.
34 *Proofs out of the word of God*: Rom. 5:14; Eph. 2:3; John 3:36.

their sins and raised again from the dead for their justification (or righteous-making), by whose power and Spirit they have walked from faith to faith, as by their whole life shall plainly appear.[35]

4th Aphorism

Now contrariwise the reprobates being conceived, born, and brought up in sin, death, and the wrath of God remaining upon them, when they go out of this world, fall into another gulf of destruction. Their souls are thrown headlong into an everlasting horror or trembling, until that day, when their body and soul being joined together again they shall go into that everlasting fire prepared for the devil and his angels.[36]

5th Aphorism

After these two ways then, and the same being clean divers one from another, shall the last end of the judgments of God lay open his glory to all men. In his elect he has declared himself to be both most exceeding just and also most exceeding merciful – namely, just in that he has with greatest severity, or sharpness, punished all the sins of his chosen in the person of his Son, and has not received them into his fellowship before he has fully and wholly made them righteous and holy in him. And this is infinitely, or without end, merciful in that he has purposed to choose them freely in himself. And afterward as he purposed he has freely adopted them in his Son, namely, by calling, justifying, and glorifying them, that faith coming in between, which he (being moved with similar gentleness) has granted unto them. Now on the other part, concerning the reprobates, their corruption and unbelief, with the fruits springing from the same, and testimony or witness of their own conscience shall so reprove them, that albeit they wrestle never so much against it, yet God's exceeding justice may appear in their just condemnation, all men approving it.

CH. 7: WHAT WAY THIS DOCTRINE MAY PROFITABLY BE OPENLY SET FORTH AND TAUGHT.

Having declared the sum of the doctrine itself it remains that we show what we think is especially to be observed or marked in the preaching and also the peculiar applying of it. For whereas it seems to many to be so hard, that they flee from it as from a rock, this is to be attributed or given partly to the lewdness and arrogance or pride of men and partly also to the lack of foresight

---

35 *Proofs out of the word of God*: John 5:24; 2 Cor. 1:22; 5:5; 1 Cor. 1:4-8; Rom. 8:24-25; Eph. 1:13-14; 5:2; Luke 23:43; Matt. 22:31-32; Luke 16:22; Phil. 1:23; Acts 3:21; Rom. 8:21; Luke 1; 1 Cor. 15; 2 Cor. 5:10; Rom. 14:10; Matt. 25:34.
36 *Proofs out of the word of God*: Ps. 51:7; John 3:36; Rom. 7:14; Eph. 2:3; Luke 16:23-24; Matt. 25:41.

in some, who go about to open these secrets unadvisedly and without any choice. And finally it is to be attributed to the lack of skill of some who know not orderly how to apply to themselves the things which otherwise are faithfully and truly declared.

Therefore as concerning those first, who sin of malice, it belongs to God alone to amend their fault which doubtless he has always done in his time and will likewise do hereafter in those whom in the end he has purposed to have mercy on. And as for the others who remain stubborn and stiff in their wickedness, there is no cause why we should be so moved either with their number or authority that God's truth should be dissembled. Now as touching the others, these things I think needful to observed or taken heed of in the preaching and setting forth of this mystery or secret.

First, as in other points and especially in this secret of predestination or foreordaining, they must diligently take heed lest instead of the plain truth of God they bring in vain and curious speculations. This they must do who, to make these hidden judgments of God agree with man's brain not only distinguish or make a difference between the foreknowledge and the purpose of God (as it is altogether needful to do) but also separate or sever them. Or else they imagine a naked and idle permission or sufferance, or else make a double purpose of God. From these errors since they must fall into other endless and fond errors they are partly constrained to deny such things as wholly fall together, partly also they invent both foolish and many dark distinctions or differences, in which the farther they wade, the more do they entangle themselves so that they can never get out of these labyrinths or mazes. These therefore must be diligently taken heed of in this argument, because none other is more meet in the church of God to be purely and sincerely or incorruptly taught. Moreover, there should be no kinds of speaking, so far as may be (for, for teaching's sake, we may sometimes godly and religiously adventure some thing) used, which are strange to the Scriptures, and that such as come to hand in the word of God should be expounded with an apt interpretation lest some ignorant person take any occasion of offence.

Also there must be great regard had of the auditors or hearers, where in again we must make a difference between the crafty and the simple, between those who are willfully ignorant and them that are taken with simple ignorance such as is usual to man. For unto the one the Lord is want plainly to denounce or threaten the judgment of his Father, and the other we must lead little by little unto the knowledge of the truth. This also in this case must be looked unto that we have not so much regard of the weak, that while we have care of them we take no keep of others, of which wisdom we see notable examples in Paul, especially in the epistle to the Romans 9:10-11, 14-15.

Also, unless some very great reason let them, they should go up from the lowest degrees to that highest, as Paul does in the epistle to the Romans (which is the method or orderly manner of teaching of all divinity). He proceeds from the law to forgiveness of sins, and from there little by little to the highest degrees, so that they stay in that which shall be fittest in that place of Scripture, which they have taken in hand to handle, rather than to come down from the highest degree to the lowest. For the brightness of God's majesty suddenly offered is want mightily to strike the eyes, in so much that afterward they are dim in beholding other things unless they have been used a long season, and oftentimes, to behold that light.

Moreover, whether they go from the lowest upwards, or contrariwise come down from the highest, you must take heed that you run not out from one extreme to the other, passing over the middle, for example from purpose to salvation, and much more from salvation to purpose, also from purpose to damnation, or contrariwise, over-stepping the nearer causes of the judgment of God, unless perhaps you have to do with open despisers of God whom it avails not once to teach except that they may be stroked with the judgments of God that there can be no just suspicion of offence.

Furthermore, this doctrine must never be in such sort set forth that it is applied to any specific person, although some need to be comforted or rebuked more than others. Unless perhaps some prophet of God be admonished by some peculiar word from God, which notwithstanding is not rashly to be believed since it comes to pass out of order, or not ordinarily.

But in visiting the sick and in familiar admonitions, it seems to be the duty of the minister, so far as he may, to comfort the conscience of the troubled with the declaration of election. And contrariwise to strike those that are obstinately wicked and disobedient with the fearful judgment of God, but so that they keep some measure [of hope] and refrain from that last sentence unto which is added no condition. For this jurisdiction pertains to God alone.[37]

CH. 8: HOW EVERY PERSON MAY APPLY WITH SOME PROFIT THIS GENERAL DOCTRINE TO HIMSELF.

1st Aphorism
Those that teach that man's salvation is grounded upon works, either wholly or in any part, utterly overthrow the gospel of God. But they that teach free justification or being made righteous by faith, stay upon a sure foundation, but yet in such sort that they lay under faith the everlasting purpose of God, in which finally both Christ himself, and also the apostle following his steps, rests and stays. For when perseverance in faith is required to salvation, to what purpose do I have faith, if I be not certain of the gift of perseverance to the end? And yet there is no need to fear that this doctrine will make us negligent and dissolute or careless. For this peace of conscience of which we speak, greatly

---

37 *Proofs out of the word of God*: Matt. 28:18, 20; 2 Tim. 2:23, 15; Matt. 25; John 8:44; 9:41; 10:26; Luke 20:46-47; Matt. 23:38; 1 Cor. 3:2; Rom. 14:1; John 8:33-34; Phil. 3:2; 1 Tim. 6:3-4; Gal. 5:12; 2 Tim. 4:14; John 6:64; 8:24.

differs from foolish security or carelessness. He that is the son of God, since he is led by the Spirit of God, will never take occasion of slothfulness by the consideration of God's benefits.

Therefore if this doctrine brings but this one fruit, that by its aid we may learn to strengthen our faith against all things that happen, it is manifest that the chief ground of our salvation is overthrown by them, who because they measure God after the small measure of their brains, oppugn or reason against this article of religion.[38]

2nd Aphorism
Now this is the way to apply this doctrine. The works of God, even the very least of them, are such that a man cannot judge of them, but after two sorts. Either after they are past, or else by the disposition of the second causes, which by long use he has known to portend some certain end, such as comes to pass in things that fall out naturally, in which notwithstanding men are wonderfully dim-sighted.

Therefore in this point, that is of all others the hardest, it is no marvel though the judgment of man be driven into such a narrow strait, that he cannot but in this order understand what is determined of him in the secret counsel of God. And now because this whole judgment consists, or stands in the observation and marking of those causes, which exceed or pass all power of nature, we must flee somewhere else. Namely, we must flee to the sentence of God set forth in his word which, whereas it is infinite, points more certain than all man's conjectures or guesses. It no doubt brings us also a more certain judgment.

The scripture therefore bears witness that whoever God has predestinated or foreordained in his eternal purpose to adopt or choose unto sons through Jesus Christ in himself the same also at the time appointed are so effectually called, that they hear and embrace the voice of the caller. By which faith since they are made righteous and holy in Christ, they must also necessarily be glorified.

Will you therefore, whoever you are, be assured of your predestination or foreordaining, and so consequently of the salvation which you look for, against all the assaults of Satan? Will you be assured, I say, not with doubtful conjectures, and such as are gathered out of man's brain, that is, with such as are no less certain and sure, than if you had gone up into heaven itself, and understood that secret decree from the very mouth of God? Take diligent heed that you begin not at that highest degree, for else it will come to pass that you will not be able to abide the exceeding great brightness of God. Begin therefore

---

38 *Proofs out of the word of God*: Gal. 2:21; Rom. 11:6; John 6:44-45; Rom. 8:29-30; Rom. 9-11; 1 Cor. 2:10; Eph. 1:4-5; 2 Tim. 1:1, 9; 1 Pet. 1:2; Matt. 10:22; Luke 21:19; Rom. 2:7; John 6:37, 39; 10:28; Acts 13:48; Rom. 8:30, 39; 2 Tim. 2:19; 1 John 2:19; Rom. 5:1, 5; Matt. 5:2; Rom. 8:14.

at the lowest degrees, and when you hear the voice of God sounding in your ears and mind, which calls you to Christ the only mediator, consider little by little, and search diligently, whether you are justified and sanctified (that is, made righteous and holy by faith in Christ) for these are the effects by which faith – the true cause of them – indeed is known. And this you will know, partly by the Spirit of adoption crying within, "Abba, Father," partly also by the power and working of the same Spirit in yourself, namely, if you feel and also show that although sin dwells in you yet it does not reign in you. Why? Is not the Holy Ghost he who makes us not purposely let loose all the reigns unto ungodly and wicked lusts, as they used to do whose eyes the prince of this world has blinded? For who moves us unto prayer, albeit being never so cold? Who stirs up in us those unspeakable sighs and groanings? Who after we have sinned, and that sometimes wittingly and willingly, engenders in us that hatred of the sin that we have committed, yes, and that not for fear of punishment, but because we have offended our most merciful Father? Who, I say, bears us witness that our sighings are heard, and moves us that we dare boldly call God, our God, and also Father, even after we have offended him? Is it not, I pray you, that Spirit, whom we have freely received, being freely given for a sure pledge of our adoption? Now if we may gather faith by these effects, it remains that we were called and drawn effectually. And by this calling (which we have showed to be proper unto the sons of God) is that which we seek to thoroughly understand, namely, that we are therefore given unto the Son because in the everlasting counsel of God which he has purposed in himself, we were predestinated or foreordained to be adopted in his Son. From which finally ensues, since we were predestinated or foreordained by that most steadfast will of God which is grounded only upon itself, that no man can pluck us out of the hand of his Son and that continuance in faith is necessary unto salvation, that the expectation or hope of our continuance and so consequently of salvation is also certain, so that it is ungodliness any more to doubt it.

So far off therefore is it that this doctrine should make us slothful and careless, that contrarily this alone opens an entry to us to search the very depths of God by his Spirit. It also helps us to understand them, as the apostle plainly witnesses, that when we know them and we know them only but in part (so long as we live here) that we must fight daily against distrust with heavenly armor. And thus we may learn not to behave ourselves negligently but to continue stoutly to honor him, to love, fear, and call upon him, so that we may daily more and more, as touching us, as Peter says, "Make our calling and election sure." And moreover, how will he abide sure and steadfast against so many noisome temptations within and without, and against so many (as the world terms them) assaults of "fortune" who has not first assuredly grounded in his mind that which is most true, namely, that according to his good pleasure God does all things, whatever they be, and what instruments he uses, to the

The Treasure of Truth 277

profit of those that are his, among whose number he must be reckoned, even when he is set in this danger?[39]

3rd Aphorism
Now touching the other part, inasmuch as the purpose of electing or choosing cannot come into any man's mind but with the contrary of it, and that in like degree, this must run in his thought. In the mean season I say nothing of that which is manifest, namely, that these two are very often knit together in the word of God. It appears (I think) that they do great wrong unto the Spirit of God, who would have this part buried as being curious or not necessary. This therefore is also to be considered, but yet such moderation being used, that the depth of God's judgments may put a bit into man's curiosity; and in such a way finallythat it be not applied privately, either to any man or to any certain multitude. For in this point it also differs from election, that election, as we have shown before, is revealed or opened, to us by the Spirit of God, not in others, whose heart we cannot see, but in ourselves. And reprobation is always for the most part hidden from men, unless it be opened by God out of order or more than ordinarily. For who knows whether God has determined at the very last moment of his life to have mercy on him, who has spent all his life in wickedness and sin? And yet there is no cause why this hope should strengthen any man in his wickedness, when I speak of those things that we ought to observe and mark in others. And such examples of God's goodness are but rare or seldom, and no wise man will promise himself upon vain security that which is not in our hand. It is therefore sufficient that we know generally that there are certain vessels prepared to destruction. Since God has not shown us who they are, we ought diligently according to our power to call everyone to salvation, both with example of life and also with words, yes, even those of whom we are almost past hope when we behold their evil acts.[40]

4th Aphorism
If we keep this mean we also will receive much fruit by this doctrine. For first by the knowledge of it we shall learn willingly to yield our neck under the majesty of God that the more we shall fear and reverence him, the more we

---

39 *Proofs out of the word of God*: Rom. 8:29-30; Eph. 1:4-5, 9; John 10:27; Rom. 5:2; 8:38-39; 1 Cor. 2:10; 1 John 3:24; Ps. 95:7-8; John 10:27; 2 Cor. 13:5; Gal. 4:6; 1 John 3:24; 1 Cor. 2:10; Rom. 6; 1 John 3:9; Rom. 6:11-12; Eph. 4:29-30; Rom. 8:26; 7:24; 8:15-16, 27; Eph. 1:13-14; 4:30; 2 Cor. 1:22; Rom. 11:29; Heb. 6:17; 2 Tim. 2:19; Rom. 8:38-39; John 3:33; Rom. 4:20-21; 5:5; Heb. 4:16; 1 Cor. 1:9; 1 Thess. 5:24; Heb. 10:22-23; 1 Cor. 2:10-12; Rom. 8:16; 1 John 3:24; 1 Cor. 13:9; 1 Tim. 6:12; Gal. 5:17; Rom. 6:1; Heb. 10:23-24; Jam. 3:18; 2 Pet. 1:10; Rom. 8:28, 31; Job 13:15; Rom. 5:3; 1 Thess. 3:3; 1 Pet. 4:19; Jam. 1:2; Rom. 8:16, 38-39.
40 *Proofs out of the word of God*: Luke 23:43; Rom. 9:21; 2 Tim. 2:20; Matt. 5:16; 1 Cor. 9:22: 2 Tim. 2:25; 1 Pet. 2:12.

may labor to make sure in us the witness of our election in Christ. Secondly, when we shall diligently consider the difference of God's mercy made between men otherwise subject to the like curse, it cannot be decided but that we must more willingly acknowledge and embrace that singular goodness of God than if we should make his grace common unto all men or should seek the cause of this inequality of grace in men only. Furthermore, when we know this gift of faith to be special – that is, such as is not given generally to all, but particularly to some – shall we not take it more cheerfully when it is offered? And shall we not be much more careful for the increase of it than if with many we should surmise it to be in all men's power as often as they will repent, because God, as they say, will have all men saved and wills not the death of a sinner? Finally, when we see the doctrine of the gospel not only to be despised almost by the whole world, but also to be most cruelly persecuted, when we behold the notable treachery and falling away of so many men, what will better strengthen us than if we make our sure reckoning that nothing comes to pass at all adventures? Or that God knows those who are his, and that those who do these things, unless it is given them to repent, are they who are ordained, not by chance but by the assured and everlasting counsel of God, in whom as in looking glasses the just wrath and power of God should appear?[41]

5th Aphorism
Yet a man can never speak so fitly of these things, but that man's reason will prattle against it, yes, and also will call the Lord himself as the chief author of all to account for it. But albeit the devil chase and all the wicked kick against the prick, yet their own conscience shall reprove them and condemn them. But our mind being strengthened with the mercy of God shall acquire us in that day of Christ, to whom with the Father and the Holy Ghost, be given glory, praise, and honor forever. Amen.[42]

---

41 *Proofs out of the word of God*: Phil. 2:12; 1 Pet. 1:17; Rom. 11:20; 9:23.
42 *Proofs out of the word of God*: Rom. 2:15; 1 Pet. 3:21.

Bibliography

Primary Sources

Ames, William. *An Exhortation to the Students of Theology.* Translated by Douglas Horton. N.p., 1958.
— *The Marrow of Theology.* Translated and edited by John Dykstra Eusden. Boston: Pilgrim, 1968. Reprint, Grand Rapids: Baker, 1997.
— *The substance of Christian religion: or, A plain and easie Draught of the Christian Catechisme, in LII. Lectures.* London: T. Mabb, 1659.
Ample Discours des Actes de Poissy. Contenant le commencement de l'assemblee, l'entree et issue du Colloque des Prelats de France, et Ministres de l'Evangile: l'ordre y gardé: Ensemble la Harangue du Roi Charles IX. Avec les sommaires, poincts des oraisons de Monsieur le Chancelier, Theodore de Besze, et du Cardinal de Lorraine. N.p., 1561.
Arminius, Jacob. *The Works of James Arminius.* 3 vols. Translated by James Nichols and William Nichols. London: 1825, 1828, 1875. Reprint, Grand Rapids: Baker, 1986.
Baduel, Claude. "Concerning the College and University of Nîmes." Translated by Theodore Casteel. In *Transition and Revolution: Problems and Issues of European Renaissance and Reformation* History, ed. Robert M. Kingdon, 179-82. Minneapolis: Burgess, 1974.
Beardslee, John W., ed. and trans. *Reformed Dogmatics.* A Library of Protestant Thought. New York: Oxford University Press, 1965.
Beza, Theodore. *Abraham Sacrifiant.* Edited by Keith Cameron, Kathleen M. Hall, and Francis Higman. Textes Litteraires Français. Geneva: Librairie Droz, 1967.
— *Ad acta Colloquii Montisbelgardensis, Tubingae edita.* Geneva: Jean le Preux, 1587-1588.
— *Ad Gilberti Genebrardi accusationem.* Geneva: n.p., 1585.
— *Apologia pro Justificatione per Unius Christi viva fide apprehensi Iustitiam gratis imputatam. Adversus Anonymi scriptoris tractatum, clam nuper ab Antonio quodam Lescalio editum et publice postea impudentissime sparsum.* Geneva: Joannes le Preux, 1592.
— "Beza's Address at the Solemn Opening at the Academy of Geneva." Translated by Lewis W. Spitz. In *Transition and Revolution: Problems and Issues of European Renaissance and Reformation History*, ed. Robert M. Kingdon, 175-79. Minneapolis: Burgess, 1974.
— "Beza's Treatise '*De triplici episcopatu.*'" Translated by W. Nijenhuis. In *Ecclesia Reformata: Studies on the Reformation*, 130-87. Kerkhistorische Bijdragen 3. Leiden: E. J. Brill, 1972.
— *A Booke of Christian Questions and Answers. Wherein are set forth the cheef points of the Christian religion in manner of an abridgement.* Translated by Arthur Golding. London: William How, 1578.
— *A Briefe and Pithie Summe of Christian Faith, Made in Form of a Confession, with a*

Confutation of al Such Superstitious Errors, as are Contrairy Thereunto. London: Roger Ward, 1589.

— *A Briefe Declaration of the Chiefe Poyntes of Christian Religion, Set Forth in a Table*. London: n.p., 1575.

— *Chrestiennes Méditations*. Edited by Mario Richter. Textes Littéraires Français. Geneva: Librairie Droz, 1964.

— *The Christian Faith*. Translated by James Clark. Lewes: Focus Christian Ministries, 1992.

— *Christian Meditations upon Eight Psalmes of the Prophet David*. London: Christopher Barker, 1582.

— *Concerning the Rights of Rulers Over Their Subjects and the Duty of Subjects Towards Their Rulers*. Edited by A. H. Murray. Translated by Henri-Louis Gonin. Cape Town: H. A. U. M., 1956.

— *Confessio Christianae fidei, et eiusdem collatio cum Papisticis Haeresibus. Adjecta est altera brevis eiusdem Bezae fidei Confessio*. London: Thomas Vautroller, 1575.

— "La Confession de Foi du Chretien par Theodore de Beza." Edited by Michel Réveillaud. *La Revue Réformée* 6 (1955): 1-180.

— *Confession de la foi Chrestienne, faite par Theodore de Besze, contenant la confirmation, d'icelle, et la refutation des superstitions contraires: Reveue et augmentee de nouveau par lui, avec un abregé d'icille*. N.p.: Conrad Badius, 1559.

— *Correspondance de Théodore de Bèze*. 21 vols. Edited by H. Aubert, A. Dufour, F. Aubert, H. Meylan, and C. Chimelli. Geneva: Librairie Droz, 1960-1999.

— *Cours sur les Épîtres aux Romains et aux Hébreux 1564-66, d'après les Notes de Marcus Widler: Thèses disputées à l'Académie de Genève, 1564-67*. Edited by Pierre Fraenkel and Luc Perrotet. Travaux d'Humanisme et Renaissance 226. Geneva: Librairie Droz, 1988.

— "Dedication" In *John Calvin's Commentaries on the Prophet Ezekiel*. Vol. 1. Translated by Thomas Myers, xxxvii-xlv. Edinburgh: Calvin Translation Society, 1849.

— *De Peste Quaestiones duae Explicatae: una sitne contagiosa: Altera, an et quatenus sit Christianis per secessionem vitanda*. Geneva: Eustathius Vignon, 1580.

— *Discours du Recteur Th. de Bèze prononcé à l'inauguration de l'Académie dans le Temple de Saint-Pierre à Genève le 5 juin 1559*. Translated by H. Delarue. Geneva: Société du Musée historique de la Réformation, 1959.

— *A Discourse, of the true and visible Markes of the Catholique Churche*. London: Robert Waldegrave, 1582.

— *Du droit des Magistrats*. Edited by Robert M. Kingdon. Geneva: Librairie Droz, 1970.

— *Ecclesiastes, or the Preacher. Solomons Sermon Made to the people, teaching every man howe to order his life, so as they may come to true and everlasting happines. With a Paraphrase, or short exposition thereof, made by Theodore Beza*. Cambridge: John Legatt, n.d.

— *Epistolae, quas Theodorus Beza ad Wilhelmum IV. Hassiae Landgravium Misit*. Edited by Heinrich Heppe. Marburg: C. L. Pfeilii, 1860.

— *Epistolarum Theologicarum Theodori Bezae Vezelli, Liber Unus*. Geneva: Eustathius Vignon, 1573.

— "Epistre." In *La Bible, qui est toute la Saincte Escriture du Vieil & du Nouveau Testament: autrement L'Anciene & la Nouvelle Alliance. Le tout reveu & conferé sur les textes Hebrieux & Grecs par les Pasteurs & Professeurs de l'Eglise de Geneve.* Geneva: n.p., 1588.

— *An evident Display of Popish Practices, or patched Pelagianisme. Wherein is mightelie cleared the soveraigne truth of Gods eternall Predestination, the stayd groundworke of oure most assured safetie by Christ.* London: Ralph Newberie and Henry Bynnyman, 1578.

— *An Excellent Treatise of Comforting Such, as are Troubled about Their Predestination. Taken Out of the Second Answer of M. Beza, to D. Andreas, in the Acte of Their Colloquie at Mompelgart.* In *A Golden Chaine, or, The Description of Theologie . . . by that man of God, Mr. William Perkins.* Translated by Robert Hill, 563-75. London: John Legatt, 1621.

— *An Exhortation to the Reformation of the Church.* In *A Confession of Faith Made By Common Consent of Divers Reformed Churches Beyond the Seas.* London: Henry Bynneman, n.d.

— *Histoire ecclésiastiques des églises réformées au royaume de France.* 3 vols. Edited by G. Baum and E. Cunitz. Paris: 1883-1889. Reprint, Nieuwkoop: B. de Graaf, 1974.

— *Icones.* N.p.: 1580. Reprint, Menston: Scolar, 1971.

— *Jesu Christi D. N. Novum testamentum, sive Novum foedus.* Geneva: Henricus Stephanus, 1565.

— *Jesu Christi Domini Nostri Novum Testamentum, sive Novum Foedus, cuius Graeco contextui respondent interpretationes duae: una, vetus; altera, Theodori Bezae. Eiusdem Theod. Bezae Annotationes, in quibus ratione interpretationis vocum reddita.* Cambridge: Roger Daniel, 1642.

— *Job Expounded by Theodore Beza, Partly in Manner of a Commentary, Partly in Manner of a Paraphrase.* Cambridge: John Legate, 1589.

— *Jobus, Theodore Bezae partim Commentariis partim Paraphrasi illustratus.* London: George Bishop, 1589.

— *The Judgement of a Most Reverend and Learned Man from Beyond the Seas, Concerning a Threefold Order of Bishops, with a Declaration of Certaine other Waightie Points, Concerning the Discipline and Government of the Church.* N.p., 1580.

— *Lex Dei: moralis, ceremonialis, et politica, ex libris Mosis excerpta, et in certas classes distributa.* Geneva: Petrum Santandreanum, 1577.

— *The Life of John Calvin.* In *Selected Works of John Calvin: Tracts and Letters.* Vol. 1. Edited and translated by Henry Beveridge, xvii-c. Edinburgh: Calvin Translation Society, 1844. Reprint, Grand Rapids: Baker, 1983.

— *A Little Book of Christian Questions and Responses, In which the Principal Headings of the Christian Religion are Briefly Set Forth.* Translated by Kirk M. Summers. Allison Park, PA: Pickwick, 1986.

— *A Little Catechisme, That is to Say, A Short Instruction Touching Christian Religion.* London: Hugh Singleton, 1579.

— *Maister Bezaes Houshold Prayers.* Translated by John Barnes. London: John Barnes, 1603.

— *Master Bezaes Sermons Upon the Three First Chapters of the Canticle of Canticles.* Translated by John Harmar. Oxford: Joseph Barnes, 1587.

— *The Newe Testament of Our Lord Iesus Christ, translated out of Greeke by Theod. Beza. Whereunto are Adioned Briefe Summaries of Doctrine upon the Evangelists* and *Actes of the Apostles, together with the methode of the Epistles of the Apostles, by the said Theod. Beza. And also Short Expositions on the Phrases and Hard Places, taken out of the large Annotations of the foresaid Author and Ioach. Camerarius, by P. Loseler, Villerius*. Translated by L. Tomson. London: Robert Barker, 1601.

— *An Oration made by Master Theodore de Beze . . . September, 1561, in the Noonnery of Poissy*. London: Richarde Jugge, n.d.

— *The Other Parte of Christian Questions and Answeares, Which is Concerning the Sacraments*. Translated by John Field. London: Thomas Woodcocke, 1580.

— *The Popes Canons: wherein the Venerable and great Masters of Sorbone are confuted in these x. discourses following, with divers other matters*. Translated by T. S. G. London: John Perin, n.d.

— *The Potter and the Clay: The Main Predestination Writings of Theodore Beza*. Translated by Philip C. Holtrop. Grand Rapids: Calvin College, 1982.

— *The Psalmes of David, truly opened and explaned by Paraphrasis, according to the right sense of everie Psalme. With large and ample Arguments before everie Psalme, declaring the true use thereof*. Translated by Anthonie Gilbie. London: Henrie Denham, 1581.

— *Psalmorum Davidis et Aliorum Prophetarum, Libri Quinque*. London: Thomas Vautroller, 1580.

— *Ratio studii theologici*. In Olivier Fatio, *Méthode et Théologie: Lambert Daneau et les débuts de la scolastique réformée*. Travaux d'Humanisme et Renaissance 147, 119-21. Geneva: Librairie Droz, 1976.

— *Response a la confession du feu Duc Jean de Northumbelande, n'agueres decapité en Angleterre*. Edited by A.-H. Chaubard. Lyon: Presses Académique, 1959.

— *Response aux cinq premieres et principales demandes de F. Jean Hay*. Geneva: Jean le Preux, 1586.

— *Response de Theodore de Beze Pour la Justification par l'imputation gratuite de la Justice de Jesus Christ apprehendé par la suele foi*. Geneva: n.p., 1592.

— *The Second Oration of Master Theodore de Beze, Minister of the holy Gospel, made and pronounced at Poissy*. London: Jhon Tysdale, n.d.

— *Sermons sur l'Histoire de la Passion et Sepulture de nostre Seigneur Jesus Christ, descrite par les quatre Evangelistes*. Geneva: Jean le Preux, 1592.

— *Sermons sur l'Histoire de la Resurrection de nostre Seigneur Jesus Christ*. Geneva: Jean le Preux, 1593.

— *Sermons sur les trois premiers chapitres du Cantique des Cantiques de Salomon*. Geneva: Jean le Preux, 1586.

— *A Shorte Learned and Pithie Treatize of the Plague*. Translated by John Stockwood. London: Thomas Dawson, 1580.

— *Sommaire, recueil des signes sacrez, sacrifices, et sacremens instituez de Dieu, depuis la Creation du monde*. Geneva: n.p., 1561.

— *Tractationum Theologicarum, in quibus plerasque Christianae Religionis dogmata adversus haereses nostris temporibus renovatas solide ex Verbo Dei defenduntur*. 3 vols. Geneva: Vignon, 1582.

— *Tractatus Pius et Moderatus de Vera Excommunicatione et Christiano Presbyterio*. London: John Norton, 1590.

— *A Tragedie of Abrahams Sacrifice*. Edited by Malcolm W. Wallace. Translated by Arthur Golding. Toronto: University of Toronto Library, 1906.

— *Traicte des Vraies essencielles et visibles margues de la vraie Eglise Catholique*. La Rochelle: Hierosme Haultin, 1592.
— *The Treasure of Truth, Touching the Grounde Worke of Man his Salvation, and Chiefest Pointes of Christian Religion: With a Briefe Summe of the Comfortable Doctrine of God His Providence, Comprised in 38 Short Aphorismes*. Translated by John Stockwood. London: Thomas Woodcocke, 1581.
— *Two very lerned Sermons of M. Beza, togither with a short sum of the sacrament of the Lordes Supper*. Translated by T[homas] W[ilcocks]. London: Robert Waldegrave, 1588.
Beza, Theodore, and Antoine de La Faye. *Propositions and Principles of Divinitie Propounded and Disputed in the Universities of Geneva, by Certaine Students of Divinitie there, under M. Theod. Beza, M. Anthonie Faius, Professors of Divinitie. Wherein is Contained a Methodicall Summarie, or Epitome of the Common Places of Divinitie*. Edinburgh: Robert Waldegrave, 1591.
— *Theses Theologicae in Schola Genevensi ab aliquot Sacrarum literarum studiosis sub DD. Theod. Beza et Antonio Fayo S. S. Theologiae professoribus propositae et disputatae. In Quibus Methodicalocorum communium S. S. Theologiae epitome continetur*. Geneva: Eustathius Vignon, 1586.
Beza, Theodore, and Clémont Marot. *Pseaumes Octantetrois de David, mis en rime Francoise par Clémont Marot et Théodore de Bèze and La Forme des Prières Ecclésiastiques et Catéchisme par Jean Calvin*. New Brunswick, NJ: Friends of the Rutgers University Libraries, 1973.
Bolsec, Jérôme. *Histoire de la vie, moeurs, doctrine et débordements de T. de Bèze*. Paris: n.p., 1582.
Bucanus, Guilielmus. *Institutions of the Christian Religion, framed out of God's Word*. Translated by Robert Hall. London: n.p., 1606.
Bullinger, Heinrich. *Commonplaces of the Christian Religion compendiously written*. Translated by John Stockwood. London: Thomas East and H. Middleton, 1572.
— *The Decades of Henry Bullinger*. 5 vols. Edited by Thomas Harding. Translated by H. I. Cambridge: Cambridge University Press, 1849-1851.
Calvin, John. *The Bondage and Liberation of the Will: A Defence of the Orthodox Doctrine of Human Choice against Pighius*. Edited by A. N. S. Lane. Translated by G. I. Davies. Texts and Studies in Reformation and Post-Reformation Thought. Grand Rapids: Baker, 1996.
— *Calvin: Institutes of the Christian Religion*. 2 vols. Edited by John T. McNeill. Translated by Ford Lewis Battles. Library of Christian Classics, vols. 20-21. Philadelphia: Westminster, 1960.
— *Calvin's Commentaries*. Edited by David W. Torrance and Thomas F. Torrance. 12 vols. Grand Rapids: Eerdmans, 1959-1970.
— *Concerning the Eternal Predestination of God*. Translated by J. K. S. Reid. London: James Clarke & Co., 1961.
— *Ioannis Calvini Opera quae supersunt omnia*. Edited by Whilhelm Baum, Eduard Cunitz, and Eduard Reuss. 59 vols. in 58. Corpus Reformatorum, vols. 29-87. Brunswick, NJ: C. A. Schwetschke and Son, 1863-1900. Reprint, New York: Johnston Reprint Corp., 1964.
— *Joannis Calvini Opera Selecta*. Edited by P. Barth, W. Niesel, and D. Scheuner. 5 vols. Munich: Chr. Kaiser, 1926-1962.
— *Selected Works of John Calvin: Tracts and Letters*. 7 vols. Edited by Henry

Beveridge and Jules Bonnet. N.p., 1858. Reprint, Grand Rapids: Baker, 1983.
— *Sermons of Maister John Calvin, upon the Booke of Job.* Translated by Arthur Golding. London: N.p., 1574. Reprint, Carlisle, PA: Banner of Truth, 1993.
— *Sermons on Election and Reprobation.* Translated by John Fielde. London: n.p., 1579. Reprint, Audobon, NJ: Old Paths, 1996.
Cicero. *De Oratore.* 2 vols. Translated by E. W. Sutton and H. Rackham. Loeb Classical Library. Cambridge, MA: Harvard University Press, 1959.
Cochrane, A. C., ed. *Reformed Confessions of the 16th Century.* Philadelphia: Westminster, 1960.
C[unningham], A. *An Essay Concerning Church Government, Out of the Excellent Writings of Calvin and Beza.* N.p., 1689.
Daneau, Lambert. *Christianae isogoges ad Christianorum theologorum locos communes.* Geneva: Vignon, 1583.
Duke, Alastair, Gillian Lewis, and Andrew Pettegree, eds. and trans. *Calvinism in Europe 1540-1610: A Collection of Documents.* Manchester: Manchester University Press, 1992.
Franklin, Julian H., ed. and trans. *Constitutionalism and Resistance in the Sixteenth Century: Three Treatises by Hotman, Beza, & Mornay.* New York: Pegasus, 1969.
The Geneva Bible: The Annotated New Testament, 1602 Edition. Edited by Gerald T. Sheppard. Cleveland: Pilgrim, 1989.
Hay, John. "Hay's *Demandes* (1580)." In *Catholic Tractates of the Sixteenth Century 1573-1600,* ed. Thomas Graves Law, 31-70. Edinburgh: William Blackwood and Sons, 1901.
Heppe, Heinrich. *Reformed Dogmatics: Set Out and Illustrated from the Sources.* Translated by G. T. Thomson. Revised and edited by Ernst Bizer. London: George Allen & Unwin, 1950.
Holtrop, Philip C., ed. *The Bolsec Controversy: Translations of Letters and Short Documents From 1551 to 1555.* Grand Rapids: Calvin College, 1984.
Hughes, Philip Edgcumbe, ed. and trans. *The Register of the Company of Pastors of Geneva in the Time of Calvin.* Grand Rapids: Eerdmans, 1966.
La Faye, Antoine de. *De Vita et Obitu Clarissviri, D. Theodori Bezae Vezelii, Ecclesiastae & Sacrarum literarum Professoris, Genevae.* Geneva: Jacob Chovet, n.d.
Martyr, Peter. *The Common Places of the Most Famous and Renowned Divine Doctor Peter Martyr, Divided into Four Principal Parts: with a Large Addition of Many Theological and Necessary Discourses, Some Never Extant Before.* Translated by Anthonie Marten. London: n.p., 1583.
Melanchthon, Philip. "On Improving the Studies of Youth." Translated by Lewis W. Spitz. In *Transition and Revolution,* ed. Robert N. Kingdon, 167-71. Minneapolis: Burgess, 1974.
Musculus, Wolfgang. *Common places of Christian Religion.* London: Henry Bynneman, 1563.
Olevianus, Caspar. *A Firm Foundation: An Aid to Interpreting the Heidelberg Catechism.* Translated and edited by Lyle D. Bierma. Texts and Studies in Reformation and Post-Reformation Thought. Grand Rapids: Baker, 1995.
— *In Epistolam d. Pauli Apostoli ad Romanos notae, ex Gasparis Oleviani concionibus excerptae, à Theodoro Beza editae: cum praefatione eiusdem Bezae.* Geneva: Eustathius Vignon, 1584.

Perkins, William. *The Work of William Perkins.* Edited by Ian Breward. Courtenay Library of Christian Classics 3. Abingdon: Sutton Courtenay, 1970.
Piscator, Johannes. *Aphorismes of the Christian Religion.* London: Robert Dexter, 1596.
Polanus, Amandus. *The Substance of Christian Religion.* Translated by Thomas Wilcox. London: John Oxenbridge, 1595.
Ramus, Peter. *Arguments in Rhetoric Against Quintilian: Translation and Text of Peter Ramus's* Rhetoricae Distinctiones in Quintilianum (1549). Translated by Carole Newlands. Dekalb, IL: Northern Illinois University Press, 1986.
— *The Logike of the Moste Excellent Philosopher P. Ramus Martyr.* London: n.p., 1574. Reprint, Leeds: Scolar, 1966.
Registres de la Compagnie des Pasteurs de Genève au temps de Calvin. 8 vols. Edited by Jean-François Bergier, Olivier Fatio, Robert M. Kingdon, et al. Geneva: Librairie Droz, 1969-1986.
Salnar. *An Harmony of the Confessions of the Faith of the Christian and Reformed Churches.* London: John Legatt, 1643.
— *The Harmony of Protestant Confessions: Exhibiting the Faith of the Churches of Christ, Reformed after the Pure and Holy Doctrine of the Gospel, Throughout Europe.* Translated and edited by Peter Hall. London: John F. Shaw, 1842.
Schaff, Philip. *The Creeds of Christendom: With a History and Critical Notes.* 3 vols. 6th ed. N.p.: Harper and Row, 1931. Reprint, Grand Rapids: Baker, 1990.
Sturm, Johann. *Johann Sturm on Education: The Reformation and Humanist Learning.* Edited and translated by Lewis W. Spitz and Barbara Sher Tinsley. St. Louis: Concordia, 1995.
Synodicon in Gallia Reformata: or, the Acts, Decisions, Decrees, and Canons Of those Famous National Councils of the Reformed Churches in France. 2 vols. Translated by John Quick. London: T. Parkhurst and J. Robinson, 1692.
Turretin, Francis. *Institutes of Elenctic Theology.* 3 vols. Translated by George Musgrave Giger. Edited by James T. Dennison. Phillipsburg, NJ: Presbyterian and Reformed, 1992-1997.
Zanchius, Hieronymus. *The Doctrine of Absolute Predestination Stated and Asserted.* Translated by A. Toplady. Wilmington: Adam's, 1793. Reprint, Grand Rapids: Sovereign Grace, 1971.
The Zurich Letters, (second series) Comprising the Correspondence of Several English Bishops and Others with some of the Helvetian Reformers, During the Reign of Queen Elizabeth. Translated by Hastings Robinson. Cambridge: Cambridge University Press, 1845.

Secondary Sources

Books

Althaus, Paul. *Die Prinzipien der deutschen reformierten Dogmatik im Zeitalter der aristotelischen Scholastik.* Leipzig: n.p., 1914.
Anderson, Marvin W. *The Battle for the Gospel: The Bible and the Reformation, 1444-1600.* Lexington, MA: Ginn, 1987.
Armstrong, Brian G. *Calvinism and the Amyraut Heresy: Protestant Scholasticism and Humanism in Seventeenth-Century France.* Madison: University of Wisconsin Press, 1969.

Asselt, Willem J. van, and Eef Dekker, eds. *Reformation and Scholasticism: An Ecumenical Enterprise*. Grand Rapids: Baker, forthcoming.

Backus, Irena Doruta. *The Reformed Roots of the English New Testament: The Influence of Theodore Beza on the English New Testament*. Pittsburgh Theological Monograph Series 28. Pittsburgh: Pickwick, 1980.

—— *Les Sept Visions et la Fin des Temps: les Commentaires Genevois de l'Apocalypse entre 1539 et 1584*. Cahiers de la Revue de Théologie et de Philosophie 19. Lausanne: Revue de Théologie et de Philosophie, 1997.

Baird, Henry Martyn. *Theodore Beza: The Counsellor of the French Reformation, 1519-1605*. N.p., 1899. Reprint, New York: Burt Franklin, 1970.

Bangert, William. *A History of the Society of Jesus*. St. Louis: Institute of Jesuit Sources, 1972.

Bangs, Carl. *Arminius: A Study in the Dutch Reformation*. Grand Rapids: Zondervan, 1985.

Barth, Karl. *Church Dogmatics*. Edited by G. W. Bromiley and T. F. Torrance. 4 vols. in 14 parts. Edinburgh: T. & T. Clark, 1956-1975.

Baum, Johann Wilhelm. *Theodor Beza nach handschriftlichen Quellen dargestellt*. 2 vols. Leipzig: Weidmann'sche Buchhandlung, 1843-1851.

Beeke, Joel R. *Assurance of Faith: Calvin, English Puritanism, and the Dutch Second Reformation*. American University Studies Series 7, Theology and Religion, vol. 89. New York: Peter Lang, 1991.

—— *The Quest for Full Assurance: The Legacy of Calvin and His Successors*. Carlisle, PA: Banner of Truth, 1999.

Benoit, Jean-Daniel. *Calvin in His Letters: A Study of Calvin's Pastoral Counselling, Mainly from His Letters*. Translated by Richard Haig. Courtenay Studies in Reformation Theology 5. Abingdon: Sutton Courtenay, 1991.

Bernus, Auguste. *Théodore de Bèze à Lausanne*. Lausanne: Georges Bridel, 1900.

Biel, Pamela. *Doorkeepers at the House of Righteousness: Heinrich Bullinger and the Zurich Clergy 1535-1575*. Zürcher Beiträge zur Reformationsgeschichte 15. Bern: Peter Lang, 1991.

Bierma, Lyle D. *German Calvinism in the Confessional Age: The Covenant Theology of Caspar Olevianus*. Grand Rapids: Baker, 1996.

Bietenholz, Peter G. *Basle and France in the Sixteenth Century*. Geneva: Libraire Droz, 1971.

Bizer, Ernst. *Frühorthodoxie und Rationalismus*. Theologische Studien 71. Zurich: EVZ-Verlag, 1963.

Bonjour, E., H. S. Offler, and G. R. Potter. *A Short History of Switzerland*. Oxford: Oxford University Press, 1952.

Borgeaud, Charles. *Histoire de l'Université de Genève: L'Académie de Calvin 1559-1798*. Vol. 1. Geneva: Georg, 1900.

Bouvier, Nicholas, Gordon A. Craig, and Lionel Gossman. *Geneva, Zürich, Basel: History, Culture, and National Identity*. Princeton: Princeton University Press, 1994.

Bouwsma, William J. *John Calvin: A Sixteenth Century Portrait*. New York: Oxford University Press, 1988.

Brady, Thomas A. Jr., Heiko A. Oberman, and James D. Tracy, eds. *Handbook of European History, 1400-1600*. 2 vols. Leiden: E. J. Brill, 1995. Reprint, Grand Rapids: Eerdmans, 1996.

Bray, John S. *Theodore Beza's Doctrine of Predestination*. Bibliotheca Humanistica and

Reformatorica 12. Nieuwkoop: B. De Graaf, 1975.
Bromiley, Geoffrey W. *Historical Theology: An Introduction*. Grand Rapids: Eerdmans, 1978.
Cameron, Euan. *The European Reformation*. Oxford: Oxford University Press, 1991.
Choisy, Eugene. *L'État Chrétien Calviniste a Genève au temps de Théodore de Bèze*. Geneva: Ch. Eggimann, n.d.
Clark, Gordon H. *Thales to Dewey: A History of Philosophy*. Boston: Houghton Mifflin, 1957.
Clavier, H. *Théodore de Bèze: Un aperçu de sa vie aventureuse, de ses travaux, de sa personnalité*. Cahors: A. Coueslant, 1960.
Conley, Thomas M. *Rhetoric in the European Tradition*. New York: Longman, 1990.
Copleston, Frederick. *A History of Philosophy*. 9 vols. Westminster, MD: Newman Press, 1950.
Cross, F. L., and E. A. Livingstone, eds. *The Oxford Dictionary of the Christian Church*. 3rd ed. Oxford: Oxford University Press, 1997.
Cunliffe-Jones, Hubert, and Benjamin Drewery, eds. *A History of Christian Doctrine*. Philadelphia: Fortress, 1978.
Dever, Mark E. *Richard Sibbes: Puritanism and Calvinism in Late Elizabethan and Early Stuart England*. Macon, GA: Mercer University Press, 2000.
Dickens, A. G. *The English Reformation*. 2nd ed. University Park, PA: Pennsylvania State University Press, 1989.
Donnelly, John Patrick. *Calvinism and Scholasticism in Vermigli's Doctrine of Man and Grace*. Leiden: E. J. Brill, 1976.
Doumergue, Emile. *Calvin, le predicateur de Geneve*. Geneva: Atar, n.d.
— *Jean Calvin: les hommes et les choses de son temps*. 7 vols. Lausanne: n.p., 1899-1917.
Dowey, Edward A. Jr. *The Knowledge of God in Calvin's Theology*. New York: Columbia University Press: 1952; enl. ed., Grand Rapids: Eerdmans, 1994.
Dückert, Armand. *Théodore de Bèze: Prédicateur*. Geneva: n.p., 1891.
Duffield, Gervase E., ed. *John Calvin*. Courtenay Studies in Reformation Theology 1. Appleford: Sutton Courtenay, 1966.
Edwards, Paul, ed. *The Encyclopedia of Philosophy*. 8 vols. New York: Macmillan and The Free Press, 1967.
Fatio, Olivier. *Méthode et Théologie: Lambert Daneau et les débuts de la scolastique réformée*. Travaux d'Humanisme et Renaissance 147. Geneva: Librairie Droz, 1976.
Fisher, George Park. *History of Christian Doctrine*. 2nd ed. The International Theological Library 4. Edinburgh: T. & T. Clark, 1908.
Fraenkel, Pierre. *De L'Écriture à la Dispute: le cas de l'Académie de Genève sous Théodore de Bèze*. Cahiers de la Revue de Théologie et de Philosophie 1. Lausanne: Revue de Théologie et de Philosophie, 1977.
Ganoczy, Alexandre. *La Bibliothèque de l'Académie de Calvin: Le Catalogue de 1572 et ses Enseignements*. Études de Philologie et d'Histoire 13. Geneva: Librairie Droz, 1969.
— *The Young Calvin*. Translated by David Foxgrover and Wade Provo. Philadelphia: Westminster, 1987.
Gardy, Frédéric. *Bibliographie des Oeuvres Théologiques, Littéraires, Historiques et Juridiques de Théodore de Bèze*. Geneva: Librairie Droz, 1960.
Geisendorf, Paul-F. *Théodore de Bèze*. Geneva: Alexandre Jullien, 1967.

_____, ed. *Livre des habitants de Genève.* 2 vols. Geneva: Droz, 1957, 1963.
George, Timothy. *Theology of the Reformers.* Nashville: Broadman, 1988.
Graham, W. Fred, ed. *Later Calvinism: International Perspectives.* Sixteenth Century Essays and Studies, vol. 22. Kirkville, MO: Sixteenth Century Journal, 1994.
Greengrass, Mark. *The French Reformation.* Historical Association Studies. Oxford: Basil Blackwell, 1987.
Greenslade, S. L., ed. *The Cambridge History of the Bible.* Vol. 3, *The West from the Reformation to the Present Day.* Cambridge: The University Press, 1963.
Grimm, Harold J. *The Reformation Era, 1500-1650.* London: Collier-Macmillan, 1965.
Hagen, Kenneth. *Hebrews Commenting from Erasmus to Bèze 1516-1598.* Beiträge zur Geschichte der Biblischen Exegese 23. Tübingen: J. C. B. Mohr, 1981.
Hamon, Léo, ed. *Un siècle et demi d'histoire protestante: Théodore de Bèze et les protestants sujets du roi.* Paris: Éditions de la Maison des Sciences de l'Homme, 1989.
Harbison, E. Harris. *The Christian Scholar in the Age of the Reformation.* New York: Charles Scribner's Sons, 1956. Reprint, Grand Rapids: Eerdmans, 1983.
Hart, Trevor A. *The Dictionary of Historical Theology.* Grand Rapids: Eerdmans, 2000.
Helleman, Wendy E., ed. *Christianity and the Classics: The Acceptance of a Heritage.* Lanham, MD: University Press of America, 1990.
Helm, Paul. *Calvin and the Calvinists.* Carlisle, PA: Banner of Truth, 1982.
Heppe, Heinrich. *Theodor Beza: Leben und ausgewahlte Schriften.* Elberfeld: R. L. Friedrichs, 1861.
Heyer, Henri. *Catalogue des Thèses de théologie soutenues à l'Academie de Genève pendant les XVIe, XVIIe et XVIIIe siècles.* Geneva: Georg, 1898.
— *L'Eglise de Genève.* Geneva: Jullien, 1909.
Hillerbrand, Hans J., ed. *The Oxford Encyclopedia of the Reformation.* 4 vols. Oxford: Oxford University Press, 1996.
Hirsch, E. D., Jr. *Validity in Interpretation.* New Haven: Yale University Press, 1967.
Holt, Mack P. *The French Wars of Religion, 1562-1629.* New Approaches to European History. Cambridge: Cambridge University Press, 1995.
Holtrop, Philip C. *The Bolsec Controversy on Predestination, from 1551 to 1555.* 2 vols. Lewiston, NY: Edwin Mellen, 1993.
Huizinga, Johan. *Erasmus and the Age of the Reformation.* Translated by F. Hopman. N.p., 1924. Reprint, Princeton: Princeton University Press, 1984.
James, Frank A. *Peter Martyr Vermigli and Predestination: The Augustinian Inheritance of an Italian Reformer.* Oxford Theological Monographs. Oxford: Clarendon, 1998.
Kendall, R. T. *Calvin and English Calvinism to 1649.* New York: Oxford University Press, 1979. Reprint, Carlisle: Paternoster, 1997.
Kickel, Walter. *Vernuft und Offenbarung bei Theodor Beza: Zum Problem des Verhältnisses von Theologie, Philosophie und Staat.* Beiträge zur geschichte und lehre der Reformierten Kirche, no. 25. Neukirchen-Vluyn: Neukirchener Verlag des Erziehungsvereins, 1967.
Kingdon, Robert M. *Adultery and Divorce in Calvin's Geneva.* Harvard Historical Studies 118. Cambridge, MA: Harvard University Press, 1995.
— *Geneva and the Coming of the Wars of Religion in France 1555-1563.* Travaux d'Humanisme et Renaissance 22. Geneva: Librairie E. Droz, 1956.
— *Geneva and the Consolidation of the French Protestant Movement 1564-1572: A*

Contribution to the History of Congregationalism, Presbyterianism, and Calvinist Resistance Theory. Madison: University of Wisconsin Press, 1967.
— *Myths about the St. Bartholomew's Day Massacres 1572-1576.* Cambridge, MA: Harvard University Press, 1988.
Klooster, Fred. *Calvin's Doctrine of Predestination.* Calvin Theological Seminary Monograph Series, no. 3. Grand Rapids: Calvin Theological Seminary, 1961. Reprint, Grand Rapids: Baker, 1977.
Knowles, David. *The Evolution of Medieval Thought.* Baltimore: Helicon Press, 1962.
Kretzmann, Norman, Anthony Kenny, and Jan Pinborg, eds. *The Cambridge History of Later Medieval Philosophy: From the Rediscovery of Aristotle to the Disintegration of Scholasticism 1100-1600.* Cambridge: Cambridge University Press, 1982.
Kristeller, P. O. *Renaissance Thought: The Classic, Scholastic, and Humanist Strains.* New York: Harper and Row, 1961.
Laplanche, François. *Orthodoxie et prédication: l'oeuvre d'Amyraut et la querelle de la grâce universelle.* Paris: Presses Universitaires, 1965.
Leith, John H. *Introduction to the Reformed Tradition: A Way of Being the Christian Community.* Rev. ed. Atlanta: John Knox, 1981.
— *John Calvin's Doctrine of the Christian Life.* Louisville: Westminster/John Knox, 1989.
Letis, Theodore, ed. *The Majority Text: Essays and Reviews in the Continuing Debate.* Grand Rapids: Institute for Biblical Studies, 1987.
Lindberg, Carter. *The European Reformations.* Cambridge, MA: Blackwell, 1996.
Lints, Richard. *The Fabric of Theology: A Prolegomenon to Evangelical Theology.* Grand Rapids: Eerdmans, 1993.
Maag, Karin. *Seminary or University? The Genevan Academy and Reformed Higher Education, 1560-1620.* St. Andrews Studies in Reformation History. Aldershot: Scholar, 1995.
Mackenney, Richard. *Sixteenth Century Europe: Expansion and Conflict.* New York: St. Martin's, 1993.
Manetsch, Scott M. *Theodore Beza and the Quest for Peace in France, 1572-1598.* Studies in Medieval and Reformation Thought, vol. 79. Leiden: Brill, 2000.
Martin, A. Lynn. *The Jesuit Mind: The Mentality of an Elite in Early Modern France.* Ithaca, NY: Cornell University Press, 1988.
Maruyama, Tadataka. *The Ecclesiology of Theodore Beza: The Reform of the True Church.* Travaux d'Humanisme et Renaissance 166. Geneva: Librairie Droz, 1978.
McComish, William A. *The Epigones: A Study of the Theology of the Genevan Academy at the Time of the Synod of Dort, with Special Reference to Giovanni Diodati.* Allison Park, PA: Pickwick, 1989.
McGrath, Alister E. *The Genesis of Doctrine: A Study in the Foundations of Doctrinal Criticism.* Oxford: Basil Blackwell, 1990.
— *Historical Theology: An Introduction to the History of Christian Thought.* Oxford: Basil Blackwell, 1998.
— *The Intellectual Origins of the European Reformation.* Oxford: Basil Blackwell, 1987.
— *Iustitia Dei: A History of the Christian Doctrine of Justification.* 2nd ed. Cambridge: Cambridge University Press, 1998.
— *A Life of John Calvin: A Study in the Shaping of Western Culture.* Oxford: Basil Blackwell, 1990.

— *Reformation Thought: An Introduction*. 2nd ed. Oxford: Basil Blackwell, 1993.
McKim, Donald K., ed. *Encyclopedia of the Reformed Faith*. Louisville: Westminster/John Knox, 1992.
McNeill, John T. *The History and Character of Calvinism*. Oxford: Oxford University Press, 1954. Reprint, New York: Oxford University Press, 1967.
Meylan, Henri. *D'Érasme á Théodore de Bèze: Problèmes de l'Eglise et de l'Ecole chez les Réformés*. Geneva: Librairie Droz, 1976.
Monter, E. William. *Calvin's Geneva*. New York: John Wiley and Sons, 1967. Reprint, Huntington, NY: Robert E. Kreiger, 1975.
Mozley, J. B. *A Treatise on the Augustinian Doctrine of Predestination*. 2nd ed. New York: n.p., 1878.
Muller, Richard A. *Christ and the Decree: Christology and Predestination in Reformed Theology from Calvin to Perkins*. Studies in Historical Theology 2. Durham, NC: Labyrinth, 1986. Reprint, Grand Rapids: Baker, 1988.
— *Dictionary of Latin and Greek Theological Terms, Drawn Principally from Protestant Scholastic Theology*. Grand Rapids: Baker, 1985.
— *God, Creation, and Providence in the Thought of Jacob Arminius: Sources and Directions in Scholastic Protestantism in the Era of Early Orthodoxy*. Grand Rapids: Baker, 1991.
— *Post-Reformation Reformed Dogmatics*. Vol. 1, *Prolegomena to Theology*. Grand Rapids: Baker, 1987.
— *Post-Reformation Reformed Dogmatics*. Vol. 2, *Holy Scripture: The Cognitive Foundation of Theology*. Grand Rapids: Baker, 1993.
— *Scholasticism and Orthodoxy in the Reformed Tradition: An Attempt at Definition*. Grand Rapids: Calvin Theological Seminary, 1995.
Nauert, Charles G., Jr. *Humanism and the Culture of Renaissance Europe*. New Approaches to European History. Cambridge, MA: Harvard University Press, 1995.
Niesel, Wilhelm. *The Theology of Calvin*. Translated by Harold Knight. Philadelphia: Westminster, 1956.
Nugent, Donald. *Ecumenism in the Age of the Reformation: The Colloquy of Poissy*. Harvard Historical Studies 89. Cambridge, MA: Harvard University Press, 1974.
O'Malley, John W. *The First Jesuits*. Cambridge, MA: Harvard University Press, 1993.
Olson, Roger E. *The Story of Christian Theology: Twenty Centuries of Tradition and Reform*. Downers Grove, IL: InterVarsity, 1999.
Ong, Walter J. *Ramus, Method, and the Decay of Dialogue: From the Art of Discourse to the Art of Reason*. Cambridge, MA: Harvard University Press, 1958.
Overfield, James. *Humanism and Scholasticism in Late Medieval Germany*. Princeton: Princeton University Press, 1984.
Ozment, Steven. *The Age of Reform 1250-1550: An Intellectual and Religious History of Late Medieval and Reformation Europe*. New Haven: Yale University Press, 1980.
Parker, T. H. L. *Calvin: An Introduction to His Thought*. Louisville: Westminster/John Knox, 1995.
Partee, Charles. *Calvin and Classical Philosophy*. Studies in the History of Christian Thought 14. Leiden: E. J. Brill, 1977.
Pelikan, Jaroslav. *The Christian Tradition: A History of the Development of Doctrine*. 5 vols. Chicago: University of Chicago Press, 1971-1989.
Platt, John. *Reformed Thought and Scholasticism: The Arguments for the Existence of God in Dutch Theology, 1575-1650*. Studies in the History of Christian Thought 29.

Leiden: E. J. Brill, 1982.
Prestwich, Menna, ed. *International Calvinism, 1534-1715*. Oxford: Clarendon, 1985.
Rabil, Albert Jr., ed. *Renaissance Humanism: Foundations, Forms, and Legacy*. 3 vols. Philadelphia: University of Pennsylvania Press, 1988.
Rainbow, Jonathan H. *The Will of God and the Cross: An Historical and Theological Study of John Calvin's Doctrine of Limited Redemption*. Allison Park, PA: Pickwick, 1990.
Raitt, Jill. *The Colloquy of Montbéliard: Religion and Politics in the Sixteenth Century*. New York: Oxford University Press, 1993.
— *The Eucharistic Theology of Theodore Beza: Development of the Reformed Doctrine*. American Academy of Religion Studies in Religion 4. Chambersburg, PA: American Academy of Religion, 1972.
_____, ed. *Shapers of Religious Traditions in Germany, Switzerland, and Poland, 1560-1600*. New Haven: Yale University Press, 1981.
Rimbach, Harald. *Gnade und Erkenntnis in Calvins Prädestinationslehre: Calvin im Vergleich mit Pighius, Beza und Melanchthon*. Frankfurt am Main: Peter Lang, 1996.
Ritschl, Otto. *Dogmengeschichte des Protestantismus*. Vol. III: *Die reformierte Theologie des 16. und des 17. Jahrhunderts in ihrer Entstehung und Entwicklung*. Göttingen: Vandenhoeck & Ruprecht, 1926.
Rogers, Jack and Donald McKim. *The Authority and the Interpretation of the Bible*. New York: Harper and Row, 1979.
Rolston, Holmes. *John Calvin versus the Westminster Confession*. Richmond: John Knox, 1972.
Rummel, Erika. *The Humanist-Scholastic Debate in the Renaissance and Reformation*. Cambridge, MA: Harvard University Press, 1995.
Schlosser, Friedrich C. *Leben des Theodor de Beza und des Peter Martyr Vermili*. Heidelberg: Mohr und Zimmer, 1809.
Schweizer, Alexander. *Die Protestantischen Centraldogmen in ihrer Entwicklung innerhalb der reformierten Kirche*. 2 vols. Zurich: n.p., 1853.
Scribner, Bob, Roy Porter, and Mikuláš Teich, eds. *The Reformation in National Context*. Cambridge: Cambridge University Press, 1994.
Seeberg, Reinhold. *Text-book of the History of Doctrines*. Translated by Charles E. Hay. 2 vols. Grand Rapids: Baker, 1952.
Spitz, Lewis W. *The Renaissance and Reformation Movements*. 2 vols. St. Louis: Concordia, 1971.
Sprunger, Keith L. *The Learned Doctor William Ames: Dutch Backgrounds of English and American Puritanism*. Urbana: University of Illinois Press, 1972.
Stauffer, Richard. *The Humanness of John Calvin*. Translated by George Shriver. Nashville: Abingdon, 1971.
Steinmetz, David C. *Calvin in Context*. New York: Oxford University Press, 1995.
— *Reformers in the Wings*. Philadelphia: Fortress, 1971. Reprint, Grand Rapids: Baker, 1981.
Stelling-Michaud, Sven, and Suzanne Stelling-Michaud, eds. *Le Livre du Recteur de l'Académie de Genève (1559-1878)*. 6 vols. Geneva: E. Droz, 1959-1980.
Strehle, Stephen. *Calvinism, Federalism, and Scholasticism: A Study in the Reformed Doctrine of Covenant*. Basler und Berner Studien zur historischen und systematischen Theologie, Band 58. New York: Peter Lang, 1988.
Thomas, G. Michael. *The Extent of the Atonement: A Dilemma for Reformed Theology*

from Calvin to the Consensus (1536-1675). Paternoster Biblical and Theological Monographs. Carlisle: Paternoster, 1997.
Trueman, Carl R. *The Claims of Truth: John Owen's Trinitarian Theology*. Carlisle: Paternoster, 1998.
Trueman, Carl R., and R. Scott Clark, eds. *Protestant Scholasticism: Essays in Reassessment*. Carlisle: Paternoster, 1999.
Walker, Williston. *John Calvin: The Organizer of Reformed Protestantism (1509-1564)*. New York: G. P. Putnam's Sons, 1906. Reprint, New York: Schocken Books, 1969.
Wallace, Dewey D., Jr. *Puritans and Predestination: Grace in English Protestant Theology, 1515-1695*. Chapel Hill: University of North Carolina Press, 1982.
Warfield, Benjamin B. *The Plan of Salvation*. Rev. ed. Grand Rapids: Eerdmans, 1942.
Weber, Hans Emil. *Reformation, Orthodoxie und Rationalismus*. Part 1: *Von der Reformation zur Orthodoxie*. 2 vols. Beiträge zur Förderung christlicher Theologie, 35, 45. Darmstadt: Wissenschaftliche Buchgesellschaft, 1966.
Wendel, François. *Calvin: Origins and Development of His Religious Thought*. Translated by Philip Mairet. New York: Harper & Row, 1963.
Williams, George Huntston. *The Radical Reformation*. Philadelphia: Westminster, 1962.
Zahl, Paul F. M. *A Short Systematic Theology*. Grand Rapids: Eerdmans, 2000.

Articles and Essays

Anderson, Marvin W. "The Geneva (Tomson/Junius) New Testament among Other English Bibles of the Period." In *The Geneva Bible: The Annotated New Testament, 1602 ed.*, ed. Gerald T. Sheppard, 5-17. Cleveland: Pilgrim, 1989.
—— "John Calvin: Biblical Preacher (1539-1564)." *Scottish Journal of Theology* 42 (1989): 167-81.
—— "Peter Martyr Vermigli: Protestant Humanist." In *Peter Martyr Vermigli and Italian Reform*, ed. J. C. McLelland, 65-84. Waterloo, Ontario: Wilfred Laurier University Press, 1980.
—— "Rhetoric and Reality: Peter Martyr and the English Reformation." *Sixteenth Century Journal* 19 (1988): 451-69.
—— "Theodore Beza: Savant or Scholastic?" *Theologische Zeitschrift* 43 (1987): 320-32.
—— "Trent and Justification (1546): A Protestant Reflection." *Scottish Journal of Theology* 21 (1968): 385-406.
—— "*Vista Tigurina*: Peter Martyr and European Reform (1556-1562)." *Harvard Theological Review* 83 (1990): 181-206.
Armstrong, Brian G. "Geneva and the Theology and Politics of French Calvinism: The Embarrassment of the 1588 Edition of the Bible of the Pastors and Professors of Geneva." In *Calvinus Ecclesiae Genevensis Custos*, ed. Wilhelm H. Neuser, 113-33. New York: Peter Lang, 1984.
—— Review of *Orthodoxie et Predication* by François Laplanche. *Bibliothèque d'Humanisme et Renaissance: Travaux et Documents* 28 (1966): 761-64.
—— "*Semper Reformanda*: The Case of the French Reformed Church, 1559-1620." In *Later Calvinism: International Perspectives*, ed. W. Fred Graham, 119-40. Sixteenth Century Essays and Studies, vol. 22. Kirksville, MO: Sixteenth Century Journal, 1994.
Backus, Irena. "'Aristotelianism' in Some of Calvin's and Beza's Expository and

Exegetical Writings on the Doctrine of the Trinity, with Particular Reference to the Terms ουσια and υποστασις." In *Histoire de l'Exégèse au XVIe Siècle: Textes du Colloque International Tenu a Genève en 1976*, ed. Olivier Fatio and Pierre Fraenkel, 351-60. Geneva: Libraire Droz, 1978.

— "The Church Fathers and the Canonicity of the Apocalypse in the Sixteenth Century: Erasmus, Frans Titelmans, and Theodore Beza." *Sixteenth Century Journal* 29 (1998): 651-65.

— "l'Enseignement de la Logique à l'Académie de Genève entre 1559 et 1565." *Revue de Théologie et de Philosophie* 111 (1979): 153-63.

— "Piscator Misconstrued? Some Remarks on Robert Rollock's 'logical analysis' of Hebrews 9." *Journal of Medieval and Renaissance Studies* 14 (1984): 113-19.

Bainton, Roland H. "The Parable of the Tares as the Proof Text for Religious Liberty to the End of the Sixteenth Century." *Church History* 1 (1932): 67-89.

Barnaud, Jean. "La Confession de Foi de Théodore de Bèze." *Société de l'Histoire du Protestantisme Français* 48 (1899): 617-33.

Beeke, Joel R. "The Order of the Divine Decrees at the Genevan Academy: From Bezan Supralapsarianism to Turretinian Infralapsarianism." In *The Identity of Geneva: The Christian Commonwealth, 1564-1864*, ed. John B. Roney and Martin I. Klauber, 57-75. Contributions to the Study of World History 59. Westport, CT: Greenwood, 1998.

— "William Cunningham." In *Historians of the Christian Tradition: Their Methodology and Influence on Western Thought*, ed. Michael Bauman and Martin I. Klauber, 209-26. Nashville: Broadman & Holman, 1995.

Bell, M. Charles. "Was Calvin a Calvinist?" *Scottish Journal of Theology* 36 (1983): 535-40.

Berry, Lloyd E. "Introduction to the Fascimile Edition." In *The Geneva Bible: A Facsimile of the 1560 Edition*, 1-24. Milwaukee: University of Wisconsin Press, 1969.

Bierma, Lyle D. "Federal Theology in the Sixteenth Century: Two Traditions?" *Westminster Theological Journal* 45 (1983): 304-21.

Bizer, Ernst. "Preface." In *Reformed Dogmatics Set Out and Illustrated from the Sources*, ed. Heinrich Heppe, xi-xiii, rev. and ed. Ernst Bizer. Translated by G. T. Thomson. London: George Allen and Unwin, 1950.

— "Reformed Orthodoxy and Cartesianism." Translated by Chalmers MacCormick. *Journal for Theology and the Church* 2 (1965): 20-82.

Boughton, Lynne Courter. "Supralapsarianism and the Role of Metaphysics in Sixteenth-Century Reformed Theology." *Westminster Theological Journal* 48 (1986): 63-96.

Bouwsma, William J. "Calvinism as Renaissance Artifact." In *John Calvin and the Church: A Prism of Reform*, ed. Timothy George, 28-41. Louisville: Westminster/John Knox, 1990.

Brady, I. C., J. E. Gurr, and J. A. Weisheipl. "Scholasticism." In *New Catholic Encyclopedia*. New York: McGraw-Hill, 1967.

Bray, John S. "The Value of Works in the Theology of Calvin and Beza." *Sixteenth Century Journal* 4 (1973): 77-86.

Breen, Quirinus. "John Calvin and the Rhetorical Tradition." *Church History* 26 (1957): 3-21.

— "The Terms 'Loci Communes' and 'Loci' in Melanchthon." *Church History* 16

(1947): 197-209.
Choisy, Eugène. "Theodore Beza." In *The New Schaff-Herzog Encyclopedia of Religious Knowledge*. Edited by Samuel Macauley Jackson. New York: Funk and Wagnalls, 1908.
Clark, R. S. "The Authority of Reason in the Later Reformation: Scholasticism in Caspar Olevian and Antoine de La Faye." In *Protestant Scholasticism: Essays in Reassessment*, ed. Carl R. Trueman and R. S. Clark, 111-26. Carlisle: Paternoster, 1999.
Clarke, F. Stuart. "Christocentric Developments in the Reformed Doctrine of Predestination." *Churchman* 98 (1984): 229-45.
Coats, Catharine Randall. "Reactivating Textual Traces: Martyrs, Memory and the Self in Theodore Beza's *Icones* (1581)." In *Later Calvinism: International Perspectives*, ed. W. Fred Graham, 19-28. Sixteenth Century Essays and Studies, vol. 22. Kirksville, MO: Sixteenth Century Journal, 1994.
Crilly, W. H. "Scholastic Philosophy." In *New Catholic Encyclopedia*. New York: McGraw-Hill, 1967.
Cunningham, William. "Calvin and Beza." In *The Reformers and the Theology of the Reformation*, ed. James Buchanan and James Bannerman, 345-412. N.p., 1862. Reprint, Edinburgh: Banner of Truth, 1967.
Danner, Dan G. "The Later English Calvinists and the Geneva Bible." In *Later Calvinism: International Perspectives*, ed. W. Fred Graham, 489-504. Sixteenth Century Essays and Studies, vol. 22. Kirksville, MO: Sixteenth Century Journal, 1994.
Dantine, Johannes. "Das christologische Problem im Rahmen der Prädestinationslehre von Theodor Beza." *Zeitschrift für Kirchengeschichte* 77 (1966): 81-96.
— "Les Tabelles sur la Doctrine de la Prédestination par Théodore de Bèze." *Revue de Théologie et de Philosophie* 16 (1966): 365-77.
Davis, Natalie Zemon. "Peletier and Beza Part Company." *Studies in the Renaissance* 11 (1964): 188-222.
de Groot, D.-J. "Melchior Volmar: Ses relations avec les réformateurs français et suisses." *Société de l'Histoire du Protestantisme Français* 83 (1934): 416-39.
Delval, Michel. "Orthodoxie et Prédication: Théodore de Bèze." *Societie de l'Histoire du Protestantisme Français* 134 (1988): 693-97.
— "La Prédication d'un Réformateur au XVIe Siècle: l'Activité Homilétique de Théodore de Bèze." *Mélanges de Science Religieuse* 41 (1984): 61-86.
Donnelly, John Patrick. "Calvinist Thomism." *Viator* 7 (1976): 441-55.
— "Italian Influences on the Development of Calvinist Scholasticism." *Sixteenth Century Journal* 7 (1976): 81-101.
— "Peter Canisius." In *Shapers of Religious Traditions in Germany, Switzerland, and Poland, 1560-1600*, ed. Jill Raitt, 141-56. New Haven: Yale University Press, 1981.
Drury, G. F. "Rhetoric." In *New Catholic Encyclopedia*. New York: McGraw-Hill, 1967.
Dublanchy, E. "Bèze, Théodore de." In *Dictionnaire de Théologie Catholique*. Edited by A. Vacant, E. Mangenot, and E. Amann. Paris: Librairie Letouzey et Ané, 1923.
Farthing, John L. "Theodore Beza (1519-1605)." In *Historical Handbook of Major Biblical Interpreters*, ed. Donald K. McKim, 153-57. Downers Grove, IL: InterVarsity, 1998.
Fatio, Olivier. "Lambert Daneau: 1530-1595." Translated by Jill Raitt. In *Shapers of*

Religious Traditions in Germany, Switzerland, and Poland, 1560-1600, ed. Jill Raitt, 105-19. New Haven: Yale University Press, 1981.
— "Theodor Beza." In *Die Reformationszeit II*, ed. Martin Greschat, 255-76. Stuttgart: Verlag W. Kohlhammer, 1981.
Fellay, Jean-Blaise. "Un Presbyterianisme de Droit Divin: l'Eglise, le Pouvoir et l'Etat dans l'Ecclesiologie de Theodore de Beze." In *Visage de l'Église: Cours d'ecclésiologie*, ed. Patrick de Laubier, 125-40. Fribourg: Éditions Universitaires Fribourg, 1989.
Foster, Herbert Darling. "Liberal Calvinism: the Remonstrants at the Synod of Dort in 1618." *Harvard Theological Review* 16 (1973): 1-37.
Fraenkel, Pierre. "Matthias Flacius Illyricus and His *Gloss* on Hebrews 9." *Journal of Medieval and Renaissance Studies* 14 (1984): 97-111.
Frost, Ronald N. "'Scholasticism, Reformation, Orthodoxy, and the Persistence of Christian Aristotelianism': A Brief Rejoinder." *Trinity Journal*, n.s., 19 (1998): 97-101.
Gamble, Richard C. "*Brevitas et facilitas*: Toward an Understanding of Calvin's Hermeneutic." *Westminster Theological Journal* 47 (1985): 1-17.
— "The Christian and the Tyrant: Beza and Knox on Political Resistance Theory." *Westminster Theological Journal* 46 (1984): 125-39.
— "Switzerland: Triumph and Decline." In *John Calvin: His Influence in the Western World*, ed. W. Stanford Reid, 55-71. Grand Rapids: Zondervan, 1982.
Ganoczy, Alexandre. "Calvin, John." Translated by Jeff Bach. In *The Oxford Encyclopedia of the Reformation*. Edited by Hans J. Hillerbrand. Oxford: Oxford University Press, 1996.
Gerrish, B. A. "Biblical Authority and the Continental Reformation." *Scottish Journal of Theology* 10 (1957): 337-60.
— "Eucharist." In *The Oxford Encyclopedia of the Reformation*. Edited by Hans J. Hillerbrand. Oxford: Oxford University Press, 1996.
Gerstner, John H. "The View of the Bible Held by the Church: Calvin and the Westminster Divines." In *Inerrancy*, ed. Norman L. Geisler, 383-410. Grand Rapids: Zondervan, 1980.
Godfrey, W. Robert. "Biblical Authority in the Sixteenth and Seventeenth Centuries: A Question of Transition." In *Scripture and Truth*, ed. D. A. Carson and John D. Woodbridge, 221-43. Grand Rapids: Zondervan, 1983. Reprint, Grand Rapids: Baker, 1992.
— "Calvin and Calvinism in the Netherlands." In *John Calvin: His Influence in the Western World*, ed. W. Stanford Reid, 95-120. Grand Rapids: Zondervan, 1982.
— "Reformed Thought on the Extent of the Atonement." *Westminster Theological Journal* 37 (1975): 133-71.
— "What Really Caused the Great Divide?" In *Roman Catholicism: Evangelical Protestants Analyze What Divides and Unites Us*, ed. John Armstrong, 64-82. Chicago: Moody, 1994.
Gomes, A. W. "*De Jesu Christo Servatore*: Faustus Socinus on the Satisfaction of Christ." *Westminster Journal of Theology* 55 (1993): 209-31.
Gordon, Bruce. "Calvin and the Swiss Reformed Churches." In *Calvinism in Europe, 1540-1620*, ed. Andrew Pettegree, Alastair Duke, and Gillian Lewis, 64-81. Cambridge: Cambridge University Press, 1994.
— "Switzerland." In *The Early Reformation in Europe*, ed. Andrew Pettegree, 70-93.

Cambridge: Cambridge University Press, 1992.

Green, Ian. "'For Children in Yeeres and Children in Understanding': The Emergence of the English Catechism under Elizabeth and the Early Stuarts." *Journal of Ecclesiastical History* 37 (1986): 397-425.

Hall, Basil. "Biblical Scholarship: Editions and Commentaries." In *The Cambridge History of the Bible*. Vol. 3, *The West from the Reformation to the Present Day*. Edited by S. L. Greenslade, 38-93. Cambridge: The University Press, 1963.

— "Calvin Against the Calvinists." In *John Calvin*, ed. G. E. Duffield, 19-37. Courtenay Studies in Reformation Theology 1. Appleford: Sutton Courtenay, 1966.

— "Review Article: From Biblical Humanism to Calvinist Orthodoxy." *Journal of Ecclesiastical History* 31 (1980): 331-43.

Hanko, H. "Predestination in Calvin, Beza, and Later Reformed Theology." *Protestant Reformed Theological Journal* 10:2 (1977): 1-24.

Harper, George. "Calvin and English Calvinism to 1649: A Review Article." *Calvin Theological Journal* 20 (1985): 255-62.

Headley, J. M. "Tommaso Campanella and Jean de Launoy: The Controversy over Aristotle and his Reception in the West." *Renaissance Quarterly* 43 (1990): 529-50.

— "Tommaso Campanella and the End of the Renaissance." *Journal of Medieval and Renaissance Studies* 20 (1990): 157-74.

Helm, Paul. "Calvin (and Zwingli) on Divine Providence." *Calvin Theological Journal* 29 (1994): 388-405.

— "Calvin, English Calvinism and the Logic of Doctrinal Development." *Scottish Journal of Theology* 34 (1981): 179-85.

Heyd, M. "From Rationalist Theology to Cartesian Voluntarism." *Journal of the History of Ideas* 40 (1979): 527-42.

Higman, Francis. "Calvin's Works in Translation." In *Calvinism in Europe, 1540-1620*, ed. Andrew Pettegree, Alastair Duke, and Gillian Lewis, 82-99. Cambridge: Cambridge University Press, 1994.

— "L'*Harmonia confessionum fidei* de 1581." In *Catéchismes et Confessions de foi*, ed. Marie-Madelaine Fragonard and Michel Peronnet, 242-62. Montpelier: Le Centre d'histoire de réforme et du protéstantisme de l'Université de Montpelier III, 1995.

— "The Origins of the Image of Geneva." In *The Identity of Geneva: The Christian Commonwealth, 1564-1864*, ed. John B. Roney and Martin I. Klauber, 22-38. Contributions to the Study of World History 59. Westport, CT: Greenwood, 1998.

Holtrop, P. C. "Decree(s) of God." In *Encyclopedia of the Reformed Faith*. Edited by D. McKim. Edinburgh: St. Andrews, 1992.

Hornik, Henry. "Three Interpretations of the French Renaissance." In *French Humanism 1470-1600*, ed. Werner L. Gundersheimer, 19-47. London: Macmillan, 1969.

Hotze, M. A. "Scholastic Theology." In *New Catholic Encyclopedia*. New York: McGraw-Hill, 1967.

Hughes, Philip Edgcumbe. "Beza as Correspondent and Poet." *Churchman* 86 (1972): 16-26.

James, Frank A. "Peter Martyr Vermigli and the Reformed Doctrine of Justification." *The Princeton Theological Review* 6 (1999): 15-20.

— "Peter Martyr Vermigli: At the Crossroads of Late Medieval Scholasticism, Christian Humanism and Resurgent Augustinianism." In *Protestant Scholasticism: Essays in Reassessment*, ed. Carl R. Trueman and R. S. Clark, 62-78. Carlisle: Paternoster, 1999.

Jardine, Lisa. "The Place of Dialectic Teaching in Sixteenth-Century Cambridge." *Studies in the Renaissance* 21 (1974): 31-62.
Jinkins, Michael. "Theodore Beza: Continuity and Regression in the Reformed Tradition." *Evangelical Quarterly* 64 (1992): 131-54.
Kendall, R. T. "The Puritan Modification of Calvin's Theology." In *John Calvin: His Influence in the Western World*, ed. W. Stanford Reid, 199-214. Grand Rapids: Zondervan, 1982.
Kingdon, Robert M. "Beza, Theodore." In *New Catholic Encyclopedia*. New York: McGraw-Hill, 1967.
—— "Calvinism and Democracy: Some Political Implications of Debates on French Reformed Church Government, 1562-1572." *American Historical Review* 69 (1964): 393-401.
—— "The First Expression of Theodore Beza's Political Ideas." *Archiv für Reformationsgeschichte* 46 (1955): 88-100.
Klauber, Martin I. "Continuity and Discontinuity in Post-Reformation Reformed Theology: An Evaluation of the Muller Thesis." *Journal of the Evangelical Theological Society* 33 (1990): 467-75.
Kolb, Robert. "Teaching the Text: Common Place Method in Sixteenth Century Lutheran Biblical Commentary." *Bibliothèque d'Humanisme et Renaissance* 49 (1987): 571-85.
Kristeller, Paul Oskar. "Humanism." In *The Cambridge History of Renaissance Philosophy*, ed. Charles B. Schmitt, Quentin Skinner, Eckhard Kessler, and Jill Kraye, 113-37. Cambridge: Cambridge University Press, 1988.
Lane, A. N. S. "Calvin's Doctrine of Assurance." *Vox Evangelica* 11 (1979): 32-54.
—— "*Sola Scriptura*? Making Sense of a Post-Reformation Slogan." In *A Pathway into the Holy Scripture*, ed. P. E. Satterthwaite and D. F. Wright, 297-327. Grand Rapids: Eerdmans, 1994.
Ledwith, Dan. "Review of *Peter Martyr Vermigli and Predestination: the Augustinian Inheritance of an Italian Reformer*, by Frank A. James." *Princeton Theological Review* 6 (1999): 31-33.
Letham, Robert. "Faith and Assurance in Early Calvinism: A Model of Continuity and Diversity." In *Later Calvinism: International Perspectives*, ed. W. Fred Graham, 355-88. Sixteenth Century Essays and Studies, vol. 22. Kirksville, MO: Sixteenth Century Journal, 1994.
—— "Theodore Beza: A Reassessment." *Scottish Journal of Theology* 40 (1987): 25-40.
Levi, Anthony. "Humanist Reform in Sixteenth-Century France." *Heythrop Journal* 6 (1965): 447-64.
Lewis, Gillian. "The Genevan Academy." In *Calvinism in Europe, 1540-1620*, ed. Andrew Pettegree, Alastair Duke, and Gillian Lewis, 35-63. Cambridge: Cambridge University Press, 1994.
Lillback, Peter. "Ursinus' Development of the Covenant of Creation: A Debt to Melanchthon or Calvin?" *Westminster Theological Journal* 43 (1981): 247-88.
Linder, Robert D. "Calvinism and Humanism: the First Generation." *Church History* 44 (1975): 167-81.
Maag, Karin. "Education and Training for the Calvinist Ministry: the Academy of Geneva, 1559-1620." In *The Reformation of the Parishes: The Ministry and the Reformation in Town and Country*, ed. Andrew Pettegree, 133-52. Manchester: Manchester University Press, 1993.

Manetsch, Scott M. "Psalms Before Sonnets: Theodore Beza and the *Studia Humanitatis.*" In *Continuity and Change: The Harvest of Late Medieval and Reformation History*, ed. Robert J. Bast and Andrew C. Gow, 400-16. Leiden: Brill, 2000.

McGrath, Alister E. "Justification." In *The Oxford Encyclopedia of the Reformation.* Edited by Hans J. Hillerbrand. Oxford: Oxford University Press, 1996.

— "Scholasticism." In *The Oxford Encyclopedia of the Reformation.* Edited by Hans J. Hillerbrand. Oxford: Oxford University Press, 1996.

McLelland, Joseph C. "The Reformed Doctrine of Predestination according to Peter Martyr." *Scottish Journal of Theology* 8 (1955): 255-71

McPhee, Ian. "Beza, Theodore." In *New Dictionary of Theology.* Edited by Sinclair B. Ferguson, David F. Wright, and J. I. Packer. Downers Grove, IL: Inter-Varsity, 1988.

Ménager, Daniel. "Théodore de Bèze, Biographe de Calvin." *Bibliothèque d'Humanisme et Renaissance: Travaux et Documents* 45 (1983): 231-55.

Moltmann, Jürgen. "Zur bedeutung des Petrus Ramus für philosophie und theologie im Calvinismus." *Zeitschrift für Kirchengeschichte* 68 (1957): 295-318.

Monter, E. William. "The Consistory of Geneva, 1559-1569." *Bibliothèque d'Humanisme et Renaissance* 38 (1976): 467-84.

— "The Italians in Geneva, 1550-1600: A New Look." In *Genève et l'Italie*, ed. Luc Monnier, 53-77. Genève: Librairie Droz, 1969.

Muller, Richard A. "Calvin and the 'Calvinists': Assessing Continuities and Discontinuities Between the Reformation and Orthodoxy." *Calvin Theological Journal* 30 (1995): 345-375; 31 (1996): 125-60.

— "Calvin, Beza, and the Exegetical History of Romans 13:1-7." In *The Identity of Geneva: The Christian Commonwealth, 1564-1864*, ed. John B. Roney and Martin I. Klauber, 39-56. Contributions to the Study of World History 59. Westport, CT: Greenwood, 1998.

— "Covenant and Conscience in English Reformed Theology: Three Variations on a 17th Century Theme." *Westminster Theological Journal* 42 (1980): 308-34.

— "'*Duplex cognitio dei*' in the Theology of Early Reformed Orthodoxy." *Sixteenth Century Journal* 10 (1979): 51-61.

— "Found (No Thanks to Theodore Beza): One 'Decretal' Theology." *Calvin Theological Journal* 32 (1997): 145-53.

— "God, Predestination, and the Integrity of the Created Order: A Note on Patterns in Arminius' Theology." In *Later Calvinism: International Perspectives*, ed. W. Fred Graham, 431-46. Sixteenth Century Essays and Studies, vol. 22. Kirksville, MO: Sixteenth Century Journal, 1994.

— "Grace, Election, and Contingent Choice: Arminius's Gambit and the Reformed Response." In *The Grace of God, The Bondage of the Will.* Vol. 2, *Historical and Theological Perspectives on Calvinism*, ed. Thomas R. Schreiner and Bruce A. Ware, 251-78. Grand Rapids: Baker, 1995.

— "Perkins' *A Golden Chaine*: Predestinarian System or Schematized *Ordo Salutis?*" *Sixteenth Century Journal* 9 (1978): 69-81.

— "Predestination." In *The Oxford Encyclopedia of the Reformation.* Edited by Hans J. Hillerbrand. Oxford: Oxford University Press, 1996.

— "The Priority of the Intellect in the Soteriology of Jacob Arminius." *Westminster Theological Journal* 55 (1993): 55-72.

— "Review of *The Bolsec Controversy on Predestination, From 1551 to 1555*, by Philip

C. Holtrop." *Calvin Theological Journal* 29 (1994): 581-89.
— "Scholasticism Protestant and Catholic: Francis Turretin on the Object and Principles of Theology." *Church History* 55 (1986): 193-205.
— "Scholasticism, Reformation, Orthodoxy, and the Persistence of Christian Aristotelianism." *Trinity Journal*, n.s., 19 (1998): 81-96.
— "The Use and Abuse of a Document: Beza's *Tabula Praedestinationis*, The Bolsec Controversy, and the Origins of Reformed Orthodoxy." In *Protestant Scholasticism: Essays in Reassessment*, ed. Carl R. Trueman and R. S. Clark, 33-61. Carlisle: Paternoster, 1999.
Nicholls, David. "France." In *The Early Reformation in Europe*, ed. Andrew Pettegree, 120-41. Cambridge: Cambridge University Press, 1992.
Nicole, Roger. "John Calvin's View of the Extent of the Atonement." *Westminster Theological Journal* 47 (1985): 197-225.
Niesel, Wilhelm. "Syllogismus practicus?" In *Aus Theologie und Geschichte der Reformierten Kirche*, 158-79. Neukirchen: K. Moers, 1933.
Olson, Jeannine E. "Geneva Academy." In *The Oxford Encyclopedia of the Reformation*. Edited by Hans J. Hillerbrand. Oxford: Oxford University Press, 1996.
Ong, W. J. "Humanism." In *New Catholic Encyclopedia*. New York: McGraw-Hill, 1967.
Overfield, James H. "Scholastic Opposition to Humanism in Pre-Reformation Germany." *Viator* 7 (1976): 391-420.
Ozment, Steven. "Humanism, Scholasticism, and the Intellectual Origins of the Reformation." In *Continuity and Discontinuity in Church History*, ed. F. Forrester Church and Timothy George, 133-49. Leiden: E. J. Brill, 1969.
Packer, J. I. "Arminianisms." In *Through Christ's Word: A Festschrift for Dr. Philip E. Hughes*, ed. W. Robert Godfrey and Jesse L. Boyd, 121-48. Phillipsburg, NJ: Presbyterian and Reformed, 1985.
Perrottet, Luc. "Chapter 9 of the Epistle to the Hebrews as presented in an unpublished course of lectures by Theodore Beza." Translated by Irena Backus. *The Journal of Medieval and Renaissance Studies* 14 (1984): 89-96.
Peter, Rodolphe. "Rhétorique et prédication selon Calvin." *Revue d'Histoire et de Philosophie Religieuses* 55 (1975): 249-72.
Pettegree, Andrew. "The Early Reformation in Europe: A German Affair or an International Movement?" In *The Early Reformation in Europe*, ed. Andrew Pettegree, 1-22. Cambridge: Cambridge University Press, 1992.
Raitt, Jill. "Beza, Guide for the Faithful Life." *Scottish Journal of Theology* 39 (1986): 83-107.
— "The French Reformed Theological Response." In *Discord, Dialogue, and Concord: Studies in the Lutheran Reformation's Formula of Concord*, ed. Lewis W. Spitz and Wenzel Lohff, 178-90. Philadelphia: Fortress, 1977.
— "Lessons in Troubled Times: Beza's Lessons On Job." In *Calvin and the State: Papers and Responses Presented at the Seventh and Eighth Colloquia on Calvin & Calvin Studies*, ed. Peter De Klerk, 21-45. Grand Rapids: Calvin Studies Society, 1993.
— "The Person of the Mediator: Calvin's Christology and Beza's Fidelity." In *Occasional Papers of the American Society for Reformation Research*, vol. 1, ed. R. C. Walton, 53-80. N.p., 1977.
— "*Probably* They Are God's Children: Theodore Beza's Doctrine of Baptism." In

Humanism and Reform: The Church in Europe, England, and Scotland, 1400-1643, ed. James Kirk, 151-70. Studies in Church History, Subsidia 8. Oxford: Blackwell, 1991.

— "Theodore Beza: 1519-1605." In *Shapers of Religious Traditions in Germany, Switzerland, and Poland, 1560-1600,* ed. Jill Raitt, 89-104. New Haven: Yale University Press, 1981.

Reid, J. K. S. "The Office of Christ in Predestination." *Scottish Journal of Theology* 1 (1948): 5-19, 166-83.

Reid, W. Stanford. "The Battle Hymns of the Lord: Calvinist Psalmody of the Sixteenth Century." *Sixteenth Century Journal* 2 (1971): 36-54.

— "Calvin and the Founding of the Academy of Geneva." *Westminster Theological Journal* 18 (1955): 1-33.

— "Theodore Dieudonne Beza (1519-1605)" In *The Encyclopedia of Christianity,* vol. 1, ed. Edwin H. Palmer, 652-53. Wilmington: The National Foundation for Christian Education, 1964.

— "The Transmission of Calvinism in the Sixteenth Century." In *John Calvin: His Influence in the Western World,* ed. W. Stanford Reid, 33-52. Grand Rapids: Zondervan, 1982.

Rice, Eugene F. "The Humanist Idea of Christian Antiquity: Lefèvre d'Étaples and his Circle." In *French Humanism 1470-1600,* ed. Werner L. Gundersheimer, 163-80. London: Macmillan, 1969.

Richgels, Robert W. "Scholasticism Meets Humanism in the Counter-Reformation: The Clash of Cultures in Robert Bellarmine's Use of Calvin in the *Controversies.*" *Sixteenth Century Journal* 6 (1975): 53-66.

Santmire, H. Paul. "Justification in Calvin's 1540 Romans Commentary." *Church History* 33 (1964): 294-313.

Schmitt, Charles B. "Towards a Reassessment of Renaissance Aristotelianism." *History of Science* 11 (1973): 159-93.

Shepherd, Norman. "Zanchius on Saving Faith." *Westminster Theological Journal* 36 (1973): 31-47.

Sinnema, Donald. "Antoine De Chandieu's Call for a Scholastic Reformed Theology (1580)." In *Later Calvinism: International Perspectives,* ed. W. Fred Graham, 159-90. Sixteenth Century Essays and Studies, vol. 22. Kirksville, MO: Sixteenth Century Journal, 1994.

— "Aristotle and Early Reformed Orthodoxy: Moments of Accomodation and Antithesis." In *Christianity and the Classics: The Acceptance of a Heritage,* ed. Wendy E. Helleman, 119-48. Lanham, MD: University Press of America, 1990.

— "The Distinction Between Scholastic and Popular: Andreas Hyperius and Reformed Scholasticism." In *Protestant Scholasticism: Essays in Reassessment,* ed. Carl R. Trueman and R. S. Clark, 127-43. Carlisle: Paternoster, 1999.

— "Reformed Scholasticism and the Synod of Dort (1618-19)." In *John Calvin's Institutes: His Opus Magnum. Proceedings of the Second South African Congress for Calvin Research, July 31-August 3, 1984,* ed. B. J. van der Walt, 467-506. Potchefstroom: Potchefstroom University Press, 1986.

Skinner, Quentin. "Meaning and Understanding in the History of Ideas." *History and Theory* 8 (1969): 3-53.

Spitz, Lewis W. "Humanism and the Reformation." In *Transition and Revolution: Problems and Issues of European Renaissance and Reformation History,* ed. Robert

M. Kingdon, 153-67. Minneapolis: Burgess, 1974.
Stauffer, Richard. "Calvinism and the Universities." In *University and Reformation: Lectures from the University of Copenhagen Symposium*, ed. Leif Grane, 76-98. Leiden: E. J. Brill, 1981.
Steinmetz, David C. "The Scholastic Calvin." In *Protestant Scholasticism: Essays in Reassessment*, ed. Carl R. Trueman and R. S. Clark, 16-30. Carlisle: Paternoster, 1999.
Stout, Harry S. "Theological Commitment and American Religious History." *Theological Education* 25, no. 2 (1989): 44-59.
Summers, Kirk M. "Theodore Beza's Classical Library and Christian Humanism." *Archiv für Reformationsgeschichte* 82 (1991): 193-207.
—— "Theodore Beza's Reading of Catullus." *Classical and Modern Literature* 15 (1995): 233-45.
Sunshine, Glenn S. "Discipline as the Third Mark of the Church: Three Views." *Calvin Theological Journal* 33 (1998): 469-80.
—— "French Protestantism on the Eve of St-Bartholomew: The Ecclesiastical Discipline of the French Reformed Churches, 1571-1572." *French History* 4 (1990): 340-77.
—— "Reformed Theology and the Origins of Synodical Polity: Calvin, Beza and the Gallican Confession." In *Later Calvinism: International Perspectives*, ed. W. Fred Graham, 141-58. Sixteenth Century Essays and Studies, vol. 22. Kirksville, MO: Sixteenth Century Journal, 1994.
Tavard, George H. "Tradition in Early Post-Tridentine Theology." *Theological Studies* 23 (1962): 377-405.
Thomas, G. Michael. "Calvin and English Calvinism: A Review Article." *Scottish Bulletin of Evangelical Theology* 16 (1998): 111-27.
Torrance, James B. "The Incarnation and 'Limited Atonement.'" *The Evangelical Quarterly* 55 (1983): 83-94.
Trueman, Carl R., and R. Scott Clark. "Introduction." In *Protestant Scholasticism: Essays in Reassessment*, ed. Carl R. Trueman and R. S. Clark, xi-xix. Carlisle: Paternoster, 1999.
Venema, Cornelis P. "Heinrich Bullinger's Correspondence on Calvin's Doctrine of Predestination, 1551-1553." *Sixteenth Century Journal* 17 (1986): 435-50.
Visser, Derk. "Zacharias Ursinus." In *Shapers of Religious Traditions in Germany, Switzerland, and Poland, 1560-1600*, ed. Jill Raitt, 121-39. New Haven: Yale University Press, 1981.
Vogler, Bernard. "Europe as Seen through the Correspondence of Theodore Beza." In *Politics and Society in Reformation Europe*, ed. E. I. Kouri and Tom Scott, 252-65. New York: St. Martin's, 1987.
Vos, Arvin. "Calvin: The Theology of a Christian Humanist." In *Christianity and the Classics: The Acceptance of a Heritage*, ed. Wendy E. Helleman, 109-18. Lanham, MD: University Press of America, 1990.
Walton, Robert C. "Heinrich Bullinger: 1504-1575." In *Shapers of Religious Traditions in Germany, Switzerland, and Poland, 1560-1600*, ed. Jill Raitt, 69-87. New Haven: Yale University Press, 1981.
Weisheipl, J. A. "Scholastic Method." In *New Catholic Encyclopedia*. New York: McGraw-Hill, 1967.
Weiss, James Michael. "Humanism." In *The Oxford Encyclopedia of the Reformation*. Edited by Hans J. Hillerbrand. Oxford: Oxford University Press, 1996.

Wilson, J. Lewis. "Catechisms, and Their Use Among the Puritans." In *One Steadfast High Intent*, 31-44. Battersea: The Evangelical Magazine, n.d.

Wolters, Albert M. "Christianity and the Classics: A Typology of Attitudes." In *Christianity and the Classics: The Acceptance of a Heritage*, ed. Wendy E. Helleman, 189-204. Lanham, MD: University Press of America, 1990.

Young, William. "Calvin and Westminster." *The Bulwark* (May/June 1980): 15-18.

Theses and Dissertations

Archbald, Paul Noel. "A Comparative Study of John Calvin and Theodore Beza on the Doctrine of the Extent of the Atonement." Ph.D. diss., Westminster Theological Seminary, 1998.

Conradt, Nancy. "John Calvin, Theodore Beza and the Reformation in Poland." Ph.D. diss., University of Wisconsin-Madison, 1974.

Godfrey, W. Robert. "Tensions within International Calvinism: The Debate on the Atonement at the Synod of Dort, 1618-1619." Ph.D. diss., Stanford University, 1974.

Kennedy, Kevin Dixon. "Union with Christ as Key to John Calvin's Understanding of the Extent of the Atonement." Ph.D. diss., The Southern Baptist Theological Seminary, 1999.

Letham, R. W. A. "Saving Faith and Assurance in Reformed Theology: Zwingli to the Synod of Dort." Ph.D. diss., University of Aberdeen, 1979.

Manetsch, Scott Michael. "Theodore Beza and the Quest for Peace in France, 1572-1598." Ph.D. diss., University of Arizona, 1997.

McPhee, Ian. "Conserver or Transformer of Calvin's Theology? A Study of the Origins and Development of Theodore Beza's Thought, 1550-1570." Ph.D. diss., Cambridge University, 1979.

Muller, Richard A. "Predestination and Christology in Sixteenth Century Reformed Theology." Ph.D. diss., Duke University, 1976.

Nicole, Roger. "Moyse Amyraut (1596-1664) and the Controversy on Universal Grace, First Phase (1634-1637)." Ph.D. diss., Harvard University, 1966.

Sinnema, Donald W. "The Issue of Reprobation at the Synod of Dort (1618-19) in Light of the History of this Doctrine." Ph.D. diss., University of St. Michael's College, 1985.

Spencer, Stephen R. "Reformed Scholasticism in Medieval Perspective: Thomas Aquinas and Francis Turrettini on the Incarnation." Ph.D. diss., Michigan State University, 1988.

Summers, Kirk Mims. "Theodore Beza on the Uses of the Mosaic Law." M.A. thesis, Reformed Theological Seminary, 1986.

Sunshine, Glenn S. "From French Protestantism to the French Reformed Churches: The Development of Huguenot Ecclesiastical Institutions, 1559-1598." Ph.D. diss., University of Wisconsin-Madison, 1992.

Ugnivenko, Regina. "Inventaire de la Correspondance de Théodore de Bèze." M.L.S. diploma, Université de Genève, 1990.

Wells, David F. "Decretum dei speciale: An Analysis of the Content and Significance of Calvin's Doctrine of Soteriological Predestination." Th.M. thesis, Trinity Evangelical Divinity School, 1967.

Subject Index

Academy, Geneva 18, 103n72, 149-50
  Curriculum 18, 19-20, 40, 106
  Plague, effect on 144
Andreae, Jacob 1, 65-66, 187, 203
Apostles' Creed 91, 130, 132
Aristotle 39, 51, 53-54, 56, 57, 61, 86, 105, 113-14
Assurance of salvation 43, 66n113, 71-81, 131-32, 137n9, 159n76, 160, 165, 180n129, 187-231
  Applied to various types of persons 188-92
  Based on Christ's atonement 194n24, 195, 205-08, 225n124
  Based on divine election 197, 198, 201
  Based on faith 208-09
  Based on God's character and promises 204-05
  Based on heaven 214-16
  Based on prayer 213-14
  Based on the church and sacraments 212-13, 225
  Based on the internal witness of the Holy Spirit 196-97, 198, 202-03, 209-11
  Covenantal focus 204, 207
  In the *Confession de la foi Chrestienne* 194-99
  In the *Petit Catéchisme* 223-25
  In the *Quaestionum et responsionum Christianarum libellus* 221-23
  Necessitated by the spiritual battle 189, 192-93, 194-96, 198-99, 200-03, 207, 213-14, 223, 226
  "Practical syllogism" 71-72, 74n147, 77-79, 203n47, 217-25
    Beeke, Joel on 220-21
    Bray, John on 217, 221
    Kendall, R. T. on 217-18, 221
    Letham, Robert on 218
    Muller, Richard on 218-20, 221
  Prayer, role of 202

Sanctification, role of 197, 198
Augsburg 143
Augustine 119-20, 121, 174
Baptism 38, 125, 187-88
Battle, spiritual 24-25, 27-30, 102-05, 110, 119, 120, 123, 129, 132-33, 151, 172, 192-93, 213-15
Bern 2, 8
Beza, Claudine 1-2
Beza, Theodore
  Biblical interpretation 39, 91-92, 106n80, 109-11, 133, 150n57
  Brother, death of 144
  Conversion 12-13
  Father, concern for 116
  Health of 1-2
  Humanism of 87, 89n14, 95-96, 104n72, 105-06, 114-15, 130, 133, 150n57, 243-58
  Letters of 3, 136-37
  Love to God 13-14, 179, 180, 186, 204-05, 229
  Pastor 5n11, 6n12, 14-18, 68, 79-80, 88-90, 91, 132, 140, 148n51, 164, 165, 187-92, 203, 228-29, 231
  Polemic against Roman Catholics 92, 102-04, 118, 119
  Preaching 14, 19, 39, 52, 88-90, 95, 99-100, 111, 116, 173, 176-77, 243-58
  Scholasticism of 20n70, 53n68, 70n130, 88, 111-14, 129n177, 130, 140, 146n46
  Self-identity 11-21
  Teaching at the Academy 16n60, 18-21, 52, 53-55, 105n73, 106, 149-50, 243-58
Beza, Theodore—Interpretation of 51-55
  "Calvin vs. Beza" theory 7n14, 17n60, 41-46, 56-63, 70, 71-75, 76n155, 219-21, 233-34
  Importance of context 7n14, 17n60, 45, 49-51, 64n108, 66n112, 81, 173, 232-

33
Importance of empathy 47-48, 84-87
Importance of genre 45, 48-49, 56-57, 60-61, 64-65, 74-75, 81, 82-83, 138, 172-77, 232-33
Beza, Theodore—Works
Altera brevis fidei confessio 122-26
Confession de la foi Chrestienne 115-22, 194-99
Jobus 149-61
De Peste Quaestiones duae Explicatae 143-49
Petit Catéchisme 130-32, 223-25
Soteriological focus 131
Quaestionum et responsionum Christianarum libellus 126-30, 221-23
  Soteriological focus 127
Sermons sur la Resurrection 88-96, 243-58
Tabula Pradestionationis 174-75, 177-79, 259-78
Vie de Calvin 21-24
Beza, Theodore—Theology
Calvinism *see* Predestination
Christ's atonement 43n27, 64n105, 93, 124, 127, 129, 144, 145n39, 185, 195, 205-08
Christology 1, 38, 124, 129, 131, 168, 169, 170, 185
Ethics 94, 101
Gospel 167-72, 179, 185
Human depravity 93, 119-21, 123-24, 128-29, 179, 179-80, 181
Imputation of Christ's righteousness 127, 197
"Means" of salvation 131-32, 182
Preaching 94-95
Reason, use of 126-30
Regeneration 93, 119, 125, 128, 175, 179-83, 188
Salvation 115-32, 167, 179-80
  Central message of Bible 121
  Necessity of response to the gospel 100, 123, 124, 127, 131, 148, 181n130, 183, 188-90
  Ultimate aim of preaching 117, 122
Sanctification 125, 197, 198, 211, 221-22, 226-28

Necessitated by the spiritual battle 228
Theological method 87-115, 117
Trinity 118, 127
View of preaching 94-95, 109-10, 116, 117, 125
View of truth 22, 25-27
Bible 98-105, 129
Allegorical interpretation 109
Central in Beza's theology 90-92, 94-95, 102n67, 113, 116-17, 120, 124, 128n170, 156, 176, 177
Christ the central message of 99
Interpretation, proper 105-14, 120
Interpretation, role of Holy Spirit in 96-98
Sufficiency of 98-102
Translation, necessity of 100
Use in spiritual battle 15-18, 25-27, 92-93, 95, 98, 99, 102-05, 110, 123
Bolsec, Jérôme 23, 66n112, 175-76, 183
Bullinger, Henry 8n19, 9, 136-37
Calvin, John 16n., 21-24, 41-45, 79n171, 148n51
Assurance, doctrine of 219-21
Biblical interpretation 16n60, 110
Catechism 115-16, 130-31
Institutes 115-16, 118
Predestination, doctrine of 131n190, 137
Scholasticism of 59n88, 70n.
Trinitarian theology 118
View of Beza's doctrine of predestination 59n88
Castellio, Sebastian 48, 66n112, 112, 139-40
Catechisms 130
Church 25, 123, 127, 212-13
Founded on Bible 107-08
History of 119
Councils of 102n67, 119
de Coligny, Gaspard 3, 30
Ecclesiology 38
Eschatological vision 3-5, 6n12, 21-30, 110, 115, 122, 129, 132-33, 156-58, 165n92, 172, 216-17, 232
Heaven 29-30, 34, 35, 121n141, 157, 165, 180-81, 214-15

Subject Index

Hell 28-29, 121n141, 127-28
Eucharist 1, 10, 38, 125, 187, 212-13
France 136-37, 161n81
  Beza's concern for 8-10
  Confession of Faith 116
  Huguenots 8-10, 136
  St. Bartholomew's Day Massacre 9
Geneva 7-8, 22, 136-37, 149-50
  Plague in 144
Heresy 25-26, 102-03, 105, 129
  Role of Satan in 129-30, 183
Holy Spirit 96-98, 125, 197-98, 202-03, 209-11
  Author of the Bible 107-08
  Illumination of 96, 125, 127, 128
  Role in salvation 131, 175, 180, 181, 210
  Role in sanctification 125, 211, 227
Huber, Samuel 2
Humanism 39-40, 52-55, 105-06, 106-10, 111n94, 114-15, 121
Justification 169-70, 196, 226n126
Kant, Immanuel 86
La Rochelle, synod of 136
London 143
Lutherans 10, 187
Montbéliard, Colloquy of 1, 65-66, 187
Nîmes, synod of 136
Perseverance 33-34, 223, 226, 228-31
Plague, the 143-44, 186
Poissy, Colloquy of 8, 90
Prayer 13-14, 179-80, 202, 212, 213-14, 227n128, 230
  For faith 32, 208-09, 227
  For heavenly life 29-30, 215-16
  For knowledge of God in Jesus Christ 208
  For illumination 97-98
  For love 210, 211n68
  For patience 4, 166
  For the Holy Spirit 96
  For the morning 180, 204-05
  For using afflictions 166
  The Lord's Prayer 163, 179n125, 204n48
  To crave God in His word 97, 99
  To the triune God 97

  Upon point of death 28, 134-35, 206-07, 209
  Upon the Symbol of Belief 181n130, 227
Predestination 1, 2, 23, 32-33, 55-71, 96, 109-10, 120, 126, 127-28, 131-32, 135, 167-85, 259-78
  "Central dogma" theory 63-65, 126
  Christocentrism 66-67, 76, 170, 178-79
  Controversies over 138, 183, 187
  Gospel, not central to 167, 169-70
  Necessitated by the spiritual battle 137n9, 167, 177-85, 187-88
  Preaching of 109-10, 135, 176-77, 178, 181-83, 272-74
  Reprobation 67-68, 174, 184, 187
  Supralapsarianism 64, 76
Providence of God 27, 126n165, 127-28, 138-66
  Attacks on 139-40, 145-46
  Definition 139, 140, 153-56
  Essential for salvation 138-39
  Faith, relation to 147-49
  God's relation to evil 126n165, 141-42, 151, 156, 158-59, 163, 164n88
  Necessitated by the spiritual battle 151-53, 156-57
  Pastoral use of 142-43, 148-49, 161-66
  Plague, relation to 143-49
  Secondary causation in 145-47, 153-54, 174
Rhetoric 90, 110-11
Sacraments 123, 131-32
Satan 24-25, 31, 100, 102-03, 110, 119, 121, 124, 129, 147n48, 151, 155, 158-59, 171, 192-94, 202, 207n55, 213-14
  Activity against Beza 12
  Activity in Geneva 22-24, 162, 183
  Activity in Roman Catholicism 123
Savoy 1, 90, 149-50, 165n92
Scholasticism 40, 46-47, 51-55, 56-63, 111-14, 118
  In Catholic schools 103-05
  Satan, role of in 103-05
Servetus, Michael 23
Sovereignty of God 11, 96, 120, 134-86, 204-227

    In Beza's life 13
    In human history 137-38
    In salvation 127-28, 167-72, 179-83
    Pastoral use of 2-4, 30-35, 140, 158, 160-61, 164, 166, 231
Suffering, Christian 157, 166, 194-95

Syphilis 144
Trent, Council of 136
Turretin, Francis 5, 178n120
Vermigli, Peter Martyr 84-85
Wollebius, Johannes 217n88
Zurich 136

Modern Author Index

Anderson, Marvin 5n11, 20n70, 44, 84-85
Armstrong, Brian 41, 42n23, 46-47, 49
Backus, Irena 38, 106n80
Baird, Henry 37
Barnaud, Jean 115
Barth, Karl 71-72, 74
Beeke, Joel 68-69, 77-78
Bernus, Auguste 115
Bizer, Ernst 41, 46, 48-50
Bray, John 61-63, 73-75, 126n163
Clark, Scott 86
Conradt, Nancy 50-51
Cunningham, William 41
Dantine, Johannes 41, 63-65
Donnelly, John Patrick 84-85
Dückert, Armand 176
Farthing, John 39n11
Geisendorf, Paul-F. 37, 115
Hall, Basil 41
Helm, Paul 42-43
Heppe, Heinrich 127
Hirsch, E. D. 86n8
Holtrop, Philip 56-59
Kendall, R. T. 41-42, 43, 63-65, 72-73, 74-75, 218n90

Kickel, Walter 41, 42n23, 46, 49, 50-51, 59-61
Kingdon, Robert 136
Kristeller, Paul Oskar 40, 89n14
Letham, Robert 42n24, 53n., 75-77, 218
Lewis, Gillian 104n72
Manetsch, Scott 37-38, 136-37, 149-50, 161
Marayama, Tadataka 38
McGrath, Alister 42n25, 86n9
McLelland, J. C. 84-85
McPhee, Ian 52-53, 68, 69-70, 79
Moltmann, Jürgen 41
Monter, William 7, 8, 136
Muller, Richard 44, 66-67, 70-71, 78-79, 88n14, 176
Raitt, Jill 38, 39, 51-52, 65-66, 70
Réveillaud, Michel 115-16
Schmitt, Charles 40
Sinnema, Donald 53-55, 67-68, 71
Skinner, Quentin 85-86
Spitz, Lewis 89n14
Stout, Harry 86n8
Sunshine, Glenn 38
Trueman, Carl 86

Studies in Christian History and Thought
(All titles uniform with this volume)
Dates in bold are of projected publication

David Bebbington
Holiness in Nineteenth-Century England
David Bebbington stresses the relationship of movements of spirituality to changes in their cultural setting, especially the legacies of the Enlightenment and Romanticism. He shows that these broad shifts in ideological mood had a profound effect on the ways in which piety was conceptualized and practised. Holiness was intimately bound up with the spirit of the age.
2000 / 0-85364-981-2 / viii + 98pp

J. William Black
Reformation Pastors
Richard Baxter and the Ideal of the Reformed Pastor
This work examines Richard Baxter's *Gildas Salvianus, The Reformed Pastor* (1656) and explores each aspect of his pastoral strategy in light of his own concern for 'reformation' and in the broader context of Edwardian, Elizabethan and early Stuart pastoral ideals and practice.
2003 / 1-84227-190-3 / xxii + 308pp

James Bruce
Prophecy, Miracles, Angels, *and* Heavenly Light?
The Eschatology, Pneumatology and Missiology of Adomnán's Life of Columba
This book surveys approaches to the marvellous in hagiography, providing the first critique of Plummer's hypothesis of Irish saga origin. It then analyses the uniquely systematized phenomena in the *Life of Columba* from Adomnán's seventh-century theological perspective, identifying the coming of the eschatological Kingdom as the key to understanding.
2004 / 1-84227-227-6 / xviii + 286pp

Colin J. Bulley
The Priesthood of Some Believers
Developments from the General to the Special Priesthood in the Christian Literature of the First Three Centuries
The first in-depth treatment of early Christian texts on the priesthood of all believers shows that the developing priesthood of the ordained related closely to the division between laity and clergy and had deleterious effects on the practice of the general priesthood.
2000 / 1-84227-034-6 / xii + 336pp

July 2005

Anthony R. Cross (ed.)
Ecumenism and History
Studies in Honour of John H.Y. Briggs
This collection of essays examines the inter-relationships between the two fields in which Professor Briggs has contributed so much: history—particularly Baptist and Nonconformist—and the ecumenical movement. With contributions from colleagues and former research students from Britain, Europe and North America, *Ecumenism and History* provides wide-ranging studies in important aspects of Christian history, theology and ecumenical studies.

2002 / 1-84227-135-0 / xx + 362pp

Maggi Dawn
Confessions of an Inquiring Spirit
Form as Constitutive of Meaning in S.T. Coleridge's Theological Writing
This study of Coleridge's *Confessions* focuses on its confessional, epistolary and fragmentary form, suggesting that attention to these features significantly affects its interpretation. Bringing a close study of these three literary forms, the author suggests ways in which they nuance the text with particular understandings of the Trinity, and of a kenotic christology. Some parallels are drawn between Romantic and postmodern dilemmas concerning the authority of the biblical text.

2006 / 1-84227-255-1 / approx. 224 pp

Ruth Gouldbourne
The Flesh and the Feminine
Gender and Theology in the Writings of Caspar Schwenckfeld
Caspar Schwenckfeld and his movement exemplify one of the radical communities of the sixteenth century. Challenging theological and liturgical norms, they also found themselves challenging social and particularly gender assumptions. In this book, the issues of the relationship between radical theology and the understanding of gender are considered.

2005 / 1-84227-048-6 / approx. 304pp

Crawford Gribben
Puritan Millennialism
Literature and Theology, 1550–1682
Puritan Millennialism surveys the growth, impact and eventual decline of puritan millennialism throughout England, Scotland and Ireland, arguing that it was much more diverse than has frequently been suggested. This Paternoster edition is revised and extended from the original 2000 text.

2007 / 1-84227-372-8 / approx. 320pp

Galen K. Johnson
Prisoner of Conscience
John Bunyan on Self, Community and Christian Faith
This is an interdisciplinary study of John Bunyan's understanding of conscience across his autobiographical, theological and fictional writings, investigating whether conscience always deserves fidelity, and how Bunyan's view of conscience affects his relationship both to modern Western individualism and historic Christianity.
2003 / 1-84227-223-3 / xvi + 236pp

R.T. Kendall
Calvin and English Calvinism to 1649
The author's thesis is that those who formed the Westminster Confession of Faith, which is regarded as Calvinism, in fact departed from John Calvin on two points: (1) the extent of the atonement and (2) the ground of assurance of salvation.
1997 / 0-85364-827-1 / xii + 264pp

Timothy Larsen
Friends of Religious Equality
Nonconformist Politics in Mid-Victorian England
During the middle decades of the nineteenth century the English Nonconformist community developed a coherent political philosophy of its own, of which a central tenet was the principle of religious equality (in contrast to the stereotype of Evangelical Dissenters). The Dissenting community fought for the civil rights of Roman Catholics, non-Christians and even atheists on an issue of principle which had its flowering in the enthusiastic and undivided support which Nonconformity gave to the campaign for Jewish emancipation. This reissued study examines the political efforts and ideas of English Nonconformists during the period, covering the whole range of national issues raised, from state education to the Crimean War. It offers a case study of a theologically conservative group defending religious pluralism in the civic sphere, showing that the concept of religious equality was a grand vision at the centre of the political philosophy of the Dissenters.
2007 */ 1-84227-402-3 / x + 300pp*

Byung-Ho Moon
Christ the Mediator of the Law
Calvin's Christological Understanding of the Law as the Rule of Living and Life-Giving

This book explores the coherence between Christology and soteriology in Calvin's theology of the law, examining its intellectual origins and his position on the concept and extent of Christ's mediation of the law. A comparative study between Calvin and contemporary Reformers—Luther, Bucer, Melancthon and Bullinger—and his opponent Michael Servetus is made for the purpose of pointing out the unique feature of Calvin's Christological understanding of the law.

2005 / 1-84227-318-3 / approx. 370pp

John Eifion Morgan-Wynne
Holy Spirit and Religious Experience in Christian Writings, c.AD 90–200

This study examines how far Christians in the third to fifth generations (c.AD 90–200) attributed their sense of encounter with the divine presence, their sense of illumination in the truth or guidance in decision-making, and their sense of ethical empowerment to the activity of the Holy Spirit in their lives.

2005 / 1-84227-319-1 / approx. 350pp

James I. Packer
The Redemption and Restoration of Man in the Thought of Richard Baxter

James I. Packer provides a full and sympathetic exposition of Richard Baxter's doctrine of humanity, created and fallen; its redemption by Christ Jesus; and its restoration in the image of God through the obedience of faith by the power of the Holy Spirit.

2002 / 1-84227-147-4 / 432pp

Andrew Partington,
Church and State
The Contribution of the Church of England Bishops to the House of Lords during the Thatcher Years

In *Church and State*, Andrew Partington argues that the contribution of the Church of England bishops to the House of Lords during the Thatcher years was overwhelmingly critical of the government; failed to have a significant influence in the public realm; was inefficient, being undertaken by a minority of those eligible to sit on the Bench of Bishops; and was insufficiently moral and spiritual in its content to be distinctive. On the basis of this, and the likely reduction of the number of places available for Church of England bishops in a fully reformed Second Chamber, the author argues for an evolution in the Church of England's approach to the service of its bishops in the House of Lords. He proposes the Church of England works to overcome the genuine obstacles which hinder busy diocesan bishops from contributing to the debates of the House of Lords and to its life more informally.

2005 / 1-84227-334-5 / approx. 324pp

Michael Pasquarello III
God's Ploughman
Hugh Latimer: A 'Preaching Life' (1490–1555)

This construction of a 'preaching life' situates Hugh Latimer within the larger religious, political and intellectual world of late medieval England. Neither biography, intellectual history, nor analysis of discrete sermon texts, this book is a work of homiletic history which draws from the details of Latimer's milieu to construct an interpretive framework for the preaching performances that formed the core of his identity as a religious reformer. Its goal is to illumine the practical wisdom embodied in the content, form and style of Latimer's preaching, and to recapture a sense of its overarching purpose, movement, and transforming force during the reform of sixteenth-century England.

2006 / 1-84227-336-1 / approx. 250pp

Alan P.F. Sell
Enlightenment, Ecumenism, Evangel
Theological Themes and Thinkers 1550–2000

This book consists of papers in which such interlocking topics as the Enlightenment, the problem of authority, the development of doctrine, spirituality, ecumenism, theological method and the heart of the gospel are discussed. Issues of significance to the church at large are explored with special reference to writers from the Reformed and Dissenting traditions.

2005 / 1-84227-330-2 / xviii + 422pp

Alan P.F. Sell
Hinterland Theology
Some Reformed and Dissenting Adjustments
Many books have been written on theology's 'giants' and significant trends, but what of those lesser-known writers who adjusted to them? In this book some hinterland theologians of the British Reformed and Dissenting traditions, who followed in the wake of toleration, the Evangelical Revival, the rise of modern biblical criticism and Karl Barth, are allowed to have their say. They include Thomas Ridgley, Ralph Wardlaw, T.V. Tymms and N.H.G. Robinson.
2006 / 1-84227-331-0 / approx. 350pp

Alan P.F. Sell and Anthony R. Cross (eds)
Protestant Nonconformity in the Twentieth Century
In this collection of essays scholars representative of a number of Nonconformist traditions reflect thematically on Nonconformists' life and witness during the twentieth century. Among the subjects reviewed are biblical studies, theology, worship, evangelism and spirituality, and ecumenism. Over and above its immediate interest, this collection provides a marker to future scholars and others wishing to know how some of their forebears assessed Nonconformity's contribution to a variety of fields during the century leading up to Christianity's third millennium.
2003 / 1-84227-221-7 / x + 398pp

Mark Smith
Religion in Industrial Society
Oldham and Saddleworth 1740–1865
This book analyses the way British churches sought to meet the challenge of industrialization and urbanization during the period 1740–1865. Working from a case-study of Oldham and Saddleworth, Mark Smith challenges the received view that the Anglican Church in the eighteenth century was characterized by complacency and inertia, and reveals Anglicanism's vigorous and creative response to the new conditions. He reassesses the significance of the centrally directed church reforms of the mid-nineteenth century, and emphasizes the importance of local energy and enthusiasm. Charting the growth of denominational pluralism in Oldham and Saddleworth, Dr Smith compares the strengths and weaknesses of the various Anglican and Nonconformist approaches to promoting church growth. He also demonstrates the extent to which all the churches participated in a common culture shaped by the influence of evangelicalism, and shows that active co-operation between the churches rather than denominational conflict dominated. This revised and updated edition of Dr Smith's challenging and original study makes an important contribution both to the social history of religion and to urban studies.
2006 / 1-84227-335-3 / approx. 300pp

Martin Sutherland
Peace, Toleration and Decay
The Ecclesiology of Later Stuart Dissent
This fresh analysis brings to light the complexity and fragility of the later Stuart Nonconformist consensus. Recent findings on wider seventeenth-century thought are incorporated into a new picture of the dynamics of Dissent and the roots of evangelicalism.

2003 / 1-84227-152-0 / xxii + 216pp

G. Michael Thomas
The Extent of the Atonement
A Dilemma for Reformed Theology from Calvin to the Consensus
A study of the way Reformed theology addressed the question, 'Did Christ die for all, or for the elect only?', commencing with John Calvin, and including debates with Lutheranism, the Synod of Dort and the teaching of Moïse Amyraut.

1997 / 0-85364-828-X / x + 278pp

David M. Thompson
Baptism, Church and Society in Britain from the Evangelical Revival to *Baptism, Eucharist and Ministry*
The theology and practice of baptism have not received the attention they deserve. How important is faith? What does baptismal regeneration mean? Is baptism a bond of unity between Christians? This book discusses the theology of baptism and popular belief and practice in England and Wales from the Evangelical Revival to the publication of the World Council of Churches' consensus statement on *Baptism, Eucharist and Ministry* (1982).

2005 / 1-84227-393-0 / approx. 224pp

Mark D. Thompson
A Sure Ground on Which to Stand
The Relation of Authority and Interpretive Method of Luther's Approach to Scripture
The best interpreter of Luther is Luther himself. Unfortunately many modern studies have superimposed contemporary agendas upon this sixteenth-century Reformer's writings. This fresh study examines Luther's own words to find an explanation for his robust confidence in the Scriptures, a confidence that generated the famous 'stand' at Worms in 1521.

2004 / 1-84227-145-8 / xvi + 322pp

Carl R. Trueman and R.S. Clark (eds)
Protestant Scholasticism
Essays in Reassessment

Traditionally Protestant theology, between Luther's early reforming career and the dawn of the Enlightenment, has been seen in terms of decline and fall into the wastelands of rationalism and scholastic speculation. In this volume a number of scholars question such an interpretation. The editors argue that the development of post-Reformation Protestantism can only be understood when a proper historical model of doctrinal change is adopted. This historical concern underlies the subsequent studies of theologians such as Calvin, Beza, Olevian, Baxter, and the two Turrentini. The result is a significantly different reading of the development of Protestant Orthodoxy, one which both challenges the older scholarly interpretations and clichés about the relationship of Protestantism to, among other things, scholasticism and rationalism, and which demonstrates the fruitfulness of the new, historical approach.

1999 / 0-85364-853-0 / xx + 344pp

Shawn D. Wright
Our Sovereign Refuge
The Pastoral Theology of Theodore Beza

Our Sovereign Refuge is a study of the pastoral theology of the Protestant reformer who inherited the mantle of leadership in the Reformed church from John Calvin. Countering a common view of Beza as supremely a 'scholastic' theologian who deviated from Calvin's biblical focus, Wright uncovers a new portrait. He was not a cold and rigid academic theologian obsessed with probing the eternal decrees of God. Rather, by placing him in his pastoral context and by noting his concerns in his pastoral and biblical treatises, Wright shows that Beza was fundamentally a committed Christian who was troubled by the vicissitudes of life in the second half of the sixteenth century. He believed that the biblical truth of the supreme sovereignty of God alone could support Christians on their earthly pilgrimage to heaven. This pastoral and personal portrait forms the heart of Wright's argument.

2004 / 1-84227-252-7 / xviii + 308pp

Paternoster
9 Holdom Avenue,
Bletchley,
Milton Keynes MK1 1QR,
United Kingdom
Web: www.authenticmedia.co.uk/paternoster

July 2005